PRAISE FOR *OUR WAY—A PARALLEL HISTORY*

"Nobel prize–winning author Toni Morrison once said, 'If there's a book that you want to read, but it hasn't been written yet, then you must write it.' Editor Julie Cajune set out to do just that, pulling together a diverse set of tribal scholars to relay their own history and their own stories, while shining light on the tribal resistance, adaptation, and persistence in the face of unrelenting settler colonialism. The result is a counterpoint to the Eurocentric histories that have dominated the conversation and a book that everyone—tribal members and nontribal members alike—should read."

—Martha Kohl, Montana Historical Society

"The United States has been needing this collection of narratives from Native scholars for a long time. Native history IS American history. There has always been an invisible and silenced Indigenous history that has run parallel to the one-sided settler history that we learned in school. Julie braids these Indigenous voices and stories together to tell our collective history from different tribal Nations and across geography and generations—and the culmination offers a new lens through which to see ourselves as a country. This epic anthology offers all of us a glimpse into a human experience that is both different from and similar to our own. Each contributor's voice and story are important and lend to the bigger narrative of reclamation of history. Contemporary Native America is experiencing a resurgence and revitalization through literature, art, fashion, movies, education, and activism. Our Way—A Parallel History *joins this movement."*

—Denise Juneau (Mandan-Hidatsa and Blackfeet), attorney, educator, and politician, former classroom teacher, former Montana State Superintendent of Public Instruction, and former Seattle Public Schools Superintendent

"Our Way *is a treasure—a lovingly curated collection of Indigenous stories and histories from an esteemed group of Native scholars and teachers who gathered on the Flathead Indian Reservation in Montana and 'collectively imagined what this book would be.' Julie Cajune's parallel history grows out of her lifelong commitment to Native education and truth-telling, and it builds on a strong tradition of counternarratives produced by the Flathead Nation, including Salish Kootenai College Press and the Séliš-Qlispé Culture Committee. Grounded in story—beginning with Séliš and Kootenai stories—*Our Way *focuses on people and places across the continent, from Montana to Georgia, and Alaska and Hawaii to Massachusetts and the Dawnland. This kaleidoscopic and accessible anthology will appeal to a broad audience of Indigenous and non-Indigenous educators, students, and community members.* Our Way *tells the stories of Indigenous people's agency and brilliance and is itself an example of that brilliance."*

—Nicholas Brown, Associate Teaching Professor,
School of Architecture and Department of History,
Northeastern University, Boston, Massachusetts,
co-author of Re-Collecting Black Hawk: Landscape, Memory, and Power in the American Midwest

"In Our Way—A Parallel History, *Julie Cajune has gathered a rich collection of stories about Indigenous people's cultures, histories, and contemporary lives. The authors offer facets of cultures, societies, historical events, and eras that have profoundly challenged Indigenous existence. These perspectives serve as an important antecedent to the stories that describe essential work that historical and contemporary Indigenous people have undertaken to preserve and perpetuate their ways. I recommend* Our Way *to educators and others looking for authentic and nuanced Indigenous viewpoints."*

—Edwin Schupman (Muscogee),
Manager of National Education (retired),
Smithsonian's National Museum
of the American Indian

"Treasure, Confront, Arise. The three section titles in Our Way—a beautiful and diverse anthology of Indigenous stories, histories, and philosophical insights—are more than organizing tools. Together, these constructs represent a theory of action and an invitation—one compellingly extended by Julie Cajune, who is brilliant as a guardian and guide of this collective work. Beginning with 'Treasure,' a section comprised of transcribed oral stories, detailed historical accounts, and personal narratives, Cajune invites us to engage with the profound wisdom and intellectual acumen flourishing within and across Indigenous communities. I was so moved by these stories and their philosophical treasures that I was already a changed and more deeply invested reader when approaching the accounts of heartbreak, dispossession, deceit, and genocide, as well as adept political strategy, courage, radical resilience, and visioning in 'Confront' and 'Arise.' As a non-Indigenous person living (and teaching) on ancestral land (Séliš), this book—through its content, its framework, and its call to action—has provided me with a more rigorous and robust education and will surely shape my work going forward. I am grateful."

—Kate Brayko, PhD, Associate Professor,
Teaching and Learning,
Phyllis J. Washington College
of Education, University of Montana

OUR WAY
A PARALLEL HISTORY

An Anthology of Native History, Reflection, and Story

Edited by Julie Cajune

Fulcrum Publishing
Wheat Ridge, Colorado

Library of Congress Cataloging-in-Publication Data

Names: Cajune, Julie, editor.
Title: Our way--a parallel history : an anthology of native history, reflection, and story / edited by Julie Cajune.
Description: Wheat Ridge, Colorado : Fulcrum Publishing, [2023] | Includes bibliographical references and index.
Identifiers: LCCN 2023012555 (print) | LCCN 2023012556 (ebook) | ISBN 9781682753323 (paperback) | ISBN 9781682754603 (ebook)
Subjects: LCSH: Indians of North America--Historiography. | Indians of North America--History. | Indians of North America--Social life and customs. | Folklore and history. | BISAC: SOCIAL SCIENCE / Ethnic Studies / American / Native American Studies | SOCIAL SCIENCE / Essays
Classification: LCC E76.8 .O87 2023 (print) | LCC E76.8 (ebook) | DDC 970.004/97--dc23/eng/20230403
LC record available at https://lccn.loc.gov/2023012555
LC ebook record available at https://lccn.loc.gov/2023012556

Printed in the United States
0 9 8 7 6 5 4 3 2 1

Chapter 1, "A Séliš Creation Story," is reprinted courtesy of Salish Kootenai College, © Salish Kootenai College. Chapter 5, "Alaska Native Education," is reprinted courtesy of the *Journal of American Indian Education*. Chapter 11, "The Peacemaker and Origins of Democracy," and chapter 18, "They Had Everything," are transcribed copies of interviews, courtesy of Direlle Calica, Institute for Tribal Government, Portland State University.

Cover artwork Credits (from top to bottom)
Hibiscus Flower, photo by John Bewlay on Unsplash, usage license: https://unsplash.com/license;
Lakota Beaded Bag, photo by Wolfgang Sauber, Creative Commons: https://creativecommons.org/licenses/by-sa/3.0/deed.en;
Makah Cedar Paddle, photo by Julie Cajune;
Acoma Water Pot, photo by de Young Museum, Creative Commons: https://creativecommons.org/publicdomain/zero/1.0/deed.en;
Floral Beaded Belt, photo by Julie Cajune;
Navajo Rug, photo by Peter D. Tillman, Creative Commons: https://creativecommons.org/licenses/by-sa/2.0/legalcode;

Cover and interior design by Kevin Piazza

Unless otherwise noted, all websites cited were current as of the initial edition of this book.

Fulcrum Publishing
3970 Youngfield Street
Wheat Ridge, Colorado 80033
(800) 992-2908 • (303) 277-1623
www.fulcrumbooks.com

Lovingly dedicated to the memory of Steve Crum (1950–2022). Steve, an expert and innovative historian, was enthusiastic and precise in his research. He was known to many as a storyteller with a twinkle in his eye as he told the most hilarious tales. He often used these stories to instruct and entertain his students. Kind and generous, Steve was a remarkable human being.

CONTENTS

PART I: TREASURE

PART II: CONFRONT

PART III: ARISE

PREFACE

I have some distinct memories of middle school social studies. I was in the seventh grade when US history was taught, and I recall an anticipation of sorts—almost an excitement for what was to come. Surely the beginning of the class would explore American Indian tribes, and I expected more Native content throughout the class. I'll admit it, I was naively optimistic, and I'll also confess—I was hopeful.

Middle school social studies turned out to be the beginning of my provocative discourse with public school teachers. My expectations went unmet, although there was some Native content in the class—the first being the infamous Bering Land Bridge. If I close my eyes, I can see the map with the arrows depicting a route from Siberia to North America. The next Indian encounter was the ever-popular "Indian Wars." This chapter of study began my animated disagreement with both the teacher and the textbook publishers. I was willing to provide the correct information that I was privy to by virtue of who I was and growing up in an Indian family. We knew our history.

I recall being placed outside the classroom in a chair, waiting for my mother to arrive. She was at work, so they had to wait until she could leave the office to come to the school. I sat in the hallway pondering my fate. My mother showed up and had a private discussion with the teacher. I was allowed back in the class and nothing more was said about the matter.

I did not read a poem, a short story, or a book by a Native author until I was a mature adult. My older sister, Luana, gave me a book of Native-authored short stories she was using for a university course she was teaching. I probably wore that book out. Over the next few years I discovered writing from Vine Deloria, Jr., Elizabeth Cook-Lynn, Joy Harjo, N. Scott Momaday, Ella Cara Deloria, and Simon J. Ortiz. Their works were life-changing for me. It is actually difficult to measure or describe the contribution of such work in my life. Language and stories are so powerful; they describe the world and our place in it. Family stories carried me through my turbulent teen and young adult years.

Upon receiving a grant to produce Native history materials, my first thought was to produce a book of narratives that I had sought out as an individual Native person, as a Native educator, and as a human being. I set out to do that by gathering a core group of Native scholars over the course of three years here on the Flathead Indian Reservation in Montana. For a week each summer we gathered, prayed, shared meals, sang, and talked story. We collectively imagined what this book could be.

We decided to contribute narratives that told stories of people and place rather than dates and events, providing a glimpse into the very human side of history. These are the stories through which we make meaning. Paramount to the writing was the intention to create accessible narratives of interest to a broad audience. We thought and talked about our own communities, with the particular objective of telling the stories of our people's agency and brilliance. Finally, we embraced one another across geographic and political boundaries to offer the fullness of stories from Indigenous America.

People brought stories from their relatives, from their homelands, from their history, their activism, their language, and their nations. I believe this collection of history, story, and reflection provokes and invites us to think and feel deeply about what it means for all of us to be human in our communities, nations, and beyond. After all, that is what a good story does.

> *Note:* The terms "American Indian," "Indian," "Native American," "Native," "Indigenous," "Tribal," and "Alaska Native" are used throughout this book, sometimes interchangeably. Understand that general terms are used for including large, diverse groups and are in no way preferred to the beautiful names of the many nations that make up Indigenous America.

PART I

Treasure

INTRODUCTION

Treasure includes stories and narratives that are the foundation of every nation. Explanations of how people came to be in their homelands, worldviews, traditional knowledge, ways of relating within and outside the human community, and relationship with place offer a beginning.

The remarkable ability of Native communities to continue with their songs, languages, histories, and lifeways is in large part due to oral tradition. The generational passing on of story and knowledge was dramatically disrupted, but individuals and communities held collective memory, at times having to guard, protect, and keep secret what was once known and shared by all.

> *The ideas and emotions contained within oral tradition shape the idea of who a given people are, what these people have experienced, and why they see the world the way they do. In sum, the important cultural knowledge contained within oral traditions not only serves as a guide for understanding the past, but also helps us to live in the present and to frame possible futures.... Respect for the teachings empowers us all to hope for deeper understanding of what makes us human, of our interconnectedness with all of creation, and of how peoples keep hope alive.*
>
> —*Kathryn Shanley (Nakoda)*

CHAPTER 1

A Séliš Creation Story

The Séliš of the Confederated Salish and Kootenai Tribes of Montana maintain and honor the cultural protocol of telling Coyote stories during the winter months. This story is a winter season story and is written as it would be told.

A long time ago, "Creator," known by our people as "Amotqn," which means "The Man Who Sits on Top of the Mountain," created the Human Beings. These people that Amotqn created were very tall people. Amotqn gave instructions to these tall people. The instructions were simple—to just enjoy this earth. As time went on, the people turned mean and bad, so Amotqn destroyed them.

Amotqn then created shorter people, thinking that these shorter people would surely have much better sense than the taller people. But, as time went on, these shorter people turned out the same as the taller people: stealing, killing, and all the other crazy wrongdoings humans do. So Amotqn destroyed them too.

Amotqn was about to create more people for the next world, but his mother, Sqwomeltn, told him, "You can't be just creating people and destroying them. When you create the people, you must give them a helper."

So, Amotqn created the animal world. Amotqn gave special instructions to all the animals. He told them, "Enjoy this earth for one full year. Don't think for yourself, just enjoy and relax. I'll come back in one year's time, and at that time I'll give all you animals your names and what your purpose will be in this world." Amotqn left the animals to enjoy the earth.

It was getting near the time when Amotqn was to come back to give all the animals their names and responsibilities. One of the animals began thinking. He thought, "If I was to be the first one in line to get the first name, I would probably be chief of all the animals. I'd probably be powerful!" So, the night before the big meeting, this animal character decided to stay up all night.

That night, this animal character tried his best to stay awake. At first it was easy, then, as the night passed, it became harder and harder for him to stay awake. He sat at the trunk of a pine tree leaning his back against it. This was getting too comfortable for him, his eyelids were beginning to shut, and he shook his head, stood up, and walked around. After a while, he stood leaning against the tree and again his eyelids began to shut, and he shook his head. Looking around, he saw a small bush off to the side. He went to the bush and broke off a couple of twigs and put them in his eyelids to keep them open. He thought, "I'll surely stay awake now." Well, this animal character fell asleep with his eyes wide open. When he awoke, it was daylight. His eyes had dried up and everything was a blur—he couldn't see anything! He looked up in the sky and could hardly see the sun. The sun had already been up for some time. This animal character thought, "I must hurry to get to the meeting. I've got to get there for the first name given." He crawled to the nearest stream, washed his eyes until he got his vision back, and went to the meeting place.

At the place of the big meeting, all the animals were there already. They were all sitting in a big circle. There was an empty space where this animal character went and sat down. As soon as he sat down, he raised his hand up and said, "I'm here! I'm here to get the first name!"

Amotqn looked at him and said, "No. There is only one name left, and that is your name." This animal character was puzzled. He looked at the other animals, looked at Amotqn, and then he said, "There is only one name left! What is it?"

Amotqn said, "Coyote. That is your name. Coyote."

Coyote didn't like this name. He looked around at the other animals. He pointed to one of the animals and asked Amotqn, "What is his name?"

"That's Grizzly Bear," Amotqn said.

Coyote went to Grizzly Bear and said to him, "Let's trade names." Coyote was trying to convince Grizzly Bear that Coyote was a much more powerful name than Grizzly Bear.

Amotqn said, "No, Coyote. All of these animals have already received their names and have already been given their instructions for their responsibilities here on earth. As for you, Coyote, I'm going to punish you. I told all of you animals at the beginning, not to think for yourself and just enjoy the earth. For disobeying my orders, Coyote, thinking you were going to be powerful if you got the first name, and maybe be chief of all the animals, this is what I am going to do. For your punishment, because you want to be so powerful, I'm going to give you special powers to help you with your assignment of responsibility. You're to go across the big waters to the new land where the human beings will live, to destroy the monsters that live there, to prepare the new land for the coming of the human beings. There are twenty-seven monsters that live there. Your brother, the Fox, will be your helper. Do you understand, Coyote?"

Coyote was ashamed. His head down, his ears and tail drooping down, he nodded his head, saying, "Yes, I understand."

Amotqn continued giving Coyote his instructions: "These items, that I give to you will help you to destroy the monsters. This blanket, you will spread out on the ground, place these items upon your blanket, sing your song, and wish. This will change you into anything, such as a leaf, a stone, a knife, and many other things to help you in destroying the monsters. But you can't use it for your own needs. There is much for you to do to prepare the new land for when there shall be human beings. When you have completed your job, we will meet again on the east coast, and it is there that I will judge you, to see if you have completed your job well. Do you understand?"

"Yes," Coyote said. Coyote was feeling much better now and was actually feeling proud of his new responsibilities.

Amotqn left, feeling satisfied with how everything had turned out.

The animals departed for the new land to begin their duties in preparation for the arrival of the human beings.

Coyote lived with his mother on one side of the mountain, and Fox lived with his mother on the other side of the mountain. Fox's and Coyote's mothers were sisters.

Coyote—Photographer Jim Peaco, Yellowstone National Park

One day, Coyote thought, "I don't need my brother Fox's help, I can do this all on my own." So Coyote went toward the east. When he reached the big waters he cut reeds and made a boat. Then he headed for the new land to begin his assignment to destroy monsters.

Meanwhile, Fox had gone to visit his brother Coyote and was told by his aunt, "Coyote left without you already."

Fox went home. He was sad and lonesome, and he lay around for a number of days until one day his mother told him, "Get yourself prepared and follow your brother. Coyote is foolish; he will be dead when you find him. Your job is to bring Coyote back to life. Here are some items that will help you complete your job. When you get to where there are people (the animals) they'll tell you where to find your brother. He'll be dead. Look all around, gather up all the hair, the little bones, the ears, tail, nose, and whatever is left of Coyote and put them in a pile, covering them with your blanket and jumping over the remains. Your brother Coyote will sit up yawning and stretching his arms saying, 'Oh, hello brother. What a long sleep I had,' and you'll tell him, 'No. You weren't sleeping. You were dead when I found you. You were beginning to rot. Your nose was over here, your tail was over there, your ears were scattered here and there along with all the rest of your body. You must have done something wrong.' Then your brother Coyote will remember what he had done. Coyote will say, 'Oh, yes I remember, I was about to fight with a monster when he must have killed me.' Then Coyote will go on from there to successfully destroy the monster. This is what your responsibility is going to be, bringing your brother back to life. Now go, my son!"

Fox said his farewells to his mother and headed east, reaching the shores of the big waters. He built a canoe and crossed the waters in search of his brother Coyote.

When Coyote had arrived on the shores of the new land, he began his journey in search of the monsters. But, Coyote, being the person he was, seemed to never have a plan. When he encountered a monster, the ending result was, Coyote always died, but then his brother Fox would bring him back to life.

But there were many times when Coyote had defeated the monsters, like when the monsters "Cold," "Famine," and "Sickness" came upon the people (animals).

Cold hated the people. He tried everything to freeze the people. Then Coyote taught the people how to make their clothing, their teepees, and their robes and also how to build their fire with flint.

Famine came along to starve the people, and Coyote went to the big waters to meet with Chief Salmon. Coyote asked Chief Salmon, "Why is it that you don't have very many of your people here?"

Chief Salmon said, "Our young people are being eaten up by the monsters as soon as they are born. That's why there aren't many of us living today."

Coyote said, "If I might make a suggestion. Why don't you take your people up the rivers and to the little streams where the water is warm and calm to lay the eggs of your people? When the little ones get big enough they can return to the big waters and your family will increase."

Chief Salmon thought this was a very good idea and agreed to do as Coyote suggested, taking his family far up the little streams to spawn.

Meanwhile, Coyote went to the people and told them that they would be able to get food by gathering the salmon. Coyote taught them how to make bows, arrows, spears, and nets. He taught them how to butcher, dry, and store the salmon.

This made Famine very mad, so he moved east to starve the people. Coyote was there again to help the people. Coyote went to Chief Buffalo who was living in the high mountains. Coyote told Chief Buffalo, "You make your people suffer way up here in these high mountains, in the deep snows where it is hard to dig up anything to eat. You should go down to the lower land where it isn't steep, and the snow isn't deep. There is plenty of water to drink and plenty of grass for your family to feed on."

Chief Buffalo thought this was a good idea and moved his family down to the lower lands. Coyote went to the people and taught them how to herd the buffalo over the buffalo jumps to gather their food; to butcher, dry, and store it; to tan the hides; to make their teepees, their robes, their ropes, their utensils, and much more.

Famine was mad and upset again, but this didn't discourage him. He came many times to try to destroy the people. Always the Coyote was there to intervene.

Sickness came to the people and destroyed many of them. Coyote taught the people how to gather the different roots and herbs to help cure themselves and others. This slowed Sickness down from destroying all the people.

There was always a law that was set for the future, for when the human beings arrived, that would be useful to them. For instance, one day Coyote got himself into mischief at a village and the people were chasing after him. As Coyote was running, he got his hair caught in the branches, and he didn't have time to stop and get loose, so, he just left his hair there and set a law, saying, "When there shall be human beings, they will gather my hair for their food." Today, the Coyote's hair is the black moss (lichen) that hangs from the branches of trees. It is gathered, cleaned, and oven-baked for three days underground along with the camas.

When Coyote arrived on the east coast for his meeting with Amotqn, Amotqn hadn't arrived yet. So, Coyote decided to create scenery of an old encampment to fool Amotqn. Coyote with his powers created some teepee poles, making them look very old, and leaned the poles up in a tree. By leaning the teepee poles in a tree, the poles stayed nice and straight and dry. If the poles were left on the ground, they would rot faster. Coyote then created a sweat lodge and made it look very old. Coyote made this encampment look very old, then he stood back and looked everything over and was pleased saying, "Good. Now I'm ready for the meeting with Amotqn."

Amotqn arrived shortly. Coyote and Amotqn stood on a little hill overlooking the old encampment Coyote had created. Then Coyote said, "It is good to see you again my little brother…" Coyote was trying to make Amotqn believe that Amotqn was younger than he was. Coyote continued, saying, "…I remember when we were little kids, you were much younger than I, you were about this tall and I was this tall. See, our grandmother's teepee poles are still leaning in the tree over there and the old sweat lodge is still standing over there. Do you remember?"

Amotqn knew that Coyote was trying to fool him, so he challenged Coyote, saying, "See those two mountains over there? If you can move those two mountains to the right and then put them back, I'll believe you."

Coyote spread his blanket upon the ground, placed his important items on the blanket, and sang his most powerful song. With all his strength, Coyote could only move one mountain, and he gave up. Amotqn calmly raised his hands in the direction of the two mountains, moved them to the right, and then replaced the two mountains in their original position. This made Coyote very ashamed. Amotqn said, "I have come to judge you for your assignment, and you have done very well, otherwise, you wouldn't be here today. I was going to gift you in bringing out the first human beings, but with your foolishness, trying to trick me, I'll punish you again. You will travel from the east to west coast to gather your people together."

My great-grandfather told me the ending of the Creation Story. He said at the end of time, Coyote will be sitting in the sunset, and Amotqn will be seated in the sunrise, both gathering their people. The ones who don't believe will be left here on earth for the next destruction of the world.

There are many stories of the Coyote from different tribes throughout Indian Country as he traveled from the west to the east coast. Along with these humorous stories came the morals of behavior and good life for the Native People. We hear our elders telling us, "Don't do this" or "Don't do that," because this is what happened to this certain animal when he did something wrong or did something foolish.

These stories that were passed on from generation to generation were told orally; nothing was written down. It is good to be a good listener, but it is just as important to pass on these stories to keep them alive for the next generation.

Séliš Creation Stories tell of the animals coming first. In our stories we call the animals "people." The animal people were sent here to prepare the new land for human beings. The elders said when it was time for the human beings to be born, all the animals gathered to have their last meeting; they all spoke one language at that time. The animals decided to go their separate ways to await human beings, to help the humans whenever they were called upon. That is why the Native People were taught to respect Mother Earth. Everything was here before us humans—the animals, trees, plants, rocks, water, everything. They all prepared everything for us. All have a special gift, and they await the young people when they seek out their strength and power. Young people were sent to the mountains by their elders on a four-day vision quest without food or water, in hopes that this young person might be pitied and gifted. It was an honor to have the name of any animal, rock, tree, plant, water, or anything connected with Mother Earth's important elements. No one animal was more important than the other, whether the largest animal or the smallest insect; each had a special gift and song to give to its seeker when sincere.

The animals came to prepare the world for us. Our ancestors lived a clean life, taking care of the land and their people. It's our turn to carry on that responsibility.

CHAPTER 2

Our Mother's Hair

A KOOTENAI STORY

Vernon S. Finley

This is a transcribed excerpt of an oral telling of the story.

Coyote Stories are really stories about Creation. There was a period of time before humans and after the Spirits that the animals were preparing the earth for the arrival of humans. That's what Coyote Stories are about. The story I am going to tell isn't really a Coyote Story per se, but it relates to how Coyote Stories were.

I was raised by my grandparents, and I used to share my grandfather's bedroom. He used to tell me all kinds of stories. This was one that he told me a long time ago. He was a great storyteller. His name was Jerome Hewankorn.

He said a long time ago when the Kootenai used to go to battle, a long time ago when there were wars among tribes, there really wasn't an awful lot of killing that happened. There was a lot of taunting and teasing—the way you see it happening now days. If you are familiar with stick game, it is usually tribe against tribe, and there is a lot of taunting and teasing that goes on and then you sit down and play. He said that's the way it used to be a long time ago. Sometimes they'd get worked up into a real battle and then people would die, but a lot of times it was taunting one another, counting coup on one another.

A long time ago it wasn't right for a person to brag. You couldn't say, "I did this" or "I did that." You couldn't say anything in a bragging manner. You couldn't tell anybody your good deeds that you had done. But you could always talk about your friends. "Gee, my friend, he is so brave. We went into battle with the Blackfeet. He counted coup on the Blackfeet War Chief. That's how brave he is."

A long time ago that's what they'd do. They would come back from our battles and tell stories about what happened. They would talk about their friends and how brave they were. So then if you think about it, the greatest war party wasn't one thousand warriors going across the mountains to raid the Blackfeet. The greatest war party was two people—two warriors. Because think about what that is saying—what that's saying is, "I and my friend are so powerful we are going to make our raids on other tribes and we're going to come back—we are both going to come back." If one of us got killed, what was the point of going? Nobody would ever hear about it. So, if you think about it, then the greatest war party was just two. The statement that's making is, "We're both coming back and we're going to have some great stories to tell." So, there were these two friends who decided to do that.

They were going across the mountains, and they had it all planned out. They would cross the mountains through the Glacier Park area, and they would raid the Blackfeet and steal horses. Then they would journey south over onto the plains. They would get a lot of buffalo out on the plains, dry it, and pack their horses full of buffalo meat. They would come back through what they now call the Hellgate Canyon, down through Missoula and come back later in the summer.

That's what they told everybody. They prepared for it, and off they went to make their raids. The raids were successful. In fact, one of the two friends counted coup on the Blackfeet War Chiefs. They both got away with a lot of horses, and they journeyed south onto the plains. As they were going out onto the plains, they knew that the Blackfeet war parties would be looking for them, so they didn't build fires at night. They took with them what they call Kiłkułka—pounded dry meat with berries, chokecherries. That's what they would eat.

At night they would tie their horses' legs together close enough so they couldn't run, but far enough apart so they could move around a bit and feed during the night. Then in the morning their horses wouldn't have wandered too far, and they could gather them back up and then continue on their journey.

There's a place that's translated from Kootenai, "Red Mountain." It's known as the Sweet Grass Hills. They were going into that area, and they came to this little valley. There was a stream running through there, there was tall grass, lots of grass for their horses—a perfect place for them to spend the night. So, they hobbled their horses and they had their little meal of Kiłkułka. There was tall grass, so they made little nests in the grass, and that's where they slept for the night.

They noticed this strong odor in the air that they hadn't smelled before—that they weren't familiar with. They were kind of wondering about it, and they made their little nests and went to sleep. In the middle of the night the grass that they were sleeping on spoke to one of them, and he started hearing this song. It was a song that he hadn't heard before. He listened and listened to it. Finally, he asked, "Who are you?"

Sweetgrass Spirit—Illustration by Antoine Sandoval

That's the way Spirits used to identify themselves to Indian people when they were coming to them. They would identify themselves by first singing their song, and in that way the people would know which Spirit was approaching. But it was a new song and the man listening said, "Who are you?" The translation of what that Spirit told him was, "I'm your Mother's hair and I'm all around you. That's what you're sleeping on. You're sleeping on your Mother's hair. I like you. I see what's in your hearts—that you know about us Spirits. You believe in us Spirits and I like that. I want to help you. You're both very brave warriors and I want to help you and your people. So, I'll tell you how I am going to do it. In the morning when you get up, walk over to the stream and all the grass that's growing there—that's your Mother's hair. Pull the whole thing out of the ground. Don't cut it. You'll have three bunches side by side." What the Spirit was teaching him was how to braid.

So that's what they did. They went and fixed all the braids of Sweetgrass that they could. The Mother's hair also told him, "Your hair is just like your mother's. You shouldn't cut it. The only time you should cut it is when your life will never be the same again. When something happens to you that from this day your life is changed forever—like when your mother goes on to join the ancestors, or someone in the family, because your story is starting over again."

So, they fixed all the braids and they brought them back. They came back and showed up with a lot of dried buffalo meat and lots of ropes and lots of braids of Sweetgrass. They taught the people and the families the song. The song is still with the Kootenai people here now.

CHAPTER 3

The Yamassee Stone Coat Giant Story

Donald Grinde, Jr.

The Stone Coat Giant named Datha or Ocasta was an important part of the philosophy and spiritual practices of the Yamassee people in the lower Savannah River Valley. Ocasta was the Creator's helper, and he was a powerful giant. When he came to earth, he observed human beings killing animals with pieces of flint on the tips of spears and arrows. This frightened him, so he picked up pieces of flint and made a stone coat to protect himself from humans. Ocasta's only magical power on earth was the ability to disappear, but he could not do that in the presence of human beings. Legends claim that Ocasta was the source of evil on earth. Some stories stated that he created witches and other bad things and also traveled from community to community causing trouble and chaos. According to tradition, Yamassee men sought to run him off with bows, arrows, and spears. However, their attempts to use arms failed repeatedly, and the entire Yamassee community was frustrated with the efforts of the men to rid themselves of his presence through warfare and violence.

Seeing the failure of men in stopping Ocasta, the women decided to use their powers to rid the community of the Stone Coat Giant. Accordingly, they stationed seven nude, "moonstruck" (menstruating) women in the woods where Ocasta would pass. When Ocasta came down the path in the woods, Ocasta became very sick seeing so many of the "moonstruck" women. When he fell down, the women picked some flint from his armor and then drove a stake into his heart to hold him down. All the men quickly gathered around him. Ocasta, seeing that the Yamassee had overcome him with the power of women, promised to leave the earth. Before leaving, Ocasta taught the humans songs and dances to please the Creator. These new rituals would help the Yamassees win wars and heal the sick. He also instructed the first medicine men and female healers. When his body began to burn, Ocasta's spirit rose, singing. He had created both good and evil and had sacrificed himself to save the people from the bad things he had made.

The story demonstrates the power of women to fight evil. It also demonstrates that the powers of women must be balanced with the powers of men in warfare and hunting to promote peace and balance in human society. Thus, the Stone Coat Giant story chronicles the origin of good and evil and the gift of medicines to treat bad things.

CHAPTER 4

The Iroquois Confederacy

Donald Grinde, Jr.

THE GREAT LAW OF PEACE

The Ganonsyoni, or People of the Longhouse, are of the Iroquoian linguistic grouping. Five Nations—the Mohawk, Oneida, Onondaga, Cayuga, and Seneca—formed a confederacy whose antecedents are shrouded in the mists of prehistory. In the early eighteenth century, these nations were joined by a sixth brother to the south, the Tuscarora—the Five Nations of the Confederacy became the Six Nations around 1735.

The Iroquois Confederacy was considered a kinship state. It was, and is, a collection of Indian nations bound together by a clan and chieftain system buttressed by a similar linguistic base. But there is much more that strengthens the League of the Iroquois. In their political life, women played a special and profound role. The structure of the Confederacy originated in the "hearth," which consisted of a mother and all her children. Each hearth was part of a wider group called an otiianer.[1] Two or more otiianers constituted a clan. This matrilineal system was headed by a "mother." All the sons and daughters of a particular clan were connected by uterine families that often lived apart. Thus, a husband went to live with his wife's family, and their children became members of the mother's clan by right of birth.[2] By uniting all the descendants in the female line of a particular woman, the Iroquois formed cohesive political groups that had little to do with where people lived or what village the hearths originated from.

The otiianer head's oldest daughter usually succeeded her mother at her death. All authority sprang from the otiianers and the various clans making up a nation. The women who headed these groups appointed the male delegates and deputies who spoke for the otiianers and clans at tribal councils. In consultation with other women within these groups, the women formulated issues and questions to be debated and acted upon in the councils.[3] These women recommended to their male spokesmen what view to express and advocate.

The philosophy of the Iroquois was based on the concept that all life is unified spiritually with the natural environment and other forces surrounding people. These forces had both good and bad aspects, and could be intangible, such as hunger, illness, and the dangers of war.[4] The power to deal with these forces came from an inner spiritual force existing in every person. The spiritual power of only one individual was limited, but when combined with the other individuals of the hearth, otiianers, or clan, the spiritual power became strong. Similarly, whenever a person died either by disease or force, through murder or war, the "public" power was reduced. To maintain the strength of the group, the dead were replaced either by natural increase or, in the event of war, by adopting captives of war. The practice of keeping clans at full strength ensured the power and durability of the matrilineal system as well as the kinship state.

The Iroquois believed in the Master of Life, the first being on earth, who directed people to live in peace and love. He was opposed, however, by an evil brother who influenced people to stray from this ideal. The Master, Teharonhiawagon, promised to send an ambassador to help fight evil when the need arose. Before the coming of Hiawatha, the Iroquois were constantly warring over hunting and fishing rights as well as over tribal territories. Even among the Five Nations, there was petty conflict—blood revenge, the killing of a man who had slain a relative—causing strife. Disunity among the tribes resulted. In this era of self-destruction, the leaders remembered the Master of Life's teachings and wondered how to persuade the people to return to those teachings. Many looked for a messenger from Teharonhiawagon. Another group proposed a council be called of all leaders to find a way to end the constant internal strife. Hiawatha was one of those who pressed for such a council.[5] By most accounts, he was living among the Onondagas and was respected for his oratory and magical powers.

But Hiawatha was pitted against a diabolical Onondaga chief called Atotarho, the symbolic figure of evil, of ferocious appearance, who used all forms of trickery such as witchcraft and wizardry to defeat the plans of Hiawatha and his followers. Some said that Atotarho was the Master of Life's evil brother, while others said he was Hiawatha's half brother. Atotarho set up a tyrannical regime with assassins and spies serving his evil purposes. He is described in the most hideous terms. His body is said to have had seven crooks, his hands were like those of the turtle, and his hair was a mass of serpents.[6]

Lithograph of Atotarho, the first Iroquois Ruler—Illustration by Seth Eastman, Plate 70 in Schoolcraft, H.R. (1851) *History of the Indian Tribes of the United States*. Philadelphia: Lippincott, Grambo & Company, 188.

Each time Hiawatha sought to form a peace council, Atotarho's spies would appear to foil the efforts of the peaceful chiefs. From the start, Atotarho viewed Hiawatha as leader of the peace chiefs and began to kill Hiawatha's daughters through magic, one by one. Finally, when Hiawatha had one daughter left alive, he made a last attempt to hold a council. As the chiefs assembled in the woods and built temporary lodges, they learned that Atotarho had heard of the council, and was already among them. The peaceful group became fearful as they awaited Hiawatha. One day, as Hiawatha's last daughter, who was pregnant, was gathering firewood, Atotarho sprang up and pointed to a large and beautiful creature flying through the sky toward the daughter. Filled with curiosity, the people ran headlong to the spot, trampling the woman to death. Atotarho had won again. The grieving Hiawatha acknowledged defeat, abandoned the Onondagas, and carried the word of peace to other Iroquois tribes.[7]

He traveled among the Iroquois villages talking to the Mohawks, Oneidas, and Cayugas, attempting to convince them to renounce war and internal strife. He spoke of the restoration of peace and brotherhood among the Iroquois. At every village Hiawatha was given lodging and an audience. However, people were slow to embrace his ideas. They could not forget the old animosities and suspicions. Tradition has it that the Oneidas agreed to accept his teachings if the Mohawks would also consent.[8] Subsequently, the Mohawks and the Cayugas embraced Hiawatha's teachings, with the proviso that he persuade the formidable Atotarho to end his rule of terror and bring the Onondagas into the covenant of peace. It was thought to be an impossible goal.

Hiawatha, it was feared, was defeated. But a man named Deganawidah entered his life and changed the nature of things through his philosophy of peace and his visionary powers. Deganawidah's words and purpose made him, in some way, a greater figure than Hiawatha in Iroquois traditional beliefs. Although Deganawidah has been portrayed as more legendary than a common man, he probably was an Indian prophet appearing at a crucial moment in Iroquois history to instruct Hiawatha.[9]

Little is known about Deganawidah's early life except that he was a Huron from eastern Ontario. Roughly translated, his name means "Man, the Thinker." He was raised by his mother who taught him to understand humankind and filled him with a philosophy of love. She also informed him that he had a divine purpose in the world.

Deganawidah was not without human frailties, however. Some accounts say he stammered so much, he could scarcely talk. But his handsome face was said to have reflected the soul of a mystic. Like most prophets, he had experienced a powerful vision that transformed him. In his vision, he saw a giant evergreen reaching to the sky and gaining strength from three counterbalancing principles of life. The principles were a stable mind and healthy body in balance, with peace between individuals as well as groups. In addition, he saw that humane conduct, thought, and speech were prerequisites for equity and justice among people. Finally, he envisioned a society in which physical strength and civil authority would reinforce the power of the clan system. The tree had four roots that stretched out to the four directions of the earth. From the base of the tree a snow-white carpet covered the surrounding countryside. This white carpet protected the lands of the people who adopted the three double principles. At the crest of the evergreen, an eagle was perched. Deganawidah recognized the tree as humanity, living within his principles governing relations among human beings. The eagle was humanity's lookout against enemies who might disturb the peace.[10] Ideally, the protective carpet could be extended to the four corners of the earth to provide a shelter of peace and brotherhood for all humankind.

Deganawidah perceived the vision as a message to him from the Master of Life. He was to bring harmony into the human condition and unite all peoples into a single family guided by the three double principles. However, his work could not begin with the Hurons because he was fatherless, an outcast with no standing. So, he bid farewell to his mother and left Huron country to carry his ideas to the other Iroquois nations. Since he was a man without a tribal bond, he moved freely from one nation to another.[11] But his words, uttered in a stammering manner, were not well received.

Events transpired in such a way that Deganawidah, in the course of his wanderings, finally met Hiawatha. Some versions of this history say that Deganawidah united all the tribes except the Onondagas, and that he persuaded the discouraged Hiawatha to attempt the conversion of the evil Atotarho. But the two men did meet, decided to work together, and complemented each other in their common cause to end the bitter strife in Iroquois country. Deganawidah gave substance to Hiawatha's vague appeals to unity, offering a practical plan of government based on specific principles. Because Deganawidah was a poor speaker, Hiawatha became his messenger to the Iroquois nations, finally gaining acceptance of the message of the Great Peace.[12] The Mohawks, Cayugas, and Oneida agreed to the Great Peace, but the Onondagas, led by Atotarho, still held out.

With Deganawidah's help, Hiawatha was now able to convert the intransigent wizard. According to one account, Deganawidah held a council of all the chiefs who had agreed to the Great Peace, including Hiawatha. They decided to go to Atotarho together. To aid in straightening out his twisted body and mind, the council members made thirteen strings of wampum and chanted the Six Songs. These were part of the Feast of the Dead. When two spies who were sent to find Atotarho returned, they told horrible stories about his physical features. Deganawidah told the wavering chiefs that it was their duty to remake the evil wizard's mind. So, the chiefs proceeded to Atotarho's village, singing.

When they reached the village, the council was ushered into Atotarho's presence. Although the dreadful shape of the evil one horrified them, they unwrapped the thirteen strings of wampum and began singing the Six Songs. This soothed Atotarho. Deganawidah then said to him, "We will straighten out your mind now." As the chiefs continued singing, they handed Atotarho a string of wampum. Deganawidah told the wizard that the song belonged to him alone, and it was called "I Used It to Beautify the Earth." Noting that Atotarho's mind was becoming transformed, Deganawidah passed his hands over the evil one's feet, changing them from their tortoise shape with claws like a bear's, to the normal feet of a man. After the prophet had restored Atotarho's distorted hands, he brushed the hissing snakes from the wizard's hair. Next, he decreed that the wizard's head should become human. Last, Deganawidah straightened the twisted body of Atotarho and pronounced him to be redeemed; the evil one was now reborn and charged with implementing the message of peace that Deganawidah spoke of.[13]

There are other versions of this redemption in which Hiawatha combed the serpents of evil thoughts from Atotarho's hair. In fact, loosely translated, the name Hiawatha means "He, the Comber." The transformed tyrant now became the Onondaga chief, the "firekeeper," the most important member of the new Confederacy.[14] To this day, the Great Council Fire of the Confederacy is kept in the land of the Onondagas. Regardless of the interpretations, Atotarho became benign and agreed to join the League, provided only that the Senecas be included. This was done soon after Atotarho's transformation, and the Iroquois were now well on the road to peace and confederation. Under the aegis of Hiawatha and Deganawidah, the clan leaders of the five tribes gathered around the council fires to fashion the laws and government of the Confederacy. Joined by the leaders of the League, Deganawidah planted a Great Tree of Peace called the Great White Pine (Tsioneratasekowa) in the land of the Onondagas. Under the shade of the tree, the down of the Globe Thistle was spread for Atotarho and his cousins in the Confederacy to sit upon. There, the leaders were to guard the League's fire. It was before this body that all affairs of the Confederacy were to be conducted, according to Deganawidah. Great White Roots spread out from the Tree of Peace, even unto the four directions. The nature of these Great White Roots was, and is, strength. Anyone outside of the Five Nations who obeyed the laws of the Great Peace (Kaianarekowa) and made this known to the statesmen of the League, could trace back the roots to the tree. If the mind was obedient and promise was made to obey the wishes of the Council of the League, they were welcome to take shelter beneath the Great Tree. The eagle was also placed atop the tree to be eternally vigilant against any impending danger.[15] Thus, the vision of Deganawidah came to pass.

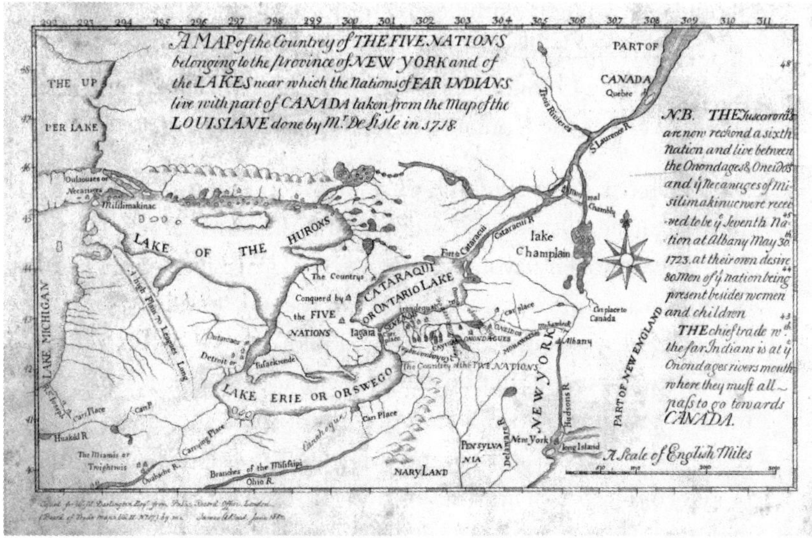

Map of the Iroquois Five Nations and Mission Sites—Map by John S. Clark in Hawley, C. (1879) *Early Chapters of Cayuga History: Jesuit Missions in Goi-O-Gouen, 1656–1684.* Auburn, NY: Knapp & Peck, front matter.

Since the fire was to be maintained by Atotarho, the League was to meet always at Onondaga. When the League was not in session, and a meeting was desired by any council members, a messenger was to be sent to the firekeepers of the Onondagas with a complete explanation of the issue to be discussed. Atotarho would then call his Onondaga chiefs together and determine whether the issue was of sufficient importance to call the attention of the Council.[16] If the business proposed for discussion was determined to merit such consideration, Atotarho sent runners to summon all chiefs to sit beneath the Great Tree of Peace. Deganawidah gave strict instructions governing the conduct of the League and its deliberations.

- When the Council is assembled, the Council Fire should be kindled (not with chestnut wood), and Atotarho should then open the meeting formally. Atotarho and the other Onondaga chiefs will then announce the purpose of the meeting and what is to be discussed.[17] The rising smoke of the Council Fire piercing the sky is a signal to the Iroquois allies that the Council is in session.

- During the course of deliberations, Atotarho and the thirteen other chiefs of the Onondagas shall keep the area around the fire clean, using the wing of a seagull (Tsiowatstekawe Onerahonstsha). Should a crawling creature come near the Council Fire, a staff presented to the leaders of the Onondagas should be used to turn it away.[18] If the Onondaga chiefs are unable to do this, they may enlist the aid of the Council's remaining members.

- The Mohawk council members are divided into three groups: Tehanakarine, Ostawenserentha, and Soskoharowane being the first. Tekarohoken, Ayonwatha, and Satekariwate are the second. Serenhowane, Teyonkekwen, and Orerekowa are the third. The first group listens only to the discussion of the second and third segments, to ensure that no errors are made. If an error occurs, the first group should call attention to it. When the dispute is settled between the second and third groups, the decision should be referred to the Seneca statesmen for their approval, in accord with the Mohawk chiefs.[19] Subsequently, the question is to be thrown across the fire to the Cayuga and Oneida chiefs on the opposite side of the council house.

- Deganawidah's instructions are precise in every way, all designed to create a form of government guided by traditions of peace and understanding.

- According to his great design, the Council is to be composed of fifty sachems (chiefs). They are obliged to meet every five years, and more frequently if necessary. The chiefs are appointed by the female leaders of the tribal otiianers. Although the sachems serve for life, they can be removed by the female leaders for misconduct, sickness, or other reasons causing them to be ineffective.

The Onondagas sent fourteen delegates to the Council. The Cayugas were permitted to send ten. The Mohawks and Oneidas had nine delegates each, and the Senecas eight. None of the sachems could be warriors. The reasoning for this was sound: they might adopt warlike positions. Upon the death of a chief, the leader of his otiianers appointed a new man, who adopted the name and functions of the man he succeeded. So, the names and duties of the first council were made permanent. An Onondaga named Atotarho was always firekeeper and moderator. The places of Hiawatha and Deganawidah were the only ones not reappointed. After their death, their seats remained empty, since they were to be present in the spirit.[20] Hiawatha and Deganawidah had founded a lasting Confederacy that functions even today.

Thus it was that the conduct and structure of the Council demonstrated the unity and completeness of humans and the environment. Whenever a Council is held, the Onondaga statesmen greet the other members and express their gratitude to the earth, the streams, the lakes and pools; to the corn and fruits; to the medicinal herbs and trees; to the trees of the forest for their usefulness; and to the animals who provide clothing and food. Thanks are given to the great winds and the lesser winds; to the Moons, the Sun, the Thunderers, and the mighty warriors; and to the messengers of the Creator who expressed his wishes. Also, gratitude is expressed to the Great Creator who dwells in the skies above, who gives all things useful to humankind, who is the ruler and source of health and life. After this thanksgiving, the Onondaga leaders declare the Council open. Council cannot be in session after dark.[21]

The laws of the confederacy are based on the teachings of Deganawidah to ensure the Great Peace and protect the lives and liberty of the participants. Individual rights, safety, and justice were assured. The blood feud, a terrible and divisive force, was outlawed. Under the new law, when an Indian killed another person, the grieving family no longer had the right to avenge the killing by taking the life of the murderer. Instead, the bereaved family was obliged to accept twenty strings of wampum from the slayer's family, ten for the dead man and ten for the life of the murderer himself. If a woman was killed, the retribution was thirty wampum strings.[22]

Wampum played several major roles in Iroquois life. Hiawatha introduced the custom of using wampum at the League's founding. He decreed and regulated its use. Wampum was designed to bring peace and unity among the Five Nations and take the place of blood. Hiawatha first used wampum with the Mohawks. After telling the Council of its use, Deganawidah used wampum to console or wipe away the tears of Hiawatha, whose heart was grieved through the loss of his daughters. This was the first Condolence Ceremony. It exists today without change. The first wampum used by Hiawatha was probably made of freshwater shells; earlier forms for decorative and communication purposes may have been wooden or constructed from porcupine quills.[23]

As the Iroquois began to trade with the New England tribes, especially the Narragansetts, wampum became more plentiful, as the Atlantic coast was a great source of purple and white quahog shells. Gradually, wampum assumed sacred connotations. It became a medium of communication as well. Wampum strings served as credentials and symbols of authority. No Iroquois chief would listen to a messenger or pay attention to a report until he had received official information through a runner who possessed the proper belt or string of wampum. Thus, wampum certified a messenger or a promise. Treaties were not recognized unless they were accompanied by wampum. Belts were exchanged at treaty ceremonies as symbols of friendship and for promises made. Often as many as forty belts would be exchanged at such a ceremony. To break a treaty under these conditions was a sacrilege. Also, all laws passed by the League were recorded with a certain string or belt of wampum. The treaty or law that was placed on wampum was memorized by trained and delegated individuals. Hence, wampum was the record-keeping function of the Confederacy;[24] it dictated credentials, protocol, and was the record of enacted laws.

Through the establishment of the new laws and the Council Fire of the League, Deganawidah had realized his vision of universal peace and brotherhood. While the new consciousness with its guarantees of an end to blood feuds applied only to the five tribes, the Great Peacemaker believed that the protective carpet of white eventually would spread to all people of the world. He visualized a Council Fire for all nations spreading toward the rising and setting sun, all over the earth. In turn, the newly converted people would teach their neighbors the message of peace and brotherhood. He did not doubt that his message would in time be embraced by all humankind.

One day, according to Iroquois tradition, Deganawidah called the people together and spoke to them. He declared he would no longer be seen by men. Then he embarked in a white canoe on Lake Onondaga and disappeared into the setting sun.[25]

Hiawatha remained to carry the word of peace to other Iroquoian tribes. Initially, the Hurons, Eriez, and Neutrals accepted the message, tentatively. Then Hiawatha and his messengers journeyed farther, throughout the Northeast and the Midwest. He is said to have traveled as far as Lake Superior and the waters of the Mississippi. When he returned to the five tribes, he brought back strings of wampum, attesting to these distant tribes' adherence to his creed.[26] These journeys increased Hiawatha's stature among his people, and the Iroquois viewed him as capable of bringing all nations on earth to the Great Peace.

Some say that Hiawatha spent his last days among the Mohawks as an elder statesman. Another tradition tells of his following Deganawidah into the mists of Lake Champlain in a white bark canoe. When Hiawatha died, the Iroquois viewed him as being very close to the Master of Life. Upon their deaths, both he and Deganawidah were rapidly cloaked in mystery and legend.[27]

THE LONGHOUSE

Throughout the time of intense settler pressure, and wars with other Native peoples, as well as with European powers, the Confederacy maintained its power and strength. Reasons for the endurance of such a confederation are many, but perhaps the idea of expanding the Longhouse is most important. This principle gave everyone under the Tree of Peace a ready analogy to everyday life in understanding the government. The physical environment and family relations had a direct bearing on the functioning of the League.

Traditional Iroquois Longhouse—Gordy, Wilbur F. (1913) *Stories of American History*, New York: Charles Scribner's Sons, 20.

The Longhouse was more than just a shelter. It was the basic unit upon which the entire society was constructed. Certain physical factors in the Iroquois lifestyle reinforced the concepts of the Longhouse, as we shall see.

The People of the Longhouse lived in stockade villages in elevated areas that were easy to defend and often were located near a water supply. Fifteen-to-twenty-foot-long palisades surrounded and protected a group of Longhouses, and a ditch was dug around palisade walls. Bark platforms at the top supplied with stones served the Iroquois' needs during attacks.[28] The palisades acted as a defensive wall and also helped to keep forest animals from foraging within the village.

Longhouses were the typical dwelling unit within the stockade. The use of the Longhouse as a dwelling, however, extended from New England to the Savannah River and westward into the Great Lakes region. A number of families were housed within each Longhouse. The size of a village might vary from four or five bark lodges to more than a hundred. The Longhouse varied in size from twenty feet by sixteen feet and fifteen feet high, to huge multiple family dwellings sixty feet by eighteen feet and eighteen feet high. In the more populous villages, Longhouses have been known to be more than three hundred feet long.[29]

To build the Longhouse, a row of forked poles was placed in the ground, between four and five feet apart. Cross poles were lashed to the forked uprights to form an arched roof. Slender poles or rafters were then secured to the roof frame, and traverse poles were added to further strengthen the overhead structure. Large pieces of bark were then tied to the frame. The bark was obtained in the spring by stripping the trees when the sap began to flow. Elm, ash, cedar, fir, spruce, or basswood were the usual sources of bark. An outer set of poles kept the bark in place on the sides and roof, and smoke holes were built into the roof at about twenty-foot intervals. These holes would usually be covered with a piece of bark.[30] The hearth beneath the smoke hole was shared by two families.

Doors were built at each end of the Longhouse. Animal hide or hinged bark was used, and this covering could be lifted up. Along the inside wall, bunks were constructed, which served as beds at night and benches in the day. Corn, dried fish, and other foods hung from overhead. The dwelling was compartmentalized to accommodate each family, and storage space was available in the corners and in closets between the compartments. At the front of the Longhouse, over the door, inhabitants placed pictures of clan symbols to represent the families living in that Longhouse.[31]

By the end of the eighteenth century, bark structures gave way to hewn log buildings; wood frame houses began to appear. However, the bark houses were built and used well into the mid-nineteenth century.

LIFEWAYS

Agriculture was reserved for the women, although the men helped in clearing the fields and other heavy work. But the actual planting and harvesting was the women's domain. The Three Sisters (corn, beans, and squash) were the traditional crops grown. The women used stone and wooden implements to till the soil. Corn was the most important crop. It could be eaten immediately, or dried and stored for the winter. Iroquois cornfields were large and planted in "hills." Beans could be dried for future use, and squash or pumpkins were stored in a cool place or cut into strips and dried.[32]

The women also gathered nuts, roots, wild berries, and fruits. Sassafras roots, birch bark, hemlock twigs, and spice wood were steeped in boiling water to serve as beverages, and maple syrup or maple sugar was used as a sweetener. Also, sunflowers were raised and pressed to extract the oil for cooking and hair dressing. They were also used in various religious rites.

Tobacco was grown and much prized, not only for smoking but also for religious purposes. Masks used in ceremonials were consecrated by attaching bags of tobacco to them. Tobacco was also burned as incense; the rising smoke was a visible prayer to the Creator. Tobacco also warded off evil. In many ways, this plant had deep spiritual meaning for the Iroquois and was widely used in religious observances and rituals.

The men were the hunters, although women often accompanied their husbands on hunting parties. On such occasions, they took charge of the camps. The hunting season began in the fall and continued until midwinter. Another hunt took place in the early spring. These expeditions frequently took the men away from the village for long periods of time. They sought moose, deer, beaver, bear, and elk using bows and arrows, tomahawks, snares, and traps. Large deer drives were common, and small animals were taken with snares or the bow and arrow.

Spring, summer, and fall were also fishing season, and lines, nets, harpoons, or weirs were the tools used. Usually, the fish was dried. Mussels were also sought and were a mainstay in the people's diet.[33]

Most of the winter festivals centered around the agricultural cycle, except for the midwinter, which concluded the fall hunting expedition. From the time the maple sap started to flow in the early spring to the fall harvest, the Iroquois had ceremonies expressing gratitude for the gifts of the Creator. Such festivals conveyed a feeling of oneness with nature. For instance, when the corn and other garden crops had ripened, the people called a meeting to give thanks with dances for the green corn. People and corn were considered sisters, and "they whispered to a person in the fields," it was said.[34] Animate and inanimate were united as one under the auspices of the Creator.

The Iroquois described natural forces in kinship terms. The thunder that brought rain was a grandparent. The moon was a grandmother who helped people in the dark and measured time. The sun was an elder brother who warmed the earth and provided daylight. The life supporters, corn, beans, and squash strengthened and sustained the Iroquois. All these things came from the Great Creator, and the Iroquois gave thanks for the gifts.[35] Not only were the people linked to the state by kinship ties but also to the environment and all living things. Since all Iroquois society was divided into clans named after certain animals, the People of the Longhouse also had a close relationship in symbolic form with the animal kingdom.

The clan was headed by a woman. This clan mother was the head of the household, and the stewardess of the affairs of the earth, such as planting and harvesting. All things were symbolically related, which produced unity and strength.[36] Unity, not only in a political sense, but also in a spiritual and environmental sense, was the binding force in Iroquois life.

Thus, the League of the Deganawidah and Hiawatha was an extension of the kinship principle. It was a symbolic as well as a physical household. Roughly translated, the League of the Ganinsyoni means, "a lodge spread out far." All individuals and all tribes were considered as one family living together. Moreover, the spiritual values and sense of unity with the environment served to strengthen this analogy, since humans were interpreted as being related to all things.

The symbolism that existed in Iroquois societal structure, in secular government, and in political union—and in religious practice as well—was deeply understood by all.

Thus were seated the nations of the Confederacy in the Longhouse: The Mohawks were Keepers of the Eastern Door of the Lodge; the Senecas were the Keepers of the Western Door. In the center, the Onondagas were named the Firekeepers and Wampum Keepers. The Mohawks, Onondagas, and Senecas were the Elder Brothers. The Oneidas and Cayugas, the Younger Brothers. The Younger and Elder Brothers sat on opposite sides of the symbolic lodge, with the Onondagas seated in the center to provide a balance between the two.[37]

Although the League was intended to be a coalition of United Nations acting with one mind, the vicissitudes of local politics often hampered its operation. Kinship concepts strengthened the League, while local autonomy often made it impotent. (Federalism is always plagued with problems of states' rights, but perhaps this problem is more tolerable than a centralized tyranny. The cost of freedom is always dear.)

To an outsider, military power and the exercise of it was the most impressive aspect of Iroquois culture. Before white contact, the Iroquois used wooden armor, but this proved ineffective when firearms and metal points for arrows and spears were introduced. The Iroquois also developed sophisticated military tactics. They would often feign retreat and draw an enemy into a trap, then rush to the foe before he could discharge his weapons. Guerilla tactics were used to destroy an enemy as an additional strategy of war. As the Iroquois obtained more and more firearms, guerilla tactics became more and more prevalent.[38]

Contrary to the usual textbook interpretation, Iroquois "war" activities were not adventuristic, chance events. There were reasons the people used force. Protection of the homeland and family, defense of the tribe's boundaries, and economic necessity, such as guarding planted fields, usually brought the so-called war parties into action.

Other than through the hereditary clan system, Iroquois men could achieve prominence by ability in war. Although the title of sachem, the peace chief, was hereditary within the lineage of a clan, ordinary men could rise to fame through military expeditions or religious crusades. Once war had been declared, anyone could form a war party. An aspiring war chief or one who was already famous would often go through the village sounding the war cry. Upon striking his hatchet into the war pole, the leader would relate his courageous deeds and begin a war dance. Men who wished to follow him joined in the dance, which was followed by a feast.[39]

But the women had a significant influence on the warriors, and frequently they could either prevent or encourage a war party by their approval or disapproval. If the women refused to give the warriors moccasins and charred corn pounded into a meal sweetened with maple sugar, they were effectively saying no to the proposed military venture.[40]

The culture and historical background of the League of the Iroquois is rich in ideals that unify people in spite of their differences. The Confederacy exemplified these concepts.

The clan system, with its ability to adopt people in order to maintain the strength of the clan and the nation, is a good example of this effort. The words of peace from Hiawatha and Deganawidah helped forge an alliance of tribes that survives even today, despite many weaknesses. The creation story and the thanksgiving festivals all played a part in bolstering this cohesion. Wampum provided the necessary mode of communication, and all these factors made the League a strong and durable coalition.

CHAPTER 5

Alaska Native Education

HISTORY AND ADAPTATION IN THE NEW MILLENNIUM[1]

Angayuqaq Oscar Kawagley

Portrait of Angayuqaq Oscar Kawagley—Courtesy of Ray Barnhardt

NATURE AS METAPHYSIC

For the Yupiaq people, culture, knowing, and living are intricately interrelated. Living in a harsh environment requires a vast array of precise empirical knowledge to survive the many risks due to conditions such as unpredictable weather and marginal food availability. To avoid starvation, they must employ a variety of survival strategies, including appropriate storage of foodstuffs that they can fall back on during the time of need. Their food gathering and storage must be efficient as well as effective. If this were not so, how could they possibly hope to survive? To help them achieve this balance, they have developed an outlook of nature as metaphysic.

Not only are humans endowed with consciousness, but so are all things of the environment. The Yupiaq people live in an aware world. Wherever they go they are amongst spirits of their ancestors, as well as those of the animals, plants, hills, winds, lakes, and rivers. Their sense of sacredness is of a practical nature, not given to abstract deities and theological rationalization. Pragmatism is the theme of their sacred ways. The *Ellam Yua*, or Creative Force, is not given the same ultimate stature as the Biblical God. Because nature is their metaphysic, Yupiaq people are concerned with maintaining harmony in their own environment. The Creative Force is acknowledged and often given gratitude, though it is the immediacy of nature that is most important.

The Yupiaq people have many taboos, rituals, and ceremonies to observe and practice that poignantly signify a harmonious ecological orientation. They behave accordingly because of what their culture has taught, as well as an abiding belief in what they and others have experienced firsthand. There are mysteries of the world that to Yupiaq are unfathomable, such as the *Ellam Yua*, but these are accepted. Such mysteries keep them humble and ever mindful of the powers around them.

There were members of the Yupiaq community who transcended all human levels of knowledge. These were the shamans, the dreamers, and others who were receptive to nature's voices and intuitively deciphered a message which was passed on by myth, taboo, ritual, ceremony, or other forms of extraordinary happening. The shamans were gifted to travel freely in the unseen world, and they often would return with new songs, taboos, rituals, or ceremonies to teach. They were skillful with their knives and were able to reify their remembrances and impressions of the gift from a spirit with wood, bone, skin, feathers, and stone. These would become sacred objects to be used in special ceremonies. Amulets were also prescribed by the shamans to those requesting and willing to trade for them. These often consisted of animal parts and/or other pieces of earthly creations. Taboos were often conferred with the amulet or medicine bag, which was usually worn as a necklace or sewn somewhere on the parka. There are many stories of how they were used when encountering an antagonistic spirit, animal, or another human being. This kind of healing is not new to the Yupiaq people. The patient's belief in its healing power most likely had a lot to do with the results.

The Yupiaq are told that if they take from another person's traps, the person may not know, but the Creative Force will see that people learn of their deeds and recognize the kind of person they really are. People may try to change a person's tendency to steal by joking and embarrassing him or her in public. However, if there is no change, then he or she might be shunned by the community. Taking another's life without cause is considered a heinous crime; banishment from the village is traditionally the justice rendered.

The Yupiaq people were admonished to never do harm, abuse, or even make fun of animals. Since Yupiaq people live in an aware world, the animals and everything else will always know. Several years ago, there was a news account of several walruses found dead on a beach with only their heads missing. The Fish and Wildlife managers lamented the fact that this was a wanton waste of meat and hides. One old Native man's comment to this was that it was unfortunate that it happened, and that the walruses had not been properly cared for. He concluded by saying that these animals would not be returning to earth. According to him, the misuse, abuse, and disrespect shown the animals would cause the spirits not to return to earth to be born and renew their kind again. From a Yupiaq perspective, this is why certain plants and animals have gone into extinction, and many others are on the endangered species list.

Certain animals represent power, for example, the bear, the wolf, raven, eagle, and beaver. Their commonality is strength and a strong will to live, along with cleanliness and care of self. Each possesses certain characteristics which set them apart from all others: the bear with its strength, the wolf with its social organization, the raven with its ability to remain airborne for great lengths of time, and the eagle with its visual acuity. The oil gland of the beaver is used for amulets, as well as for medicinal purposes. If a person has a shortness of breath, they can chew on a small piece and swallow the juice, thus relieving the stressful feeling. It is also thought to be particularly strong against spirits, so that merely having it in the hand is enough to keep a spirit at bay.

WHEN THE EARTH'S CRUST WAS THIN

Stories and myths abound from Distant Time, when the earth's crust was thin, when it was easy for people and animals to communicate or transform from one to the other. Some tell of animals and birds wearing special parkas with hoods. If they needed to communicate with man, all they needed to do was raise the hood, very much like taking off a mask. Lo and behold, there would be a human face underneath able to communicate in human language. This was an excellent way of learning about animals and how they wanted to be cared for once they gave themselves to the hunter. There is one important difference between human beings and animals. The animals seem to have not been given the knowledge of death. It is only the human who possesses this dubious knowledge. However, the Yupiaq person does not consider death the end but rather a completion of a cycle which continues. As such, most have no fear of death.

The following story, told by William Oquilluk,[2] an Inupiaq Eskimo from the Bering Strait area whose ways are very similar to the Yupiaq, provides an illustration of how observations of the characteristics of animals are integrated into the fabric of the Native mythology.

> *It is a story of "Two Brothers" living with their mother and father. They are young boys always roaming around their environment. One day the boys are walking amongst the trees when they spot a camp robber nest. The younger boy says to his brother that these birds always steal from the camps and that he will sharpen a stick and kill the young birds. This he does. He climbs the tree and as each bird opens its mouth, he thrusts the stick down their throats killing them. Finally, there is only one left and the older brother forces the younger boy down, thereby saving one bird. Meanwhile, the parents are flying around making frantic noises.*
>
> *One winter, when the boys are hiking around, they spot a rabbit. They give it chase. They get separated and are lost. Many animals help each boy during the year. They are invited to homes very often housing small people. They are housed and fed for a few days. When it is time for them to leave, they are told to go a certain distance before looking back. One time when leaving a home, they looked back and saw a beaver house with two beavers swimming about.*

The younger brother ended up in a large community house with many couples living inside. He stayed with them many days. Finally, the eldest man said that he hasn't much time to live, and that the boy will have to leave. The wife tells him how he had killed her children, save one. Because one had been left alive, she would spare his life, but he would have to take the girl as his wife. The little human beings changed to a variety of birds, and left in pairs each singing its own special song. He turned to look at the girl. She had changed to a full sized human being. They departed and went to their camp which turned out to be quite close by.

The older brother is shown by others the direction to go home. He soon joined the other brother. They grew to a ripe old age, and eventually the older brother died followed closely by his younger brother. The latter slipped into another world and immediately saw his brother walking toward him. He could see that his brother had a cut on his lip. He noticed that he too had a similar cut. He told his brother that this was his punishment for killing those birds. They pondered the question of where they should go. The older loved the land, while the younger felt at home in the ocean. They decided that they would separate and go to the place of their liking. The older brother became a rabbit, the younger a seal. To this day they are classified together as they both have cleft lips and are brothers!

Harbor Seals in Kenai Fjords National Park—
Photographer Kaitlin Thoreson, National Park Service

Mythology is an invaluable pedagogical tool that transcends time. As the storyteller talks, the Yupiaq listeners are thrust into the world of imagination. As the story unfolds, it becomes a part of their present. As you imagine and visualize in the mind's eye, how could you not become a part of it and it a part of you? There is no separation. The story and words contain the epistemological webbing; how is it we got to know these truths? The storyteller's inflections, play on words, and actions give special meaning to the listener. How the participants are to act and interact in the whole are clearly conveyed. To the outsider attempting to understand the meaning of the experience, it may appear to be merely a story, but to the insider it becomes reality leading to a spiritual orientation in accord with nature. This is quality knowledge whose end is happiness and a long life.

The Yupiaq people are admonished not to take themselves too seriously, but to laugh at themselves and with others, and to make light of a lot of life's triumphs and tribulations. Joking is a necessary part of life. No matter how serious a ceremony, there will be joking and laughing interspersed between singing, dancing, and moments of silence. Silence is embraced as a time for introspection and collective mindfulness for a greater and better life. Because of this collective mindfulness, the individual man or woman becomes greater as a provider or as a homemaker. And as rational thinking would have it, the whole is always greater than the sum of its parts.

Through the millennia of their existence, the Yupiaq people worked as stewards of their world and maintained a balance between their culture, technology, and the environment around them. Their psychological satisfaction with their nature-mediated technology was on an even plane with their technological attainments. This allowed for nature as their metaphysic. However in the last sixty years or more there has appeared an ontological discontinuity. This is the period of time in which they have participated in the destructive acts of misuse, abuse, and disrespect of the ecological processes that produce life in their environment. How did they come about making this destruction of life? What has happened to cause their social organization to disintegrate with concomitant decay of their morality and disillusionment with their way of life?

YUPIAQ LIFEWAYS

Traditionally, men and women had very defined roles. The man was the provider, the one to work with nature in hunting and trapping. It was a solitary effort—solitary in that he did many activities by himself, but in reality was always accompanied by spirits and in close contact with the animals and earth. His role as provider was to learn as much as possible from his father, extended family members, elders and others, so as to be a success.

The woman, on the other hand, had to learn womanly duties from her mother, grandmother, and others. This included child rearing, food preparation, garment making, observing taboos having to do with menses and giving childbirth, and mindfully supporting her husband. The man's success as hunter was just as much her responsibility. They made up a team, complemented one another, and were very much equal in standing. The community members' bondedness to each other was mutual, adding to their wholeness and vitality.

When a child was born, the name of a recently deceased person was anointed to the newborn by pouring a little water into the mouth or sometimes sprinkling onto the head. Thereafter, that was his/her name. The gender was unimportant. The relatives called the baby by that name and the kinship term associated with the person whose name was bestowed on the child. For example, if the deceased person's wife addressed the child, she would address it by name then follow it with "my husband". Thus a "new relative" was made whether blood related or not.

The traditional houses in which families lived were constructed of sod in a semi-subterranean fashion. A high, dry location was chosen, a circular hole dug down three to four feet in depth, and then a framework of driftwood was constructed. Sod was cut and carried to the site and placed on the wood frame with the vegetation-covered side next to the wood. Sometimes grass was placed between to serve as a natural vapor barrier. An opening at the top was covered with a seal or walrus gut canopy. This was removed when a fire was made in the firepit for cooking or a fire bath. The house was a circular and domed structure with an enclosed entranceway much like the snow igloos of Northern Canada.

The structure of the Yupiaq sod house has been likened to the woman's reproductive system. The ceiling's name in the Yupiaq language means "the above covering," a term which is now used to mean "heaven." The skylight is likened to the umbilical cord leading to the *Ellam Yua*, the interior to the womb, and the tunnel-like entrance to the birth canal, or "the way to go out." In the old days, when a person died, he or she was never removed through the entranceway, but through the skylight. The body was lifted and passed through the opening to the place of interment. The act was very symbolic of the spirit's journey to the spiritual land. The body was then placed with knees to the chest and arms around the knees bound together at the wrists—a fetal position, signifying completion of the life cycle and readiness for reincarnation and renewal. The body was then covered with driftwood or rocks, or sometimes with wooden planks, a canoe, or kayak overturned with the body inside.

The *qasegiq*, or community house, was mainly the domain of men and boys prior to puberty. This is where much of the storytelling, teaching of arts and crafts, tests of skill and strength, and learning of rituals and ceremonies took place. It was the site of reintegration and renewal of spirit and where balancing occurred. When special ceremonies were conducted, participants from other villages were invited. The whole community and visitors from invited communities all participated and enjoyed the generosity of the host village. They renewed acquaintances and made new friendships, acknowledged the unseen greater powers, paid respects to their ancestors, celebrated the animal spirits, and even made a few marriage arrangements. The ceremonies reaffirmed the truths that the people chose to live by.

Much of man's and woman's activities were patterned to the landscape. For those living on the upper riverine systems, the activities were bound to catching and preserving fish and hunting for land animals. Those on the coast hunted sea mammals, fish, and seasonal birds and eggs. The technological tools and implements were made from natural resources most abundant in their location, or were gained in trade from other areas. The materials consisted of wood, bone, stone, and skin, or, sometimes, nature-refined copper. They may have intuitively known that their technology would be restricted to unrefined natural resources, and that this would conform to their nature-adaptive orientation. They may have observed themselves and others aging, tools wearing out, rivers getting shallow and changing course, trails where nothing grew, and that death and decay occurred everywhere. When a certain amount of matter and energy are no longer in usable state, some degradation is inevitable. Were they to refine natural resources, they would speed up the entropic process.

A few years ago, there was an old Native man on the Kobuk River speaking about the tundra fires raging about the state. He said that the earth is like a human being; it is aging, its skin is drying and graying. Therefore, the fires never burn themselves out, rather they have to have firefighters or heavy rains put them out. He recalled fires years ago that naturally burned themselves out because of lush greenery and moisture. He talked of the earth as a living being, aging, decaying, and perhaps, needing to be renewed. The Creative Force has not the patience nor compassion to accept a people that defile and destroy, and will take the shortest route to heal a festering sore.

CONSEQUENCES OF ADAPTATION

The encroachment of western civilization in the Yupiaq world changed a people that did not seek to be changed. The Yupiaq peoples' systems of education, governance, spirituality, economy, being, and behavior were very much in conformity with their philosophy of life and provided for harmonious living. The people were satisfied with the quality of their life and felt that their technology was in accord with it. Culture- and nature-mediated technology was geared to a sustainable level of self-sufficiency.

The people in general were sufficiently content with their lifestyle that they did not readily accept Eurocentric education and religions when the first envoys of the dominant society set foot in their land. Eurocentric knowledge and technological might did not bring the Yupiaq people to compliance—rather it was the incomprehensible diseases that decimated the people. A great number of elders, mothers and/or fathers, shamans, and children succumbed to these new diseases. Whole villages were wiped out. The missionaries began to open orphanages and schools for the newly dislocated exiles in their own land. A hospital was located on the Kuskokwim River near Akiak, and the Moravian Church established a "Children's Home" a short distance up river. The Federal Bureau of Education established "contract schools" with religious organizations. Money was paid to these organizations to establish schools and pay for the missionary teachers. The children were taught a new language (English) along with new knowledge and skills to become servants to the newcomers' needs and as laborers for newly established businesses. The Compulsory School Attendance Law was enacted, requiring families to remain in one location for many months of the year, thus ending the Native peoples' practice of moving from place to place according to the seasons and migration patterns. The restrictive law initiated a twelve-year sentence given all Native children to attend school. Today, that sentence has increased to thirteen, including kindergarten. This has greatly reduced the freedom of people to be who they are, to learn traditional values, and to living in harmony with their environment. It has meant that the families and children no longer experience the great freedom of earlier times.

The schools do not require that the Yupiaq children learn their own languages and lifeways, but rather they are expected to learn a foreign language and the related humanities and sciences. The majority of teachers are from the outside world and have little or no knowledge of the people with whom they are going to be working. To the original people of the land, these are an immigrant people with a different way of being, thinking, behaving, and doing from the Yupiaq. Few teachers recognize that the indigenous Yupiaq are not like other European ethnic groups, such as the Irish, French, or Italians, who have chosen to leave their homeland. By not teaching the Yupiaq youngsters their own language and way of doing things, the classroom teachers are telling them that their language, knowledge, and skills are of little importance. The students begin to think of themselves as being less than other people. After all, they are expected to learn through a language other than their own, to learn values that are in conflict with their own, and to learn a "better" way of seeing and doing things. They are taught the "American Dream" which, in their case, is largely unattainable, without leaving behind who they are.

The messages from the school and the media, and other manifestations of Eurocentric society present Yupiaq students with an unreal picture of the outside world as well as a distorted view of their own, which leads to a great deal of confusion for students over who they are and where they fit in the world. This loss of Yupiaq identity leads to guilt and shame at being Yupiaq. The resultant feelings of hurt, grief, and pain are locked in the mind to emerge as depression and apathy, which is further reinforced by the fear of failure in school, by ridicule from non-Natives, and by the loss of their spirituality. There are many contributing factors as to why Native children do not excel in school. I advance the following as a possible variable. I will do this by telling you a Yupiaq story:

> *Aka tamani, ellam kainga mamkitellrani. In distant time, when the earth's crust was thin, a crane is flying around looking for a likely place to eat. The sky is blue; the sun is shining, the tundra is warming. The crane decides to check out the weather. He begins to fly in a circle. Each time he completes the circle, he gains altitude. He looks at earth from a very high altitude. He then decides to descend and look for food. He flies over a river and sights a skin boat with Yupiat in it slowly paddling down the river. He continues his flight and sees a lake. He flies to it, and finds many kinds of berries. He is very hungry.*
>
> *He lands on the riverbank. He contemplates going back to the tundra to eat berries, but his mind cannot forget the Yupiat coming down the river. He knows that he could be hunted. He must think of a way to warn him when the people approach. He sits there and thinks. He finally decides that he will use his eyes as sentries. He removes his eyes and puts them on a log. He instructs the eyes by telling them, "Now when you see people coming down the river, you warn me. I will come down and get you and fly off."*
>
> *After telling them so, he goes back to the tundra and starts to eat berries. Soon he hears his eyes shout, "Crane, crane, there are people coming down the river!" He hurries down, finds his eyes and plucks them back in the sockets. He looks. There is only a log drifting down the river. The branches must have resembled people. He gets upset and says to his eyes, "Now you be very careful and make sure they are people before you call for me." He goes back to the tundra and eats. Soon, he hears his eyes calling him, "Crane, crane, there is a boat with people in it coming down the river. Come quick!" He hurries down to the log and picks up his eyes and looks. There is only a chunk of tundra drifting down. Tufts of grass move up and down with movements of the clump of tundra.*
>
> *"Now, look eyes you have made a second mistake. Look very carefully before you call for me. I'm going back to eat some more berries."*

> *Soon afterward, the eyes call, "Crane, crane, people are coming down the river in a boat." This time the crane does not heed the call. He is thinking, "Well, I suppose they see something else that might resemble a boat and people. This time I won't respond." He continues to eat. Soon the eyes call, "Crane, crane, the people are almost upon us. Come quick." He does not answer.*
>
> *Some time elapses, then he hears the eyes calling from a distance, "Crane, crane, the people have us, and they're taking us down the river."*
>
> *The crane runs down to the riverbank and finds the log. He feels around, but there are no eyes. He sits down and thinks, "What am I going to do for eyes?" After much thought and consternation at not being able to see, he ambles back to the tundra. A thought occurs to him, "Why not try berries for eyes?" With that he finds blackberries. He plops them into his eye sockets. Lo and behold, he sees, but the world is different shades of black and grey. This can't be, so, he disposes of the blackberries. He finds salmonberries, and tries them. But the world is orange with its color variations and does not look right. So, he gets rid of them. He tries cranberries, but again the world is not the right color. It shows a place of red hues.*
>
> *Finally, he tries blueberries. This time, the skies are blue, the tundra is green and varied in color; the clouds are white. Whew, these are to be his eyes. And, that is how the crane got BLUE eyes.*

This is very mythical, as defined by Joseph Campbell (1969) and magical. The myth is an analogical way of relating to one's environment. It reflects the human mind's response to the world; it has to do with understanding. It tells people that we humans have the heavy load of intelligence and responsibility to have a beautiful world to inspire them. It is healing. The Yupiat people accepted this on faith because of the need to know and understand. To them, it made beautiful sense. If these people believe in a worldview that includes a language, an ecosophy, epistemology, and ecopsychology all contingent on Nature, so why should the things of Nature not be understandable and interchangeable. All have a spirit therefore, a consciousness, an awareness of the world around them. So, the eyes are able to communicate, perhaps, not verbally but maybe through unsaid words. To the Yupiat, listening not only with the ears, but also with the mind and heart, was essential to become aware of patterns of events that natural laws describe. The sun will rise and descend each day; the earth will continue to revolve around the sun; the spruce seeds will germinate; and so forth. These recurring phenomena will continue to occur in a given way. We accept these on faith—that life is science.

A case in point is the crane flying in circles and ascending. The Yupiat knew that the tundra warms under the sun. This becomes visible as one looks out across the tundra. One can see a disturbance over the tundra, heat waves rising. They know the scientific principle that hot air rises. This is the principle that the crane is using to get high into the air to look around. Is he not a scientist? Nature is science, science is nature. The Eurocentric scientists tell us that a gene or a combination thereof will produce an eye. After seeing this happen time and again, we accept on faith. We will never understand the creative design behind the genetic mechanism for producing the eye, just as we will never know what creative forces or what entity started the physical laws into motion to bring about the "big bang". The scientific laws of nature merely explain or describe what physicists, astronomers, astrophysicists, and others have observed. The preconditions leading to this phenomenon have not been seen and are unimaginable. The Yupiat accept that which is unknowable, uncontrollable, and immeasurable.

The Eurocentric scientists tell us many things, such as that there are particles in the atom that are so small that no one will ever be able to see. They exist only in mathematical statistics. But, we as a people accept these on faith. Do mathematics and physics really exist in Nature, or are they merely constructs of the human rational mind to try to make sense of this world? The important aspect to consider is that the modern creative scientist only deals with the physical and intellectual essences, in other words, the outer ecology. In addition, the modern scientist makes theories based on sometimes limited facts, and these theories are made to fit their constructed technocratic societies. They do NOT necessarily fit reality. If these socio-politico-economics and scientific theories do not describe reality, they most certainly will not work in tribal societies because they are trans-rational. Perceptions can be far removed from what is real, and in Yupiaq thought are incomplete and often erroneous knowledge. This fragmentary approach disassociates the parts from the whole. In trying to understand the parts to understand the whole, their scientific methods skew their way of looking at things. Their assumptions and expectations muddle their efforts to see things as they really are. The Native creative mythology deals with the whole—the physical, intellectual, emotional, and spiritual of inner and outer ecologies. The Native person realizes that he/she is a microcosm of the whole, the universe. Therein lies the ultimate difference between the two.

Another problem is that the scientist's own identity remains a mystery. They try to control nature for narrow dehumanizing purposes. They invent antibiotics and weapons of mass destruction. Their lack of self-knowledge leads nature to keep its secrets when we most need to let the book of Nature speak for itself.

The above Yupiaq story is a creative mythology of our ancestors. But is not the physicist who creates the statistics of unseen particles a creative mythologist? Is not the genetic microbiologist who determines what gene(s) cause Alzheimer's a creative mythologist? Is not the microbiologist who creates a clone of a dog a creative mythologist? This latter thrusts me into the technomechanistic world whereby things discovered are rendered into useful tools and gadgets, such as the 747 jet, the snow machine, outboard motor, cloned living things, antibiotics, fluoride toothpaste, skyscraper buildings, and the plastic raincoat. All of these are intensive in the use of natural resources and energy. They do not consider that the natural resources and energy sources of Mother Earth are finite. The ultimate goal is to gain control over Nature and manipulate it for the purposes of humankind. Supposedly, in the Eurocentric eyes, technology will produce more food, energy, and natural resources when they are used up. "Technology is the answer! (But what was the question?)" is a quote from Amory Lovins. Often, the industrial leaders are mainly concerned about the financial, driven by greed and ambition. Technological products and inventions are improved means to an often foggy or meaningless end. When a product such as a talking doll, cellular phone, or new material for clothing are made, it does not change a small segment of life, but all of life. Psychological and economic changes are impossible to measure, just as bad and evil cannot be quantified. Because of this, technocracy has no conscience.

Mathematics, and the disciplines of science have their own languages and areas of expertise. Each is isolated from the other so that there is no understanding of interrelationships and interconnectedness of all phenomena of this universe. In fact, each area of study has its own contrived language, which make disassociation with other disciplines and Nature easy. In these fields of study are an abundance of well-funded research projects generating rampant information and technological devices. But, to what means do these lead? Surely, not to abundance of natural resources, natural beauty, and diversity, but maybe to natural degradation and poverty and confusion, not only of humans, but creatures too. Our education skews our view of reality because of expectations and assumptions it produces as to what it should be.

I now delve into the Yupiat ways of knowing and being in harmony with Mother Earth. I have enclosed a diagram of a tetrahedral metaphor of the Alaska Native worldview:

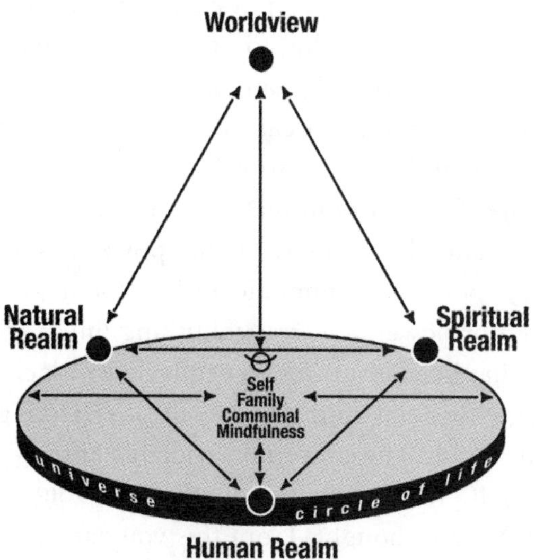

Circle of Life—Oscar Kawagley

I have drawn a circle representing the universe or circle of life. The circle represents togetherness, which has no beginning and no end. On this circle are represented the human, natural, and spiritual worlds. There are two-way arrows between them as well as to the worldview at the apex of the tetrahedral. These two-way arrows depict communications between all these functions to maintain balance. The Yupiat say *Yuluni pitallkertugluni*, "Living a life that feels just right." One has to be in constant communications with each of the realms to know that one is in balance. If the feeling is that something is wrong, then one must be able to check to see what might be the cause for unease or dis-ease. If the feeling of being just right comes instinctively and this feeling permeates your whole being, then you have attained balance. This means that one does not question the other functions intellectually, but that one merges spiritually and emotionally with the others. The circle brings all into one mind. In the Yupiat thought world, everything of Mother Earth possesses a spirit. This spirit is consciousness, an awareness. So, the wind, river, rabbit, amoeba, star, lily, and so forth possess a spirit. The human consciousness, with its ability to merge into one with all consciousnesss of this world, produce the holotropic mind. The holistic mind is given to the nurturance of health and an environmental ethic.

Thus, if all possess a spirit/soul, then all possess consciousness and the power that it gives to its physical counterpart. It allows the Native person to have the ability to have the aid of the spirit to do extraordinary feats of righting an unbalanced individual psyche or to deal with community disease or the loss of communication with the spiritual and natural world through irreverence toward beings of Nature. Harry Robinson[3] calls this nature power, the life-sustaining spirituality. Dr. Grof refers to "power animals"[4] that give the possessor the power to communicate with them, adopting aspects of their wisdom or power, and re-establishing links with them when the connection has been lost through negligence or lack of reverence, or by offending either the animal spirits or one of the greater spirits of the natural world. These are not available through Eurocentric scientific research methods but only through the ancient art of shamanism or Nature thought. From this you can see that when we rely on Eurocentric means of research, it is a limiting factor, and this is what our institutions of higher learning espouse and teach. All areas of social and scientific research teach one way of trying to learn and understand phenomena. Our technological and scientific training imprisons the students' minds to its understandings much to the detriment of the learners who enter the mainstream Eurocentric world to become its unerring members of progress and development.

The Alaska Native needed to take lives of animals to live. To give honor, respect, dignity, and reciprocation to the animals whose lives were taken, the Native people conceived and put into practice many rituals and ceremonies to communicate with the animal and spiritual beings. These are corroborated through the Alaska Native mythology, which are manifestations of fundamental organizing principles that exist within the cosmos, affecting all our lives.[5] It then behooves the Alaska Native person to leave something behind such as a piece of dry fish when getting mouse food from the tundra. The mouse food is gathered in the early fall so that the mouse and its family will have opportunity to collect more food for the winter. The seal, when caught, is given a drink of water so that its spirit will not be thirsty when it travels to the animal spiritual kingdom. This is done to show respect to the animal for having shared and given its life to the hunter. Medicinal plants are gathered respectfully knowing full well their power to heal and recognition that these were given freely by Nature and that it thus requires that we share these freely. The Alaska Native person is aware that if we do not use these gifts of Nature regularly, mindfully, and respectfully, they will begin to diminish through disuse or misuse. Earth, air, water, fire, and spirit must always be in balance. Its elements and creatures each have an important niche in the ecological system. With this concept in mind, it then requires that we carefully examine the lifestyles and technology that are extant in this world. Our lifestyles have become materialistic and given to technological devices and gadgets galore that are not geared to sustainability. Our modern cities with their network of buildings, transportation, communications, goods and services distribution centers are destructive and given to conformity. Likewise, the studies of natural resources are given to conformity. They are approached in a fragmentary way such that an expert in harbor seals does not know what the expert in herring fish is doing or has discovered. This type of research is geared for measuring and objectifying the species studied for commercial purposes and not for sustaining Mother Earth.

In the Eurocentric world of science and technology exist many alternative approaches that are nature-friendly and sustainable. They await the time when the global societies evolve from consumerism and materialism to ones that are oriented to conservation and regeneration. As Alaska Native people and other indigenous societies, we have much to share with the modern world. I believe it is much more difficult to live in tune with and in concert with Mother Earth than it is to plunder earth, air, fire, water, and spirit using the sciences and their offspring, the technologies, as tools of destruction. Eurocentric mathematics and sciences and the resulting technomechanistic inventions impact and change our ways of thinking and present new tools to think with, including the computer and other means of communications. These modern inventions and thinking are inimical to living in nature, with nature, and being of nature. It behooves us as indigenous and minority peoples to learn both ways of knowing and doing, so that we can begin to develop a caring consciousness and a technology that is kind to our being as humans, to the spiritual and the natural.

The question now is: How do we counteract the depression, hopelessness, and despair that derive from the unfulfilled promises of the modern world, and what role can schooling and education play in this effort? To address this question, it will be necessary to take a closer look at how traditional education and Eurocentric schooling have fit into the lives of the Yupiaq people.

LEARNING FROM NATURE

It is through direct interaction with the environment that the Yupiaq people learn. What they learn is mediated by their cultural cognitive map. The map consists of those "truths" that have been proven over a long period of time. As the Yupiaq people interact with nature, they carefully observe to find pattern or order where there might otherwise appear to be chaos. The Yupiaq peoples' empirical knowledge of their environment has to be general and specific at the same time. During their hunting trips into the tundra or on the ocean in the winter, they must have precise knowledge of the snow and ice conditions, so over many years of experience and observation they have classified snow and ice with terms having very specific meanings. For example, there are at least thirty-seven terms for ice, having to do with seasons, weather conditions, solar energy transformations, currents, and rapid changes in wind direction and velocity. To the Yupiaq people, it is a matter of survival. This knowledge is passed down from generation to generation by example, by showing, and by telling with stories to reinforce the importance of knowing about the varying conditions. This comprises the rational side of the Yupiaq people.

The rational mind has the ability to see and store many bits of observed information, which can then be mulled over and shared with others for more ideas of what it may mean. This may evolve into a tentative assumption of how and why something is the way it is. Being self-aware of the subconscious and intuition, the Yupiaq people let it play in their minds until a direction or answer evolves. They observe nature's indicators and come to a tentative supposition, followed by testing with further observation of variables that may affect the conclusion. They know that nature is dynamic and they have to change with it. Thus their conduct of life changes with nature. They pass on the truths to the next generation, knowing fully well changes in interpretation will occur, but that certain values, such as caring, sharing, cooperation, harmony, and interconnectedness with the created whole of their environment will continue. This then validates and gives dignity to their existence.

One cannot be conscious of the world without first being aware of oneself. To know who you are, what your place in the world is, and that you are to strive to seek life is what self-awareness is all about. It is the highest level of human knowledge, to know oneself so intimately that you are not afraid to tell others of life and to help those that need help with compassion without being dragged down by the troubles of those being helped. Knowledge of oneself is power, and you acquire it by looking into yourself to see what strengths and weaknesses you have. You accomplish this through looking at your own reactions to everyday situations, both good and bad.

To achieve a secure sense of oneself involves meditation, visualization, intuition, and tempering all thoughts and actions with the "heart," which is on a higher plane than knowledge of the mind. "Heart" can best be explained by giving examples: to give freely of oneself to help a person with personal problems; to bring a little bird home with a broken leg and care for it to restore its health; to come upon a moose mired in soft snow and shovel the snow away to free it; to be motivated by kindness and care—these all involve the exercise of heart. You can recognize people with heart by the respect shown to them by others through kind words, inclusion in community activities, and acceptance as a stable and common-sensical member of the community.

The Yupiaq's careful and acute observational ability taught them many years ago the presence of a Creative Force. They saw birth and death in the human, and in nature. This Creative Force flowed through everything—the years, months, days, rivers, lightning and thunder, plants, animals, and earth. They were awed by the creative process. They studied, they connected, and nature became their metaphysic. It gave them empirical knowledge. Products of nature extended to them ideas for developing their technology. The spider web provided the idea for the net; the snowshoe hare's feet and tracks, their snowshoes; the mouse's chamber lined with grass, their houses. The moon's phases were their calendar; the Big Dipper and the North Star served as their timepiece at night; wind directions were their indicators of weather; and flint and slate were their cutlery. Certain plants and herbs gave them their healing powers and they discovered that certain living things were adapted to live in certain areas, while others were able to make physical adjustments through changes in coloration, forming a heavier coat for winter, hibernation, estivation, etc., all under trying conditions. They noticed change across time and conditions and they recognized that they too would have to change with time and conditions to survive.

It was meaningless for Yupiaq to count, measure, and weigh, for their wisdom transcended the quantification of things to recognize a qualitative level whereby the spiritual, natural and human worlds were inextricably interconnected. This was accomplished through the Creative Force having endowed all earthly things with spirits, which meant that they would have to deal with all things being alive and aware. Having a Raven as creator of man and woman and everything else ensured that humans would never be superior to the other elements of creation. Each being endowed with a spirit signified that it possessed innate survival skills. It had the will to live, propagate, and care for itself, thus the need to respect everything and to have taboos, rituals, and ceremonies to keep the three realms in balance.

Nature's indicators and voices give much knowledge for making a living, but intuitive and spiritual knowledge gives wisdom to make a life. Therein lies the strength and tenacity with which the Yupiaq people continue to maintain their identity, despite assaults on the philosophical, epistemological, ontological, economical, and technological fronts. Their template has certainly eroded, but the continuity of their ways to comfort and create harmony persists. As long as the Yupiaq peoples' spirituality is intact, they will withstand.

CHAPTER 6

My Mother's Clan(s)

THE INLAND TESLIN TLINGIT

Norma A. Shorty

My mother is the late Emma Joanne Shorty, and she went to mission school at Carcross Yukon and Lower Post British Columbia from 1937 to 1950. Mother's mother, Olive Sidney, is from Teslin Yukon and is an inland Tlingit; Olive's mother, Annie Fox, could still remember her childhood connections to Juneau and Taku, Alaska. My clan is G̲aanax̲.ádi and my house is Kook̲hittaan. My ancestral homelands include Teslin, Taku, Douglas, and Angoon.

Among Yukon First Nations, clan systems are matrilineal, and who you are is established by your mother. My name is Yesk̲eitch Anntookwasaak. I am a Tlingit woman, and I have two brothers, two sisters, and one beautiful daughter who recently blessed us with a beautiful new granddaughter.

Using Indigenous constructs, we repeat our (hi)stories so that our grandchildren will know where they belong and so that they will not be strangers in their own land.[1] We are cautioned to speak carefully because when we tell our ancestral history, we are honoring our place as children and grandchildren of our maternal and paternal ancestors.

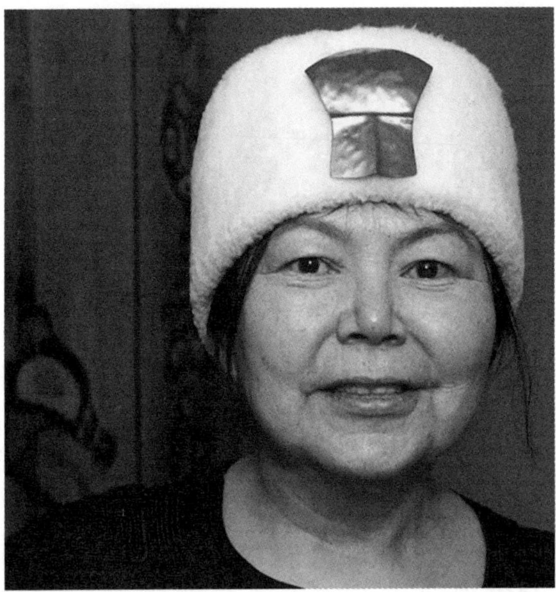

Portrait of Norma Shorty in Juneau, Alaska—Courtesy of Cathy Ruddy

MY RESEARCH

February 18, 2012, my daughter shared her nightmare: "You passed away,[2] and I was saying over and over again: I don't know who I am! I don't know who I am! I don't know who I am!"[3] Rae's interpretation of her ominous dream is that I would not finish my research. Her fears are great because I do not know the stories of my mother's clan, our clan ancestors, or our clan connections and clan contributions to our collective Tlingit lands in Yukon, Alaska, and elsewhere. My research seeks to ensure the preservation and perpetuation of Tlingit knowledge on Mom's clan(s) stories of origin while expressing our clan connections to the land, trade, trails, and more.

As the eldest of four siblings, I have entry-level fluency in the Tlingit language.[4] I do not know our ancestral history and stories about my mother's first great-great-grandparents and on. Personally, I am seeking ways to fulfill eldest child and mother duties by ensuring the stories and knowledge about my mother's clan live on into the future. Hence my work strives to record and perpetuate inland Tlingit history as well as generate ideas and discussions around the methodologies employed in gathering, recording, and discussing Mom's clan from an inland Tlingit perspective. Today, Teslin Tlingit people have five clans: three are from the raven moiety and two are from the wolf moiety. My thesis may or may not bring more clarity to a statement that was made by Mom's sister, Gladys Johnston, at Yukon Native Language Literacy Session in 1985. Mom's sister stated that she is from the G̱aanax̱.ádi[5] clan. Mom always said we are Kookhittaan. The reason the research focuses on my mother's clan is because we are a matrilineal society. Like many Indigenous communities, Teslin Tlingit people have strict copyright laws[6] within their culture, regarding their stories[7] and inland Tlingit clan names, clan crests, songs, and knowledge.[8] As evidenced in early books and publications, inland Tlingit history appears to begin when explorers, gold seekers, scientists, and others discovered us.[9] Tlingit oratory, artifacts, and genetic mapping tell otherwise.[10]

Teslin Tlingit elders have not published their own stories because of culture laws. "The Tlingit people forbid the writing of Tlingit history; we did not talk about it [our past events]. Those that wrote about it [the history] didn't always record it right and the tellers only told it just so far. Knowing the culture stories, this is what I see. Teslin will stand up and say it the way they want it."[11] Considering Tlingit clan laws[12] and Canada's past policy on "Indian"[13] people, this internally placed ban on writing down the inland Tlingit culture is not surprising. The writing of our culture is viewed by many of our Teslin Tlingit elders as a finalizing step toward colonization.[14] Yet at the same time, these same elders are gravely aware that we need to take immediate measures to preserve and perpetuate our stories.[15] Many of us Teslin Tlingit people have carefully hidden the most valuable parts of our culture by keeping and guarding culture stories and histories to ourselves.[16] Some Teslin Tlingit elders are now engaging in dialogue about how to write down our stories on and about us.[17]

Mom, now seventy-nine, experienced deep cultural trauma due to Canada's policies to assimilate the Indian.[18] Prior to 1920, my mother's people maintained their identities, land and trail stewardship, Tlingit language, and culture by practicing intergenerational methodologies for transmitting and preserving Indigenous knowledges on land tenure, ancestral history, place names, and more.[19] Connections to the land were fiercely upheld between generations of Tlingit people by way of story, war, and migrations.[20] The Klondike Gold Rush, the building of the Alaska Highway, the influx of outsiders, the federal and territorial government policies, the mission schools,[21] the diseases, and other events overwhelmed and displaced Indigenous people's stories on and about themselves.[22] In 1920, doing away with Canada's Indian problem included enfranchisement, assimilation schemes, reservations, and government-enforced policies on the removal of children for the purposes of attending residential schools. The story about my mother's clan cannot be told without alluding to the impacts of residential school upon my mom and others from her era, but this is not the focus of my research. Today Mom is talking about writing her autobiography. This work will reflect on her life, including her residential school and other experiences. Mom has recently been saying that she wanted to do this clan research work, and since I was now working on our personal clan stories, she could now concentrate on her personal stories.[23] Rather than focusing on Mom's residential school stories, my research will focus on inland Tlingit understandings about my mother's clan(s). This clan history work is done to ensure intergenerational perpetuation of our inland Tlingit stories and our ancestral connections to our place, our land, and our knowledge. Mom was born in 1933, and during the 1940s it was not uncommon for Indigenous children to be forcefully removed from their homes and community in order to attend government-funded mission schools. Mom learned some of the stories about her clan origins, her ancestors, and her clan heroes and heroines. Mom does from time to time share what she can of these stories, histories, and ancestral connections with me, my siblings, and our children. From the age of four to sixteen, Mom was sent to two residential schools. The first was situated in Carcross, Yukon, and the other in Lower Post, British Columbia. Both of these schools are hundreds of miles away from the community of Teslin, Yukon.[24] Mom had contracted tuberculosis while she was at residential school—at age sixteen she was sent home without a treatment plan. Due to the loving actions of a nurse in Teslin, Mom spent nearly four years at Charles Camsel Hospital in Edmonton, Canada. When she returned home from the hospital, she was twenty-one, and she and my dad married—they had met at the hospital, and I was on the way.

WHO AM I AS THE RESEARCHER?

At birth, my grandmother Olive Sidney gave me her Tlingit name—Yesk̲eitch (Works Well with Her Hands). Dad was a Crow and mom is a Raven—they broke Indian law so the people would not name me.[25] I received my second name, Aantoox̲.usaax̲ (The Cry of the Raven above the Trees) when I was thirteen.[26] Today I am a fifty-six-year-old Tlingit woman. I have a master's[27] degree from the University of Hawaii at Manoa, 2004, and it was during this time that I first heard[28] about Indigenous researcher Linda Smith. In 2016 I completed my PhD at the University of Alaska Fairbanks. What Dr. Smith had written about decolonization schemes resonated with me because of where Yukon First Nation peoples were politically in terms of self-governance here in the Yukon. Our Yukon land claim agreements were kicking in, and many Yukon First Nations were beginning to articulate decolonization schemes in order to define, implement,[29] and evaluate our Indigenous ways of governing ourselves. As mentioned, documentation[30] almost always portrays Yukon history as beginning at the time of the Klondike Gold Rush. And it is here where the processes of contact and colonization began, and as a result, my and many others' family ancestral history are on the verge of being lost.[31] This research journey will enable me to contribute more fully to the story of where my mother's ancestors came from. Based on my previous experiences with cultural learning, I know that this renewed sense of self, family, clan, and nation will increase our collective sense of identity. I hypothesize that increased cultural, historical, and place-based knowledge about inland Tlingit contributions to history, knowing, and doing will positively enhance and promote our own Tlingit beliefs and ideas around ourselves.

This project will identify and articulate inland Tlingit clan knowledge and clan histories. Teslin Tlingit government, as per the implementation of their land claims agreements, has begun articulation processes in areas such as language, place-name development, education, and social justice. Linda Smith, Margie Maaka, Shawn Wilson, and Bryon Brayboy[32] all talk about decolonizing our Indigenous methodologies. Articulating and validating our Indigenous knowledge and methodologies is essential to ensuring that our Indigenous culture and practices live on. My clan origins project strives to perpetuate our inland Tlingit knowledge about G̲aanax̲.ádi and Kook̲hittaan clan history. My research will contribute to the body of knowledge about clan migrations into the Teslin area as well as preserve knowledge about Mom's clan origins, clan structures, clan stories, and so on. My research will define inland Tlingit governance processes over our education, lands, history, place names, spiritual areas, clan objects, and clan names. My PhD coursework has helped me realize that as Indigenous researchers, we need to seek ways to document and validate our local and Indigenous place-based histories.[33] It is hoped that my research can serve as dialogue tables toward our own decolonization efforts in the area of governance and can help us as we "unpack" our cultural ways. My coursework has shown me that there are Indigenous worldviews, ways of knowing and doing, including Indigenous research methodologies, copyright and property considerations, and so on. I have learned that Indigenous languages lend worldviews and images that cannot always be replicated using the English language.[34] Much of my coursework for Indigenous studies helped me to develop a toolbox with which to research, implement, and critique current and past work on or about Indigenous peoples.[35]

WHO ARE THE INLAND TLINGIT?

The inland Tlingit communities Atlin, Tagish, and Teslin are distinct, each with their own "moieties, clans, house groups and k̲wáan."[36] In understanding how long Tlingit people have been inland it appears for as long as legend remembers.[37] With few published scholarly works about the inland Tlingit of Teslin, it is increasingly important to preserve and perpetuate history and stories as presented by inland Tlingit people by and about us. As discussed, most documentation portrays Yukon history as beginning at the point of contact.[38] Exploration and mapping, the Klondike Gold Rush, the building of the Alaska Highway, government reports, and scholarly articles assume that the Yukon lands were terra nullius at the time of contact. On the surface, it appears that the Tlingit people have not responded to these early testimonies. Indigenous oratory[39] and collections of oratory[40] artifacts,[41] marks on trees,[42] and mountain features including early Tlingit letters,[43] and maps[44] tell otherwise. In the late 1700s, explorers from Russia, America, and France sailed into the Northwest Passage.[45] Known as fierce[46] middlemen in the trade industry, the Tlingit people traveled inland to the interior to trade for furs. The trails that lead from the salt water to the inland were (1) Klukwan to Fort Selkirk, (2) Skagway to Tutshi Lake,[47] (3) T'aaḵu Ḵwáan to Teslin, and (4) Stikine River to Tahltan Country.[48] It is said that all these trails met up, and that the First Nation people followed these trails just like we follow the highways today.[49] The Teslin Tlingit Council website points out that the Teslin Tlingits are descendants of the T'aakú Kwáan. The descendants' of T'aakú Ḵwáan[50] lived along the Taku River. "The Taku [River] was an important migration route and trade corridor to the interior; with the exception of Douglas, Alaska, no settlement remains in this Ḵwáan."[51] The Taku River tributary begins a few miles southeast of Juneau. Mom said that the T'aakú Ḵwáan has descendants from Juneau, Douglas, and Seenáa,[52] which she heard this from her late sister, Gladys. Thornton, quotes Emmons, who writes that T'aakú Ḵwáan was made up of those Tlingit who gathered around Juneau and was one of the later Tlingit communities to settle.[53] McClellan emphasizes the research of Emmons, Swanton, and de Laguna,[54] telling the reader that these researchers find striking parallels between the coastal Taku and Teslin.[55]

McClellan[56] continues to quote Emmons, who reports that the Yanyeidí claim to have been the first people to come down the Taku River from T'aaḵu Ḵwáan.[57] Emmons also states that the raven moiety has five sibs among the coastal T'aaḵu, and these are

- G̱aanax̱.ádi, who emigrated from Hutsnuwu on Admiralty Island
- Ishkeetaan, who separated from the G̱aanax̱.ádi at either Chilkat or T'aaḵu
- Kooḵhittaan are described as unimportant sibs who came down the T'aaḵu River to the coast
- Kah yah utdi (?)[58]
- Tooḵa.ádi[59]

As can be determined, trade trails near Klukwan were monopolized among the coastal Tlingit[60] and are well represented in history based on Davidson's account of Kohklux Map, including cultural validation as heard through story. The Taku River route inland is lesser known, and is virtually unexplored. Harris[61] writes that in 1891, Schwatka was commissioned by southern US newspapers to trek inland via the

Chilkoot Trail; Schwatka was convinced while on board the "Pacific Coast Steamship Company's vessel City of Topeka"[62] to "explore and map the obscure Taku River trail to the Interior."[63] As I was reading about Schwatka's exploration inland, an expert in Tlingit story and culture simultaneously shared a story with me about Tlingit packers and Tlingit trails. The following story explains one of Schwatka's many journeys inland.

> *My father was Mark Jacobs, Jr., whose father was Mark Sr. and was the son of Emma Johnson. Emma's mother was Anna Cane-teen, who was married to a man of the Dagistinaa Clan of Klukwan whose name was T'eik. Keinteen had a sister named Yeitkhin.aawtí whose husband was Yíndayáank. The latter two raised Emma (S'eiltín).*
>
> *Yíndayáank was a guide. One story about him tells of his snowshoe prints being on one side of a ravine and appearing on the other side, looking as though he had jumped across the ravine. Walking across a sapling tree it snapped back up when he stepped off of it!*
>
> *He led Lt. Schwatka on his expedition to map the boundary. THIS is the Tlingit version of course, and it is said that "where Lt. Schwatka's legs gave out is where the boundary was set" and that the boundary actually should've been much further Inland (also bearing in mind that this is THEIR boundary.)*
>
> *Yíndayáank was promised a large payment for his work but was never paid. In Tlingit fashion, other payment was made by the clan of Yíndayáank "taking his name as payment." The name Schwatka was "Tlingit-ized" to Swáatk'i, which became one of the names of Yíndayáank. They also created the name Sóonjee koosá, or "Slender Soldier," because Lt. Schwatka was a thin man. Another name is Shaakwéinsi, or "Mountain Marker," referring to the boundary expedition.*[64]

This story demonstrates how the coastal Tlingit people responded to the explorers and historians who came to our great northern land. As an Indigenous scholar, there is a great need to work with elders and story bearers in order to validate, respond, and contribute to the body of literature on or about the inland Tlingit from Teslin. The Taku River trail leads from near

Juneau to Teslin, Yukon, and then follows a well-known interior river route to Fort Selkirk and then back down to the coast by Klukwan. To date, not enough is known about the inland Tlingit from Teslin, and there continues to be an ever-growing number of resources among our coastal brethren.

At the time of this writing, it is not known why some Tlingits moved and settled inland. Mom remembers her paternal grandfather talking of Russian raids in which women and children were being killed, so some Tlingit people migrated inland. Others whom I spoke with speculate that the move inland was because trade was a lucrative business. Others make reference to a forced move due to something over a woman. Other sources give the environment[65] or war (with the Russians) as reasons. Some Teslin elders say that the Teslin Tlingit have always been here. Another source tells of clan migrations from the inland (Teslin) via the Stikine trail to Wrangell, Alaska.

Robert Zuboff tells a story about when the people were moving from Teslin to Stikine, which is near Wrangell.

> *They walked for years and some of the people did not survive. There were two old women among them. The two old women were sent down under the glacier which was by the river. The two old women began to sing on the other side of the river. Some people were afraid to go. They went all the way to Chilkat and Taku.*[66]

This is a Deisheetaan story. Robert Zuboff's story of migration from Teslin to Wrangell takes into account the Stikine River trail to the coast. Daniel Henry of Haines, Alaska, is constructing place-based history for the Haines, Alaska, region. He has developed a timeline of Tlingit stories and events to aid his writing.[67] According to Henry's timeline, I could possibly date Robert Zuboff's Deisheetaan story to circa 1200 to 1500 based on Klukwan migration histories. At times of migration, did many clans leave at once, or was it only one clan at a time? Daniel Henry's timeline suggests a possible timeframe for the Kaagwaantaan migration stories in Klukwan circa 1200 to 1500. During this timeframe, what were the climate conditions? Could the Deisheetaan have migrated from the inland to the coast during this time too, or are these two separate stories? I suspect all reasons stand.

WHAT DOES THE LITERATURE SAY ABOUT MY MOTHER'S CLAN(S)?

At the onset of the literature review, I had the following questions: Why are there no references to the G̲aanax̲.ádi clan in Teslin today? There are five totemic structures at Teslin Tlingit Heritage Center, there are five totemic clan flags, and there are five recognized clans in the Teslin Tlingit Constitution, which was updated in 2009. These clans are Dak̲l'aweidí (wolf moiety), Ishkahittaan (raven moiety), Kook̲hittaan (raven moiety), Deisheetaan (raven moiety), and Yanyeidí (wolf moiety). What are the origins of the G̲aanax̲.ádi and Kook̲hittaan[68] clans in Teslin? Why did the members of the G̲aanax̲.ádi clan in Teslin become absorbed into a clan house of itself—Kook̲hittaan?[69] Why did Mother not discuss the origins of the G̲aanax̲.ádi or the Kook̲hittaan clans with us? Why did Mrs. Gladys Johnston, my mom's blood sister, say she is from the G̲aanax̲.ádi clan? Previous to reading this statement in the Tlingit Literacy Workshop, May 6–8, 1985, Yukon Native Language Centre results, there was no previous reference by Mom or others made to me about the G̲aanax̲.ádi clan existing in Teslin except for this statement.

In some uncanny way and a few days after reading the statement, I had a visit from someone in an opposite clan in Teslin. This person validated Gladys Johnston's information by retelling (unsolicited)[70] how the G̲aanax̲.ádi were absorbed into the Kook̲hittaan clan of Teslin, Yukon. This individual said that "there were too few G̲aanax̲.ádi, and to balance it out, some clan elders and people said to make them G̲aanax̲.ádi all Kook̲hittaan [Children of the Raven]."[71] When looking at the participants list at the Tlingit Literacy Workshop in 1985, the late Clara Schinkel, a respected and beloved Tlingit woman from Tagish,[72] is listed as Yanyeidí, and today her clan is known as Dakl'aweidí. At first glance, there appeared to be errors in this clan information, and now I am beginning to understand how these perceived errors are in large part because of my own limited cultural knowledge. From a cultural perspective, Mrs. Schinkel is neither from my clan nor from my community, and I have no business "questioning" these kinds of details, especially from an elder. My "schooling" answer is that each of our inland Tlingit communities has separate and similar clan origin stories; after all, we used different trails to get inland, we intermarried, we migrated, and we had age-old trade connections. McClellan's earlier work among the Teslin Tlingit in 1953[73] points out that there was only one wolf clan in Teslin, and this was the Yanyeidí. Today it is known that there was an internal feud,[74] and now there are tracts of land that fall under the stewardship of the Old and New Yanyeidí clans. These clans are now known as Dakl'aweidí and Yanyeidí.[75]

In *My Old People Say*, McClellan gathers stories from Southern Tutchone, Tagish, and inland Tlingit, covering the last quarter of the nineteenth century up to the 1970s. McClellan writes that the Tlingit clans in Teslin are

- Deisheetaan (the Deisheetaan clan [from Teslin] has a strong presence at Angoon)
- Kook̲hittaan (branch of the G̲aanax̲.ádi)
- Ishkeetaan (branch of the G̲aanax̲.ádi)
- Old (now Dakl'aweidí) and New Yanyeidí.[76]

In the 1970s, McClellan reports that there were few G̲aanax̲.ádi, and that the important sib in Teslin is Kook̲hittaan.[77] McClellan's publication on the inland Tlingit reports that "the Kuqhitan derive their name from kuq (hole) which refers to a hole in the center of a Ganaxadi house in Angoon where the women and children hid in case of an enemy attack."[78] There appears to be a shift in McClellan's findings on the status of the G̲aanax̲.ádi clan in Teslin between the years of 1950 and 1970. In the 1950s McClellan reports that the Kook̲hittaan and Ishkahittaan in Teslin were branches of the G̲aanax̲.ádi clan. In the 1970s McClellan says the Kook̲hittaan are the important clan in Teslin, and she reports that the G̲aanax̲.ádi and the Ishkahittaan did not own any land in the Teslin area.[79] From what I can determine it appears that some of the coastal G̲aanax̲.ádi who were in Teslin in the 1950s may have migrated from southern areas in Alaska to Angoon, then to T'aak̲u K̲wáan, then to Teslin Yukon, while other G̲aanax̲.ádi married into Teslin from Juneau, Alaska, and beyond.[80] Much of what is written about inland Tlingit clans today relies on the work of Emmons, de Laguna, and McClellan. As an Indigenous researcher I am greatly indebted to these ethnographers for their notes, publications, tapes, and maps. These early ethnographic studies provide a basic framework and timeline of events about Teslin life, some of which, to my humble surprise, correlates with some of the stories Mother and others told me. I have found these early works about the inland Tlingit to be hugely important to my current understandings and ideas about the origins of my mother's clan.

At a local level, I am aware of a genealogy chart here at Yukon Archives, and this was completed by Bonner and Bessie Coolie of Teslin. Recent preservation work by Dr. A. Taff and Dr. R. Dauenhauer, 2008–2011, includes an Excel spreadsheet of Tlingit stories about the great flood, migrations between Teslin and Wrangell, and so on.[81] This worksheet yields cassette tape numbers and Tlingit tellers, including their Tlingit name(s), clans, and villages. These stories were gathered by Nora Marks Dauenhauer in the 1970s. Included in this data series are stories about Teslin (find Tom Peters, George Davis, David Hammonds Potlatch in Carcross, and the Deisheetaan clan story by Robert Zuboff).

Oratory collections and personal communication are incredibly useful and will be foundational for the study of my mother's clan. I have heard most recently[82] and for the first time the clan origin stories of the Kooḵhittaan from Jimmy Johnson, Kooḵhittaan clan leader. Sam Johnson, the Ishkahittaan clan leader, told me this same story, a shorter version at another time and place. From the perspective of Indigenous research methodologies, Jimmy Johnson and Sam Johnson need to endorse publishing the clan origins information shared with me. Until then I will document, keeping records of the story. I am uncomfortable with this, as I acknowledge the sensitive nature of these stories and the fact that express permission is not given, although from a culture perspective, here lies my authority (but with concomitant tension) to have voice in my clan. On November 30, 2012, I asked Jimmy if I could write down the story. He said yes, but it can only be told publicly when all the other clan stories are told publicly. It is important to note here the scholarly tension that exists between academic disclosure and the "telling" of potentially sensitive cultural information. As a Tlingit woman, I have authority to wear our clan symbols, to research our clan origin stories. From the 1950s to the 1980s, when McClellan did her research, it appears she received a lot of culturally sensitive information. As an outside ethnographer, McClellan was able to write and publish stories about both the wolf and raven moieties in the Teslin area. Now among the inland Tlingit, the wolf and raven stories, histories, and lands[83] are considered clan property (Aat.oow)[84] and are fiercely protected. Many of our clan stories have resulted in a renewed understanding about our "traditional" lands; stories are one of the foundations of our Yukon land claims.[85] The Teslin Tlingit Council has negotiated for programs and services with the federal government of Canada. Tlingit elders agree that the most important learning is to know who you are.

In my case, because of my mother's early mission school traumas, we did not spend our growing years immersed in Tlingit culture and language. In the early days, government policies and laws were designed to keep Indigenous peoples from participating as equals in a fast-developing society.[86] Today, it is crucial to research and publish our Indigenous stories—if we don't, these stories and their intent may be lost to us forever.[87] So far, my literature review is uncovering and reframing a story, a deeply personal and unknown story. As Mother and I traveled together throughout coastal Tlingit communities in Juneau and Sitka, it was known that we were searching for our clan origin stories and our coastal family. During this time, I marveled at what Mom remembered. Mom's "erased" cultural memory was slowly returning, and my previously held beliefs were shifting. Mom told me stories about how I got my "Indian" name; in fact, in the 1970s she authored *How Emma Got Her Indian Name*. In this story, Mom, as a four-year-old girl, is in day school and has the ability to run home every day. In reality, Mom was taken to Carcross Residential School at age four. Mom's real story is not reflected in this children's book because it was edited out.

As we ferried from place-to-place, Mom talked about her mother, and Mom told me the stories that she remembered about Tlaanak' (her mother's mother). As I get deeper and deeper into my research, gaps began to surface. Yukon Indigenous peoples are barely mentioned in current historical understandings about the Yukon. Today, as Alaskan researchers publish their findings and understandings of Tlingit nations, clans, and communities, they include what they can about the Canadian Tlingit. The inland Tlingit are barely represented in Alaskan materials on the Tlingit because these materials are so scarce.[88]

A problem with the literature on Indigenous peoples from my region is that the sources are few and outdated. I continue to experience inner and cognitive conflict due to western (outsider) ways of knowing juxtaposed with Indigenous ways of knowing. That is, I had learned early on to be suspicious about outsider views because of the colonizing nature of those views.[89] Now that I have experienced how our Indigenous stories can work side by side with western views, I am eager to incorporate our stories, and I am eager to show how these stories may in part support what early ethnographers found among us. The culture and the story are the most important elements of my research.[90] The benefit of hearing our stories has greatly impacted how I live my life. This year, for the first time, I netted salmon, and I cut, smoked, and dried it without Mom's and Auntie's tutelage. I set gopher traps and skinned my first moose head. I assisted in retrieving eulachon, our revered and respected fish. I picked berries, mushrooms, and medicines. I thought a lot about what I had been learning and took many personal notes, including field notes of elders Martha Vanheel, Pearl Keenan, Emma Shorty, and Jimmy Johnson. Mom and I established strong ties and life-changing relationships with each other and with the Tlingit and resource people from Juneau and beyond.

During a summer trip to Yakutat, I began to realize the power of our knowledge, our history, our language, and our relationships with one another. When Elder George Ramos pointed in a southwest direction and said Haines Junction is 180 miles that way—it suddenly dawned on me. Our stories are real—they go beyond being myth, distant and no longer relevant. It is at times like this that I realize the impact of the job ahead of me, and it feels overwhelming. My research activities have included increased travel to Alaska, more time with Mom, and hearing and reading stories, history, and dialogue on the inland and coastal Tlingit from elders and resources. The benefit of searching for resources beyond books has increased Mother's and my connections to our Alaskan Tlingit relatives in Juneau, Angoon, and possibly Sitka.

CONCLUSION

Will this project revitalize Tlingit learning and teaching methodologies among family and clans? Will the trail from Teslin to Juneau lead to an enhanced sense of family and community history? Will this research revitalize Indigenous teaching methodologies for family and clan learners while out on the land? I propose to engage in a research project that allows me as the researcher to experience a fuller sense of community belonging. I hope to explore place-based oral learning methods with our Tlingit knowledge bearers. This research journey will enable me as an adult learner and PhD student to more fully understand where my ancestors came from. Based on previous cultural learning, I know that this renewed sense of self, family, clan, and nation has already increased my confidence and self-esteem. I am hoping that this project will foster this same feeling among the participants. I hypothesize that increased cultural and place-based knowledge about our contributions to knowing and doing will enhance and promote decolonization of our own beliefs and ideas around ourselves. This project needs to articulate Tlingit decolonizing processes. Hence, what are the elders' thoughts on the revitalization of our knowledge about our trails, environment, culture, knowledge, and languages? There are numerous contributions of Indigenous peoples' voices in our meeting minutes, oratory, found objects, and spiritual places. Tlingit researchers, such as Nora Dauenhauer, have contributed a lot of print materials that have assisted us, as Tlingit learners, in decolonizing our Indigenous learning methodologies. This project is in part a result of a comment made by Nora Dauenhauer. She said, "Thank you for greasing the Tlingit trade trails." This comment was offered after I had given her some home-tanned slippers—made in the Yukon. She said, "Maybe you can work on recording our stories about the inland trade trail—it will be good to grease that trail again."[91] Despite my initial feeling of angst and distress due to not knowing about our past, I have learned to be patient. My mother's clan stories will perpetuate Indigenous worldviews, Indigenous knowledge systems, Indigenous property and processes, and Indigenous ways of teaching, living, and learning.

I hope that my research will encourage other Indigenous scholars to research their own family and clan origins, their stories, and their heroes and heroines who have contributed to the development and enhancement of the Yukon as we know it today. The big picture issue is Indigenous identity. Who are we, and why does it matter and to whom? I have found a surprising amount of material about my mother's clans, and what I find most surprising is that I barely had to scratch the surface; the stories came tumbling out.

CHAPTER 7

To Perpetuate the Knowledge of Our Elders into Our Future Generation

Annette Wong

This is a story about my grandfather, whom I admire for the person he was and the work he did helping and caring for the people in the Ni‘ihau community. He was raised in this small community where basically everyone on the whole island knew each other. Ni‘ihau is a very remote island of Hawai‘i. My grandfather raised me, and he was my teacher, my mentor. I grew up admiring him for working hard for his family. While watching him do the work he did, it did not occur to me that one day I would be wearing his shoes in order to keep his knowledge alive. I want to continue the work he loved into the next generation. I want to continue the work he loved to make sure that his knowledge will continue to live into the next generation and the generation after that. In fact, I believe that it is my kuleana, or responsibility. He is no longer here in the present, but my memories of him are still fresh, as though he was just gone yesterday. I feel his presence especially when I am doing his work, preparing the Hawaiian herbal medicine for postnatal mothers. This is the reason I decided to write his story and share it with you. You might find that somehow his story intertwines with yours.

Portrait of Ernest Enoka Nohokula Kaohelaulii—Courtesy of Annette Wong

My grandfather's name is Ernest Enoka Nohokula Kaohelaulii. He was born at Wainiha, Kaua'i. He was the son of my great-grandfather, Enoka Nohokula Kaohelaulii of Pu'uwai, Ni'ihau, and great-grandmother, Poipe Naapuwai Nuuhiwa of Wainiha, Kaua'i. Grandfather was raised on the island of Kaua'i. Great-Grandfather was born and raised on the island of Ni'ihau. While working on the Robinson family's ship from Ni'ihau to Kaua'i, Grandfather met my grandmother, Rowena Ponikani Beniamina of Waiaka, Ni'ihau. They were married on Ni'ihau in a church named Ho'omana Iā Iesu. They resided at Pu'uwai, Ni'ihau, and had six children. The Robinson family is the owner of the island of Ni'ihau.

Grandfather worked as a beekeeper, a shepherd, and a pigeon keeper for the Robinson family. Besides fulfilling his duty for the family, he loved to farm. He cultivated his one-acre plot of land, and the whole yard was filled with all different types of edible plants such as mangoes, oranges, sweet potatoes, papaya, and of course Hawaiian herbal medicinal plants. I remember many occasions helping him dig out sweet potatoes from his garden, and they felt like they weighed ten pounds. Since I was not familiar with other farmers' sweet potatoes, I thought that my grandfather's sweet potatoes were the common size. I have not seen any enormous sweet potatoes like my grandfather Enoka's sweet potatoes since. I often heard him sharing stories about what caused the enormous size of his sweet potatoes. Of course, like many farmers, they tend to follow the cycles of the Hawaiian moon calendar. He prepared the plants beforehand and planted them on the night of mahealani (full moon); the cycle of full moon was well known to the Niʻihau people as mahealani. The other reasons for the enormous size of sweet potatoes, papayas, bananas, and watermelons were revealed in stories from both of my grandfathers. They said they stripped naked on the night of mahealani and went into the garden to plant the fruits and vegetables; they would supposedly bear the enormous size that reflects the male penis. My first impression when hearing their story was that they were joking to make us laugh. But, when I saw with my own eyes the actual size of the fruits and vegetables, I began to think that maybe what they said was the truth.

Many Niʻihau elders farm, as that is the only way they will have fresh fruits and vegetables. Niʻihau does not have a supermarket like outside here where fresh fruits and vegetables can be purchased. The only store that exists on Niʻihau sells canned goods and dry goods like flours, sugar, rice, and detergents. It is for that reason the Niʻihauan people farm for fresh fruits and vegetables. The introduction of foreign things to the island made the people dependent on packaged foods, canned goods, and pre-baked goods. Today, there are a few people who still farm the land, but the majority of them do not. When I think about what is happening to the life and health of the people of Niʻihau, I am constantly reminded of the hard work done by my kupuna (elders). These are the things that I miss, and I hope that one day the people will go back to farming the land and eating the fruits of their labor, like my grandfather did. He did not depend on the labors of others, only on his very own. He farmed the land and raised his family with the fruits and vegetables that he grew.

Besides his busy schedule working and farming the land, Grandfather found time to have other hobbies, like weaving lauhala hats and reed baskets, making fish nets, or picking Niʻihau shells. All my life growing up on Niʻihau, I never saw my grandfather sit idly or sleep in. I never saw him wear a foreign hat or a straw hat—he made his own hat by weaving the pandanus leaves. Like many kupuna, they are creative people. They did not depend on store-bought things but instead created things they needed and used throughout their lives.

Shoreline of Ni'ihau—Courtesy of Ni'ihau Cultural Heritage Foundation

I was fortunate to be raised in the presence of my grandparents who were experts in cultural knowledge. There was no need for me to go out and seek the knowledge of others. With the knowledge that was planted in me, I will share with those who want to learn the knowledge of our kupuna. As long as I live, I will always remember the ways my grandfather Enoka specially prepared the Hawaiian herbal medicines, apu hala, for postnatal mothers. I just loved watching him picking and preparing the medicines. He was well-known throughout the island of Ni'ihau as a kahuna laau lapaau, or a Hawaiian herbal medicine practitioner.

Being raised on a remote island like Ni'ihau where the language and culture flourish, I was taught many skills at a very young age. While I did not think that I would walk in the footsteps of my kupuna and practice the work they did, it felt like they had already chosen me to carry on their knowledge. At a very young age I learned the process of gathering and preparing many Hawaiian herbal medicines to cure sore throats, headaches, fevers, cold sores, and so forth. I am also familiar with the places where my grandfather gathered the herbal medicines. Places on the upland, on the plain, or on the seaside, and what plants grew there that were needed for different ailments. My grandfather taught me what and how to pick, and how much was needed. When you gather, you are to take only what you need. Never take more than what you need. Our kupuna told us that if we take more than what we need, there would be nothing for others. This wise teaching of our kupuna is something that I have taken and shared with my siblings, cousins, nieces, and nephews. I think that it is our kuleana, responsibility, to make sure that the teaching of our kupuna has been passed on to our children.

As I mentioned, my grandfather was particularly well-known for the Hawaiian herbal medicine he prepared for postnatal mothers. A week after the birth, the mother would partake of the arrowroot medicines called apu hala. I remember he prepared the apu hala for my mother when she gave birth to my younger brother. He went to his garden and gathered the herbal plants that he needed for the apu hala. From his garden, he gathered sweet potatoes, banana flowers, and sugarcane. He went upland to collect coconuts from a coconut grove called Halaliʻi and the arrowroots from a pandanus tree. He shared with me that on the whole island of Niʻihau there were only three pandanus trees.

As I think back on what has been taught to me, I am thankful that I took interest in Hawaiian herbal medicine from my grandfather. Sitting and watching a kupuna doing something is not an interesting thing to any young child, especially one the age of ten. They would rather play with their siblings or friends. For me, though, it was interesting—sitting and watching him whenever I had the chance.

There were only two grandchildren who practiced and took interest in watching him go through the whole process of making apu hala. The reason I was interested in apu hala was so that I could have a taste of it after my grandfather finished cooking. Just smelling the sweet aroma of the apu hala made my mouth get watery. Others might say, "Who wants to take medicine?" We all know that medicine is not something that people are fond of, especially the Hawaiian herbal medicines. There are medicines that I do not want to take because of their bitterness, but if you are sick, let me tell you that there is no other medicine that will cure your ailment *except* the one that our kupuna gives us. I know for sure if you taste a bit of the apu hala, you will love it. For me, the sweetness and aroma of the apu hala is like coconut candy.

As usual, my grandfather would prepare just enough apu hala for the birth mother and no extra. I often thought, "Why didn't he make extra for those who wanted to taste it?" He always prepared only enough for the birth mother. Whenever a Ni'ihauan gave birth to a child, it was almost like my grandfather knew that the apu hala was needed for the birth mother. There was no request—he just made it. After a week, he gathered everything that was needed for the apu hala and prepared it. As a young girl, I often thought to myself, "Man, why doesn't anybody else help him prepare the apu hala? This is hard work!" But I never heard my grandfather complain while preparing the medicines. I probably watched him prepare apu hala more than a hundred times, and he always sat in the same spot. Sometimes I thought to myself, "Why is my grandfather the only person throughout the Ni'ihau community who knows how to make apu hala? Does anyone else know how to make it, or are they just plain lazy? Or maybe my grandfather did not want anyone to know the process of making the apu hala. Wouldn't he want to teach anyone about the Hawaiian herbal medicines so he would not carry the burden alone?" These questions were always on my mind, even at a very young age. I could see that it was not an easy task.

There was a lot of muscle and love that came with the preparation of apu hala. In my own learning experience from my kupuna and parents, there was no direction to "come here, sit down, and learn." The elders just did what they needed to do to get the task done. It was the responsibility of the children to assist the elders with the chores. Since it wasn't something that a child would understand, it wasn't until I was an adult that I learned there was actually a protocol that came with the preparation of Hawaiian herbal medicines. It starts with the gathering of the plants, then the preparation, and last, the partaking of the medicine.

Apu hala was not the only medicine that the Ni'ihauan used. They also used *Morinda citrifolia* (noni), guava, coconut, sugarcane, tealeaf, *Ipomoea indica*—mountain morning glory (koali), waltheria ('uhaloa or hi'aloa), and many others for medicinal purposes. The noni fruits are used to lower high blood pressure. I remember my grandfather picked noni fruits and placed them in a one-gallon mayonnaise jar and put it on the roof of the house. When the sun heated the noni fruits, the juice extracted from the heat accumulated in the jar. As I watched, the jar with the noni fruits filled with liquid. My grandfather would take a shot orally of noni juice every morning before breakfast. Since Ni'ihau did not have any hospital, doctors, and nurses, they depended heavily on the Hawaiian herbal medicines to cure or to heal any illnesses that affected their internal and external body.

The other use from noni plants were the leaves. I remember on numerous occasions my grandfather picked noni leaves and flipped them on the fire for a few minutes. Then he placed them on my sister's knees and wrapped them with a cloth to drain out the water. Whenever she had water on her knee, this is what my grandfather would do to drain out the liquid.

As we lived, watched, and learned, my grandfather took care of us whenever we got sick. We knew that whatever we were told to pick and eat, it was good for us. We knew from our own personal experiences that whatever our kupuna gave us, it cured or healed whatever sickness we had. And now today I am following in the footsteps of my grandfather and his teaching, doing the same thing he did during his life.

Not only did my grandfather do the work I have mentioned, he also served as a midwife. On Ni'ihau, it was not common that every family or a member of the family were trained to help the birth mother deliver her child. As Mary Kawena Pukui explained, "A family member, perhaps the husband, might take charge of the delivery." I was present during the occasion when my mother gave birth to my younger brother. He was born at the home of our great-grandparents, the same home where all of my siblings were born at Pukaiki Ni'ihau. I was eleven years old when my brother was born. While the adults were preparing for his birth, my grandmother took the six grandchildren in the kitchen and laid blankets on the floor for us to sleep on while the adults assisted my mother. Even at that young age, I remembered everything. As we lay close to each other in the quietness of night, it was so peaceful. Ni'ihau did not have cars or buses to distract us while we were sleeping at night. As we waited patiently for the arrival of my brother, no sound or noise was heard from my mom giving birth until we heard my brother crying as he entered this world. During the birthing process, the children were not allowed in that space. Only the adults that were trained or midwives were allowed to be with the birth mother. As Mary Kawena Pukui explains, "Aiding her were adult members of the family."

What really appalls me today, and what I have witnessed in twenty-first-century birthing, is that nonrelatives and children are allowed in that space. During an interview session I had with my mother, she told me that on Ni'ihau, when the birth mother pushes the child in the process of birthing, those who assist the mother push too as though they are also giving birth. In the Hawaiian epistemology, this process is called "Kau ka 'eha ma luna o ha'i." The pains of labor are transferred onto the elders or adults to ease the pain of the birth mother. This concept of assisting the birth mothers is common to the people of Ni'ihau; every mother who gave birth on Ni'ihau went through the same process. The question that always comes to mind is, "How do we teach this knowledge to the next generation so that it can continue on?"

Learning from my kupuna and parents is something that I cannot get anywhere else in the world. They pass their knowledge down to me. And it becomes my responsibility to pass down to the next generation.

THE PASSING OF KNOWLEDGE TO THE NEXT GENERATION

What does it mean, the passing of knowledge to the next generation? For me, it means that the next generations practice and then pass the knowledge of their kupuna down to their children. To continue on the knowledge and legacy of my grandfather, I have taught my sons what is needed for and how to prepare different Hawaiian herbal medicines for different ailments. I had to walk through the whole process with my sons, gathering the plants to prepare apu hala for my cousin when she gave birth to her daughter. In my family, I and one of my brothers continue the tradition of Hawaiian herbal medicines for apu hala. The tradition on Ni'ihau when someone in the family gives birth is for an adult family member to take on the role for the preparation of apu hala. Since I was the only close relative that my cousin had on O'ahu, I knew that it was my responsibility. Most of our family lives on Kaua'i and Ni'ihau.

The passing of knowledge comes by practicing with our kupuna. I sat with my grandfather numerous times not only to watch him prepare the medicines but to listen to him tell his stories. I think the generations of today do not take into consideration the value of sitting with our kupuna. I believe it is essential for us to teach our children what is important. What will happen if our new generations take no action or responsibility in our kupuna's knowledge? We need to make sure that they are aware of it and that they know what will happen if they don't take responsibility.

Another way of passing the knowledge of our kupuna to the next generations is to be in that space where everything took place. Although I did not physically see my mom give birth to my brother but was in the space where it happened, I could feel the mana, or power, from her. I consider that a transfer of knowledge because I could sense what happened and what took place. To feel the energy of my kupuna while my mom gave birth to my brother is still fresh in my mind.

I have noticed in this generation, giving birth is not an important event like in the days of my kupuna. I remember my mom shared her story during the labor of my older sister. Before I continue this story, I would like to point out that both of my grandparents' homes were about seven miles away from each other. To the outside world, seven miles is nothing. On Ni'ihau, seven miles is very far. Because there are no cars or buses on Ni'ihau, the only transportation is done either by walking or by horse. Because of the long distance between the two homes, my dad put my mom on his mule named Kay-Bee, and he walked as she rode the seven miles to my maternal grandparents' home. She wanted to be with her parents when she gave birth to my sister. She was longing for her mom and dad to be with her. In the Hawaiian worldview, this is called, "Kau ka maka." It literally means to long for loved ones. I do remember on one occasion while interviewing my parents, my mom said; "kahi manawa, mamate kula no ho'i 'oe i tau tāne me 'oe i tou wa e hānau ai. No ta hiti 'ole te hānau, wala'au 'ia mila 'oe, 'ahe nānā i tau tane, nānā mai iā mātou ta po'e i mua o tou alo.'" (Sometimes you long to be with your husband during labor. The elders would say, don't think of your husband, think of us, the ones before you). Hearing her story,

I thought these were such powerful words. These are teachings that you cannot find anywhere else unless such teaching exists in stories or publications. This is what I mean when I think about teaching the next generations. Now, it is my responsibility to make sure that this knowledge will be passed on. It is something that I will care for, practice, and share with those whose interest or desire is to practice the Niʻihau birthing in their life.

I believe that the knowledge of my kupuna was meant to be shared so it can thrive into the next generation. This knowledge cannot continue on to the next generations if we don't take care of it. For me, this is one of my goals, to live and walk in the footsteps of my kupuna.

PART II

Confront

INTRODUCTION

Native people and nations confronted a tidal wave of change that moved across the continent. These essays share ways that specific nations and individuals met and continue to meet the challenges of that change. The severity of issues facing Native people with the onslaught of settler colonialism was relentless in its ferocity. These stories explore resistance, adaptation, and persistence, portraying the complexity of decision-making for one's self and one's people.

> *In spite of the crimes of history, we write. We continue as artists, poets, novelists, fictionists, parents, grandparents. We continue to want the story. We have little power, but that does not mean we have no influence.*
>
> —*Elizabeth Cook-Lynn,*
> Notebooks of Elizabeth Cook-Lynn[a]

CHAPTER 8

The Doctrine of Discovery

Robert J. Miller

As Europeans began to explore and claim rights over Indigenous peoples and lands outside of Europe, Spain and Portugal looked to the Catholic Pope to ratify their discoveries and their claims over these lands and peoples. Spain and Portugal had made conflicting claims to the Canary Islands off the northwest coast of Africa from 1341 forward. King Duarte of Portugal finally convinced the pope in 1436 to grant him control of the Canary Islands to civilize and to convert the non-Christian Canary Islanders. In 1436, Pope Eugenius IV issued a papal bull (a church order), *Romanus Pontifex*, to both manage and control the islands on behalf of the pope and to convert the natives.

Other popes reissued this bull in succeeding decades and extended Portugal's jurisdiction and geographical rights over the Indigenous peoples along the west coast of Africa. In 1452 and 1455, Pope Nicholas V issued significantly more aggressive orders that authorized Portugal "to invade, search out, capture, vanquish, and subdue all Saracens and pagans," and place them into perpetual slavery, taking all their property.

> *The Roman pontiff, successor of the key-bearer of the heavenly kingdom and vicar of Jesus Christ, contemplating with a father's mind all the several climes of the world and the characteristics of all the nations dwelling in them and seeking and desiring the salvation of all, wholesomely ordains and disposes upon careful deliberation those things which he sees will be agreeable to the Divine Majesty and by which he may bring the sheep entrusted to him by God into the single divine fold, and may acquire for them the reward of felicity, and pardon for their souls.... We [therefore] weighing all and singular the premises with due meditation, and noting that since we had formerly by other letters of ours granted among other things free and ample faculty to the aforesaid King Alfonso—to invade, search out, capture, vanquish, and subdue all Saracens and pagans whatsoever, and other enemies of Christ wheresoever placed, and the kingdoms, dukedoms, principalities, dominions, possessions, and all movable and immovable goods whatsoever held and possessed by them and to reduce their persons to perpetual slavery, and to apply and appropriate to himself and his successors the kingdoms, dukedoms, counties, principalities, dominions, possessions, and goods, and to convert them to his and their use and profit—by having secured the said faculty, the said King Alfonso, or, by his authority, the aforesaid infante, justly and lawfully has acquired and possessed, and doth possess, these islands, lands, harbors, and seas, and they do of right belong and pertain to the said King Alfonso and his successors.*[1]

After Columbus encountered and claimed islands in the Caribbean, Spain looked to the pope to ratify its ownership of these lands. In May 1493, Pope Alexander VI issued three papal bulls, including *Inter caetera divinai*, and ordered that the inhabited islands Columbus landed on, which according to the Pope had been "undiscovered by others," now belonged to the king and queen of Spain. The pope also granted Spain any lands it might discover in the future, provided they were "not previously possessed by any Christian owner."

Copia dela bula del decreto y concession q̃ hizo el papa
Alexandro sexto al Rey y a la Reyna nuestros señores de las Indias conforme al capitu.
Per venerabilem. §. rationibus qui filij sint legitimi/ y al cap. ... xxiij. q. iiij.

Pope Alexander VI Demarcation Bull 1493—
Courtesy of the Gilder Lehrman Institute of American History, GLC014093

Pope Alexander also issued another bull to settle Spanish and Portuguese claims and drew a line of demarcation from the North Pole to the South Pole three hundred miles west of the Azores, which are off the west coast of Europe. The Pope granted Spain title under the authority of God to all the lands it had discovered or would discover west of that line. Portugal was granted the same rights east of that line and allegedly granted Portugal the rights to control, convert, and dominate Africa, most of Asia, and Brazil.

> *Among other works well pleasing to the Divine Majesty … that in our times especially the Catholic faith and the Christian religion be exalted and be everywhere increased and spread, that the health of souls be cared for and that barbarous nations be overthrown and brought to the*

> *faith itself ... by the authority of Almighty God conferred upon us in blessed Peter and of the vicarship of Jesus Christ, which we hold on earth, do by tenor of these presents, should any of said islands have been found by your envoys and captains, give, grant, and assign to you and your heirs and successors, kings of Castile and Leon, forever, together with all their dominions, cities, camps, places, and villages, and all rights, jurisdictions, and appurtenances, all islands and mainlands found and to be found, discovered and to be discovered towards the west and south, by drawing and establishing a line from the Arctic pole, namely the north, to the Antarctic pole, namely the south, no matter whether the said mainlands and islands are found and to be found in the direction of India or towards any other quarter, the said line to be distant one hundred leagues towards the west and south from any of the islands commonly known as the Azores and Cape Verde.... And we make, appoint, and depute you and your said heirs and successors lords of them with full and free power, authority, and jurisdiction of every kind.*[2]

TESTING THE OWNERSHIP OF LAND IN THE UNITED STATES

The newly created US government quickly adopted the principles of Discovery and preemption. This is by no means surprising in light of the widespread acceptance of this power by the colonial and state governments. By 1790, after a period of competition and struggle with its states, the federal government assumed the dominant position in Indian affairs and the exclusive Discovery and preemption authority over Indian tribes. Long before 1823, when the US Supreme Court agreed that Discovery was the law of the United States, all the various permutations and branches of the federal government had already adopted and were operating under Discovery. In actuality, the Supreme Court was the last governmental entity of any form in the United States—colonial, state, or federal—to expressly adopt the Doctrine and the preemption power.

Johnson v. M'Intosh, 21 U.S. (8 Wheat.) 543 (1823)

In 1823, 1831, and 1832, the US Supreme Court published three cases that created the basic outlines of federal Indian law that still apply today. These cases are known as the "Marshall Trilogy" because the primary opinions in all three cases were written by Chief Justice John Marshall.

In 1823, the Supreme Court was faced with the long-anticipated question of whether the international law principle that today we call the Doctrine of Discovery was American law. The court also had to answer questions about the nature of Indian land ownership, and whether individual Americans could buy Indian lands directly from Indians and tribal governments. In essence, the court had to define the nature of "Indian title" (or the legally recognized right of tribes and Indians to own and possess land).[3]

Johnson v. M'Intosh is an extremely important case not only because it was the first Indian law case to reach the Supreme Court but also because it tested the ownership of all lands in the United States. It continues to be a crucial case because Indian title is the original link in almost all land titles in the United States, and *Johnson* also continues to control the relationship between the United States and Indian tribes.

In June 1773, before the United States existed, William Murray, a partner in a land speculation company, bought land from Illinois Indians. Despite being warned by British officers that he was violating English law, Murray allegedly purchased two large tracts of land from the Kaskaskia, Peoria, and Cahokia tribes. In October 1775, Murray bought two more large tracts of land from the Piankeshaw tribe. These lands are located in modern-day Indiana and Illinois.

The land companies worked for decades to get these purchases ratified by the English colonial and royal governments, and then by the American state and federal governments. When these political attempts failed, the issue ended up in federal court.

In the intervening years, however, the United States pursued its own policies to acquire Indian lands and to expand across the North American continent.[4] In fact, in 1803 and 1809, the federal government negotiated treaties with the same tribal governments that William Murray had allegedly dealt with, and the United States purchased enormous areas of land in what is now Illinois and Indiana, including the lands Murray had purchased. The United States immediately began surveying the area and selling land to settlers. The defendant in the case of *Johnson v. M'Intosh*, William McIntosh, purchased his land in 1815 from the United States and received his title to the land in 1818 from the federal government.

The plaintiffs in *Johnson v. M'Intosh* were descendants of an investor in one of the land speculation companies. They filed a trespass lawsuit in federal court against William McIntosh to force him off his land. McIntosh won the case in the trial court.

On appeal to the US Supreme Court, the plaintiffs' attorneys argued that Indians and tribes had a natural law right to sell the lands they had owned and occupied since time immemorial. Even these attorneys, however, did not think that the "savage tribes" possessed full title to their lands.[5] Instead, they called the Indian title a "title by occupancy," and one that was held in common by the entire tribe. They argued, though, that since England and the treaties it signed with American Indian tribes recognized a tribal right to land, then Indians could sell their land rights to anyone they wished. In contrast, McIntosh's attorneys argued that all European countries denied that Indians and tribal governments had permanent property rights in land and denied Indians the right to sell land to private individuals: "Discovery is the foundation of title, in European nations, and this overlooks all proprietary rights in the natives."[6]

Chief Justice John Marshall began the court's opinion by stating that the plaintiffs claimed to have purchased land from the chiefs of Indian nations in 1773 and 1775, and that these transactions raised "the question [ ] whether this title can be recognised [sic] in the Courts of the United States?"[7] Marshall restated the issue: "The inquiry, therefore, is … confined to the power of Indians to give, and of private individuals to receive, a title which can be sustained in the courts of this country."[8]

Marshall then searched for the legal rule to apply to this case. He stated that a nation or society where land is located has to make the rules about how property can be acquired, and a court cannot look to "principles of abstract justice" or natural law and instead must look to the principles of its own government.[9] Marshall then methodically investigated the European rules of property that had been applied in North America to see what rule should be used in *Johnson*. The court noted that the rule of property acquisition and transfer applied by Holland, Spain, Portugal, France, and England in

North America was the Doctrine of Discovery.[10] All these countries "relied on the title given by discovery [even] to lands remaining in the possession of Indians."[11] Marshall then traced the English king's title to lands in North America from first discovery, through the royal charters granting land to the thirteen colonies, and finally to how the American states and the United States had acquired these same rights from European countries.[12]

From the foregoing, the court reasoned that the English Crown had "absolute title" in Indian lands "subject only to [the] Indian right of occupancy" and that this situation was "incompatible with an absolute and complete title in the Indians."[13] Since the American states and then the United States acquired this same title as the Crown, Marshall wrote: "It has never been doubted, that either the United States, or the several States, had a clear title to all the lands … subject only to the Indian right of occupancy, and that the exclusive power to extinguish that right, was vested in that government which might constitutionally exercise it."[14]

Marshall then arrived at a succinct statement of the rule that all European and American governments had accepted for buying Indian lands in North America: The "principle [ ] that *discovery gave title* to the government by whose subjects, or by whose authority, it was made, against all other European governments, which title might be consummated by possession"[15] (author's emphasis). He also stated that "the original fundamental principle" governing land titles and transfers of title was "that discovery gave *exclusive title* to those who made it"[16] (author's emphasis). Thus, European and American governments claimed that they acquired the legal title to the lands in North America by discovering those lands, and that Indians retained the rights of use and occupancy of the lands under the European or American government who gained those legal rights from the tribal governments.

The *Johnson* case was easy to decide once the court applied the Doctrine of Discovery rule. It follows naturally from the above statements that if discovering European governments owned the exclusive title to Indian lands, how then could tribal chiefs sell their lands to private individuals? In fact, Chief Justice Marshall stated that this case was easy, but that a long opinion was required "by the magnitude of the interest in [the] litigation ... [more] than by its intrinsic difficulty."[17] In light of the Discovery rule, the court's answer to the issue presented in *Johnson* was obvious: the sale of land directly from Indian tribes to private individuals did not transfer a title "which can be sustained in the Courts of the United States."[18] Consequently, the private land speculators lost in their long battle for the right to buy tribal lands.

Even though this legal struggle was only between non-Indians, and the Doctrine of Discovery itself allegedly applied only to Europeans and American colonists, it was Indian peoples and tribal governments who lost significant and valuable property rights that were confiscated by Euro-Americans. The court clearly recognized that under the Doctrine of Discovery Indian tribes lost two very important rights, without their knowledge or consent and without any payment, based on the "discovery" of their territories by Euro-Americans. While tribes continued to have the right to use and occupy their lands, they lost the valuable governmental and property right to sell their lands to whomever they wished for whatever amount of money they could negotiate.[19] In addition, tribal governments lost significant sovereign and commercial powers because they were no longer allowed to engage in international diplomacy and trade with any country other than their "discoverer."[20] The following statement best describes the rule of the *Johnson* case:

> *"The United States, then, have unequivocally acceded to that great and broad rule [Discovery] by which its civilized inhabitants now hold this country. They hold, and assert in themselves, the title by which it was acquired. They maintain, as all others have maintained, that discovery gave an exclusive right to extinguish the Indian title of occupancy, either by purchase or by conquest; and gave also a right to such a degree of sovereignty, as the circumstances of the people would allow them to exercise."*[21]

Thus, European countries and later the United States gained "the ultimate dominion" over tribal lands and claimed the "power to grant the soil, while yet in possession of the natives."[22]

It bears repeating that this 1823 Supreme Court decision determined the validity of 1773 and 1775 purchases of Indian lands by non-Indians. The US Supreme Court invalidated those land purchases because the Doctrine of Discovery was the controlling law in the colonial era for buying Indian lands. In *Johnson*, the Supreme Court adopted the Doctrine of Discovery and ratified the prior actions of the American colonial, state, and federal governments in using Discovery to control the purchases of tribal lands and all political and commercial interactions with tribes. The Doctrine and *Johnson v. M'Intosh* are still the law in the United States today. Tribal governments still cannot sell, lease, or develop their own lands (if they are held in "trust" by the United States) without the permission of the United States, 25 U.S.C. §§ 177, 415, and the United States is considered to be the legal owner of tribal and Indian lands, and the tribes and individual Indians are considered to be only the beneficial owner.

> *Colonialism was legalized by the law of nations developed by Europeans during the colonial era. That body of law was developed largely to facilitate the conquest and colonization of the New World.*
>
> —*Walter R. Echo-Hawk*[23]

TEN ELEMENTS OF THE DOCTRINE OF DISCOVERY

Johnson v. M'Intosh, 21 U.S. (8 Wheat.) 543 (1823).

Here are the ten elements that I think constitute the Doctrine and are useful in analyzing and comparing how settler/colonizer societies have used this international law against Indigenous peoples around the globe.[24]

1. **First discovery.** The first Euro-American country to discover lands unknown to other Euro-Americans claimed property and sovereign rights over the lands and Native peoples. First discovery, however, was usually considered to have created only an incomplete title.

2. **Actual occupancy and possession.** To turn first discovery into recognized title, a Euro-American country had to actually occupy newly found lands. This was usually done by building forts or settlements. Physical possession had to be accomplished within a reasonable amount of time after a first discovery to create a claim to the complete title.

3. **Preemption/European title.** Discovering Euro-American countries also claimed the power of preemption; that is, the sole right to buy the land from Indigenous peoples. This is a valuable property right similar to an exclusive option to purchase land. The government that owned the preemption right prevented or preempted any other Euro-American government or individual from buying land from the Native owners. The United States still claims this power over Indian nations and their lands today. 25 U.S.C. § 177.

4. **Indian or Native title.** After first discovery, Euro-American legal systems claimed that Indigenous peoples and nations had lost their full property rights and full ownership of their lands. Euro-Americans claimed that Indigenous nations only retained the rights to occupy and use their lands. Nevertheless, these rights could last forever if they never consented to sell to the country that claimed the preemption power. If Indigenous nations did choose to sell, they were only supposed to deal with the government that held the preemption right. Thus, "Indian title" in the United States, "Maori title" in New Zealand, and Native titles elsewhere allegedly define limited ownership rights.

5. **Tribal limited sovereign and commercial rights.** After a first discovery, Euro-Americans considered that Indigenous nations and peoples had lost some aspects of their inherent sovereign powers and their rights to international free trade and diplomatic relations. Thereafter, they were only supposed to deal with the Euro-American government that had "discovered" them and claimed the preemption power.

6. **Contiguity.** Euro-Americans claimed a significant amount of land contiguous to and surrounding their actual discoveries and settlements in the New World. Contiguity became very important when different Euro-American countries had settlements somewhat close together. In that situation, each country claimed to hold rights over the unoccupied lands between their settlements to a point halfway between their settlements. Moreover, contiguity held that the discovery of the mouth of a river gave the discovering country a claim over all the lands drained by that river, even if that was thousands of miles. For example, refer to the boundaries of the Louisiana Territory and Oregon country.

7. **Terra nullius.** This phrase literally means land that is null, void, or empty. This element stated that if lands were not possessed or occupied by any person or nation, or even if they were occupied but they were not being used in a fashion that Euro-American legal systems approved, then the lands were considered to be "empty" and available for Discovery claims. Euro-Americans eagerly applied this element and often considered lands that were actually owned, occupied, and being used by Indigenous peoples to be "vacant" and available for Discovery claims if they were not being "used" according to Euro-American laws and cultural mores.

8. **Christianity.** Religion was a significant aspect of the Doctrine of Discovery. Under Discovery, non-Christian peoples were not deemed to have the same rights to land, sovereignty, and self-determination as Christians.

9. **Civilization.** The Euro-American ideals of civilization were important parts of Discovery and of ideas of superiority. Euro-Americans thought that God had directed them to bring civilized ways, education, and religion to Indigenous peoples and to exercise paternalism and guardianship powers over them.

10. **Conquest.** Euro-Americans claimed they acquired Indian titles by military victories in "just" and "necessary" wars. In addition, conquest was also used as a term of art to describe the property and sovereign rights Euro-Americans claimed to have acquired automatically over Indigenous nations simply by making a "first discovery."

A Letter from Beatrice Long Visitor Holy Dance to Pope Benedict XVI

Delivered to the Vatican by Beatrice in 2008 and used with permission from her daughter, Loretta Afraid Of Bear Cook.

I am Grandmother Beatrice Long Visitor Holy Dance. I am from the Oglala Lakota Nation. My original homelands are the Black Hills of South Dakota.

I want to speak to the issue of "Healing Our Relations."

We believe our ancestral ways of prayer, peacemaking and healing are needed today. We still rely on the teachings of our ancestors for our survival.

We the International Council of Thirteen Indigenous Grandmothers were brought together by a common vision:

1. To form a global alliance of prayer.
2. (For) education and healing for Mother Earth and all her children.
3. To protect our lands and cultures upon which our peoples depend.

Unfortunately, relationships between national-states and tribal peoples in the Americas, Africa and Oceania rests on the foundation of the "doctrine of conquest" or the "doctrine of discovery." These governmental doctrines can be traced directly to the following Papal Bulls—Dum Diversas, June 18, 1452; Romanus Pontifex, January 8, 1455; Inter Caetera, May 4, 1493.

These papal bulls gave dominion to European nations over lands that our tribal nations have occupied for thousands of years. They also laid the basis for the European "Age of Discovery" that resulted in the outright theft of entire continents from our indigenous people worldwide.

It has been over 500 years since these papal bulls were written, yet they remain the spiritual, legal and moral foundation for exercising jurisdiction over tribal people by nation states today.

Our tribal nations must still live with the denial of our right to be treated as equal participants in the world community of nations. In other words, our people are still struggling for the right to live on earth and practice our cultural and spiritual traditions as our ancestors did.

As a very concerned Grandmother, I'm asking Pope Benedict the XVI, a servant of God, to remove these Papal Bulls. An act like this would create a global healing of all the injustices suffered by indigenous people all over the world.

A Reflection on Beatrice Long Visitor Holy Dance and the Doctrine of Discovery from Beatrice's Daughter, Loretta Afraid of Bear Cook

Many years have passed since I escorted my mother, Beatrice Long Visitor Holy Dance, to the Vatican in 2006–2007. Mama had very strong prayers, hopes, and dreams in her life. She joined the International Council of Thirteen Indigenous Grandmothers in the fall of 2004. During that inaugural meeting held in Phoenicia, New York, in the beautiful Catskill Mountains, we were privileged to gather together. Each of the Grandmothers set out their mission and goals for the world. For the first time in my years as the oldest child in my family I wondered, "What is Mama wanting to do in this grandmother capacity?" As the oldest child, it was my duty as a Lakota woman and daughter to carry forward my mother's vision after her passing. My heart rose and sank as I heard her utter the words, "I want the papal bulls rescinded and the Black Hills returned to our People." These tasks felt monumental.

Much work has been done by Indigenous Peoples and scholars around the world with regards to raising awareness about the papal bulls and getting them rescinded. Awareness was raised in 1972, when Vine Deloria, Jr. wrote about the *1493 Inter Caetera* papal bull in his book *God Is Red*. Since that time, global campaigns have been made, proclamations signed, letters written, resolutions drafted, and meetings with Vatican officials have been attended. Many Indigenous people have directed their energy to this battle, such as the late Birgil Kills Straight, and we have Steven Newcomb, Tony Castanha, Oren Lyons, and many others who continue this fight. Still, our quest to have the Catholic Church officially and formally rescind the applicable papal bulls has not been realized.

In July of 2008, the International Council of Thirteen Indigenous Grandmothers traveled to the Vatican to call for the revocation of the bulls *Dum diversas, Romanus Pontifex,* and *Inter Caetera* from the fifteenth century. In 2016, shortly after the passing of my beloved mother, Beatrice

Long Visitor Holy Dance, I traveled to Rome along with Indigenous scholar Steven Newcomb and many others as part of the Long March to Rome campaign to continue her prayer, as well as the prayer of countless others. There our group met with Pope Francis and Archbishop Tomasi, head of the Vatican Council for Peace and Justice, to once again call for the formal revocation of bulls *Dum diversas*, *Romanus Pontifex*, and *Inter Caetera* from the fifteenth century.

Still today, our quest continues. To date, the church's position, as explained in a 2005 letter by the Archbishop Celestino Migliore, states that "taken from the context of the political climate at the time, the notion of international law and the geographical notions then extant, the bull *Inter Caetera*, like other documents of that era, has become *ipso facto* obsolete and with no effect."

However, each day I hear my mother's words in my mind, "I want the papal bulls rescinded and the Black Hills returned to our People." Today, I am preparing my own daughter to carry this prayer in the event that the Vatican continues to evade this request, rather than to act upon it. It is my hope that during my lifetime, these papal bulls can formally be rescinded so the healing of Indigenous Peoples, and those who colonized them, can move forward and become complete. Mitakuye Oyasin.

CHAPTER 9

The Dispossession of Titticut

THE STRUGGLE OF THE WAMPANOAG AND MASSACHUSET PEOPLE OF THE TITTICUT VILLAGE AND RESERVATION TO KEEP THEIR LANDS, 1669–1790

George Price

Titticut was one of only two Indian reservations in colonial Massachusetts that were designated as such by the Massachusetts Bay Colony government. The first was at Freetown in 1701, and Titticut was reserved in 1724. It was the home of many families from both the Massachuset and Wampanoag tribal nations. Several types of interactions between American Indians and non-Indians that occurred in the nineteenth-century American West happened in similar ways about one hundred years earlier at Titticut—including legal battles over land, land loss due to economic struggles, and issues of identity, allegiance, and betrayal. This is a story of Titticut's origins, and its demise.

What does "dispossession" mean? Is it the successful outcome of an exorcism? No, this chapter does not deal with the topic of exorcisms at all. In this case, "dispossession" is a word used to describe how the English colonists of Massachusetts Bay Colony "acquired" land from the people who had been living on those lands for possibly thousands of years before English arrival—the Wampanoag and Massachuset Indian nations. Some questions that will be raised and explored in this article include:

1. In what ways did Native American and English cultural concepts about living with the land differ from each other?

2. Can land be "dispossessed" if it is not previously possessed? Can land really be "sold" if it is not actually owned? Can words such as "stealing" or "taking" be legitimate substitutes for the word "dispossessed?"

3. Why did English law and customs prevail over the laws and customs of the people who originally lived in Massachusetts?

4. What could possibly give one group of people the right to take anything away from another group?

To better understand the components of this struggle to keep their remaining lands, it will be useful to first briefly explore the history of land use and land ownership at Titticut. Massachuset and Wampanoag cultural traditions concerning the use and care of the lands preceded the arrival of Europeans, and the introduction of their concept of land ownership, by several thousand years. Understanding the differences between Native American and European cultural concepts regarding land and how to live upon it is crucial to understanding the roots of Anglo–Native conflicts over land, such as the conflict at Titticut.

Traditional Native American cultural concepts relating to the land upon which we live express a sense of belonging to the land, rather than owning it as property that we can dispose of or transfer ownership of to others. While they did have a tradition of protecting territory and recognizing tribal homeland boundaries, it was more as the hereditary caretakers of those lands than as owners in the western legal sense. The tribal origin stories within their oral traditions describe the establishment of permanent reciprocal relationships between spirits, land, and all of the species (including humans) that were placed in specific locations. Those locations, or "territories," were recognized and understood by all the tribal nations within a region as the specific homelands of the specific tribes who, according to their beliefs, were placed upon those lands back when the first people were formed out of the very land itself.

All members of every tribe were responsible for making the proper prayers and offerings to the spirit guardians of their particular lands and resources, and for following closely the spirit-given directions for caring for and using them *sustainably*. The sense of responsibility to the land that is generated by such a cosmology gave Indian people a deep concern for maintaining the balance and integrity of the ecosystem, so that it would continue to provide sustenance for them and the generations of their descendants to come. To do otherwise would mean to break their relationship with everything that was sacred to them and threaten the continuation of life itself.[1]

In light of such a long-held cultural perspective on the correct relationship of humans to land, the European concepts of ruling over, ownership, and the buying and selling of land must have been so different from their own experience as to be incomprehensible to the Native people—which is precisely what many Native Americans, both then and now, have claimed. Consider the following example from the Sauk leader, Black Hawk:

> *My reason teaches me that land cannot be sold. The Great Spirit gave it to his children to live upon, and cultivate as far as necessary for their subsistence; and so long as they occupy and cultivate it, they have the right to the soil—but if they voluntarily leave it, then any other people have the right to settle upon it. Nothing can be sold, but such things as can be carried away.*[2]

It is primarily because of this traditional cultural perspective that the validity of these early colonial land deeds and bills of sale are suspect, especially when they involved English translators for Indians who spoke very little or no English. Many of the earliest so-called Indian land grants to the English were based on nothing more than an erroneous, and perhaps overly optimistic English interpretation of Indian sign language or hand gestures.[3] During the early English land acquisition period in the seventeenth century, Wampanoag and Massachuset leaders may have understood the land deeds as nothing more than an English way of establishing peace and friendship or bonds of alliance between neighbors, which was a very important tradition among Native Americans. The deed-signing ceremonies in those early years of colonialism often involved an exchange of gifts, eating food together, and smoking tobacco, all of which closely resembled traditional alliance-making and peace-making ceremonies between tribes.[4] Even so, the Native American people of Massachusetts became painfully aware before long—perhaps within the first decade or two after the English arrival—that the English understood their "talking papers" to mean something much more invasive and unfriendly than the Indians first thought.[5]

The Concept of Ownership

The concept of land ownership was completely foreign to Native American understandings about the land. Perhaps in the earliest transactions there was little understanding of the dispossession of land through sale to Europeans, but Native American sophistication grew rapidly. European power soon drove home the lesson that a land sale involved full and final alienation of rights.

Not all English colonists in America thought the same way about how to acquire and rightfully settle in American lands. Some Englishmen, like Massachusetts Bay Colony's first governor, John Winthrop, held to a concept called vacuum domicilium regarding Indian hunting and gathering territories outside their villages and cultivated lands. Under that concept, Indians only had legal property rights to lands that had been "subdued" (cultivated) or "improved" (built upon, containing homes, storage facilities, etc.). The Native peoples of New England were not nomadic. They lived in permanent villages and cultivated a great variety of vegetable crops. But they also hunted, fished, and gathered wild plant foods and medicines on the lands and waters surrounding their villages, within their traditional territories. Winthrop did not consider those hunting and gathering areas to be Indian property, and therefore he thought they required no deed of purchase for the English to start living there. But other Englishmen, such as Roger Williams, who was kicked out of the Massachusetts Bay Colony in 1635 and walked nearly one hundred miles to the southwest to establish the Rhode Island colony, were compelled by their own moral sense to execute deeds of sale and pay what they considered to be a fair price to acquire any Indian homelands. Williams believed that the English conviction in their right to settle on "unsubdued" American lands without regard to Native American territorial traditions was invalid in the eyes of God.[6] When Edmund Andros became royal governor of the United Colonies of New

England in 1686, the use of legal deeds and establishment of title became required for all subsequent acquisitions of Indian land. Many Indian land deeds after that point, as well as some before, were written to affirm and amend the early colonial land grants and purchases and legally resolve any disputes over those previously acquired lands.[7]

Nevertheless, legality and moral issues were often evaded or disregarded completely in the actual practices of appropriating Indian lands. English colonialists were usually ethnocentric in their attitudes toward people of other cultures. The colonialists' sense of innate superiority over other humans—combined with their insatiable "need" for the Indian lands—meant they disregarded whether the Indians understood English land ownership concepts and laws; nor did they bother to find out anything about Indian concepts and laws. Most colonial-era English had little or no respect for, or understanding of, Native cultures, laws, and customs.[8] In their zealous pursuit of American Indian lands and resources, some English even showed little regard for their own laws. Many examples can be found in the colonial records of illegal methods used to acquire Indian lands. Such methods included allowing their livestock to roam into Indian gardens and wild food gathering areas in hope that the Indians would move, getting Indians drunk before persuading them to sign a land deed, persuading individual Indians to sign a deed for the sale of some other Indian's land—sometimes a whole tribe's land—and even using the threat of violence and forcing or pressuring Indians to sell land to pay off their debts.[9]

ENGLISH LAND ACQUISITION AND THE ORIGIN OF THE BIG CHIEF CONCEPT

The most common and convenient method of acquiring land from Indians in the early colonial period was to get one Indian to sign a deed on behalf of the whole tribe. In order for that to happen, the English had to impose their own cultural norms onto the Native American people, as the Native people had no such traditional practices in their own cultures—neither land sales nor absolute rulers. With few exceptions, the English had failed to learn much about the social structure of Native societies and their customs regarding leadership and government, which conveniently allowed them to create land deeds based on two pivotal false assumptions.

First, the English assumed that American Indian nations were monarchies. Second, they assumed that the Indian monarchs held the same or similar powers of authority that belonged to their own monarchs, including the right to take, buy, or sell lands. In reality, traditional Native American leaders in most tribal nations were representatives of small extended family or clan social units who met in councils to solve social problems through discussion and consensus. They were servants of the people who performed their leadership roles as needed—when problems arose or decisions had to be made.

They were *not* full-time politicians, nor were they kings, queens, princes, or any other type of monarchs. Nevertheless, English colonial histories, documents, and especially land deeds consistently refer to Wampanoag and Massachuset sachems (male leaders) and squasachems (female leaders) as "kings," "queens," "princes," or other types of rulers. The term "chief" eventually replaced the other labels but did not become the common label until the late eighteenth or early nineteenth century.

Misconception of Leadership

The concept of Indian leaders as monarchs became so prevalent after its introduction by the English that it has become a generally unquestioned "fact." Many anthropologists and historians have amended the misconception by speaking of "high sachems" and lower or "sub-sachems." The myth of "supreme" or high sachems gradually became internalized by partially deculturalized tribal people, which may have also been in part a survival tactic as they were pressured to prove their "Indianness," as understood in the minds of most Americans during the nineteenth and twentieth centuries.

From Ruth Wallis Herndon, and Ella Wilcox Sekatau, 1997, "The Right to a Name: The Narragansett People and Rhode Island Officials in the Revolutionary Era," *Ethnohistory* 44(3); and Daniel Denton, 1670, *A Brief Description of New York, Formerly Called New-Netherlands*, London, 11–c12.

Had they not made those assumptions, how could the English write up the deeds of sale for Indian lands? Who would the sellers of the land be? Could they persuade an entire tribal council to—after careful deliberation that typically went on for days or weeks at a time—come to a consensus that they should immediately embrace English culture and sell their source of life and well-being, which they had not ever imagined could be "owned" or "sold"? It was much easier for the colonists to pull aside one Indian council member, declare that person to be a monarch, have him or her place their mark on a piece of paper that they did not fully comprehend, and then let them find out the meaning of that act later, through painful experience. By use of this method, the English could proclaim that they had legally (in English law and English culture) acquired the signature of the "king" and "rightful owner" of the Indian land on a document that the English wrote and that only they understood.

Money—A Foreign Concept

Money, or currency, was also a foreign concept to the vast majority of Native American nations (possibly all, except the failed megasocieties, such as the Moundbuilders). Small-scale, sustainable societies live directly from the natural resource base, both wild and cultivated, with no need for buying, selling, or the use of currency. Wampum beads, in contrast to popular mythology and opinion, were not "the Indians' money," as used by tribes in the Northeast, although they were exchanged in trade and used as gifts.

From George Price, 1996, *Wampumpeag: The Impact of the 17th-Century Wampum Trade on Native Culture in Southern New England and New Netherlands*, Missoula: University of Montana Press.

THE ORIGIN OF THE TITTICUT INDIAN RESERVATION

Before Titticut became a reservation, it was a Wampanoag Indian village in the northern part of Wampanoag territory, near their traditional boundary with Massachuset territory. However, some colonial records say it was Massachuset Indian land. Claims varied depending upon whether land deeds signed by Wampanoag or Massachuset sachems were recognized. In 1645, the English claimed that the Wampanoag sachem, Massasoit Ousamequin, who had welcomed and assisted the Pilgrims during the 1620s, had sold them a large mass of land west of Plymouth. That land deed was later interpreted to include the lands that became the towns of Middleborough and Bridgewater, and the boundaries of Middleborough encompassed the Indian villages of Titticut, Assawompsett, and Nemasket. The English laid out their town boundaries like counties, with no open or unclaimed land in between the towns.

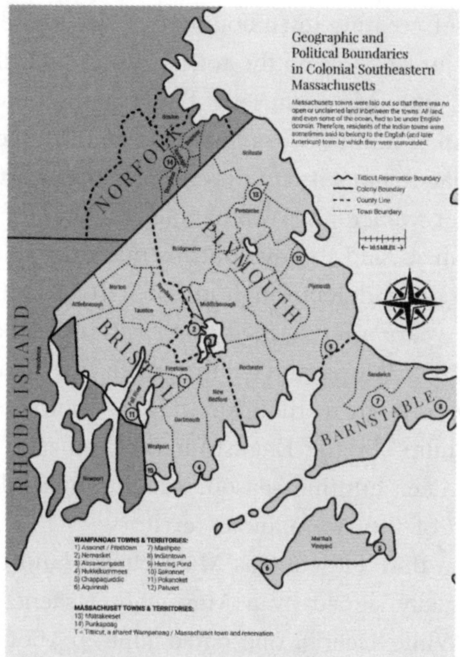

SE Massachusetts Town and Boundaries—Map by George Price and Kevin Piazza

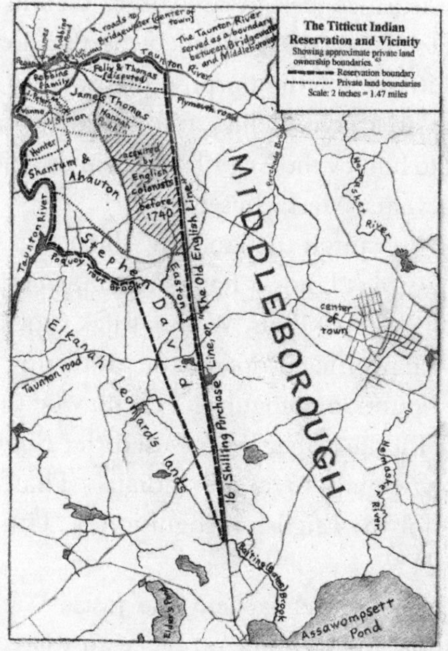

The Titticut Indian Reservation and Vicinity—Map by George Price

That method of creating town boundaries placed the Indian villages under the legal jurisdiction of the towns, along with the jurisdictions of the counties, the Massachusetts Bay Colony, and the King of England. Nemasket and Assawompsett are undisputedly regarded as Wampanoag villages, but Titticut may have been a shared Wampanoag and Massachuset village. A Wampanoag sachem of Assawompsett named Tuspaquin is said to have put his mark on land deeds for the expanding town of Middleborough in 1663, 1664, 1667, 1669, 1672, and 1673. Two years after signing that last land deed, during King Philip's War in 1675, Tuspaquin led the attack that burned most of the town of Middleborough to the ground. Massasoit's son, Metacomet (called "King Philip" by the English) had a home in Titticut that he lived in during deer hunting season, which would also suggest that Titticut was part of the Wampanoag territory.

The suggestion that Titticut was Massachuset land comes from two land deeds allegedly signed by a Massachuset sachem named Josias Wampattuck ("White Deer"), one dated June 9, 1664, and the other December 23, 1686.[10] The signature of Wampattuck on the 1686 document was either a forgery or possibly signed by another Indian with the same name, since Josias Wampattuck died in 1669. The 1664 deed is of crucial importance to Titticut as that deed was initiated by Wampattuck himself for the purpose of protecting the land of all the Indians in the area surrounding and including Titticut, using the authority granted to him by the English to sell lands adjoining Titticut to the town of Bridgewater, Massachusetts.

Wampattuck also granted the land on which the Native village of Titticut already lay, plus lands a few miles on each side of the town to the Indians living there. Thus, Wampattuck provided the Tittticut Indians with an English legal document protecting their lands that the English were bound to recognize. This may be the earliest known case in which an Indian tribal leader used the English legal system to grant land ownership to other Indians. That document later became the basis for the English recognition of Titticut as an Indian reservation in 1724.[11]

Why would a Massachuset sachem like Josias Wampattuck seek to protect a Wampanoag village? The probable answer is that Titticut was by then a mixed Wampanoag and Massachuset Indian town, located on the border between the two tribes' ancestral territories. It may also have been land designated as shared territory by a long-standing agreement between the two tribal nations. The practice of sharing territory, especially along the borders of the ancestral territory of two tribes, was not unusual. A well-known example of this in Massachusetts involves the Nipmuc and an unknown other tribal nation (or, perhaps two different divisions or villages within the Nipmuc nation) and a lake they shared that bordered both of their territories near the present-day town of Webster, Massachusetts. The lake was originally called, in the Nipmuc Algonquian language, Chaugoggagoggmanchauggagoggchaubunagungamaugg, which means, according to some, "You fish on your side of the lake and we'll fish on our side and nobody fishes in the middle." The exact translation is disputed, but it is generally acknowledged that there was an agreement between the two tribal groups to share the resources of the lake. More recent scholarship has revealed that intertribal alliances, mutual respect, and skilled diplomacy were much more the norm in pre-European-contact American Indian societies than the popular mythical image of "warlike peoples" that has prevailed in the American imagination to this day.

After the arrival of Europeans, several other factors contributed to an increase in intertribal alliances and mergers. There was a need to restore populations after the many deadly epidemics from foreign diseases. Tribes also united as warriors for their mutual protection from increasing attacks by the colonists and by some Indians from other nations who had either joined with the English or were forced to seek new lands. The influence of Christianity was yet another factor.

Sometime before 1672, and possibly before Wampattuck deeded their land in 1664, Titticut was designated by English missionary John Eliot as one of the "praying towns" for Christian Indians of both the Wampanoag and Massachuset tribes. About fourteen Indian towns in eastern Massachusetts were so designated where the missionaries felt they had had considerable success. Indians who had been displaced from their lands were encouraged by the missionaries and colonial authorities to settle in those towns, and they were told that if they conformed to Christian teachings and English culture, the villages of Christian Indians would be safer and more protected from English attacks and incursions.[12] Wampattuck, who resided most of the time in the Massachuset village of

Mattakeeset (near present-day Pembroke, east of Bridgewater), probably had relatives in Titticut, and it is certain that he had descendants there by the 1740s. An examination of the Indian family surnames on various Titticut-related documents of the early through mid-eighteenth century, shows a nearly equal mixture of Wampanoag and Massachuset names.

Surnames

Massachuset family surnames at Titticut in the mid-eighteenth century include Shantum, Ahauton, Thomas, Sachemus, and Robbins—a family name that was also taken by some of the Nipmucs twenty miles west of them, in the area north of Providence, Rhode Island.

Wampanoag family surnames at Titticut during that same era include Wanno, Simons (aka Simon, Symon, and Symons), Felix, Anthony, and Easton. Several other surnames are of uncertain tribal origin. Obviously, some of these names are of European origin but had been adopted by Native individuals and families at some point.

Exactly why the Massachusetts Bay Colony set aside about 3,500 acres (or 5.5 square miles) of the land that Josias Wampattuck deeded as a reservation for the Indians at Titticut is not completely clear. Motivations and attitudes among the colonial leaders toward Indians and their land rights surely varied in some ways. But the prevailing belief among the English colonists in early eighteenth-century Massachusetts was not much different from that of Winthrop, when he said,

> *As for the Natives in New England, they inclose noe Land, neither have any setled habytation, nor any tame Cattle to improve the Land by, and soe have noe other but a Naturall Right to those Countries, soe as if we leave them sufficient for their use, we may lawfully take the rest, there being more than enough for them and us [sic].*[13]

The common belief was that the land would be put to better, or more "profitable," use in the possession of "civilized" people like themselves, and if the Natives of America would become more like the English culturally, then they might be able to put the land to good use too. About nine years before the Titticut lands were formally declared a "plantation," "reserved" for the Indians who lived there, two Titticut sachems, Isaac Wanno and Joshua Shantum, petitioned the colonial government to prevent their citizens from attempting to take Titticut lands under false premises. Beginning in the 1720s and 1730s, the Massachusetts General Court appointed what they called "guardians" over most of the remaining Indian communities in the colony, claiming that this was to protect the Indians from those who wanted to exploit them. Under that system, individual Indians had to have the permission of the guardians and the General Court itself in order to sell any of their lands. Petitions for such permission were almost always granted.

Titticut Land

The boundaries and status of Titticut as a "reserve" were formally laid out in March of 1724, which is documented in a rare map (for the colonial era) of an Indian community land holding, that includes a written description of all of the boundary markers, as was done on any land deed of that period. The Titticut Indian Reservation and Vicinity Map is based on this map, as well as information gathered from careful examination of fifty-nine Titticut Indian land deeds executed between 1732 and 1784. For more on the Indian reserves of Massachusetts Bay Colony, including two nongovernment-created reserves at Gay Head and "Indiantown," see Daniel Mandell, 1996, *Behind the Frontier: Indians in Eighteenth-Century Eastern Massachusetts* (Lincoln: University of Nebraska Press), 51, 75.

The bulk of the reservation lay on the Middleborough side of the river, which is why the Titticut Indians were often referred to as the "Middleborough Indians."

From *Acts and Resolves, Public and Private, of the Province of the Massachusetts Bay, Vol. X, Appendix, Resolves, etc., 1720–1726*, Boston: Wright & Potter Printing Co., Sate Printers, 1902, 464 (Ch. 88) and 492 (Ch. 174); John Winthrop, 1629. "Generall Considerations for the Plantation in New England," in the *Winthrop Papers*, ed, Allyn B. Forbes, Boston: Massachusetts Historical Society, 1929–47, Vol. 2, 118; and Petition of Benjamin Wanoo [sic] and Joshua Shantum, May 25, 1715, Massachusetts State Archives, Vol. 31, 91–93. This document is in the Massachusetts State Archives, colonial towns collection, Vol. 113, p. 653. See Daniel Mandell, 1996, *Behind the Frontier: Indians in Eighteenth-Century Eastern Massachusetts*, Lincoln: University of Nebraska Press, 51 and 75.

As happened in the late-nineteenth and twentieth century American West, warfare became futile for the Native peoples of New England because the Europeans had come to outnumber them so significantly. So the legal arena became the new battlefield, and Indians who had knowledge of the English laws became the new warriors. The legal act of Josias Wampattuck in 1664—whether ingenious or simply an act of desperation—apparently inspired other Indians to use the English land laws for their own protection. Beginning in the early 1700s, Indians who were not necessarily sachems or squasachems began to appear in land deeds as individual owners of lands. These deeds usually involved sales of land to English individuals and towns, but they also involved the sale or granting of lands to their own children, grandchildren, or other tribal citizens, providing them with a legal document that would, it was hoped, protect those lands from further English attempts to dispossess them.

In the cases of Richard and Mingo Gonduary (aka Gunderway) in 1732, Thomas Felix in 1745, and Caesar and Mercy Easton in 1748, the tribal elders of Titticut (possibly their entire council of leaders) jointly granted tracts of land to individual tribal members. Unlike the Allotment Act of 1887, which forcefully imposed the practice of individual land ownership on the Native peoples of the West, this earlier movement toward individual land ownership seems to have been directed by Native Americans themselves as a strategy for protecting their remaining lands and communities. But, even though the Wampanoags and Massachusets found some legal protection in acquiring individual deeds to their lands, the conversion of tribal lands to individual Indian ownership primarily benefited the English, as they no longer needed to seek out or claim some Indian to be a monarch in order to purchase Indian land. Any Indian's mark on a paper would do, and in many cases, they found it easier to acquire Indian land one parcel at a time than to try to stake claim to a vast territory from an entire tribal nation. Moreover, by the early eighteenth century there were no vast Indian territories left in eastern Massachusetts.

THE FIGHT FOR TITTICUT LANDS IN THE PLYMOUTH COUNTY COURT

Faced with this new English strategy for dispossessing them of their remaining lands, the Titticut leaders took additional steps toward protection. They made their own land rights laws, in defiance of English legal jurisdiction over them. Under those laws, "foreigners," or nontribal members (including Indians of other tribes or communities) who married into the Titticut community, had no right to sell off any Titticut lands without permission of their tribal member spouse and the tribe itself. If the Titticut Indian spouse died, and the couple had no surviving children, the outsider spouse had no right to sell the land at all. Since this Indian law was in conflict with Massachusetts colonial law, the "foreigners" would generally win their cases if it went to the courts. Such court decisions made it possible for any nontribal male who married a Titticut woman to have the legal rights to own and/or sell that woman's property, as was the patriarchal custom and law in all of England and its colonies. As Massachusetts colonists sought eagerly to acquire lands from the dwindling remnant tribal communities in the mid-eighteenth century, outsiders (usually Indian men from other tribes or other Wampanoag or Massachuset communities who were economically desperate and ethically challenged) would sometimes marry into tribal communities in order to benefit personally from the English demand for Indian lands.[14] The English "guardians" would occasionally intervene to prevent those and other such fraudulent land claims, but more often than not they would either approve the claim or defer to a ruling by the court that was favorable to the particular Englishman intent on purchasing Indian land. When the colonists could not successfully acquire the land itself, they sometimes would lease or just brazenly take the resources on those lands, such as trees or hay, which also prompted many Indians and their guardians to bring them to court.[15]

Of all the Massachusetts Englishmen who were intent on acquiring Titticut Indian lands during the 1740s and 1750s, perhaps none was more aggressive and resourceful in this pursuit than Elkanah Leonard, Esq., of Middleborough. Leonard was at one time one of the wealthiest men and largest landowners in Middleborough, and his lands bordered the southern edge of the Titticut reservation. His lands also bordered the Wampanoag community of Assawompsett to the east of him, pursuing and buying Indian land here as well. Leonard was a lawyer, and he shared an interest in his uncle's iron foundry; he also had a small foundry, or "bloomery,"[16] of his own. Iron foundries used tremendous amounts of wood as fuel to run their furnaces, and the pursuit of wood often led to the pursuit of land. But wood was not Leonard's only motivation for a seemingly insatiable appetite for more land. During the early 1840s, a failed large-scale business venture put him deeply into debt.

The Leonard family had a long history of various relations with the Indians of this part of Massachusetts, dating back to the time just before King Philip's war of 1675–1676. At that time, the Leonard family ran a large iron foundry in Taunton, which was just west of Middleborough and in the heart of the western Wampanoag territory. According to one popular legend about the family, the Leonards were friendly with the Wampanoags and would often repair their firearms and make hatchets for them at their foundry. For that reason, the legend goes, during King Philip's War, Metacomet himself ordered his warriors to spare the town of Taunton, lest any harm should come to any member of the Leonard family.[17] One of Elkanah Leonard's relatives, Uriah Leonard, is said to have hidden the head of Metacomet (King Philip) at the old Leonard family home a few miles west of Titticut "for some time" at the end of the war.[18] Why he possessed the head is uncertain, but the colonial authorities eventually retrieved it and displayed it on a pike in several Massachusetts towns over the next twenty-five years.

During the 1740s and 1750s, Elkanah Leonard used a variety of methods, both legal and illegal, to acquire Indian as well as other English colonialists' land. In one incident that occurred in 1751, Leonard invited a Massachuset Indian of Titticut named Job Ahauton into his home, where he plied him with alcohol and coerced him into signing a deed of sale for some of Ahauton's land.[19] Based on the fraudulent manner in which his signature was procured, Ahauton later petitioned the General Court for a nullification of that land deed, but his petition was dismissed. Leonard had an Indian accomplice who helped him to manipulate and deceive Ahauton named Stephen David, who filed a counter-petition claiming that Ahauton was a "common drunk," and that it was nobody's fault but his own that he signed that deed.[20]

Stephen David was a "foreign" Indian (tribe unknown) who acquired Titticut land through marriages to two different Titticut Indian women. David sold more Titticut lands to the English than any other Indian in Titticut, and in 1753, the tribe petitioned the General Court to ban David from selling any more.[21] David's land lay between the lands of Elkanah Leonard and a Wampanoag man named Caesar Easton, at the southern end of the reservation, and David assisted Leonard in trying to acquire part of the Easton family's land by including part of it in a sale of his own land to Leonard.

Elkanah Leonard made a claim to seventeen of Caesar Easton's ninety acres through the Plymouth County Court of Common Pleas in May of 1753, alleging that he had been "seised" (legally in possession) of those seventeen acres of land since May of 1751, when he bought the disputed tract of land from Stephen David. In spite of Leonard's high standing in the community and his familiarity with the courts,[22] Caesar Easton won this first case against Leonard. This was probably due largely to the strength of his land deed document of 1748, which included a copy of the deed of the previous owners (Caesar's in-laws) and to which all the tribal elders had signed.

Less than one year later, in March of 1754, Elkanah Leonard's wife, Elizabeth, and his son, Elkanah, Jr., acting on behalf of Elkanah, who was at this time described as "non compos mentis" (a legal term for "crazy" or insane), registered a land deed with Plymouth County claiming that Caesar Easton had quit claim to the property in question and relinquished it to the Leonards in exchange for ten shillings "and for diverse other good causes and considerations." Although registered at that later date, the signatures on this new deed, which allegedly included Caesar Easton's mark, bore the date May 16, 1753, which was the day after Elkanah had lost to the Eastons and the Titticut Indians in court. In May of 1755, on the basis of this new land deed, which was probably fraudulent and never agreed to by the Eastons—certainly not on the day after their victory in court—Elkanah Leonard's wife and son took Caesar Easton to Plymouth Court again. This time the jury returned a verdict for the plaintiff, Elkanah Leonard, and ejected Caesar Easton from sixteen acres of his land.[23] There was no appeal filed, and no further legal actions regarding those lands have been found to date.

Whether or not Elkanah Leonard lost his mind due to his defeat in Plymouth Court by a group of "Indians and Negroes" (the Eastons and many other Titticut Indians were part African), or if it was the cumulative effect of the stress from over a decade of personal financial disaster, or both, is uncertain. A story is told that, in his later years, Leonard began to wear his shoes with the soles facing upward and the tops of the shoes facing the ground. When asked why he did so, Leonard answered, "Because the world has turned upside down." Understandably, it seemed so to him.[24]

Another "foreign" Indian (though likely a Massachuset), who came to Titticut in 1743, was James Thomas. Thomas became second only to Stephen David in the amount of Titticut land that he sold to the English. When he first arrived at Titticut, a Massachuset woman named Mary Mooet (aka Mooit, or Sachemus, a descendant of Josias Wampattuck) who lived on sixty acres in the northern part of the reservation gave (without charge) the bulk of her land (fifty acres) to Thomas, and kept ten acres, including a fruit orchard, for herself. Thomas soon began selling portions of his land to neighboring Englishmen, and one of those men, Captain Nehemiah Washburn, wrote up a deed that included Mary Mooet's ten acres as well, without her consent. Mary's daughter, Katherine Sachemus, who lived in a different community, probably Mattakeeset, petitioned the colonial government twice on her mother's behalf, seeking a return of the stolen land. According to Katherine, after Captain Washburn informed her mother that he had purchased her home and orchard from James Thomas, Mary Mooet was "obliged to leave the place and wander from town to town," as a homeless person. In Katherine Sachemus's second petition she claimed that, after she filed the first one, James Thomas came to her and forced her, "partly by threats and partly by entreaties," to sign a quit claim deed on her mother's land, which she then asked the Massachusetts General Court to nullify.[25]

James Thomas filed his own counterpetition in May of 1754, in which he claimed, among other things, that Katherine had lied regarding the size of the portion of land her mother had kept for herself, and that "it was always understood" that Washburn had "justly purchased the land." The General Court then dismissed Katherine Sachemus' petitions, based on Thomas' claims and on a supplemental request filed by Washburn's son-in-law, Josiah Dean, who held the land at that time.[26]

At about the same time that Katherine Sachemus filed her first petition, one of the most respected sachems at Titticut, John Simon, who was also a Christian pastor for the "praying-town" that became a reservation, filed a petition against both Stephen David and James Thomas, to ask the colonial government to prevent them from selling any more Titticut land. Before this petition, the most recent sale made by James Thomas included the Titticut church building, which was also John Simon's house. But it is clear that Simon's concerns expressed in this petition were not merely personal. He expresses a deeply held fear for the future of his people, for whom he was both a civil and spiritual leader, and whom he believed would be "broken up" and scattered—no longer a people—if things continued as they had been, and they became landless.

John Simon's petition gives us the most detailed account found to date of the dispossession of Titticut from the point of view of a Native person who was caught up in the midst of this struggle. In it you will find that Simon served in the English military five times during what were called the French and Indian Wars of the first half of the eighteenth century, as did many men from nearly all of the tribal communities within the Massachusetts Bay Colony. John Simon lost a leg during his fifth term of service. Whether or not that gained him much respect in the eyes of the colonial government is unclear, but they did respond favorably to his petition, and the response of the government officials is also printed here, after the petition.

TRANSCRIPTION OF THE PETITION OF JOHN SIMON TO THE GOVERNOR OF MASSACHUSETTS

Bay Colony, September 14, 1753[27]

To His Excellency William Shirley Esq. Captine and Governer in Cheif in and over his Majesty's Provice of the Massachusetts Bay in New-England and the Hon. His Majesty's councll & house of Representatives in the Gen. Court Asembled at Boston

The Humble Petition of John Simon of Titecutt Indian man and preacher their to Indians at this present time approved of by the Corporation[28] *in his own name and behalf of the little flock he has their with him~*

Humbly begs leave to enform this Honoured Court of the great grievances that we now ly under~ That notwithstanding the care that was taken by our Antient Ansestors to prevent our selling of Land and coming to want as will appear by the Records if examin'd into~

Yett by the repeated entreaty's of us Indians and the Indulgence of this Honour'd Court, we have parted with almost all our Lands in that place. And when some of us by sickness or by other Accidents has been reduced to great want and Nessecity and to prevent our Suffering it may be right to sell some Land but the great sale of Lands by some of our Indians have obtain'd at this Court of late we apprehend to be rong for two reasons~ First that they got in Debt by a Laisey & indolent life, and the encouragement of some of our English Neighbours who prompt them on to run in Debt on purposes to sell their land

Secondly two Indians who has sold large tracts of land we Aprehend had no write to any Land at all further than to sitt down and improve with us. This argument we have offer'd to the Honourable Committee's that came from this Court to sell Lands but they tell us it is too late for the sale is granted and they must do the work, but if we would stop these Indians from selling Land we should have come to the General Court sooner~ The two Indians I now speak of are Stephen David and James Thomas who tho' they have sold more Land than would fetch us five Hundred pounds Lawfull Money, Yett we Understand they have offer'd a petition to the Guardians for approbation for the sale of more lands, we Humbly pray may not be granted. for the two reasons above mentioned~ In the first place that Stephen David has led a very bad and Wicked life. and never had any rite to sell Land in Titecutt further than an Artfull Write that some of the English Neighbour's found out for him to gett away our Lands as we think

As to James Thomas he never had any rite to any of our Titicutt Lands till before the year 1743. When he got a deed of gift from Mary Mooet of about Sixty Acres and soon after He came to this

Court for Liberty to sell it which accordingly was done and he [sold?] all that he had any rite too. And our English Neighbour's [illegible] that he could have leave for sale prompt him on to run in Debt and he being very prood & Laisey was willing to do it~

And now for near ten years he has lived that life, and we believe has never done one months work in the whole time. But constantly comes to this Court for the sale of Lands which has always been granted and Since that first sale he has sold five different Sales. The last of which takes in the Meeting House in which we meet to Worship in and where I now live, So that I even cant have Liberty to gett a little wood for my Fire, although I am now very unable to gett it as I have but one Legg left~ And your humble petitioner would humbly pray your Excellency and Honour's to take these things under your Consideration and do what in your Wisdom you shall think fit. And that the little Society of us be not wholly brock up. For all the Support your petitioner has is only twelve pounds old tenor a year as a preacher paid me by the Corporation, and a Small pention of fifteen pounds old tenor for the loss of my Legg in the late Expedition which was the fifth time I ventur'd my Life in Defence of the English people~

And this James goes now Clothed in Broad Cloak Beaver Hatt Watch in his pockett and his Coffee Tea & Chocklate and appears very much like a gentleman at home & abroad and as we understand is now in Debt Seven or Eight Hundred pounds old tenor to one Gentleman who no Doubt intends to have a good Peneath [Legibility unclear] of land for it. Which we humbly pray may not be granted before wee have a hearing at this Court, or some other methode that your Excellency and Honours shall think fit~

And that some other Methode may be taken to improve the Indian Lands more for our benefitt than has been~

And your humble petitioner for himself and his Small Flock as in Duty bound Shall ever pray

—*John Simon*

REPLY OF THE GENERAL COURT TO JOHN SIMON'S PETITION

In the House of Representatives Sept. 14th 1753~ Ordered that the Guardians for the Titicut Indians Take Special Care that they approbate no petition from Stephen David or James Thomas for sale of Land until they Strictly Examine into the right which they may respectively have to the Lands they may petition to Sell. Inasmuch as it is Suggested to this Court that the said Stephen & James have sold Considerable Lands that they had no right to and are now applying to the said Guardians for their approbation for the sale of more

Sent up for Concurrence

T Hubbard Spkr. [signature]

In Council Sept. 14, 1753 Read & Concur'd Thos. Clarke [illegible] [signature]

Consented to, W Shirley [signature]

In this petition you will also find a very detailed and unflattering account of the deeds and character of James Thomas, which tends to corroborate the claims made by Katherine Sachemus, except for the exact amount of land granted him by her mother. Simon describes Thomas as a lazy man who had spent less than one month in total doing any work during the whole ten years that he had lived at Titticut. Apparently, Thomas supported himself and his wife through selling land and borrowing money. Like many of the Titticut people who sold land, one of the main reasons he did so was to pay off debts. John Simon states that he was sympathetic to those people who did so out of absolute necessity, as a last resort, but he had no sympathy for those who were in poverty because of laziness. Simon also blamed "the encouragement of some of our English Neighbours who prompt them on to run in Debt on purposes to sell their land."[29]

Throughout the colonial era, the Massachusetts colonists encouraged Indians to pay off their debts by selling their lands, and would often order them to do so through the courts. Native people who were convicted of crimes under English law had no choice—either pay off their fines with land, or, if they had no land with indentured servitude. Simon also described Thomas as somewhat of a "dandy," or a person who dressed in a flashy manner, usually in an attempt to appear wealthier than they actually were:

> *And this James goes now Clothed in Broad Cloak Beaver Hatt Watch in his pockett and his Coffee Tea & Chocklate and appears very much like a gentleman at home & abroad and as we understand is now in Debt Seven or Eight Hundred pounds old tenor to one Gentleman.*[30]

Regarding Stephen David, Simon had less to say, but he minced no words and got right to the point: "Stephen David has led a very bad and Wicked life and never had any rite to sell Land in Titecutt further than an Artfull Write that some of the English Neighbour's found out for him to gett away our Lands as we think." In other words, David was an evil tool of the English.

The Titticut Indians were dispossessed of most of their reservation lands during the 1750s and 1760s, and the remaining lands were gone by the late 1780s. In the 1790 census, there were no Indians counted living in Titticut. Although Indians living in intact, sovereign, tribal communities, who fit the constitutional category of "Indians not taxed," were often not counted in the census, it is not likely that a tribal community was still in place at Titticut at that time.

A state report on the Indians of Massachusetts published in 1827 stated only six Indians were counted within the boundaries of the town of Middleborough, which included Titticut and Assawompsett.[31] It is unknown which year the Eastons were dispossessed of their remaining Titticut lands, but records from during and after the Revolution show the known adult children of Caesar and Mercy Easton had dispersed to Bridgewater, Taunton, and Dartmouth. Within thirty years after the second Easton court case, the Titticut and Assawompset Indians had been dispossessed of all or nearly all of their lands.

CHAPTER 10

Our Ancestors as Decision Makers

RETURNING TO HOMELAND—TOLOWA CONTINUANCE, PERSEVERANCE, ADAPTATION, AND RESISTANCE, 1858–1868

Annette Reed

Since time immemorial Native peoples have passed down through oral tradition creation accounts and stories that root specific Native groups to specific geographic places. These places are sacred and are the points by which creation of those particular tribes originated. At times, these sacred places of origin are called the "Center of the World." More than five hundred Native Nations across the United States—and even more if one looks at the larger Western Hemisphere—have their own place of creation.

My name is Annette Louise Reed or "Day-na-tre" (Woman Who Does Hard Work). I am Tolowa or Dee-ni and am both enrolled and a member at Smith River Rancheria in far northwestern California.[1] My husband is Steven James Crum, who is Western Shoshone or *Newe*, which means "people" in their language. He is both enrolled and a member of Duck

Portrait of Annette Reed—Courtesy of Hulleah J. Tsinhnahjinnie

Valley Reservation in Nevada and Idaho.[2] We have been together since 1990 and married since 1991. We are two Native historians, who enjoy hearing historical stories and passing along these histories to present and future generations. Humor is one gift that we share. Driving eastward on Highway 80 through Reno, Winnemucca, Battle Mountain, and finally Elko, Nevada, we turn north into Wild Horse Canyon on the way to the Duck Valley Reservation. Steve, while watching the highway before us, smiles slightly and says, "We are at the Center of the World." We both chuckle softly, knowing this is true and using a bit of humor. According to the Newe oral tradition, this is how they came to be:

> *The Newe were placed in their homeland by the Creator (Uteen Taikwahni), whose complexion was the same color as that of the natives. Once placed on the land, two native women instructed the coyote to carry a large, pitched water-basket with him on his journey into the [Great] Basin area. Coyote was specifically told not to open*

> *the lid. Moved by irrepressible curiosity, he periodically opened the basket during his trip. The beings concealed inside jumped out here and there. The Newe believe this explains why they live over a large area. Today, family groups can be found in Death Valley, the Reese River Valley, Ruby Valley, the South Fork Valley, and numerous other places primarily in Nevada.*[3]

Therefore, this beautiful desert area in Nevada is the heart of Western Shoshone and the "Center of Their World." Now, again with a slight humor in play, when we drive up Highway 101, northward through Eureka, Crescent City, the main town of Smith River, and then finally to Smith River Rancheria, I say, "We are at the Center of the World." Steve and I both smile at those words so common to us over the years. For Tolowa people the place of creation is Yontocket, which is a village on the south bank of the Smith River. My family are from the village of Howonquet, which was a large village on the north bank of the river and is currently known as part of the Smith River Rancheria. In our oral tradition, life began at Yontocket, and it became the place of many sacred ceremonies. Native people traveled from all around the area to attend and participate in the ceremonies at Yontocket. Our sacred places and the place where life originated for our people is extremely important. These creation accounts and oral tradition have been passed on from generation to generation since time immemorial.

This chapter will discuss the sacrifices, courage, and utter determination to remain in our Tolowa homelands. Our ancestors faced "a world turned upside down" by white invasion into Native lands.[4] Their lives were forever changed, as they faced diseases, massacres, forced removal from homelands, colonization of entire nations, and in the end, survived plummeting numbers in population. It would be easy for Native Americans to be viewed as helpless victims. However, nothing could be further from a Native reality. Our Ancestors, while they endured horrific conditions, also maintained their powerful role as "decision makers." In fact, their decisions, their responsible ways of taking actions, and their deep connection to homeland ensured our lives as Native peoples today.

This chapter focuses on the history of Indian–white relations between the Tolowa and Euro-Americans between 1858 and 1868. Despite white invasion in the mid-1800s, the Tolowa people of northwestern California and southwestern Oregon remained Native over the years because of their cultural persistence and a deep-rooted attachment to their land. Through resistance efforts, Tolowa people shaped their own destiny and that of their future generations. This chapter seeks to illuminate Native responses to non-Indian invasion of their homeland, and demonstrates, up to the present, how Native people, our Ancestors have been active agents, decision makers in their own tribal histories.

In the history of federal Indian policy, at least three threads emerge: massacres, forced removal, and assimilation. Many actions taken against Native people can be viewed as genocidal in nature. When I refer to genocide, I reach to the United Nations definition, the Convention on the Prevention and Punishment of the Crime of Genocide, adopted by Resolution 260 (III) A of the United Nations General Assembly on December 9, 1948. In article 2, it defines the act as follows:

> *Genocide means any of the following acts committed with intent to destroy, in whole or in part, a national, ethnical, racial or religious group, as such: (a) Killing members of the group; (b) Causing serious bodily or mental harm to members of the group; (c) Deliberately inflicting on the group conditions of life calculated to bring about its physical destruction in whole or in part; (d) Imposing measures intended to prevent births within the group; (e) Forcibly transferring children of the group to another group.*[5]

In the 1850s, local militia units massacred entire Tolowa villages, often during times of ceremony while they were praying for all good things of the past year and thanking Creator for all of the next. In order to aid local whites, the state of California authorized the formation of six different local militia units from 1854 to 1856: the Coast Rangers (1854), the Klamath Mounted Rangers (1854), the Mounted Coast Riflemen (1855), the Salmon Guard 1855), the Klamath Rifles (1855), and the Crescent Rifles (1856).[6] It is from these local militia units that Tolowa villages faced massacres during the 1850s. Surviving Tolowa hid in the rivers or lakes breathing up through reeds, while the waters ran red with the blood of their family and friends. Other Tolowa sought refuge in other villages or by escaping upriver. After enduring several massacres, Tolowa still remained in their traditional homelands, which are today defined as:

> *Their Taa-laa-waa-dvn (Tolowa-Ancestral-Land) lays along the Pacific Coast between the water sheds of; Wilson Creek and Smith River in California and the Winchuck, Chetco, Pistol, Rogue, Elk and Sixes Rivers, extending inland up the Rogue River throughout the Applegate Valley in Oregon. Their Taa-laa-waa-dvn roughly covers what are today Curry, Josephine and Del Norte Counties. The Dee-ni' population exceeded ten-thousand. Their tribal neighbors are the Coquille and Umpqua to the north, Takelma, Shasta and Karuk to the east and the Yurok to the south.*[7]

The Pacific Ocean near Annette's mom's house—Courtesy of Annette Reed

From the mid-1850s and into the 1860s, the Tolowa of northwestern California experienced the federal government's removal and reservation policies. This historical narrative recounts both the removal of Tolowa from their homelands in these decades and their decision to return. The removal policy emerged in the 1830s and the reservation blossomed in the 1850s, respectively.

Years before the establishment of the Smith River Reservation in 1862, the American government enacted two Indian policies: removal and reservations. The federal government first applied removal to

Native American tribes east of the Mississippi River. In the 1830s, the government removed approximately 75,000 tribal people of the Southeast, including Cherokees, Choctaws, Chickasaws, Creeks, and Seminoles to Indian Territory (now Oklahoma). Congress made Indian removal official in 1830 with the passage of the Indian Removal Act.[8]

Removing tribes to the West affected Native groups living there. And once westward expansion hit the Pacific Ocean, whites faced the question, "Where do we remove the Indians to now?" They could not keep removing them past the barrier of the "Great Pacific," or could they? Beginning in the early 1860s, the government considered gathering up tribal groups in California and removing them to particular reservations. In 1862, Senator Milton Latham of California submitted a bill into Congress, which, if passed, would have gathered up all the tribes west of the Sierra Nevada mountains in California and placed them on one big reservation located in Owens Valley, California.[9] This idea failed, but others continued to be proposed. Two years later, some white Californians suggested gathering up all California Indian tribes and placing them on some offshore island. Specifically, they had in mind the Santa Catalina Islands, not far from Santa Barbara.[10] Again, this idea fell to the wayside. However, the federal government successfully carried out Indian removal in 1863 when local whites accused a few Indians in Butte County of stealing white-owned cattle. The military gathered up 461 Indians of the Concow Maidu tribe around Chico and removed them to Mendocino County on the newly established Round Valley Reservation.[11]

By the late 1840s some American policy makers began to question the policy of removing tribes farther west. In 1848, William Medill, the commissioner of Indian Affairs of the Bureau of Indian Affairs (BIA), suggested creating "colonies" for Indians. He had in mind setting aside large reserves of land in the American heartland and then removing tribes to those reserves. Medill wanted one reserve located in the northern Great Plains region and the second reserve on the southern plains.[12] By creating these sizable colonies, the American people would open up the middle part of the continent as a major travel artery to move from east to west.

Eventually, Medill's idea of colonies became the new reservation policy for Indians in the 1850s, although many of these did not include large areas of land. During this period, the government negotiated treaties with the tribes of the Great Plains area, which brought into existence reservation land for Indians to move to. For agreeing to surrender their large hunting ranges and consenting to move to reservations, the United States agreed to pay the Indians in the form of annuity goods (clothing, food, etc.) and services (education, health services, etc.). Once the government acquired Indian land by land cession treaties, it created new western territories. In 1854, Congress passed the Kansas-Nebraska Act, which created these two territories. Thus, the reservation policy came into existence in the 1850s and largely replaced the earlier policy of removing Indians farther west.[13] However, Indian removal was not eliminated completely, for it continued to be carried out, as the government wanted all Indians to remove to newly established reservations located throughout the far western region. The notion of Indian removal therefore became intertwined with the reservation policy.

By the late 1850s, both policies became evident in the far West. The federal government removed many Indians from southwestern Oregon and northwestern California to the Siletz Reservation in west-central Oregon due to the Rogue River War, which lasted from 1855 to 1856.

The American government forced the Tolowa to leave their homeland and move to a variety of places already inhabited by Native peoples from other tribal groups. Local white citizens sought the rich agricultural lands of the Smith River Valley. The beginning of removal took place from 1852 to 1856, when the federal government, with local white support, removed some Tolowa to Wilson Creek, approximately twenty-five miles south of Smith River. But the significant removals of Tolowa started in the mid-1850s and thereafter. And it was in 1857 that the military forced most Tolowa to move to the newly established Klamath Reservation in northern California.

In June 1855, Stephen Gerald Whipple, a federal Indian agent, proposed Tolowa removal to a reservation at the lower Klamath River. Whipple and other Indian agents, along with the US military, decided that the Indians in the area needed to be moved to the Klamath Reservation to make the Smith River Valley available for white "settlement."[14] The US Army thus moved the Tolowa onto the Lower Klamath Reservation, but without food or supplies and with few belongings. In Tolowa traditional society, each family possesses the "rights of usage" to their own fishing, hunting, and gathering areas. This move took the Tolowa to the Yuroks' homeland, leaving them without resource areas to obtain food and without the ability to pay for "rights of usage." The Tolowa and Yurok often intermarried, yet the Yurok did not have enough resources to take in all of the Tolowa placed upon their lands.

In October 1857, the US Army established Fort Ter-waw on the lower Klamath River under the command of Lieutenant George Crook, and Crook and approximately fifty soldiers arrived at the Klamath River Reservation on October 13, 1857.[15] Lieutenant Crook explained to his superior, Major Mackall, in a letter dated October 21, 1857, that upon his arrival to the Klamath River Reservation he found Tolowa dissatisfied with their new location on the Klamath River, and that they were escaping in small groups to return to their homeland on the Smith River. Crook and his men, however, forcibly removed approximately one hundred Tolowa from Smith River back to the Klamath Reservation.[16]

Lieutenant Crook quickly assessed the state of Tolowa and Yuroks on the Klamath Reservation and incorrectly gave his reasons why Tolowa returned to Smith River:

> *As far as I can learn of present, the Indians [Yuroks] who have allways [sic] lived in the land occupied by this Indian Reservation, are perfectly contented, and it is only those moved here from Smith River and its vicinity, who are discontented and that this disaffection is principally caused from misrepresentations of ill disposed whites, whose interest it is to have the Indians back on Smith River.*[17]

While some whites did urge Tolowa to return to Smith River so they could have laborers or kill them outright, the main reason for Tolowa returning to Smith River was their deep-rooted connection to their ancestral homeland. A secondary reason was the lack of food and supplies on the lower Klamath. Tolowa, acting upon their own initiative, repeatedly escaped Klamath Reservation and returned home. In a letter from Lieutenant Crook to Major Mackall, November 21, 1857, Lt. Crook wrote:

> *Major,*
> *I have the honor to report, that, since my communication to you of Oct 21st, the Smith River Indians here, have made repeated attempts to leave the reservation, and a large number succeeded by*

> *stealing off in small parties: they said they were not afraid of one, as the white men told them I would not dare fire on them, and that they were going back to their country.*[18]

Indeed, Tolowa viewed the area around Smith River as "their country" and made every effort to return. After several attempts to escape, they were finally rounded up by the army and forcibly returned to the Lower Klamath Reservation. So the Tolowa developed a different plan.

Tolowa leaders and elders most likely gathered to discuss the best strategies to escape to their homeland. Facing a military force with their families, including children, must have been of great consideration, and the massacres of the 1850s would have been fresh in their minds. Surely, when they closed their eyes, they could still hear the cries of the babies being thrown to their deaths. One account from the Yontocket massacre, just a few years prior to the removal to Lower Klamath is still recounted through oral tradition as such:

> *People gathered for Needash (dancing and praying), after fall harvest, at the center of the world, Yontocket. Indians from all over gathered to celebrate creation and to give thanks to the creator. On the third night of the ten-night dance, whites slithered into the village in the early morning hours. They quickly torched the redwood plank houses, and as the Indians attempted to escape through the round holes in the houses, the militia killed them. This village existed as the largest native settlement consisting of over thirty houses. The whites would cut off the heads of the Indians and throw them into the fire. They lined their horses on the slough and as the Indians sought refuge, they were gunned down. One young Indian man ran out of a house with a "big elk hide" over his body, fought and escaped to the slough. He stayed down there two or three hours: "All quiet down, and I could hear them people talking and laughing. I looked in the water, and the water was just red with blood, with people floating around all over." The center of the world, Yontocket, burned for days. They were not armed since they were in the middle of praying and ceremony.*[19]

Al Logan Slagle, Native American lawyer and author, wrote: "This was the sacking of the Tolowa sacred center. There is no mention anywhere that this could have been a 'war dance.' The whole point of an attack by the Coast and Klamath Rangers at such a time was the complete demoralization of a defenseless civilian population."[20] Definitely, all the massacres weighed heavily upon the hearts and minds of Tolowa leaders as they discussed and formed a plan to leave and return home—even in the midst of life-threatening danger, they decided to implement their plan of escape. Lieutenant Crook learned of the plan in time to alter it but remained unable to stop the Tolowa efforts.

> *Finding however that they could not all get away by this method [escaping to Smith River in small groups] they formed a conspiracy, first to kill me, destroy the boats between here and Man-kill and leave for Smith River. Being apprizece [sic] of this conspiracy, and that a large number of warriors had already arrived from Smith River, for the purpose of carrying their plat into execution. I posted a guard at Man-kill on the 7th inst. to await the issue. On the 17th inst. the Indians sent for the agent to come to their houses, to see a sick Indian: the agent went accompanied by one white man! Immediately upon their arrival, the Indians made an attack from all sides with knives and bows and arrows, fortunately the two succeeded in keeping them off until the guard came to their rescue, who after firing two or three volleys succeeded in driving the Indians to the brush. A dispatch was sent for me, but after my arrival, I could only get an occasional shot at them in the bush.*[21]

In their struggle to return to the Smith River area, the Tolowa did not kill Crook and the Indian agent, but they did leave the Klamath Reservation in record numbers, approximately six hundred to seven hundred, and returned to Smith River.[22]

Tolowa men, women, and children returned to the Smith River to make their stand in their sacred homeland. They chose to not submit to the federal government policy of removal and remained determined. In a letter dated December 25, 1857, Lieutenant Crook wrote: "The number of warriors on Smith River are about one hundred and they say they will not come back here alive and if I want to fight, I will find them on Smith River."[23] As a result of this and subsequent stands, Tolowa played an active role in remaining within their ancestral homeland. They refused to submit to removal policy and continued to escape in small groups back to their homeland.

These powerful responses ensured the continuation and survival of Tolowa people in the place where they now reside. If they had submitted to removal to the Klamath River Reservation, they would have perhaps intermarried far more with Yurok. Also, they could have effectively assimilated or at least acculturated to a greater degree into the dominant society. It can be speculated that they would have ceased to be a culturally distinct group, known as Tolowa.

Later, Indian Agent Stephen Whipple attempted to obtain $2,000 from the federal government to purchase "rights of usage" from the Yuroks; however, it appears he was unsuccessful. The Tolowa were starving and therefore the remaining numbers returned to Smith River. A year later, only a handful of Tolowa resided at the Lower Klamath Reservation. H. P. Heintzleman, sub-Indian agent, reported to Thomas J. Henley, superintendent of Indian Affairs in San Francisco, on July 1, 1858: "Of the Tolana [Tolowa] Indians who were removed to the reservation during the past year about eighty of them remain, the balance have returned to their old haunts."[24]

It is rather ironic that whites commonly used the term "old haunts" in reference to Tolowa returning to their homeland. They did not realize how accurate a term this became to reflect the perspective of Native people. Smith River area remained their Indigenous homeland with the graves of their ancestors embedded in the very soil since the beginning of time, hence the irony of using the word "haunts," ghosts, and thereby ancestors. So, they returned to the land of their ancestors. Also, most Tolowa returning to their Native homeland demonstrated that the ancestors made the decision to return home, and they carried out their decision even in the face of US military forces in the area.

After the Klamath Reservation experience, Tolowa also experienced removal northward, especially after the Rogue River War broke out between Indians of southwestern Oregon. Local militia groups and white settlers targeted all Indians of the area, including Tolowa, for removal to distant reservations. White citizens and military officers repeatedly expressed concern that Tolowa would join their southwestern Oregon tribal cousins in open warfare against non-Indians. The federal government, as well as local militia units, used the Rogue River War of the mid-1850s as a springboard for Tolowa removal policy.

In 1860, the military force marched six hundred Tolowa to Siletz Reservation in Oregon. During the march, a woman gave birth, but she was allowed to stop only long enough to squat down and bear the baby.

The woman died, and other women took the baby and nursed it.[25] The military herded Tolowa onto Battle Rock at Port Orford and stayed there for nearly a year. Many Tolowa died on the forced march or during the internment at Port Orford. After near starvation, the government removed them to Siletz, but most hid and returned to Smith River Valley.

By this time, the Tolowa were scattered in various directions, but many made their way back to their homeland. Finally, on May 3, 1862, the federal government created a reservation at Smith River, as well as Camp Lincoln, a military fort in Elk Valley, near Crescent City, to "supervise" this reservation and act as a buffer between the Tolowa and Crescent City white settlers. It was clear that the Indian women needed protection from unruly white men. In a letter to William Dole, commissioner of Indian affairs, Indian Agent George Hanson wrote, "It was quite apparent that more *married men* should be brought into the service as soon as possible and those who are unmarried discharged."[26] Of course, "married men" would rape Indian women, just like unmarried men might rape Indian women; however, the point of the letter was that Indian women lived in constant danger of assault.

By the beginning of the 1860s, it became clear that the Tolowa people remained deeply rooted to their homeland. Even after the devastating massacres and more than one removal, the Tolowa continued to return to their "old haunts."[27] The reasons they returned were based on their spiritual beliefs and culture. These reasons are part of a collective memory of the Tolowa people. The creation account embedded religious significance between the land and people. The physical land was tied in with traditional stories that connected the Tolowa people to their land. Used for education, the stories of the land and animals cemented the Tolowa with their land.

With the California Gold Rush in the 1850s came the invasion of non-Indians with contrastingly different views of land use and ownership. They envisioned Indian removal as a humane way of gaining possession and ownership of the entire Smith River Valley. The whites did not or would not seek to understand why Tolowa would not trade their homeland for land in another region. Removal placed Tolowa into a region unfamiliar to them, and this new region had no significance in their religious ceremonies, stories, or worldview. One piece of land was not the same as another. Each area supported its own Native people, and the Native people of that region were given the responsibility to care for the land, as related through the creation account.

The federal government did not create the Smith River Reservation as a place specifically for the Tolowa living there. Instead, the government wanted the reservation to be the home for various tribes living in the larger region, including the Yurok and other tribes living on the Klamath Reservation at the mouth of the Klamath River, forty miles south of Smith River. Talk about a reservation at Smith River began only after the Klamath Reservation was flooded out in December 1861. With the topsoil washed away and replaced by gravel and debris, BIA officials decided to abandon the reservation and place the Indian occupants elsewhere. Indian agent George Hanson suggested establishing a large reservation in the Smith River Valley, which would become the new home for the former Klamath Reservation Indians, for other tribes living along coastal Humboldt County, and also for the Tolowa already living in the Smith River Valley. Because of animosities between coastal Indians and interior mountain Indians, Hanson wanted Smith River to be the home for only coastal tribes.[28]

Hanson first proposed a sizable reservation that would include all the land between the Smith River and the Oregon border (six to eight miles in distance), and from the Pacific coast to some fifteen miles inland along the coastal mountain range. This area would be a comfortable home for several tribes living along coastal northern California. Some white settlers owned plots of land within this area, and Hanson offered to buy them out for a price of $56,000. They willingly accepted his offer, but for reasons unknown, the government never purchased all the land as a reservation for the Indians.[29]

When the Smith River Reservation did come into existence on May 3, 1862, the BIA, originally called the Office of Indian Affairs, ended up renting farmland from some local white ranchers. Ultimately, the reservation ended up being about 1,100 acres, with 450 as good quality farmland. In the first year, roughly 2,000 coastal Indians ended up at Smith River. At least 850 came from Humboldt County from the vacated Klamath Reservation and included Yuroks and Matolles whose Native homes were along the Klamath, Mad, and Eel Rivers. There were also some Wylackies removed from below the Klamath River. Additionally, there were local Tolowa from the Smith River itself.[30]

Deeply attached to their former Native places, most Indians removed to the Smith River Reservation ran away the first year and returned to Humboldt County to the Klamath River and other southern places. Most left in large groups, with one group of four hundred leaving in October 1862.[31] When the BIA abolished the reservation in 1868, only 370 Indians remained, most of whom were Tolowa, with a smaller minority of Yurok from the Klamath River area.[32]

Many whites of the region criticized the BIA for removing Indians of northwestern California to Smith River because of the nearness of removal. In other words, Indians from the abandoned Klamath Reservation were moved only forty miles northward, making it easy for them to run away and return home. The whites argued that the BIA was wasting its money by removing the Indians only a short distance. One of the biggest critics of removal was the *Weekly Humboldt Times*, whose editors wrote that the removed Indians would "be back before the 'leaves fall.'"[33] Their prediction proved largely correct. In November 1862, the newspaper wrote that "most of the Indians sent there from this country have returned."[34]

Besides the Smith River Reservation, the federal government also established a small military garrison called Camp Lincoln, located between Crescent City and Smith River. The military established the fort at the request of local whites who became threatened by the Indian population living on the new reservation. As early as April 1862, the residents of Crescent City wanted a "garrison" built "to keep the savages quiet." The members of the Crescent City Guards, a local volunteer militia organization, also asked for US military support in May 1862.[35] Their concern was over the Humboldt Indians who were to be brought to Smith River whom the whites considered to be aggressive. In response to white concern, the military established Camp Lincoln on September 11, 1862.[36]

Camp Lincoln's major objective was to deal with the Indians of the Smith River Reservation. The camp commander mentioned that he had at least three duties: (1) to prevent Indians from escaping the reservation, (2) to capture runaways, and (3) to deal with any aggressive Indians.[37] The military had both successes and failures. It failed to capture most Indians who left the reservation, including the four hundred who left in October 1862. But on occasion it tracked down some runaways and returned them to Smith River. In May 1865, it captured and brought back 150 Indians. The military also dealt with runaway Indians who escaped from the Siletz Reservation and returned to northwestern California. On occasion, military officials punished reservation Indians for committing crimes. In October 1863, troops executed one Indian for murdering another Indian. It carried out the execution to send a message to all Indians that crimes would be dealt with publicly.[38]

The roughly four hundred Indians who made the reservation their new home in the 1860s became farmers and laborers. They were taught how to farm and do American-style work by the BIA agent George Hanson and other agents who followed him. In July 1863, 363 Indians grew crops and by September 1864 had roughly 481 acres under cultivation. A major crop was oats. The Indians also hauled gravel and built houses to live in. At the same time, they could not survive completely from American-grown foods. For this reason, Indians convinced the agents to "allow" them to secure Native food sources. Most of the Indians therefore caught salmon from the Smith River. Others caught smelt, a small fish that swims in large schools, along nearby coastal areas. The agents also issued food rations at other times when there were no salmon runs. To reward hardworking individuals, one agent even "gave" certain Indians a month off to procure Native foods. Some agents "allowed" the Indians to practice Native customs, providing Native ways took place during patriotic holidays. In July 1868, three hundred Indians dressed in Native regalia to participate in the Fourth of July celebration.[39] While the agents viewed the July Fourth celebrations as a way for Natives to participate in an "American" holiday, while moving toward assimilation, Natives viewed it much differently. They viewed it as yet another way to maintain their songs, regalia, and dance activities for their own spiritual practices and for future generations. Native people actively utilized the holiday as a reason to openly practice their dances.

Life, however, remained difficult on the new reservation. The whites, including government agents, looked down upon the Indians as a lower form of human being. They called Indian men "Bucks" and the women "Squaws."[40] These were of course derogatory names given to Indian people in general. Some Indians continued to contract new American diseases that Native medicine people could not deal with. In March 1866, there were seven reported cases of venereal diseases, a new kind of disease introduced by white sexual contact with Indians.[41] Because different tribes lived on the reservation, some people became suspicious of each other at times. In February 1868, there was talk that the death of an Indian woman was the result of intentional poisoning.[42] Additionally, many felt uneasy because of their fear that the Smith River Reservation would never be a permanent home for the Indian residents. This concern became evident in September 1866 when a BIA agent reported that "they are under the firm belief that the government does not intend to purchase the valley lands for a reserve."[43] The fear proved to be legitimate, for as early as December 1867 the BIA considered abolishing the Smith River Reservation and removing all the Indians, including the local Tolowa, to another reservation.[44]

The BIA in fact abolished the reservation in July 1868 as a way to save money. It first considered taking about 370 residents of the reservation and removing them to the Round Valley Reservation in Mendocino County. But the government concluded that the trip would be too far and expensive. Therefore, it removed the Indians to the Hoopa Valley Reservation, established in 1864 and located some 150 miles southeast of Smith River.[45] On December 6, 1868, the government moved Smith River Indian residents out of the valley, and they arrived on the Hoopa Reservation on December 20. About one hundred of this number ran away before arriving but were soon captured and also brought to Hoopa.[46] As previously discussed, this was not their first removal from their ancestral homelands.

After settling down at Hoopa, the BIA agent commented on the Tolowa and other former Smith River Indian residents now at Hoopa. He reflected that they were hardworking, industrious, and had good behavior compared to the local tribe, the Hupa. The agent stated the following:

> *The Smith River Indians have been of great service at Hoopa, in clearing and fencing new land, building Indian houses, cutting saw-logs, teaming, and general farm work. They are much more industrious and skillful in all kinds of farm labor than the Hoopa.*[47]

But the agent's kind words for the Tolowa proved to be short-lived, for the Tolowa eventually chose to act against government policy and reject their new home. By 1871, not one Tolowa remained at Hoopa; they had all left over a two-year period and returned to Smith River. Only fifty former residents of the former Smith River Reservation remained at Hoopa in the early 1870s, but they were all prior Natives of Humboldt County—perhaps Yurok.[48]

Thus, up to 1870, the Tolowa had lived on three different Indian reservations: first the Klamath Reservation (1857–1858), then the Smith River Reservation (1862–1868), and finally the Hoopa Reservation (1868–1871). The nation's Indian policies certainly had an impact on the Tolowa in the 1860s. Interestingly, the abolition of the Smith River Reservation in 1868 came at a time when the federal government favored reservation land for Indians. One year earlier, in 1867, the government's special commission, the Taylor Peace Commission, produced a sizable report and made various recommendations for how life could be made better for all Indian tribes. One recommendation was the establishment of Indian reservations where Indians could be protected from unscrupulous whites. Yet the government turned right around and abolished the Smith River Reservation.

Tolowa would not become reservation Indians until the first decade of the twentieth century. In 1908, the federal government established a small, 163-acre reservation at the mouth of the Smith River along the Pacific coast. The government purchased the land for $7,200 from William Westbrook, a white landowner whose family owned considerable amounts of property in the Smith River Valley. Payment was made possible by the congressional appropriation of June 21, 1906.[49] With the creation of this small reservation in 1908, the Tolowa in the Smith River Valley officially became reservation Indians, roughly forty to fifty years after many other Indians across the nation had established their reservations.

Regardless of whether Tolowa from Smith River lived on their own reservation or where the federal Government removed them, they still maintained a sense of deep connection to the land of their ancestors. At every attempt to remove Tolowa, they made decisions to return to their homeland. If they had not stood strong and actively carried through with their plans to escape and return home, today's people of Smith River Rancheria most likely would not have remained a culturally distinct people. When I return, I see my family, including my mother, Adrienne Thomas, daughter of Andrew Whipple and Louise Moorehead Whipple; as well as my sister, nieces, cousins, and friends, and I know I am truly home. I attend Tolowa Night and Day, the March General Meeting, Nay-Dosh, our ceremonial dances, and watch the young people singing and giving thanks to Creator. I have gone for walks with my uncle to gather plants used by our people. I constantly think of the great sacrifices made, the determination and decision-making of our ancestors that ensured we exist today. I hope the decisions we make today will be ones by which future generations will look back and say, "Our ancestors way back in 2014 made decisions and actions that ensured our continuance in a good way, as Native people."

Reconstructed Tolowa Dance House—Courtesy of Annette Reed

CHAPTER 11

The Peacemaker and Origins of Democracy

Oren Lyons

An excerpt of a 2003 interview with Portland State University's Institute for Tribal Government, from Great Tribal Leaders of Modern Times.

GROWING UP

I grew up on the Onondaga Nation territory. The time that I was growing up they called it the Onondaga Reservation. My mother was Seneca, Wolf Clan. She was married to my father who was Onondaga, Eel Clan. As the process of keeping track follows the mother, I was Seneca, Seneca Wolf, as was our whole family. In 1972 I was adopted into the Onondaga Nation. So now I'm Onondaga—still Wolf but borrowed into the Turtle Clan. I've been sitting in for the Turtles since 1967.

We were brought up Indian style. My early childhood was just running about the nation. I don't think I saw a white person until I was four years old. We didn't travel downtown. Syracuse is just down the road.

All your family is around. Grandmother is down the road. You've got all your relatives everywhere, a real community. So that even though you may not be related, wherever you happen to be at dinnertime, that is where you ate. People just sat you down wherever you were.

If you lived off the main highway, which is where the spigots were, you had to go to the springs and carry water. So, we carried water all our lives growing up. Cut wood, hunted, hunted for food. We were very good at it. Everybody was planting. I remember my father planted fields in the back using the old style of plow that held the handles behind the horse. It was hard work.

Cold winters—there was no such thing as an insulated house. There was a school on the reservation. Still is. Kind of like an extension of white people into our land. There was no such thing as a parent-teachers association. You just sent the kids and left them, and then picked them up. There was no interaction. For us it was like going into this outpost with all white people, strange ideas, and different talking people. It was a trial every day. We were pretty independent rambunctious kids. School was something to be endured. Most of the kids quit in sixth grade and went on to work.

The reservation, the nation itself was very traditional. It still is. As far as I know we are part of the last traditional chiefs and leaders in North America who are still in charge of land. There is no Bureau of Indian Affairs. We don't allow them on our territory. We don't allow the state police or any police except our own people. We have working arrangements, and it is not unusual. It's just the way we were brought up to be who we are. As I travel about, I see the differences. The longhouse was the center of activities all the time. Ceremonies were going on. There were always dances. There were feasts going on. There was always community activity.

THE STORY OF THE GREAT LAW OF PEACE AND THE PEACEMAKER

We didn't learn that story. We lived it. The Great Law of Peace is what governed our people. You learned by participating and watching. The Great Law of Peace is a daily event, it is how you live, how ceremonies are performed, how leaders work, how the community operates. That's how we were brought up—very free, very independent, and very aware of who we were in terms of our clan and our nation. People kept close track of our clans.

The Great Law of Peace is our second gift, our second message. The first message that our people received was how to live—what non-Indians call religion. We don't have a word for religion; it is how you live day to day. The ceremonies were given to us way back. We don't know when, but we know the stories and we know how it came.

The Great Law of Peace came when we were in battles, when we were neglecting the first message, which was how to live. It was a terrible time for the Five Nation people. We were battling, we were fighting one another, and we were fighting internally. Children and women, they were hiding in the woods, they were not even in their homes because they were afraid. And here comes the Great Peacemaker. His intent and purpose was before he was born. His mother was a virgin. She didn't know how she got pregnant. When the baby was born, her mother tried to kill the baby three separate times. The third time she received a visit from spiritual beings who told her, you are not going to be able to do that. They told her, don't do that because this person has a mission. So the story of him growing up was one of being different and being singular in who he was.

The Peacemaker's process was thought, not force. He moved from the Mohawk to Oneida, to Onondaga, Cayuga, and Seneca, and he said, "My business is peace, I want to talk to your leaders." And they laughed. They said, "You've got a lot of work." He was really insistent, and that impressed them, so they said, "Alright, we'll take the message." And so they left. They started out.

And there's the story of Aionwatha. Aionwatha [Hiawatha] was Onondaga, who was exiled from his own land because of the fierce leadership. A fierce leader by the name of Tadodaho, he was evil incarnate, and powerful, and had killed three of his [Hiawatha's] daughters. Hiawatha was mourning—he just left. He was in the woods all the time and the Mohawks knew about him and he drifted up their way. They said, "You should go talk to this man, he talks like you do about peace." So he did, and there is a whole epic story of how they became a partner with Peacemaker, and they convinced the leaders—they changed their minds. And they moved west to the Oneidas. The Oneidas were going through the same thing and so the story goes. After convincing the leaders of the Oneidas to come with them they went to the Onondaga, and they couldn't deal with Onondaga, he was too strong—Tadodaho. He did all kinds of things. They couldn't get to him. He lived in a swamp. They couldn't get near him. His hair was covered with snakes. He was twisted. He was evil and powerful and a cannibal. He didn't want to talk to anyone about peace.

> *[The Peacemaker had stayed at a lodge where the woman who was the lodgekeeper required weapons be left outside. She was Erie, Cat Nation. When the Peacemaker and leaders could not find a way to approach Tadodaho, they called upon the woman for her advice. She taught them a song for approaching Tadodaho.]*

They learned the song and then they all approached him, and they said the song affected him. Even as they approached, they could see him transforming, could see the snakes dropping from his head. He was transforming into something like a human being. Eventually they talked with him. They bargained with him, "And your title will be the leader of the Five Nations, and they will always come from the Onondaga, and this will always be the central fire." They bargained with him, and he agreed with that.

They transformed him, the Peacemaker transformed him, the most evil of all beings. The lesson there is that you should not give up on anybody. Anybody can be redeemed.

ORIGINS OF DEMOCRACY

Then he [Peacemaker] began a discussion on governance and how you shall operate and how you will function. The women were chosen as the Keepers of the Nation. The identity of children is directly what the woman is. That is the law. That is one of our oldest laws, and that continues today. It is still her duty to choose the leaders and oversee the conduct and activities and oversee the general welfare of the clan itself. Indeed, act like the mother of the clan, of the people—very hard work. We have clan mothers today doing that, just as they have always been. It's difficult work. You give your life over to the people.

I think that is the genius of why we are still here. That's what makes the Iroquois strong. The balance of relationship and governance was between male and female—between men and women. They had equal responsibility and much work to do. The essence of it was that leadership was chosen by the woman. Then it had to be ratified by the clan by consensus. There was no voting. You had to all agree, which is the harder way to do things. But of course, when you come to a total agreement, you are much stronger.

The Peacemaker laid out the foundation, he said, "There will be elder brothers and younger brothers. They will have two houses. This is how you will work together. This is the dynamics of your governance. Even in your nation there will be two houses." This is how the clans are set. This is how the houses operate together.

We are talking about governance now. We are talking about the establishment of a democratic government, which I believe is the basis of western society. The democracy they talk about that comes from Greece was not here. They learned what we knew.

Now when the Peacemaker had them throw these weapons of war into the currents under the Earth, he said "They will be carried away—to nobody knows where—and you will now rely on the rule of law and the rule of peace and the process of governing people by consent. I would say that democracy, western democracy, was based on that.

I talked about this meeting in Lancaster, Pennsylvania, when the Onondaga chief talked to the leaders about having a union—in 1744. All of that was heavily recorded. It was recorded very well. There is a very

Mohawk Chief Hendriuk Theyanoguin, Mayor Abraham Yates, Jr., and Benjamin Franklin at the Albany Conference 1754—Illustration by John Kahiones Fadden

thick and large book on just that 1744 Treatise. This book was printed by Benjamin Franklin. All those words were taken down to Philadelphia. Benjamin Franklin read the reports and he said, "This is a good idea." Ten years later he called the Albany Plan of Union, and he asked the Six Nations to preside and talk about governance and talk about democracy.

The Albany Plan of Union transformed into the Continental Congress. The Continental Congress was formed very much along the lines of the Confederacy. They called themselves the thirteen fires. They called themselves the Grand Council. They used all the euphemisms and they also used wampum.

Canassatego, Iroquois Sachem, speaks on Iroquois unity to colonial governors—Illustration by John Kahiones Fadden

REMINDING THE COUNTRY

All that history, all those meetings—hundreds of hundreds of meetings that we had—we knew each other well—our leaders. If you go down to Philadelphia, [you] will see the Hall of Independence where the Liberty

Bell is. You'll see a square of greens out front. That is Six Nations land. We visited there so often we camped right there. It is our land today even.

The two hundredth anniversary of the Constitution of the United States was coming up. They were making no consideration or place for Indian people. We said, "How can you do that?" We went to Washington and we said, "Where do you want the Iroquois to stand in your celebration?" They said, "Why?" They had no idea. It is not in your books. They don't teach it. It is not in the schools. Nobody teaches the history I am talking about.

Onondaga Sachem at Independence Hall—Illustration by John Kahiones Fadden

We said, "We gave you this idea of democracy. We held your hand through the process—our leaders." So, it was presented to the Congress. We took it to Senator Inouye. The result of it was the passage of S 76, recognizing the contribution of the Iroquois to the Constitution of the United States on the principle of democracy.

Western democracy is directly from our roots. Democracy didn't come over on a boat—Democracy was here, and it was all over the country.

S.Con.Res.76 – A concurrent resolution to acknowledge the contribution of the Iroquois Confederacy of Nations to the Development of the United States Constitution and to reaffirm the continuing government-to-government relationship between Indian tribes and the United States established in the Constitution.

100th Congress (1987–1988) congress.gov

We The People, Iroquois Confederacy Flag—Illustration by John Kahiones Fadden

Oct. 21, 1988 [H. Con. Res. 331]

Iroquois Confederacy and Indian Nations—Recognizing Contributions to the United States

Whereas the original framers of the Constitution, including, most notably, George Washington and Benjamin Franklin, are known to have greatly admired the concepts of the Six Nations of the Iroquois Confederacy…

Whereas the confederation of the original Thirteen Colonies into one republic was influenced by the political system developed by the

Iroquois Confederacy as were many of the democratic principles which were incorporated into the Constitution itself; and...

Resolved by the House of Representatives (the Senate concurring),

That—

(1) the Congress, on the occasion of the two hundredth anniversary of the signing of the United States Constitution, acknowledges the contribution made by the Iroquois Confederacy and other Indian Nations to the formation and development of the United States;

Agreed to October 21, 1988

CHAPTER 12

The Alaska Native Claims Settlement Act (ANCSA)

ORIGIN, PURPOSE, CONSEQUENCES

Jeane Breinig

The Alaska Native Claims Settlement Act (ANCSA) is a historic piece of legislation enacted on December 18, 1971. Its primary purpose was to determine aboriginal title and to resolve disputes among the State of Alaska, environmental activists, the oil industry, and Alaska Natives. In this legislation, all past and future claims of Native title were extinguished except as provided for within ANCSA. Alaska Natives gave up their rights to over 300 million acres of land in Alaska and in return were paid $962.5 million in compensation. In exchange for clear title to 44 million acres in traditionally utilized areas, the United States extinguished Native title to the remaining land.[1] The act has been lavishly praised and roundly criticized. Some view it as a vehicle for cultural genocide, forcing the alien concepts and structures of capitalism and modern for-profit corporations on Alaska Natives, and others have lauded it for freeing Natives from paternalistic governmental oversight. The truths rests somewhere between.

HISTORICAL BACKGROUND

Alaska Native peoples—Aleut/Unangan, Alutiiq/Sugpiaq, Athabascan, Eyak, Haida, Tlingit, Iñupiat, Central Yup'ik, and Siberian Yupik—occupied and used the land for at least eleven thousand years, prior to the arrival of immigrants to their land and waterways.[2] Because of Alaska's vast size and its relative isolation from the continental United States, the encroachment of American immigrants upon Indigenous lands came later to Alaska than it did for American Indian nations of the lower forty-eight states, avoiding for the most part, the reservation system that still exists.[3] The American occupation of Alaska was preceded by a period of Russian expeditions into various regions. Russian fur hunters first entered the Aleut area in 1745, massacring many and enslaving others. In their quest for sea otter skins, the Russians expanded southward along the Pacific Rim, as far as California, finally concentrating at Sitka, the Russian-American capital until the 1867 Treaty of Cession, when Alaska was sold to the United States.[4] Russia sold Alaska for $7,200,000 (about 1.9 cents per acre), without regard

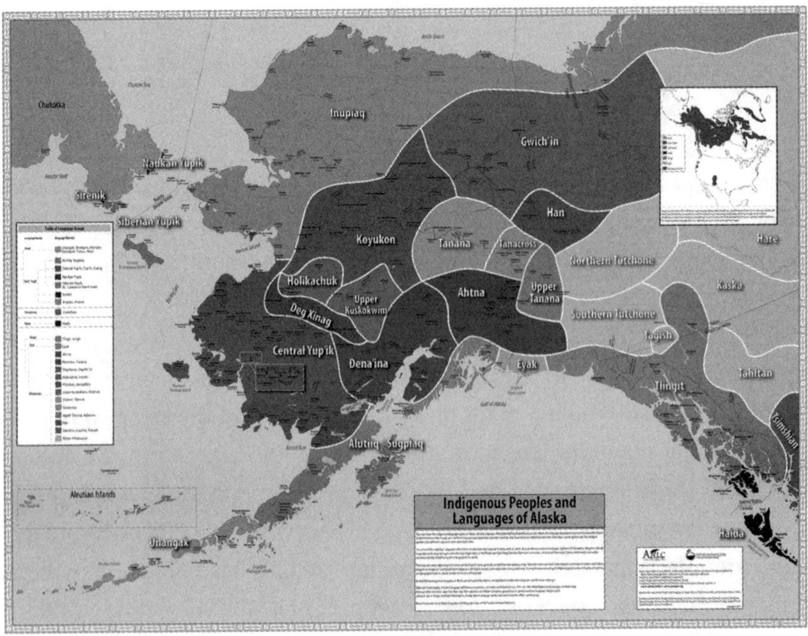

Alaska Native Language Map—*Indigenous Peoples and Languages of Alaska* (2011) compiled by Michael E. Krauss for the Alaska Native Language Center and the Institute of Social and Economic Research, University of Alaska Anchorage (https://www.uaf.edu/anla/collections/map/).

to the Indigenous people, transferring title to all "public and vacant" lands not owned by individuals. The treaty with Russia "provided that those tribes would be subject to such laws and regulation as the United States might from time to time adopt to aboriginal tribes."[5]

By the time Alaska Natives began to understand the consequences of America's sovereign claim, treaties had been ruled illegal. In the first few decades after the United States assumed jurisdiction of Alaska, Alaska Natives remained fairly undisturbed in their homeland. The United States continued to recognize these rights in subsequent legislation adopted for the Territory of Alaska. As the American population grew and expanded, however, conflicts with immigrants over land use and ownership intensified.

THE BEGINNING OF LAND CLAIMS AND ALASKAN STATEHOOD

In 1912, the Natives of Southeast Alaska—Haida, Tlingit, and Tsimshian (who migrated from northern Canada in 1880)—had mobilized politically and founded a pan-Native, pan-Christian organization to fight for the human rights denied its aboriginal population. The Alaska Native Brotherhood (ANB), founded in 1912, and its companion organization, the Alaska Native Sisterhood (ANS) founded in 1923, won crucial political battles, including the right to vote and the right for Native children to attend public schools.[6] However, continuing frustration over non-Native encroachment upon the lands and waterways of Southeast Alaska led the ANB/ANS to recommend that the Haida and Tlingit peoples unite to pursue a legal suit against the government for lands taken.[7]

In 1939, the Central Council of Tlingit and Haida Indian Tribes of Alaska was formed. William L. Paul Sr.—the first Alaska Native (Tlingit) attorney and first Native elected to the legislature—was instrumental in paving the way for the successful conclusion of the landmark Tlingit and Haida land claims suit filed against the United States for lands taken without compensation.[8] While the suit was not settled until 1968, it coincided with another lawsuit filed by a group represented by Paul Sr.—one that ultimately provided significant legal groundwork for ANCSA, enacted in 1971. In *Tee-Hit-Ton Indians v. U.S. (1955)*, Paul Sr., who secured a Washington attorney to press the case, petitioned for due compensation for US removal of timber from Tlingit lands in the Tongass National Forest in Southeast Alaska. Although the Supreme Court denied the United States was obligated to pay compensation for lands taken, it did confirm aboriginal ownership existed, eventually allowing for the recognition of aboriginal title in Alaska.

The Tlingit and Haida land suit (1935–1959) spanned the period in which Alaskans were contemplating whether Alaska should join the union. Alaska Native people held mixed views on whether this would be beneficial to the Indigenous population. In Southeast Alaska, both Paul Sr. and his son, William Paul Jr., were important voices in opposing various statehood enactment bills that could have denied recognition of aboriginal land title and were the key issues in arguments both for and against statehood. This stance was intimately connected to recognition of Native rights and land claims.[9] Paul Sr. was a prolific writer and activist for Native rights and a staunch advocate for Native land claim issues. In addition, Paul Jr. also earned a law degree and was attorney for the ANB in the early stages of the Tlingit and Haida land claims movement.

Paul Sr. often argued "against" statehood, primarily based upon numerous statehood enactment bills in Congress that abolished aboriginal title. However, he also voiced concerns about the economics of it. In June 1958, Paul Sr. noted in a letter that "the Organized Natives of Alaska are definitely opposed to immediate statehood because ... they belong to the group in the U.S. census reports as having less than $500 income per year," and he had grave concerns about taxes rising.[10]

In contrast, Victor Haldane (Haida), ANB secretary, voiced the views of many other Southeast Natives who supported statehood. In the March 1959, Voice of Brotherhood, Haldane, anticipating statehood, made the case that Natives would no longer be "second class citizens" because of "dependen[cy] upon the Bureau of Indian Affairs,"[11] mirroring others who looked forward to casting off federal control.

ALASKA NATIVES AND ATTITUDES TOWARD RESERVATIONS

Significant issues, like aboriginal property rights and how Natives might fare under state or federal control, helped determine whether people felt "reservations" would be beneficial or detrimental to Native control of resources. Depending on which alternative afforded better protection of their lands and waters, Southeast Natives were variously for or against reservations. That is, reservations—as they existed in the lower forty-eight states—did not have a good reputation among Alaska Natives. However, the idea of "reserving" certain areas for their own use was seen in a more positive light.

A good example of this problem occurred in Hydaburg (located in southern southeast Alaska, near Ketchikan). In 1939, Alaska Natives viewed reservations "as a degradation of their social status as American citizens ... [yet] a reservation offered them a chance to regain considerable control over some part of their fishing industry."[12] Later that same year, the Hydaburg council petitioned the secretary of the interior for a reservation of 800,000 acres, to include "all water extending three thousand (3,000) feet from the shoreline," which was viewed as a way to protect their land base and fishing resources.[13]

However, Bureau of Indian Affairs officials and Hydaburg disagreed as to the amount of land and water to be set aside; the local office in Juneau forwarded a request to the national office, which was only about one-fifth the size of the area requested in Hydaburg's petition. Initially, Hydaburg was unwilling to accept the offer, and protested the reduced land and water allotment. However, in 1949, when US interior secretary Julius Krug signed an order to create a 101,000-acre reservation, the people of Hydaburg voted 95 to 29 in favor of the reservation.[14]

Yet even with reservation status, Hydaburg was unable to control their fishing boundaries from unscrupulous cannery owners who placed within their waters huge commercial fish traps, able to capture thousands of pounds of salmon in one fell swoop. Hydaburg attempted to charge cannery owners a fee, but they refused to pay, and federal authorities were unable to enforce payment. A legal suit was filed against the Chicago–based trap company Libby, McNeil, and Libby, but Hydaburg's allegation was not upheld.[15] In fact, this case held that the Hydaburg reservation was illegally established, and this effectively ended the Indian Reorganization Act (IRA) reservations in Alaska.[16]

Eventually, the Tlingit and Haida lawsuit was pursued and won in 1959, the year in which Alaska became a state. While the settlement provided some monetary compensation for lands taken, it did not return any land to Native peoples. Therefore, in the 1960s, the Tlingit and Haida Central Council joined with the new, larger, statewide Native organization formed in 1966 known as the Alaska Federation of Natives (AFN) to pursue the questions of legal ownership of Alaskan lands. From 1966 to 1971, AFN was led by a group of fiery young Alaska Native activists, including Athabascan Emil Notti, AFN's first president.

Because of Alaska's vast size and long distances between villages, the *Tundra Times*, founded in 1962 by Iñupiat Howard Rock, became one of the primary means to spread the word about the Alaska Native movement.[17] Others prominent in land claims and AFN as it evolved include John Borbridge Jr. (Tlingit), Robert Rude (Athabascan), Eben Hopson (Iñupiat), William L. Hensley (Iñupiat), Byron Mallott (Tlingit), Marlene Johnson (Tlingit), Brenda Itta Lee (Iñupiat), and Janie Leask (Haida/Tsimshian), among others.[18] Today, the AFN remains the largest statewide Native organization in Alaska. It is governed by a thirty-eight-member board that is elected by its membership at the annual convention held each October.[19] The AFN continues to advocate for Alaska Natives and has achieved some political clout within the state.

ANCSA AND ITS IMPLEMENTATION

Fortuitously, the 1959 Alaska's Statehood Act contained language that renounced all right and title to any lands held by any of Alaska's Native peoples clouding the issue for the state who sought to develop its natural resources. Section 4 of the Act disclaims:

> *all right or title in or to any property, including fishing rights, the right or title to which may be held by or for any Indian, Eskimo, or Aleut, or community thereof, as that right or title is defined in the act of admission. The State and its people agree that, unless otherwise provided by Congress, the property, as described in this section, shall remain subject to the absolute disposition of the United States.*[20]

The disclaimer clause recognized undefined property and fishing rights held by Alaska Natives, but the resolution of these rights was the responsibility of the United States. The newly sovereign state was eventually obligated to clarify what portion of the Alaska territory was actually owned by its Native inhabitants before the state could develop its lately discovered and potentially lucrative natural resources—notably the oil discovered in the Prudhoe Bay field. As a result, the state was forced to negotiate with its Indigenous population through the AFN. The negotiations between the AFN and the state ultimately led to the enactment of ANCSA.

Governor Hickel meeting with Alaska Native Leaders—
Courtesy of Alaska State Library Collection, ASL-P01-4686

Under provisions of ANCSA, any US citizen who could prove at least one-quarter Aleut, Eskimo, or Indian blood—and was born before the act was signed into law on December 18, 1971—was eligible to enroll in newly established business corporations formed along the boundaries of twelve regional Native associations listed in the settlement act, or the special thirteenth corporation for people living outside Alaska who did not receive land.[21]

Natives enrolled in corporations based upon where they considered their permanent home. Some people who only enrolled in regional corporations were known as "at large" shareholders, because their permanent homes were away from villages. Shareholders in village corporations could also enroll in their regional corporation, but village shareholders would ultimately receive smaller corporate dividend payments from the regional corporation than the "at large" shareholders. Sometimes this choice between "village" and "at large" enrollment resulted in family members becoming members of different corporations.

Corporations received title to a total of 40 million acres, divided among some 220 Native Village and 12 regional corporations established by the act. The regional corporations shared in payment of $462,500 from the US Treasury and $500 million in mineral revenues from Alaskan lands. Eligible Alaska Natives were issued one hundred shares of corporation stock, and monies from ANCSA went to the newly created corporations rather than directly to individuals, tribes, or clans.

All eligible Native villages were required to form corporations but could choose whether to incorporate as "for profit" or "nonprofit." Eligible villages were defined as communities, half or more of whose population were Natives, having at least twenty-five Natives who were residents, and not being modern or urban in character. Two hundred were listed in the act; however based on the criteria, not all were found eligible. Villages in southeastern Alaska could choose only a single township (23,040 acres), a limitation due to the earlier cash award of the Tlingit-Haida settlement. Other villages were limited

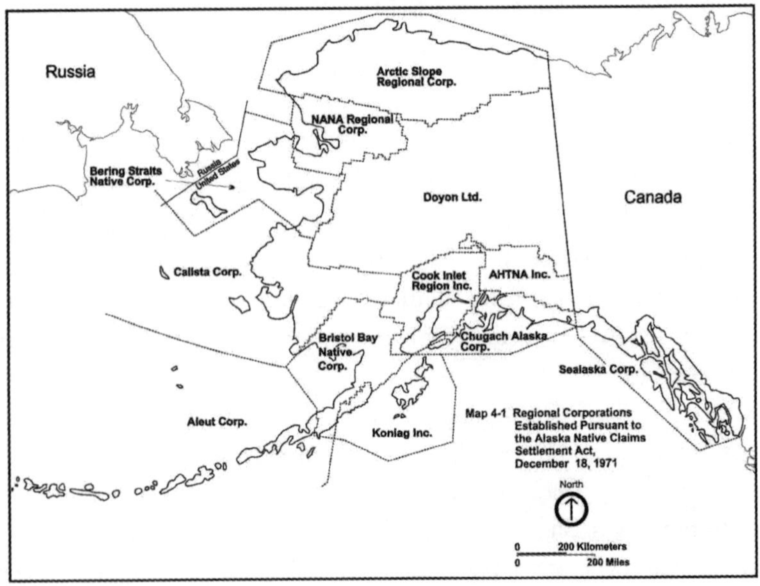

ANCSA Map—Courtesy of the US National Park Service

to land selection outside national forests or wildlife refuges, or lands not chosen by the state. The village corporations would own only the rights to the surface portion of their land; belowground mineral rights—the subsurface estate—would belong to regional corporations.[22]

At the outset of ANCSA, many Native people did not understand the function or purpose of corporations and expected to receive large checks after they enrolled. Since corporations were charged with making a profit, many corporations did not distribute much money initially, instead using the funds to establish a business enterprise. Natives faced many problems implementing the act, including deciding how to invest millions of dollars, selecting lands for surface and subsurface values, as well as educating themselves and their shareholders about corporation business practices. In addition, corporations faced a shortage of Native individuals with business and legal experience to implement the act properly. Sometimes inexperienced corporate boards faced unscrupulous people who took advantage of them, proposing questionable business schemes designed to line the pockets of the initiator rather than shareholders. Additionally, not all the lands available for selection included areas that contained the lands and waters traditionally used by the people. For example, in southeast Alaska, the area from which Kasaan Village Corporation (KAVILCO) was required to select did not include Karta Bay or Grindall Island, the areas upon which Haida people hunted, fished, and gathered food. Had shareholders been more business or legal savvy, they would most likely have protested these areas not being included in their potential choice and would have negotiated to include them.

While the $962 million distributed through ANCSA may sound large, in truth it was distributed over a period of about eleven years, and in the first five years, just 10 percent of the money distributed went to all individuals who were shareholders. The regions retained 45 percent of the total, and the remaining 45 percent was distributed to the villages and the "at large" shareholders.[23] In addition, depending upon the development potential of lands conveyed, different corporations had different investment prospects. Oil discovered in Prudhoe Bay, for example, set the stage for Arctic Slope Regional Corporation to generate steady profits. Likewise, some village corporations in Southeast Alaska were able to capitalize on the rich timber in their regions. Other corporations, however, faced lack of readily developed resources.

Moreover, many shareholders expected to secure jobs in the newly created corporate businesses but often did not possess the required skills, nor were there enough jobs created for every shareholder to have one.

UNRESOLVED ANCSA ISSUES

ANCSA left three major issues unresolved: (1) stock alienation (or the potential for stock to be lost through sale to non-Natives); (2) children born after the December 18, 1971, cut-off date—also known as "afterborns"; and (3) land taxation and protection. The ANCSA amendments enacted in 1988[24] addressed these three major issues. The original act prohibited transfer of shareholder stock, and denied rights to non-Natives who might acquire stock through inheritance, until the end of 1991. At that time, all stock was to be liquidated and new stock reissued. The amendment provided for a procedure to extend stock restrictions unless specifically removed by the majority of stockholders in each corporation. Afterborns, or children of original ANCSA shareholders born after the December 17, 1971 date,[25] were ineligible to enroll in the original established corporations, but the new amendment allowed a majority of stockholders in each corporation to vote to issue stock to afterborns, designated "new Natives." The stock could be restricted or unrestricted and may or may not possess voting rights. The amendments also allowed for issuance of extra elders' stock. In addition, the amendment provided the means for corporations to issue stock to ANCSA-eligible Natives who missed the deadline.[26]

Some corporations have voted to include their afterborns, have issued elders stock, and voted to include eligible Natives who missed the deadline. Other corporations have elected to maintain the status quo. As one can imagine, whether or not each corporation should open their enrollments to their children and descendants has sometimes created disputes and hard feelings among people. Some corporations have decided not to do so because they fear dilution of what are considered meager profits and argue the shares will ultimately be inherited by their descendants. Other corporations want to include their children because they feel inclusion in the corporation is important to their children's sense of contemporary Native identity and belonging. Phyllis Fast (Koyukon Athabascan) describes it this way:

> *ANCSA has had a tremendous and ongoing impact on Alaska Natives identity with its cutoff date of birth (December 18, 1971) for inclusion into its provisions. All Alaska Natives born after that date were expected to assimilate into the mainstream population and/or inherit ANCSA shares from their parents and grandparents. In cultures where huge families and longer lives have become the norm, many original shareholders are alive and well and continue to own their own shares.*[27]

Of the twelve regional corporations, four (Arctic Slope Regional Corporation; NANA; Doyon Limited; and in 2007, Sealaska) have voted to grant descendants shares. These shares differ among the four corporations, but generally speaking, they are life-estate stock that cannot be passed on. Older afterborns are now middle-aged, and many do not own shares of any sort. Even the corporations that voted to include their afterborns followed American laws by incorporating a cutoff date and number of new shareholders.[28]

In *Growing Up Native in Alaska*, commissioned by CIRI Foundation (the nonprofit arm of CIRI corporation), interviewees born between 1957 and 1976 were asked about their relationship to ANCSA and its effect on them. Those born after the cut-off date often noted how the exclusion deeply affected their sense of belonging. Matt Nichol (Eyak) born in 1976, notes being an afterborn "messes with Native identity" and "it's not so much the status but 'why do you get this? And why don't I.' We have the same blood quantum. I don't understand."[29]

In addition to the afterborn issue, under ANCSA, Native corporations were protected from taxation for only twenty years. With the amendment, shareholders could elect to protect their undeveloped land indefinitely by putting it into a "land bank trust." The amendments also offered some protection from corporate debt or bankruptcy, unless shareholders vote to mortgage their land. Additionally, the amendments do not protect the land from the federal or state government exercising their right of "eminent domain," or the taking of private property for the benefit of public good.[30]

While these three issues were resolved in the amendments, the US Congress declined to comment on tribal control or sovereignty. But in May 1988, the Alaska Supreme Court ruled in a split decision that Alaska Native groups and communities, except the Annette Island Reserve, do not have tribal sovereignty.[31]

The decision was appealed, but in 1998, the US Supreme Court ruled in *Alaska v. Village of Venetie Tribal Government* that because ANCSA conveyed lands to state-chartered and state-regulated private business corporations, the lands did not meet the requirements for dependent Indian communities. As a result, the court held that ANCSA severed tribal territorial jurisdiction over ANCSA lands. Village governments, operating under the IRA, were not designated as landowners under the act.[32]

What this means in practicality is that corporations often own the land surrounding the villages, and the village-based tribal councils must negotiate with corporations about access and use. As Alaska Natives increasingly move from villages to urban centers, often for economic reasons, some corporations have many shareholders who do not live in or near their villages. In a sense, they are absentee landlords. The potential exists for shareholder decisions about appropriate land use to be based on profits rather than what is good for the people who live there.

Additionally, in Alaska, tribal territorial jurisdiction is limited. In 1953, the US Congress directed some states, including Alaska, to share jurisdiction with tribes over tribal members. Shared jurisdiction has had severe consequences for tribal authority because often the state does not recognize tribal authority.[33] Although recognition of Indian tribes is a federal decision, state governors are in control of all state agencies that work with tribes. Depending on the particular governor in office, Alaskan tribes have found more or less recognition and support. In 1990, Governor Steve Cowper issued an administrative order, recognizing tribal authority. The next governor, Walter J. Hickel, rescinded the order, and in 2000, Governor Tony Knowles recognized tribes and developed the Millennium Agreement to provide a framework to establish government-to-government relationships. After this point, governors came to accept that tribes exist in Alaska primarily because they bring in billions of federal dollars, but the state continues to challenge tribal jurisdiction. In 2004, Governor Frank Murkowski rescinded the Millennium Agreement and issued an opinion that tribes cannot initiate children's cases. Former governor Sarah Palin supported this, as did former governor Sean Parnell.[34]

In addition to the three major unresolved issues, ANCSA also left unresolved Alaska Native rights regarding hunting, fishing, and gathering on traditional land bases and waterways, used by their peoples—commonly known as "subsistence" in Alaska. Although ANCSA originally appeared to extinguish aboriginal hunting and fishing rights, Congress—recognizing that Alaska Native subsistence was inadequately protected—later included provisions for rural subsistence hunting and fishing preference in the Alaska National Interest Lands Conservation Act (ANILCA) of 1980. The state of Alaska then enacted a rural subsistence preference in order to maintain control of hunting and fishing laws. However, in 1989, the Alaska Supreme Court ruled against the rural preference after a group of urban sport hunters filed a suit based on discrimination against urban residents.[35]

ANILCA was enacted to protect subsistence on federal lands. As a condition of giving management of all fish and wildlife within Alaska to the state, ANILCA required the state to enact laws to guarantee subsistence under state jurisdiction. The state attempted to accommodate the subsistence needs of Alaska Natives or rural Alaskans, but the "equal access" clauses of the constitution, as they would become known, posed an intractable problem for the state. Since the constitution could not allow for a subsistence priority based on rural residence, the State of Alaska lost management of fish and wildlife authority on federal lands. In 1999, the federal government assumed management, thereby creating a dual management system, which continues until the present day. Accordingly, subsistence has remained a politically sensitive issue in the state, with Native people feeling pressured to reduce access to their traditional foods.

Given Alaska's vast size and the distances separating small villages from urban areas, subsistence hunting, fishing, and gathering activities are important aspects of physical and economic survival for most rural Alaskans—Native and non-Native alike. Yet most Alaska Natives, regardless of where they now live, view traditional Native subsistence foods as much more than means of physical survival; they are a crucial aspect of cultural survival and spiritual sustenance. Regaining control of subsistence rights has remained a priority for the AFN, tribes, and many Alaska Native corporations.

COMMENTARY

Some Alaska Natives view ANCSA as a positive step toward economic empowerment. Others see it as a necessary compromise to prevent total loss of lands. Others consider it a continuation of the US government's allotment and assimilation policies. In some respects, ANCSA was like treaties the United States negotiated with American Indian tribes in the lower forty-eight, and in other respects, it was different. In return for grants of limited land, ANCSA extinguished aboriginal title to much more extensive lands used by the peoples. Yet ANCSA was not negotiated with leaders from each individual tribal nation within Alaska, and the majority of traditional lands are owned by corporations, not tribes.

ANCSA has had a positive effect for some, but not for all corporations and their shareholders. Economic development most often depends on whether the corporation has been able to develop natural resources located within corporate landholdings. Some corporate lands included oil, minerals, or timber, while other lands contained little that might be developed. Two provisions within ANCSA, known as 7(i) and 7(j) were meant to address this imbalance. These provisions provide for revenue sharing among the corporations. 7(i) requires that every year 70 percent of revenue from timber and subsurface estates are to be divided equally among the twelve corporations. 7(j) requires revenue derived from 7(i) be distributed to village corporations. Because of lack of clarity in the law's language, expensive litigation kept the funds from being deployed as they were intended.[36] ANCSA's revenue-sharing aspect is different from most western-based corporate models, and some might say, in line with the Indigenous value of sharing, while others might view it as undue burden that hinders a corporation's profit-making ability.

Moreover, when corporations were first established, the profit imperative based upon resource development was a foreign concept for most, especially those living in the rural villages where subsistence livelihood was the norm. Perhaps the largest issue from the perspective of Ilarion (Larry) Merculieff, an Aleut, is that "corporate laws and U.S. accounting systems do not place any value on well-being, subsistence ways of life, and cultural survival, so there is no place for such things when corporations calculate the 'bottom line.'"[37] Yet Paul Ongtooguk (Iñupiaq) recognizes that "The Alaska Native Claims Settlement Act was a giant act of compromise on the part of Alaska Native peoples; we had to make huge sacrifices of our lands in order to arrive at any kind of settlement."[38] He further notes that Natives "wrestle with the huge challenge of how to help lift the economic boats of Alaska Native peoples while simultaneously protecting the cultures, lands, and waters of our people."[39]

Margie Brown (Yup'ik) reinforces that while not perfect, Native people, prior to ANCSA, were "generally disenfranchised, disrespected, and sidelined and often poverty stricken."[40] She cites statistics from Willie Hensley's testimony before Congress that put the average life expectancy of Alaska Natives, in 1966, at 34.5; Native infant mortality at twice the national average; and median Alaska Native family annual income was below $2,000 while the costs of goods in remote parts of Alaska were the highest in the country.[41] A recent report supports Brown's claim that corporations have contributed to improving economic conditions for Alaska Natives, although not always in direct cash payments. Corporate dividends paid during the past ten years range from $5.50 to more than $600 per share, and they do help defray expenses such as high heating and transportation costs for those still living in the villages, or supplement other sources of income for all shareholders. Many corporations, whose headquarters are most often located in urban centers, have implemented shareholder hiring preference. Regional corporations have also taken steps to foster economic development within their regions. One corporation is working with a regional Native Health Association to build a dental and health clinic on corporate land, leased at $1.00 per year. Another regional corporation developed a joint venture with a village corporation to reestablish a seafood plant, and several other corporations are exploring developing alternative energy sources on corporate land to help ease high village heating costs.[42]

Brown also argues that most Alaska Native corporations *do* attend to Alaska Native values in their corporate decision-making processes, citing the millions of dollars the nonprofit arms of corporations provide to their shareholders for cultural, educational, health, and social purposes, including scholarships, language and cultural revitalization projects, and elder benefits. Brown points out the economic effect Native corporations have had on the state, diversifying its economy, and she highlights executive director of Alaska's Permanent fund, Michael J. Burns's statement that Alaska Native corporations "absolutely control the economic destiny of the state." Brown disagrees with the notion that ANCSA and the corporate model are not appropriate for Alaska Native people, and that Alaska Natives through their corporate boards, elected by their shareholders, will collectively make decisions about appropriate levels of development. She thinks that Alaska Natives are best suited to make those decisions.[43] As these varied views suggest, whether ANCSA has been a brilliant success or dismal failure, it remains a topic of debate four decades after its passage.

CHAPTER 13

Genny and Lundy

Annette Reed

Genny (Karok-Yurok) and Lundy Mitchell (Yerington Paiute) served as outstanding teachers and role models for their families and generations of youth in the American Indian Education Programs in California. They spent much of their early lives at the federally run Stewart Indian Boarding School near Carson City, Nevada. In order to tell their story, there is a need to place it within the context of the US government assimilation policies, in particular the Federal Boarding School system.

In the 1880s, the United States implemented assimilation through the policies of reservation land allotment, religious suppression, and government boarding schools. The US government's goal of assimilation at this point in time was to completely end the practice of Native language, culture, religion, and ways of life and to have it all replaced with that of the dominant society, which was white, Christian, and English speaking. This onslaught served to be devastating to Native American people. The US government did not seem to value Native American language, political systems, and ways of life; in fact, they sought to exterminate them through government policy and acts.[1]

In 1879, the federal government assigned Captain Richard Pratt, a military officer, to establish Carlisle Indian Boarding School in Carlisle, Pennsylvania. He ran the school in military style and forbade all that was Native. By 1900, twenty-five off-reservation government boarding schools had been established across the United States. In 1890, the United States established Stewart Indian Boarding School near Carson, Nevada. In 1892, Sherman Institute opened its doors in California, followed by Chemawa Indian Boarding School in Oregon in 1880, and Hoopa Indian Boarding School in California around 1900. The reason I mention these particular schools is twofold.[2] First, Genny and Lundy Mitchell, whose story I will share later in this chapter, attended Stewart Indian Boarding school. The second reason is to place emphasis upon how widespread boarding school attendance was across Indian Country. My grandfather attended Hoopa Indian Boarding School, and my uncle and cousins attended Chemewa. My great aunts attended Sherman in southern California, and my great uncles attended Stewart Indian Boarding School in Nevada. My uncle Charlie Whipple served as class president in 1940 at Stewart. My husband, Steven Crum, is enrolled Western Shoshone from the Duck Valley Reservation in Nevada. His father, Earl, attended Stewart Indian Boarding School, and his aunts attended Sherman Indian Boarding School. These are only a few examples of our relatives who attended various boarding schools. We are not the exceptions but rather the norm with regard to the large number of Natives attending.

While the schools did provide basic skills education, they also put forth strict policies of assimilation. School officials forbade religious practices and culture and the speaking of Native languages, while attempting to replace them with practices of the larger white society. Beatings and punishment for display of Native ways were common. Indian boarding schools sought to forever change Native peoples and their culture. Some students did assimilate. Other students resisted and retained their Native identities and traditions while taking on some ways of larger society, thus acculturating rather than assimilating. I define acculturating as retaining our culture, while taking on parts of larger society. I will discuss more about federal boarding schools as Genny's and Lundy's stories are shared. Genny's and Lundy's life experiences took place within this context.

This is a story, a history, and a biography about a person who is no longer with us. However, she is always in the heart of her family and friends. She was one of my dearest friends and to me, like another mother. I have been blessed in my life by having more than one mother figure. I deeply love my mother of birth for all that she has done and continues to do to make me a better person. In addition, I love those who helped teach me about life. I will be weaving a story of Genny Godfry Mitchell, with historical events of the time and with current day. Both Genny and her husband, Lundy, were American Indian. As previously mentioned, Genny was Karuk and Yurok from northern California and Lundy Mitchell was Yerington Paiute from Nevada. I asked Genny's permission to interview her and expressed to her that later I planned to develop a presentation, chapter, article, or book about her life in part or in whole. She agreed, and we conducted several interviews. This part of the chapter is based on those interviews and others, my own primary research in archives, secondary sources, and my own personal accounts.

I met Genny in the mid-1980s when I worked with American Indian Education Programs with school districts in the Oakland/San Francisco Bay Area. I sought to become either an elementary or high school teacher—I really wasn't at all sure at the time which way I wanted to go with my career. The American Indian Education Programs brought skilled people to the schools, and they taught mostly Native American children aspects of culture, including storytelling, traditional dance, traditional jewelry making, or more contemporary Native arts. Genny and her husband, Lundy, by this time had retired from their careers and worked as consultants with the Indian Education Programs.

They taught art and cultural classes at more than one of the Indian Education Programs and created beautiful Native items to share with others or to sell at various events in the area. Teaching a beadwork course to ten to twenty young people, when one is dealing with small beads and a specific pattern, can be quite difficult. Even using larger materials when teaching children ages six to twelve was very hard. Therefore, they had a teaching assistant as an aid, and I served as one of those aids. I was in my early to mid-twenties with a thirst for learning traditional beadwork and shellwork. I loved and still do love creating traditional Native regalia. I learned so much from both Genny and Lundy.

At times we traveled together with me as their chauffeur. Later in life they both had heart conditions; however Lundy's was more serious at that time. Lundy phoned me secretly and said, "Hello, are you doing anything this coming weekend?"

Lundy, Annette, and Genny—Courtesy of Annette Reed

I answered, "What do you have in mind?"

He responded, "Well, the doctor told me not to drive. That with my heart condition it would cause too much stress. This weekend there is a Powwow and reunion at Stewart Indian School, and we wanted to go. If I drive, like I said, the doctor said too much stress, so I am supposed to let Genny drive. Have you ever been with Genny driving?!"

He continued,"If she drives I would have far more stress than if I had driven" (Lundy laughed at this point, and I chuckled too).

I said, "Oh, yes, I have been with Genny driving, and I agree. Do you want me to drive?"

Lundy said, "Yes, I want you to drive our car. If I suggest this to Genny she will get upset about me not wanting her to drive, but if you phone her and say you want to drive us, she will be happy about you joining us."[3] Many times I became their driver, good friend, and to me, their family. I wanted to tell you about the relationship to place this narrative within context. Now to speak of Genny and the story I have attempted to weave together, strand by strand as a basket begins its creation.

Born in the town of Yreka, in far northern California in 1924, Genny lived with her mother until age four when her mother died. Genny then went to live at the Salmon River, in Forks of Salmon, which is an unincorporated community. She lived with her great-grandmother, who was also Karuk and Yurok.

Genny saw a book that I was reading, *Genocide in Northwestern California: When Our Worlds Cried* by Jack Norton (1979).[4] She commented, "That reminds me of my childhood." The cover of the book she was pointing to had a drawing of a white man on a horse with a Native woman holding her baby, trying to run away from the man and horse, while he was reaching out for her. The Native woman's face was terror filled, and it was a life-or-death situation. I asked her thoughtfully why that reminded her of her childhood. Genny responded with a faraway look in her eyes:

> *In those days you didn't want to be caught on the road because they would kill Indians if they could. If you got caught on the trail or road you ran and went somewhere you could hide. Whether it was a car, truck, or a horse they would try to run you over. We could not talk and play on trails; we had to listen carefully to hear what was coming. If you heard someone on the trail or road, we would run off the trail so they didn't know we were there. We would hide wherever we could and be very quiet.*[5]

Such abuse of American Indian women and children, in particular, was common in northern California. Many cases of rape and murder were very common in the 1850s with the influx of non-Indians invading our homelands.[6] In Jack Norton's book the author states,

> *The patterns of genocide in Northwestern California repeat what has occurred in the rest of North America, and is an echoing cry down the corridors of time from the genocide practiced in the entire Western Hemisphere by the Spanish Conquistadores, the Catholic missionaries, and the United States through the miners, settlers, and the federal government itself.*[7]

Genocide is indeed what occurred in many forms in the United States with regard to American Indians. Many Native people and scholars of American Indian studies would argue that genocide continues today.

Noted scholar Luana Ross (Confederated Salish and Kootenai Tribes located at the Flathead Indian Reservation in Montana), in the article entitled "Introduction: Native Women and State Violence" in *Social Justice* (2004), makes the point that Native American women and children faced violence in numerous ways.

UN Genocide

Resolution 260 (III) A of the United Nations General Assembly

Adopted December 9, 1948

Convention on the Prevention and Punishment of the Crimes of Genocide

ARTICLE 1

The Contacting Parties confirm that genocide, whether committed in time of peace or in time of war, is a crime under international law which they may undertake to prevent and to punish.

ARTICLE 2

In the present Convention, genocide means any of the following acts committed with intent to destroy, in whole or in part, a national, ethnical, racial or religious group as such.

(a) Killing members of the group;

(b) Causing serious bodily or mental harm to members of the group;

(c) Deliberately inflicting on the group conditions of life calculated to bring about physical destruction in whole or in part;

(d) Imposing measures intended to prevent births within the group;

(e) Forcibly transferring children of the group to another group.

David Stannard (1992) points out that control over women's reproductive abilities and destruction of women and children are essential to the destruction of a people. If the women of a nation are not disproportionately killed, then that nation's population will not be severely affected. According to Stannard, Native women and children were targeted for wholesale killing to destroy the Indian nations. Consequently, colonizers such as Andrew Jackson [Seventh

> *President of the United States and army general] advocated killing the women and children of Native tribes as part of massacres to ensure the destruction of the tribe. The constant sexual violations of Native women during such massacres further demonstrate the colonial desire to control Native women's sexuality.*[8]

In addition to violence against Native women in the 1800s and the first half of the 1900s, Native scholar Myla Vincenti Carpio (Jicarilla Apache, Laguna Pueblo/Isleta Pueblo located in the southwestern part of the United States) in her article "Lost Generation: Sterilization and American Indian Women" in *Social Justice: A Journal of Crime, Conflict and World Order* (2004) demonstrates that during the 1970s, US-funded Indian health facilities performed sterilization on Native women without their understanding, knowledge, or consent. I have heard that two of my great aunts and many other women of my own tribe went through this experience and therefore never had children. And so, as Genny speaks of horses or motor vehicles trying to run over or stamp out Indians in the 1920s and 1930s, we see that in other ways the government has attempted to stamp out future generations of Native people.

Genny continued and spoke of the importance of baskets when she was a young girl. Gathering all of the materials for baskets takes a long time, then the materials need to cure for a year and dry out prior to use. Genny said, "I picked willows with my aunt, and she made baskets. I remember my great-grandmother and others went to gather roots. We went fishing and caught fish, salmon, and eels, mostly in the summers." Later in life, Genny would learn to weave baskets from other great weavers. She taught basket weaving to generations of Native youth, including myself when I was in my twenties. Genny met and exchanged styles of weaving with many other Native women.

Genny enjoyed living with her great-grandmother, who eventually passed away. Genny thus went to live at one family member's household, then went to another. She was around six years old at this time. She went to the federally operated school at Hoopa, then, after a year, she said it was closed and she returned to Forks of Salmon. The year she spent at Hoopa was a difficult one for her. "I wasn't happy living there. All had big families and I was always 'the one who did it.' It was always my fault no matter what it was." She felt that since she was the new child to enter a household that all of the other children blamed her for any negative thing that happened. For example, if a dish broke, it was her fault, so that they wouldn't get in trouble. The children already in the family house stuck together, and she was the new one and therefore easier to blame.

Genny observed many events and ways of life at a young age up in northern California. During this time, traditional ceremonial Indian dancing became seen as an "Indian Offense" by the US government. In response and in an effort to retain their own Indian way of life, Indian dances went underground and were conducted away from the watchful eyes of Indian agents who were the ones who served under the commissioner of Indian Affairs. Genny notes,

> *The dances went underground and no one except Indians knew where they were at. I remember staying with an aunt, and her husband was sick. I remember the medicine doctors came to heal him. They had all-night sessions, singing and praying. I was about seven years old at the time. This was at Forks of Salmon. They held the healing upstairs even though the sick person's bedroom was downstairs.*

In this way, American Indians continued their traditions even though the government had banned them. Native people are resilient.

Genny observed other ways of life as a young girl. She was fascinated with the gold mining that her Native family conducted and in general the hard work that everyone participated in.

> *Most people around were miners or farmers. My people had their own vegetables and cows. Some worked in logging. My brother-in-law was a miner. He had a big mine. I don't know what kind of mine that would be. Older people did what they called sniping, panning for gold, and they had a rocker thing for the water run into it; the gold got caught in the bottom. I remember doing that a lot. A slough box I think was about thirty-six inches wide and six feet long. One end you put the dirt in and put the water on it and wash the dirt down. The other part of it, about three feet of it, had gunny sacks at the bottom, then the next layer was some kind of fine rocks, then the screens. As water was washed down, gold would settle in the bottom and the rest would wash out. My aunts, uncles, everyone worked, everyone worked hard.*[9]

There are many stereotypes about American Indians that are false. People read them in books or see them in the popular media. One is that Indians are lazy, but nothing could be further from the truth. Native people worked hard to provide for their families. Genny did a lot of work as a child helping with housework and even some cooking. Native families asked their children to do age-appropriate work, so that they would learn important life activities. Genny laughed when she told a short story about her making biscuits. "I could not make biscuits good, they turned out hard. My dogs would bury my biscuits!" She recalled that most days her family ate beans, rice, day-old biscuits, and a lot of salmon. She cleaned salmon and put them on sticks in the smoke house. Even today, a smoke house stands behind my own mother's house at Smith River Rancheria. Most Indian families in northwestern California smoke salmon and cook it a variety of ways. It still stands as a staple part of the diet.

Finally, Genny ended up with a family she liked living with. She was happy. However, this was short lived, for an aunt decided to send her to Stewart Indian Boarding School at Carson City, Nevada. She was about seven at that time.

> *I liked them [her family] and was real happy with them. Then this government agent came to get me, he just threw me in the car and slammed the door and away we were going. I didn't want to go. There was no choice. The government agent drove me to Stewart the whole way by car. His name was Grange or Gage. I don't remember the trip to the school. I was scared.*

As mentioned previously, the government sought to change the American Indians' philosophy. Strict discipline accompanied the boarding school system. If the school officials found an Indian child speaking their own language, they might beat them, lock them in closets, or even worse forms of punishment. One elder woman who attended Chilocco Indian School in Salem, Oregon, explained a cruel way to teach her not to speak her language. She said the school officials took her and put a propane pipe up to her lips and burned her lips off. She reflected, "I had my lips burned off many a time at that Indian School." However, she continued to speak her language and practice her Native religion in secret, as did many Indian students. They resisted efforts of assimilation. Many students ran away from the schools, even if they were far from home. Noted Native historian Brenda Child wrote that "girls were just as likely to run away as boys, and one year the matron at Flandreau [South Dakota] reported that Mary Badboy had the distinction of holding 'the run away record for the year.'"[10]

The schools were often hundreds of miles from their homelands. Some students went home during summer breaks, while others stayed at the school. When students first arrived at the schools, the officials cut their hair, which for many Native people is a sign of death in the family. They assumed every Indian had lice so poured kerosene over their hair and body. Their own traditional clothing was replaced with uniforms. It was a difficult time to be Indian, yet Indian they did remain. The federal government attempted to completely assimilate American Indian people. They tried to force Indians into being "white" in all ways except color, yet they would still not accept them as white. They both succeeded and failed. Many Native people lost their language and culture, while others retain it today. Since the ultimate goal was to completely assimilate Indians, they failed because ceremonies are still preformed.

Boarding schools deeply impact Native people today. While many of the original boarding schools have closed or changed to a "Native friendly" type of teaching style, the original schools left a tragic legacy. Since they taught that whenever a child did something that was deemed "wrong," they were hit or severely punished. They grew up a very different way from traditional Native societies. Usually, children were not beaten or even yelled at. Instead, there were different forms of teaching. But people usually learn how to parent from those who raise them. Because the children might be taken from their home and placed into boarding schools by age five, some even as babies, and remain at the schools until they were eighteen to twenty-two years old, the boarding school was where many were raised. During this time, they learned how to be punished and how to punish. This abuse has been passed down from generation to generation. Unfortunately, it has led to an increase in child abuse, violence against women, suicide, alcoholism, and substance abuse.

Genny rode that long ride to Stewart, traveling through northern California, down through Nevada. She didn't want to leave her family she loved. She rode in the car and had a long time during the drive to think through her situation. She decided that no matter what she would like it, since she had no choice. In a pain-ridden voice, Genny described her first memories of Stewart Indian Boarding School.

I had a long drive to make up my mind that I was going to like it. It was a nice building and warm bed. It was a dormitory. There must have been about 150 girls in the small girls' building and about that many in the large girls' room. All in one room, a large square room with beds, all beds. The matron rooms were in the same building… I can't seem to remember my first days, everything blended together. I had made up my mind that I was going to like it. It was a beautiful place with green lawns and rock buildings. You had to line up, stand in line, all of us stood in line, we had to march from the dormitory building to the dining hall then march back. If you could put up with it all and not say anything it could be nice, but a lot of people could not put up with it. I had made up my mind to put up with it.

The school turned into kindergarten through twelfth grade by that time. I was in first grade. Reading, writing, and arithmetic—it was that type of education. What a lot of people didn't like was lining up and marching. We had to march everywhere—one, two, three, four, one, two, three, four—all the way over to wherever we were going, even to the classes. To building to school to building again we marched. Some would run away, they always ran away. I didn't run away because I didn't have any place to run to. My friends would ask me to go, but I told them usually don't tell me when you are going or what window you are going to crawl out 'cause I don't want to know. I never did run away.

They would say, "You could come stay at our house." I said, "I have already been in houses. I was always the one who ate too much, slept too long, didn't do the dishes, or whatever it was it was always my fault. So I don't want to go…." We had to wear a uniform, overalls. They were usually striped. When I arrived there I had long hair like your hair [she was talking about my hair that has always been long], but when I got there they cut it all off. They shingled it up the back and it was all frizzy; they kept my hair short, they always kept the hair short. I didn't like it at all. I had long hair, but I went along with the program. They said when children came from their home they had lice so in order to control things they cut the hair, everyone's hair was short."[11]

Genny went to Stewart when she was about seven years old, which would have been approximately 1931. It would have been very strict at that time. The boarding schools began to change in 1933 with a change in administration. John Collier became the commissioner of Indian Affairs, and he held more respect for Native culture than did the commissioners before him. Genny continued, "In the early days we marched until the third grade. That's when the system changed and wasn't so military. As time went by the system changed and they didn't insist on you knowing how to march. You didn't have to stay in step anymore."

I asked Genny "What did you do for fun?" She responded:

> *Got up at six a.m. and stayed by your bed until the matron checked your bed to make sure you didn't wet it. Then we got dressed, made your bed, then marched to breakfast, of course marched to breakfast and back again. Got in line and went to school, but some people had chores to do. Little chores, sweeping or picking up things were common. We had to pick up the grounds—every little bit of piece of paper or stick and put them in the garbage cans. Then we dressed for school and went in line and marched to school at about eight a.m. After school we went to our lockers and changed. We wore a school dress uniform at school, then when we got back, we changed into overalls for working. There was a little bit of time to play with swings and sandbox, you could check out a ball, but wasn't too much time to play, so we either played on the swings or played jacks and little games. We worked after school. There was very little time to play. After dinner, if it [was] light we could play till 7 p.m.*[12]

Genny described one Christmas:

> *I liked the food but the older girls would say give me your apple or orange. But I never gave it to them. They could slap me or hit me, push me, but I didn't give it to them. They could not intimidate me. At Christmas I didn't get presents except what the school gave me… I can't remember what they gave me. One year a cousin sent me a bracelet, a sparkling bracelet, and a doll. I know I was surprised! Who would give me a doll? I didn't expect anything, but I got the pretty jewelry and a doll that year.*[13]

The apples have come up with many boarding school children. They served as a desired treat. The girls learned to slap, hit, and push from their own punishments, which later some inflicted upon others.

The school disciplinarians carried out swift and harsh punishments for any infraction of school rules, including any speaking of Native language or practicing of culture in the late 1880s and early 1900s. Noted artist and emeritus professor from California State University, Frank LaPena spoke about a method for discipline of boys at Stewart Indian Boarding School:

> *They had the boys line up in two parallel lines. The boy who was being disciplined would start at the beginning between the lines and each boy standing there would take a turn hitting or kicking the boy as hard as they could. If a friend let up and didn't hit as hard, then he would have to go through that gauntlet line themselves. This ensured the boy being disciplined would receive the hardest hits.*[14]

In one interview, Genny and I were traveling up to Humboldt State for a California Indian Conference and to have Genny see her homeland one last time. During this ride I mentioned to Genny about current Native historians, such as Brenda Child, writing about children running away from the schools. Genny said, "Oh, did I tell you about the near-riot at Stewart? A couple of the girls saw the cook for the school take his pipe and empty it into the pot of stew we were to eat later that day. They told the rest of us, and many students tore up the kitchen then ran away. I never did because I didn't have anywhere to go. But I did get hit at that school." Later she talked about how things changed when she became older. "Just like other kids, they used to beat me with a stick and put me into a closet, then lock the door. When I grew up and was nearly a woman, the matron again tried to do this, but that time I fought her and grabbed the stick myself. Both of us fought in that closet and she never tried that with me again."[15] Beatings at the boarding schools were common.

Genny never mentioned about being sexually molested; however, another elder woman who I interviewed did talk about a male teacher touching her and having her sit on his lap. She said he had her touch him inappropriately. She gave permission to tell of this; however, she did not wish to be named.[16] Sexual molestation in the schools was common. If we think of how often people get through the screening system today to work with children, and some still molest them, just imagine a world without screening. To think of these children far from home, some not speaking the language and at a time when no one could speak against a white male in courts, it is not difficult to see how these acts could happen on a regular basis without much consequence.

Unfortunately, through research we know today that some people pass down experiences they were taught at a young age. The boarding school experience has led to higher rates of child abuse, domestic violence, and sexual abuse. It is amazing that any kind-hearted people have emerged from such a negative system. However, not all students shared the same experiences.

Genny shared that the boarding schools did teach trades to some of the students, which they later used for a career. The schools served as meeting places for intertribal friendships and some relationships. Through the schools, young Native people learned to interact with other Native people from different tribes, and later that helped to form alliances in urban areas. From these alliances Native people formed the early community centers.

Genny has many more stories to tell of her boarding school days; however, they are for another time. She grew up within Stewart Boarding School and went home for a few summers during her stay there. Growing into a young woman, she decided to leave Stewart and move to Hayward, California, where her brother lived. Genny went to a United Service Organization dance in Oakland. It was in the forties that she met the man who was to become her husband, Lundy Mitchell. They both shared this story of their meeting.

Lundy said, "I saw this beautiful young woman and wanted to meet her."

Genny continued, "He didn't know who I was, but I recognized him because he went to Stewart too. He was older than I, so we didn't hang around at that time together."

Lundy smiled and added, "When I learned who she was I thought 'wow' she was that snot-nosed little girl, I didn't pay attention to her because she was a little one."

Genny at this point rolled her eyes since she knew he said that in good humor to tease her. He clarified, "But when I saw her then at that dance, she was beautiful like I said."

Portrait of Genny and Lundy Mitchell—Courtesy of Annette Reed

They had children and grandchildren, and if they had lived longer they would have seen their great-grandchildren who are alive today. They both worked hard and raised their family. Genny and Lundy became powerful and active members of the urban Indian community of the Oakland/San Francisco Bay Area. People respected them, each for their own skills and ways. They taught classes for Native youth, were active in community organizations, and were two of the early ones who entered the urban area. Many of this generation of urban Indians had already met or had experiences of the boarding schools. They became part of a movement to resist assimilation and retain Native heritage.

CHAPTER 14

"Look Out Cleveland"

A COMMENT ON NATIONAL LEADERSHIP IN CRITICAL TIMES

Jonathan Osorio

"Look out Cleveland, the storm is coming through, and it's rolling right up on you."

—*Robbie Robertson*

Kanaka Maoli, (Indigenous Hawaiian peoples) have no trouble identifying whether an Ali'i[1] is a worthy or unworthy leader. We draw our inferences about their character from what they do, especially those who lived in the centuries before literacy. Little is remembered of what they said, although we do remember the mele[2] composed by Ali'i who have written beautiful and often heart-rending love songs to another. This is not to say that an Ali'i Nui's[3] words were politically insignificant. If we know anything about the great chiefs that ruled over the land and the people, it is that their words, their wishes, their declarations were regarded by the people as manifests requiring their most prodigious efforts to ensure that the chief's desires and commands were met. Words were only idle amusements in riddling games like Ho'opāpā; otherwise they were serious projections of the chief's own realities, and when the Ali'i spoke, the people endeavored to make their words—whether a command to build a heiau (sacred structure) or to vanquish an enemy—a reality.

Words were important in nineteenth-century American politics as well, but in a different way. Words made up the frameworks of laws and treaties, calculated to create advantages for one party or another. Words also framed the ideologies of Whig and Federalist, Democrat and Republican, slave owner and abolitionist. The democratic polity of America was moved by words as much as anything.

So, it is important to remember, when looking at two leaders, one American and one Kanaka Maoli,[4] that one cannot judge both of them by the same criteria. Grover Cleveland, seventeenth and nineteenth president of the United States, and Lili'uokalani, eighth and final monarch of the Hawaiian Kingdom, exemplified the best things about their respective societies and demonstrated the stark differences between the two nations.

Even now, we know these two leaders represent two very different ways of thinking. We Hawaiians know Cleveland in large part for his speech denouncing the actions of John Stevens and the State Department under Benjamin Harrison as "An Act of War."[5] In January 1893, the senior American official in Hawai'i, US minister John L. Stevens, called American troops ashore to protect a few hundred white men who were attempting to unseat our country's sovereign and make themselves the government. When the queen refused to attack American troops in order to arrest the insurrectionists for treason, the US minister promptly recognized the group as the de facto government of Hawai'i. It was this bit of mischief that brought Cleveland's denunciation in his speech to Congress:

> *It has been the boast of our government that it seeks to do justice in all things without regard to the strength or weakness of those with whom it deals. I mistake the American people if they favor the odious doctrine that there is no such thing as international morality, that there is one law for a strong nation and another for a weak one, and that even by indirection a strong power may with impunity despoil a weak one of its territory.*[6]

By an act of war, committed with the participation of a diplomatic representative of the United States and without authority of Congress, the government of a feeble but friendly and confiding people has been overthrown. A substantial wrong has thus been done, one that we should work to repair as a due regard for our national character as well as the rights of the injured people.

We are moved by Cleveland's words and the inherent sense of fairness they signify. We are even moved by the thought that America was a place where at least some of the most powerful individuals in the land could evoke such compassion and conscience when dealing with a small and vulnerable nation such as ours. I think that we understand that Cleveland's speech was a profound political act, and there is kaona (multiple meanings) in that English word "act", is there not?

Politics in the representative democracy were constructed by speeches and postures. A president's speech was comparable to a king leading warriors into battle. He was challenging the legislature to take action, and he was exposing his political neck to the ridicule that he actually received. Under the limitation of his own political society, he acted bravely.

He opposed imperialism, and the stark truth was that the events in Hawai'i in 1893 were simple enough demonstrations of American imperialism. Yet Cleveland's opposition to imperialism had more to do with his uneasiness about America's increasingly complicated relationships with foreign nations than with the belief in some kind of national or ethnic egalitarianism. Indeed, he refused to use federal pressure to back the Fifteenth Amendment and force southern states to allow African Americans to vote. When it came to issues of race, as one historian put it, "He agreed with white southerners in their reluctance to treat African Americans as social and political equals, and made special efforts to reach out to Democrats and former Confederates in the South to assure them that they had a friend in the White House."[7]

His support for Lili'uokalani was genuine, I believe, though his attitude toward Native people in his own land was largely paternalistic and, to be fair, almost arrogant. He was the president who signed the Dawes Act in 1887, causing many of the tribes to dissolve, out of his conviction that the Indians had to become proper Americans. In the course of the next seventy years, the American Indian lost vast territories, and those that remained were largely impoverished.

And yet Kanaka admired this man, if for no other reason than, for a few months in 1893, he stood squarely with our queen and called on his country to deal fairly with our kingdom. If he was unable to restore her to the throne, we should remind ourselves that neither was Her Majesty. Lili'uokalani had nothing but praise for the American president in her book *Hawaii's Story* saying,

> *But, none the less, my grateful people will always remember that, in his message to Congress and in his official acts, Mr. Cleveland showed the greatest anxiety to do that which was just, and that which was for the honor of the nation over which he had been elected chief ruler. He has always had from me the utmost respect and esteem.*[8]

I think the president and the queen had much in common, including a deep sense of personal honor and courage, both of which Her Majesty demonstrates with such magnificence in her hour of trial on January 17, 1893. Both seem to act from an inner commitment to choose right over wrong, regardless of how little reliable support they had from their own political communities. Cleveland had a vicious partisan struggle in Washington to contend with, along with bitter enemies on the left and right on Capitol Hill and on Wall Street. Lili'u had the Hawaiian League[9] and its despicable constitution that complicated her every political move.[10] But she also had serious opposition from her own Kanaka politicians such as John Bush and Robert Wilcox—and even a possible informer in her own circle.[11]

What sustained the queen then, flanked by American troops and the Committee of Public Safety, was not her marshal and her ministry arguing over whether to fire on American troops and arrest the traitors. She could have drawn no confidence from her ministry, which had initially given their support for a new constitution only to withdraw it at the first sign of aggression from Thurston, Smith, and Dole. All three were members of the Committee of Safety, a thirteen-member group of the Annexation Club. Once she made the decision to refrain from violence she was very much alone.

In that sense, the actions of Her Majesty cannot be compared with those of the American president. Cleveland after all did not face execution as a result of his political decisions. Moreover, he did not pursue the restoration of Lili'uokalani as far as he could have. Having agreed to a restoration in exchange for an amnesty of the Committee of Public Safety, he refused to use troops to dislodge them from power and ultimately turned the problem over to Congress. His presidency seemed even to be repudiated by his own country, when Republicans were elected overwhelmingly to the House and took the majority in the Senate in 1894. The president's support for the Hawaiian monarchy was made to look ridiculous on one hand and sinister on another; and the annexationist William McKinley would defeat him in 1896.

But the queen faced a totally different situation in Honolulu. She had no idea what would become of her once she yielded her authority to the United States. Indeed, the US soldiers did not take her into custody, and she was very much left to the mercy of the haole (white) traitors who flirted with the notion of having her condemned.

A few years ago, in a sermon that I wrote for one of her birthday celebrations, I speculated that a profound faith in God sustained Liliʻuokalani, and I believe that still. I said that I was certain she was not really putting her faith in the American people when she placed herself in the hands of her enemies. I think she simply refused to do evil and trusted God to be with her. And I think she also knew that her Lāhui (people) would never desert her. While her cabinet and some of her closest relatives would disappoint her with their political intrigues and lust for her property, the queen lived out her life fully experiencing the aloha, the fullest and deepest regard her people had for her. While there would be discouragements ahead for her personally, she never had reason to question her faith in the Kanaka Māoli, or in her Lāhui.

I don't know if the same thing can be said for Grover Cleveland. His country's behavior over the next decade and a half of his life had to have been deeply disappointing to the old anti-imperialist: the gratuitous war with Spain; the constitutionally contorted annexation of Hawaiʻi; the brutal slaughter of thousands of Filipino warriors defending their homeland, as the Americans began to model the most vicious of European colonizers.

I wonder if looking back on his tenure as president, Grover Cleveland did not wonder if he might have done more. I doubt that the queen was so troubled. In the end, she did not simply speak of her ideals and beliefs. She acted on them. It is the consistency between what she believed, said, and how she behaved that makes her the beloved historical figure that she is. As for the president, it is noteworthy that he is not a more beloved and remembered leader in the United States. And that is due more, I think, to the deeply divided society that America has come to be.

It seems ironic that I should speak about Kanaka Maoli unity when our unwillingness to unite in one single political movement has occasioned the suspicion that we are not serious about nationhood. But the truth is that there is nearly universal admiration among Hawaiians for the queen—not the conqueror who created the unified state, but the stateswoman who protected her people from American arms and never surrendered her values or her dignity. That tells me that Kanaka Maoli are serious about having our nation and our government on our own terms; that we will resist, like Her Majesty, denying the Americans governance over our spirits and over our memories. Look closely, and you will see that we are on opposing trajectories, with Americans losing themselves in their ideologies and their avarice, and Hawaiians finding our strength and unity in the example of our queen.

As Hawaiians, we should be supportive of and grateful for national leaders, such as Cleveland and even former President Barack Obama, who both attempted to tap into the more compassionate and idealistic natures of their countries. But we have a special admiration for those who place their people and their ideals before their own lives. In the end we understand that words uttered by a leader are not enough, and that leaders must so value the ideals and the purpose behind those words that they will risk and even sacrifice themselves to defend them. That, for Kanaka Māoli, is what defines Ali'i.

"MY OFFICIAL PROTEST TO THE TREATY"

I, LILIUOKALANI OF HAWAII, by the Will of God named heir-apparent on the tenth day of April, A.D. 1877, and by the grace of God Queen of the Hawaiian Islands on the seventeenth day of January, A.D. 1893, do hereby protest against the ratification of a certain treaty, which, so I am informed, has been signed at Washington by Messrs, Hatch, Thurston, and Kinney, purporting to cede those Islands to the territory and dominion of the United States. I declare such a treaty to be an act of wrong toward the native and part-native people of Hawaii, an invasion of the rights of the ruling chiefs, in violation of international rights both toward my people and toward friendly nations with whom they have made treaties, the perpetuation of the fraud whereby the constitutional government was overthrown, and, finally, an act of gross injustice to me.

BECAUSE the official protests made by me on the seventeenth day of January, 1893, to the so-called Provisional Government was signed by me, and received by said government with the assurance that the case was referred to the United States of America for arbitration.

Yielded to Avoid Bloodshed

BECAUSE that protest and my communications to the United States Government immediately thereafter expressly declare that I yielded my authority to the forces of the United States in order to avoid bloodshed, and because I recognized the futility of a conflict with so formidable a power.

BECAUSE the President of the United States, the Secretary of State, and an envoy commissioned by them reported in official documents that my government was unlawfully coerced by the forces, diplomatic and naval, of the United States; that I was at the date of their investigations the constitutional ruler of my people.

BECAUSE neither the above-named commission nor the government which sends it has ever received any such authority from the registered voters of Hawaii, but derives its assumed powers from the so-called committee of public safety, organized on or about the seventeenth-day of January, 1893, said committee being composed largely of persons claiming American citizenship, and not one single Hawaiian was a member thereof, or in any way participated in the demonstration leading to its existence.

BECAUSE my people, about forty thousand in number, have in no way been consulted by those, three thousand in number, who claim the right to destroy the independence of Hawaii. My people constitute four-fifths of the legally qualified voters of Hawaii, and excluding those imported for the demands of labor, about the same proportion of the inhabitants.

Civic and Hereditary Rights

BECAUSE said treaty ignores, not only the civic rights of my people, but, further, the hereditary property of their chiefs. Of the 4,000,000 acres composing the territory said treaty offers to annex, 1,000,000 or 915,000 acres has in no way been heretofore recognized as other than the private property of the constitutional monarch, subject to a control in no way differing from other items of a private estate.

BECAUSE it is proposed by said treaty to confiscate said property, technically called the crown lands, those legally entitled thereto, either now or in succession, receiving no consideration whatever for estates, their title to which has been always undisputed, and which is legitimately in my name at this date.

BECAUSE said treaty ignores, not only all professions of perpetual amity and good faith made by the United States in former treaties with the sovereigns representing the Hawaiian people, but all treaties made by those sovereigns with other and friendly powers, and it is thereby in violation of international law.

BECAUSE, by treating with the parties claiming at this time the right to cede said territory of Hawaii, the Government of the United States receives such territory from the hands of those whom its own magistrates (legally elected by the people of the United States, and in office in 1893) pronounced fraudulently in power and unconstitutionally ruling Hawaii.

Appeals to President and Senate

THEREFORE I, LILIUOKALANI OF HAWAII, do hereby call upon the President of that nation, to whom alone I yielded my property and my authority, to withdraw said treaty (ceding said Islands) from further consideration. I ask the honorable Senate of the United States to decline to ratify said treaty, and I implore the people of this great and good nation, from whom my ancestors learned the Christian religion, to sustain their representatives in such acts of justice and equity as may be in accord with the principles of their fathers, and to the Almighty Ruler of the universe, to him who judgeth righteously, I commit my cause.

DONE at Washington, District of Columbia, United States of America, this seventeenth day of June, in the year eighteen hundred and ninety-seven.

LILIUOKALNI

JOSEPH HELELUHE

WOKEKI HELELUHE

JULIUS A. PALMER

From Lili'uokalani. 1898. *Hawaii's Story by Hawaii's Queen*. Boston, MA: Lee and Shepard Publishing, 354–357.

Portrait of Queen Lili'uokalani—Courtesy of the National Portrait Gallery, Smithsonian Institution: Gift of the Bernice Pauahi Bishop Museum, Menzie Dickson, NPG.80.320

CHAPTER 15

Henry Roe Cloud

ACTIVIST, INTELLECTUAL, AND MY GRANDFATHER

Renya Ramirez

Henry Roe Cloud (c. 1884–1950), a Ho-Chunk, was my grandfather. An important activist, policy maker, and intellectual in the early twentieth century, he argued that Native Americans should attend college to become educated warriors for their people, a major intellectual contribution of the time. He founded a college preparatory high school for young Native men, the American Indian Institute, a revolutionary educational approach, as during that same time the US government usually sent Indigenous youth to federal boarding schools, which offered an exclusively vocational curriculum. As an intellectual, Cloud challenged assimilation and argued for flexible and fluid notions of culture and identity. I argue that his educational experiences encouraged him to combine traditional Ho-Chunk and modern identities. First, I will discuss the lack of published writings about Cloud. Second, I will examine his Ho-Chunk and educational training. Next, I will consider his founding of a college preparatory high school. Finally, I will examine some last motivational thoughts he shared with Alaska Native students.

Overall, this chapter revolves around a speech Cloud gave to graduating Alaska Native students from Mt. Edgecumbe High School in Alaska in 1949. By analyzing his speech to Indigenous students, I hope to follow in my grandfather's footsteps and encourage contemporary Natives to attend college and become warriors for their Native communities.

Only very recently has Cloud been recognized in published writings, including five books, including my own book, and three published articles.[1] This is surprising, since he has been hailed as the most important Native policy maker of the early twentieth century:[2] he coauthored the Meriam Report of 1928 and was centrally involved in the Indian Reorganization Act of 1934, which founded modern tribal governments. One potential reason no books had been written about him until very recently is that some, including Hazel Hertzberg, called him "assimilated," because he was "progressive." This label is based in static notions of identity, in which one cannot be simultaneously Native, Christian, and modern.[3] It is also stuck in a binary, in which a "progressive" is assumed to assimilate into society, while a "traditional" is viewed as upholding deep linkages with their tribal traditions and nations. Hoxie, Iverson, and Porter have freed progressives from this binary that saw them with little connection to their tribal communities.[4] My work builds on these scholars by demonstrating how Henry Roe Cloud combined Native and modern identities. Too many scholars, including anthropologists and Pfister, a literary scholar, have studied Indigenous peoples by placing them within larger contexts, such as modernity, globalization, late capitalism, and neoliberalism.[5] Their primary focus on larger forces has meant there is not enough emphasis on Indigenous peoples' response to these forces from their own point of view. Indeed, the possibility that a "Native point of view" might be grounded in an Indigenous worldview is not explored enough. In contrast, this chapter will examine Cloud's creative response to the larger force of modernity, including founding a college preparatory high school for Native young men.

Cloud's Ho-Chunk name was Wo-Na-Xi-Lay-Hunka, meaning War-Chief, and described by him as "the Chief of the Place of Fear."[6] He was a member of the Thunderbird Clan—the clan he discusses, "obstructed and permitted war." According to my mother, Cloud's father told a significant prophecy about him. During a winter when food was scarce, Cloud did not eat for ten days. Then his father found a frozen beaver hut, killed the animals, traded some of their skins for corn, boiled the beaver meat, and arranged a feast. During the feast, his father discussed his prophecy. He told Cloud, "Eat, War-Chief, for I am hungry but will not eat until you have tasted food. I am old and

Portrait of Henry Roe Cloud—Courtesy of the Wisconsin Historical Society, ID# 140795

it makes no difference if I starve, but you are young. The future of the Winnebagoes (Ho-Chunks) lies within you." According to my mother, these words motivated Cloud throughout his life to always fight as a Ho-Chunk warrior for the survival of his people. This story also shares an essential value of a Ho-Chunk warrior identity, putting the survival of the young before one's own continued existence. At around twelve or thirteen years old, flu epidemics swept through our reservation, killing Cloud's grandmother and parents. According to my mother, her father suffered from much loneliness and grief after losing his close family members. These terrible losses influenced his decision to adopt the Roes informally, a white missionary couple, as his "mother" and "father" when he was a freshman at Yale University. This informal adoption fit within the Ho-Chunk cultural custom to adopt others to take the place of those who had passed away.

Cloud's name and clan membership were central to his identities as a Ho-Chunk man, leader, and modern-day warrior. From a Ho-Chunk perspective, a warrior not only fought in war for the survival of his people but also was a servant to his people, placing the needs of others first, including elders, children, and women. My mother taught me that pivotal to a Ho-Chunk warrior identity is learning strength and self-discipline, one reason the traditional practice of fasting was taught to children at an early age. Going without food and water for four days is not an easy task, but something that Ho-Chunk boys and girls practiced to become strong, self-disciplined, and close to "Ma-un-a" (Ho-Chunk word for Earthmaker or Creator).[7]

In a speech to graduating Alaska Native students in 1949, Cloud, for example, discusses the crucial role of fasting, and connecting to Ho-Chunk spirituality, including one's guardian spirit, the Great Spirit, and the four great spirits from the four directions. Cloud's examination of Ho-Chunk spirituality underscores the significance of fasting as a regimen and an institution that acts as a conduit to communicate to the spiritual world. His use of the words "institution" and "regime" underscores Ho-Chunk spirituality as a philosophy to be taken seriously rather than automatically discounted as pagan. He explains:

> *I was taught there were four great spirits in [the] universe, commanding the four corners of the universe, and under them there were a hierarchy of spirits innumerable and certain definite authorities and responsibilities were given these spirits to govern their section of the universe, and under these spirits there were other spirits who could communicate with human beings on the face of this earth and to those the Great Spirit intended that the Red men of America should approach and become acquainted with and have fellowship with in due time. And the institution that was set up for*

> *this communion and fellowship was fasting periods, eating nothing four days and nights. So I passed through that regime, and after the fourth day hunger seized my brother and me and thirst. And father and mother promised that we would have something to eat at the end of the fourth day's fasting. In the meantime, we went into the deep woods on the banks of the Missouri River to pray to these spirits that some (one) of them might take pity and speak out of the eternal heavens and to our souls.... We were encouraged not to be common men but to become uncommon men that the common man of this world without supernatural assistance did not amount to anything and success is prohibited at this time ... there must be in your soul a guardian spirit to assist you and that was what we were seeking and trying to achieve.*[8]

Cloud's arduous Ho-Chunk warrior training, which included fasting and learning to rely on spirituality, enabled him to weather many difficult challenges during this time period, including going without food when food was often scarce. It is also interesting that Cloud emphasizes that his Ho-Chunk traditional training encouraged him to become an "uncommon" man, since as a teenager he became a Christian and learned that Ho-Chunk spirituality was pagan. His discussion of fasting at sixty-five years old is much more Ho Chunk–centric as compared to his writing in a missionary journal in 1915, highlighting in a skeptical tone that he never did have a fasting vision.[9] These divergent perspectives point to a relaxing of his strict Christian position one year before his death, and his desire to connect to an Indigenous audience rather than a white missionary readership. His sharing of Ho-Chunk knowledge also reflects his respect for his tribal philosophy, encouraging young Alaska Natives to value their Indigenous philosophy. Furthermore, his discussion points to his development of a strong Ho-Chunk spiritual foundation upon which he later added his Christian training. In other words, rather than totally rejecting his Ho-Chunk spiritual training, Cloud greatly relied upon various aspects, such as learning self-discipline, strength, and self-control through fasting, and learning to gain strength from a spiritual power greater than himself.

Along with his training as a Ho-Chunk warrior, another pivotal aspect of his traditional Ho-Chunk education included listening to his grandmother tell him Ho-Chunk stories during winter. He recounts:

> *In winter times, our grandmother … would say if you grandchildren want any stories you must first get the wood and so we went into the woods and gathered all the dry wood and sticks that we could find because we lived in the woods…. And grandmother was very wise indeed to reserve her stories for the winter season when 50 degrees below zero was experienced and the ice-coated limbs were creaking above our heads above the wigwam. So we carried in the wood and we supplied all that she needed, and we were warm in the wigwam as we listened to the stories. She used to tell us about these four great spirits. We called it cosmology, and the world became a world full of spirits to me.... She often said that no child should eat the marrow of the bone because if he did he would lose his teeth. I later discovered that she had no teeth and could eat nothing but the marrow of the bone. She used to say that no child should eat a long ear of corn for … the long ear would be too long for the width of his stomach here. The long-eared corn would stick too far out and give him a pain in the side.... So we had nothing but short ears and grandmother and all the old people got all the long ears of corn.*[10]

Cloud's narrative portrays a sense of warmth and comfort, sitting together with his grandmother and family in their wigwam protected from the extreme Nebraska winters, challenging colonial representations of traditional Indigenous homes in negative terms as primitive, dirty, and disorganized.[11] Cloud emphasizes his grandmother's wisdom and how she taught him about Ho-Chunk spirituality, cosmology, and important values, including contributing to the well-being of the community by bringing firewood, helping tribal members stay warm during the frigid Nebraska winters. His grandmother also taught Ho-Chunk children to put the needs of elders first so they would have enough nutritional food to eat. By telling these stories, he shows the importance of Ho-Chunk humor, encouraging his audience of young Alaska Natives to laugh about his grandmother outwitting him, while she protected the elders' food supply. He also accentuates how central his grandmother was to his spiritual and intellectual development as a Ho-Chunk person.

Cloud switches the tone of his speech to Alaska Native students from humorous to somber when he discusses his brother being forcibly taken to Genoa, a federal Indian boarding school. The purpose of these schools was to assimilate Natives into American society, punishing Native students for speaking their Indigenous languages, and teaching subservience to whites rather than the leadership of their own people.[12] Cloud recounts:

> *One day a policeman came to our lodge in the wigwam in the deep woods and seized my older brother. They were taking him to [a federal boarding] school.... I was only 5 years of age. [H]e was my only playmate. I cried a great deal in losing him so my mother agreed that I would go along with him. He [the policeman] took me to a government institution called Genoa, Nebraska and I stayed there for awhile [sic] and then came back to the reservation boarding school where we played all manner of games and learned to speak English and [later] they took me to Santee Mission School in Northeastern Nebraska and there I was taught to learn a trade.*[13]

Cloud's emphasis of his tremendous suffering and grief regarding "losing" his brother, is an example of the terrible sorrow Native children experienced because of the federal government schools that separated small children from their parents. Because a policeman forcibly took Cloud's brother, and his mother allowed Cloud to accompany him, their parents became separated from two sons rather than only one. This separation must have caused enormous sadness for the entire family. Cloud recounts being forcibly taken, using the word "seized," to a federal boarding school, Genoa, while speaking more positively about attending a school on the Winnebago Reservation, probably because he was close to his extended family and tribe, saying, "We played all manner of games." The words "taken" and "seized" speak volumes regarding the lack of control, distress, and anguish Cloud experienced. His incredibly difficult federal boarding school experience encouraged him to struggle to end this policy by coauthoring the Meriam Report of 1928, which documented the abuses of the federal boarding schools.

After Santee Indian Mission School, Cloud attended Mount Herman College Preparatory School. In his speech to Alaska Natives, he discusses an experience there, combining knowledge gained from his Ho-Chunk traditional education with his white schooling. He also emphasizes his loneliness as an orphan, separated from his extended family and tribe. His sense of loneliness must have been profound, especially since whites surrounded him and he must have experienced disrespect and racism as a young Native man at Mount Herman. He explains:

> *[The] spirit [and importance of labor] went with me to the Mount Herman School in Massachusetts. And there they had a work hour system where they were also taught the dignity of labor, learning things intellectually by doing things, and knowing how to bear responsibility for each individual, day by day. One winter I had to dig a ditch. It was Christmas time; my father and mother had passed away. I had no home. I could not go to any home. While all the other students went back to their home to celebrate Christmas, they set me to digging a ditch and we had to dig that ditch 15 feet deep.... Without this, the pipes would freeze during the winters in Massachusetts. I stood digging that ditch with pickaxe and shovel and I felt sorry for myself. They put me in here to dig this ditch because they knew I had no home to go to and I had to stay here. I had that spirit in my heart. When one day a young lad was placed beside me by the name of James McConaghy. He lived on the campus. He did not need to go away to school. His father and mother were there and his father was one of the great teachers of that institution and they sent him with me to dig the ditch. He did not have to work in that ditch. And I began to revise my feeling. Perhaps they put this young fella with me to dig this ditch because the water pipe that we are laying here will be a source of great joy to the whole community. It will bring about contentment, health, and satisfaction to thousands of people in this neighborhood.... I learned that I wasn't placed in there because I was an orphan lad, but because of the great blessing my job would result in the entire community.*[14]

In this quote, his discussion of labor is not so much about the white notion of individual self-improvement, but rather about contributing to the overall community, which is a Native-oriented concept. Thus, he refashions a Eurocentric notion about the importance of individual labor into a Native idea about the significance of work in order to contribute to the community as a whole. Indeed, contributing to Native community well-being is an essential Ho-Chunk warrior value. He also teaches these Alaska Native students the dignity of labor and its ability to teach people, whatever one's class status. Thus, Cloud combines a white concept about individual labor with his Ho-Chunk traditional values, supporting the creation of a Native male modern identity. Another lesson he teaches these students is that one should view the world "half full" rather than "half empty." In other words, it is important to see the positives in one's experience rather than the difficulties. Whites ordering Cloud to dig a huge ditch during Christmas break could have sparked deep feelings of oppression and disrespect. Rather than discussing these kinds of feelings, however, he chooses to focus on his contribution to the overall community, accentuating his lack of victimhood.

After graduating from Mount Herman College Preparatory School, he attended Yale University, becoming the first full-blooded Native American to graduate with a bachelor's degree (1910) and a master's degree (1914). He recounts:

> *As I entered [Yale] I began to work my way through the institution. I didn't have any money. I entered it with only 60 dollars in my pocket and they required in those days something over 1000 dollars a year. I had the confidence that laboring with my hands, doing all sorts of jobs, waiting on tables, doing jobs for the rich people, selling Navajo rugs, selling all kinds of articles to the student body, selling tickets at the great university games that I could somehow make ends meet. When I graduated I was still 60 dollars in debt, but having paid all the other expenses from my own labors.... I went into all kinds of athletics.... I gained confidence because I could compete in athletics. I gained confidence because I could compete in oratory and debate. And one of my competitors was the president Robert Taft's son.... When I stood up against him, debated against him and won prizes on the same platform with a man whose father had been President of the United States before, I began to feel a welling up of confidence in myself. Why I began to realize that I can do things just as this man can and somehow my spirit became ready for the battle or any sort of a battle that might come my way.*[15]

Cloud describes himself as a hard worker and self-supporting, challenging dominant ideas that Natives were indolent. He talks about selling Native cultural objects among other things, in order to support himself financially. Native Americans selling cherished cultural objects, unfortunately, was a common practice, especially when poor.[16] He learned quickly how precious Native artifacts were to curious whites, and he used it to help support himself.[17] This self-supporting theme is inextricably linked to Cloud's proclamation of his masculine influence as a "self-made" man of importance who came from humble beginnings.[18] During the nineteenth century, the "self-made" man personified economic and personal success, exemplifying a new type of daring white American man. In the nineteenth century, author Horatio Alger Jr. was a "self-made" man, who was a hero integral to individualism. During the late nineteenth and early twentieth centuries, racial justice movements created leaders as examples of heroic masculinity. Men such as Frederick Douglas, Booker T. Washington, and W. E. B Du Bois were heroic combatants for racial equality. Distinct from white ideas of the "self-made" man, these men were heroic because they came from modest beginnings to achieve personal success, and demonstrated a strong public dedication to their racial communities.[19] Similarly, Cloud indigenized the idea of the "self-made" man, becoming a heroic fighter for Natives, and helping him increase his power in the public sphere during a time when white society viewed Native men as "non-men."[20]

This quote also emphasizes Cloud's prowess as an orator and a debater, which was grounded in his Ho-Chunk grandmother's storytelling and oratory training. He carried his Ho-Chunk oratory skills with him to Yale, and honed them by rehearsing speeches and creating arguments. His public speaking competition with the president's son improved his confidence and prepared him for "battle." Indeed, he highlights his Native masculinity and warrior identity, using word battles to defeat his rich white male adversaries, demonstrating his verbal and intellectual abilities, defying dominant notions that Natives were inarticulate and slow. He also highlights his poverty as compared to Yale's rich white community, while emphasizing that his lower economic status did not interfere with attending college or achieving in an elite white institution like Yale. In this way, he attempts to motivate Alaska Native students to go to college, who very likely were poor, and college must have seemed out of reach.

By indigenizing the popular white notion of the "self-made" man, Cloud asserted a Native heroic masculinity during a time period when the American western novel had greatly reduced Native male power. This masculine power was encapsulated into opposites between those who remain standing and those who fall down, between erect men on horseback and those whose "natural" position is viewed as lying down. Those lying down were portrayed as "non-men," a category that generally included Indians, Mexicans, small children, and women. Even though Natives defeated Custer, for example, Custer is always portrayed as dying on his feet, asserting his white male masculinity.[21] Cloud's assertion of his "self-made" masculine character was an innovative strategy to increase his masculine power so that he would not be viewed as a Native "non-man."

Cloud's involvement in athletics was another strategy to be viewed as a *real* man instead of a Native "non-man." At the turn of the century, white masculinity not only relied on the image of the frontiersman, but also stereotypical notions of Native masculinity. White men embraced an ideal that stressed physical prowess, including stereotypical notions of Native warrior identity, while creating a linkage between white supremacy and male dominance. Custer, for example, embodied masculine notions of a warrior, and a masculine drive to conquer and succeed.[22] Cloud's involvement in athletics could be linked to the popular Native male stereotype of a man with innate physical prowess. At the same time, involving himself in athletics could also be viewed as his attempt to reappropriate the male prowess imagery stolen from stereotypical Native notions of masculinity, and in the process increase his own masculine power.

Cloud's participation in sports was also a way for him to connect to his Ho-Chunk identity while being away from his tribe in Winnebago, Nebraska. Native Americans have been involved in physical activity and games since before colonization. Lacrosse, for example, is a game that the Haudenosaunee (Iroquois) and other Northeast tribes, as well as the Ho-Chunk, played. It was and is a very physically demanding sport, as players must run fast, cover much distance, and have much dexterity, and because players catch and throw a ball using a net attached to a long stick. The Ho-Chunk also competed against each other with bows and arrows, a sport now called archery, and played the game "Chunkey." In "Chunkey," a round "chunkey" stone was rolled over the ground or ice, while several players threw spears to try to demonstrate where the stone would stop. The closest player, whose spear did not hit the stone, won the game. These games were important for the Ho-Chunk, because they contributed to dexterity, improving hand-eye coordination and endurance, both skills needed for hunting and waging war.[23] Cloud played baseball on the Winnebago Reservation, so his involvement in athletics at a white school was a continuation of his reservation athletic activities and, therefore, a way for him to feel a connection to his Ho-Chunk tribe and his people when he was away at school.

After graduating from Yale, Cloud returned to the Winnebago Reservation to work with his people, including preaching Christianity. He recounts, "After these experiences, I went back to my tribe, because there was a provocation upon my soul to do something for them. I could not always receive, receive, receive."[24] His decision to return to Winnebago, Nebraska, challenges the purpose of the federal boarding schools, which was to encourage Natives to assimilate and live away from their tribe among whites. He was also involved in founding the American Indian Institute, a Christian college preparatory school for Native young men, which occupied him from 1910 to 1931. He describes:

> *I founded the American Indian Institute for young [Indian] men in the states. And there I taught them the work system. They had to work, rich or poor—that was the life of the institution. An Osage boy came [to the school] from the Oklahoma country and he had money from oil, royalties. We had him work along with the other boys. We harvested great fields of wheat. He stood at one end of the field of wheat and looked way down yonder and had to shuck this wheat. After perspiring heavily at the end of one row, he turned to me and said, "I now know what goes into a loaf of bread." He had been receiving $3000 every three months. He did not have to work, but after graduation he took a job just like any boy would and rose in that job until he became an official in the Greyhound lines.*[25]

Cloud again discusses the importance of labor for Native students, while arguing that one's upper-class status should not stop a Native person from benefiting from work experience. Cloud's belief in the white idea of the work system was consistent with his Ho-Chunk warrior training regarding the significance of hard work. It was also similar to traditional Ho-Chunk education regarding the pivotal importance of working hard and working fast. Helen Lincoln of Little Priest Tribal College discusses how Ho-Chunk traditional education revolves around "wadesak." "Wade" means work and "sak" means fast, and it also means to enjoy working and do it well.[26] Thus,

Cloud combines a Ho-Chunk notion about the importance of hard work with a white idea regarding labor, ultimately building upon his traditional Ho-Chunk educational training.

Similarly, in 1911, Cloud argues that rather than try to erase Native knowledge as part of the federal boarding school's civilization training, one should build upon existing Indigenous knowledge. He explains:

> *Certain government Indian employees come into the Service and look upon the Indian and his ways of thought as beneath them, and think [they] are so common as to merit very little respect and therefore anything that is Indian is not worth preserving and not given much thought.... The right way to look at this question of Indian philosophy is to examine it very carefully and see how it contributes to the happiness and satisfaction of this individual. You make it possible for the Indian to build on to what he already has. You have to proceed from the known to the unknown. You bring him a new philosophy entirely unknown to him. This mistake is being made in the attempt to civilize the Indian.*[27]

Cloud challenges the lack of respect federal government employees had for Native thought and philosophy, while he argues against assimilation and instead for a flexible and fluid notion of culture where Natives could combine Indigenous and white knowledge. His flexible and fluid notion of culture is a radical departure from static notions of culture, which the federal government policy of assimilation was based upon. Assimilationists assumed that dominant culture would overpower subordinated culture. Assimilation was viewed as a one-way process in which the oppressed would be forced to give up their own ways and replace it with dominant culture and ideas.[28] Rather than erasing Indigenous knowledge and thought, Cloud incorporates white knowledge regarding labor that was consistent with his traditional Ho-Chunk educational training about working hard.

Cloud's objective of a high school for Indigenous boys was very rare. During this time, many argued that secondary education was not necessary for everyone. Many of the high schools served whites—only a few were available for African Americans, and even fewer permitted Native Americans.[29] At the same time, his choice to admit only Native males was problematic, since Native women and their need for leadership training was not provided, potentially adding to power disparities between women and men in tribal communities. These power differentials were partially caused by government boarding schools, where patriarchal notions of gender norms were emphasized, teaching Indian girls to be subservient to Native males. The school held powwows and encouraged the study of Indigenous stories and arts,[30] a radical approach to education during a time when everything Indian was to be abolished in government boarding schools. Indeed, the school's Literary Society inspired students to consider the relationship between their own traditional tribal stories and Shakespeare. This comparison was an approach for them to comprehend a complicated Eurocentric story.[31] His educational philosophy worked to build on Native knowledge rather than erase it as he had experienced in the federal boarding schools.

Cloud proposed a Native-centric educational approach for Indian boys. He wanted to educate a new generation of Native American leaders by providing Native young men a Christian-based nondenominational high school education. Harry Coonts, a Pawnee, and a student at the school, explains his grasp of Cloud's leadership training: "[The American Indian Institute] taught Christian leadership, that is to say an Indian man was to fight for his people to get justice."[32] Thus, Cloud combined his Ho-Chunk notion of a warrior identity with Christianity, changing the white notion of Christianity into an instrument for Native goals and objectives. In this way, Cloud indigenized a male modern Christian identity. Cloud's teaching of a Christian warrior identity certainly was not taught in government boarding schools, which encouraged Indians to assimilate and be subservient to whites, and concentrated on vocational training. Cloud also dreamed that his school could become a junior college in the future. It had classes that began in the sixth grade and went through high school.

Cloud discusses other pivotal Ho-Chunk warrior values with the graduating Mt. Edgecumbe High school students, including pride and courage. He emphasizes:

> *And the [Indian] race needs pride in your origin. Never be ashamed that you are an American Indian or Native of Alaska. Never be ashamed. I am thinking of the Iroquois [Haudenosaunee] tribe in the States. They had self-government.... They had a constitution followed upon that of the clan organization.... Benjamin Franklin took lessons from their tribal organization and put [these lessons]*

> *in the U.S. Constitution of the United States of America. Your [Indian] race has accomplished things of that sort of world import. You should lift your head and be proud that you are a Native American. And then you should have courage. The Indian race despises a coward.... There is philosophy among my [Ho-Chunk] people when the smoke of battle clears away let the enemy see the scars on your face [not] on your back. Face forward in the fight [against] all odds and costs. That is applicable to your vocation and anything you propose to do in this life.*[33]

Cloud challenges the colonial notion that Natives were an inferior race by emphasizing that these young Alaska Native students should not be ashamed of their Indigenous identity but rather should be very proud. He disputes the settler colonial historical narrative about a heroic struggle between good and evil, viewing Indigenous peoples as evil and settlers as good. Cloud challenges this good versus evil binary by arguing that one of the founding fathers of the United States, Benjamin Franklin, learned from the Haudenosaunee Constitution, and introduced Indigenous concepts into his formulation of the US constitution. In Cloud's historical rendering, Natives were not evil, but instead had ideas of "world import" that were so powerful they influenced the writing of the US Constitution. In this way, Cloud portrayed Natives as intellectuals in their own right, who had systems of government that were equal (if not better) than the colonial government. Cloud also emphasizes that the Haudenosaunee had "self-government." It is important to note that self-government has a settler colonial connotation, in which tribal governments become subsets to the US colonial nation as part of the Indian Reorganization Act of 1934. Regardless of the colonial connotation of self-government, Cloud's discussion assumes that, before the coming of the whites, Natives had their own governments that were just as important as the US government. Cloud also highlights the Ho-Chunk warrior value regarding courage. He encourages the students to connect to this warrior idea and to work hard in their vocations. By combining an Indigenous idea with a modern one, he indigenizes the modern concept of a vocation.

Furthermore, Cloud tells an inspiring story to motivate Alaska Native students to rely upon their educational training to reach their goals in life. Cloud makes a connection to Edgecumbe Mountain that overlooks the school, comparing the goal of mounting its summit to the Alaska Native students reaching their educational goals. He discusses:

> *Lastly … I have been admiring this wonderful mountain over here, Edgecombe Mountain, for which this institution is named, the peak for all of you to strive after, the top of that ridge of that mountain of learning. An Indian chief when he was dying … would give his chiefdom-ship to the man who gave him the best present. So a young Indian ran out and one brought him a deer. Another brought him not only food but [also] clothing. The next man brought him a pine bough. The third man brought him an aspen leaf [from] higher up the mountain. These men wanted to demonstrate that they worked hard for the gifts they brought to him. The fourth man came, and he said, "Oh Chief I come with empty hands. I have no present to give thee, but I have seen the Sun." He had been on top of the mountain and experienced the glory of seeing everything in its relationship to the wide expanse of the world in front of him and he gained wisdom as well as intellectual power having reached the summit of that mountain. So it will be with the education that you received in this institution.*[34]

Cloud conveys a story about young Native men who were competing with each other to become chief by bringing their leader various gifts. The last man did not bring a material possession, but brought something that was more powerful than any possession, and that was knowledge and wisdom that comes from "seeing everything in its relationship to the wide expanse of the world," which, according to Cloud, was what the students' education had given them. The meaning of this Indigenous story is that knowledge and wisdom are more important than material possessions, which is a Native-centric idea.

Cloud finishes his speech with an encouraging and a prophetic vision about Alaska Natives and the state's future. He states:

> *Here in Alaska if you the Native Americans will build up your economic conditions.... You have a good boat, plenty of fish, or … your timber resources whatever they maybe.... Labor and work are the greatest things in the world today.... You will grow up*

> *with young, fresh, Alaska. We in the states look with great hope and anticipation to your young people with visions and ambitions and make this young Alaska what it shall be. I dare say United States will not make what Alaska will be, it will contribute much, but Alaska is going to be made by Natives who live here and … determination will make Alaska what it will be. I congratulate you and your institution and the wonderful opportunities to achieve something of world import.*[35]

While Cloud looks over the fresh, young faces of Alaska Native students in the high school auditorium, he imagines what Alaska could be from an Indigenous perspective. He envisions these Alaska Natives building up their economic base, relying on fishing, timber, and other industries, to make "young Alaska" into an economically formidable force throughout the world. He spoke these words before the passage of the Alaska Native Claims Settlement Act of 1971, which authorized the establishment of Alaska Native for-profit corporations as a tool of economic development.[36] Here, Cloud rethinks economics from an Indigenous viewpoint, envisaging how Alaska Natives could build a strong economic base for their people. In this way, he indigenized modernity for the survival of Alaska Native nations.

In sum, Cloud was an intellectual, who argued that Natives should attend college so they could become educated warriors—warriors who could fight for their people. He discussed flexible and fluid notions of culture and identity, challenging static notions common during this time period. He challenged the federal boarding school's vocational nature by founding a college preparatory high school for Native young men. He developed a sense of a Native male modern identity by adding white concepts that were consistent with his core Ho-Chunk philosophy and educational training. His additive, as well as flexible and fluid, cultural, and intellectual methodology disputes the subtractive and static approach of the incredibly painful assimilation campaign of the federal boarding schools.

CHAPTER 16

In the Tradition of Honor

NATIVE AMERICAN VETERANS OF THE TWENTIETH AND TWENTY-FIRST CENTURIES

Steven J. Crum

Throughout Indian Country, veterans receive a particular status of respect. The tradition of warrior and protector evolved from protecting one's people and territory to serving in the US military in every major conflict.

Native Americans were involved in the first major war of the twentieth century—World War I. Upon entering the war, non-Indians debated whether Indians should be integrated into the regular armed forces, or to serve in all-Indian segregated units like African Americans. Those who favored all-Indian units were Edward Ayers, member of the Board of Indian Commissioners, a federal watchdog board established in the nineteenth century to police the activities of the Bureau of Indian Affairs (BIA); Julius Kahn, US House of Representatives of California, who submitted H.R. 3970 in April 1917 to create Indian military units; and Joseph K. Dixon, American Clergyman, lecturer, and philosopher, who wanted to honor

Indians with the construction of a large statue in New York to be called the "National American Indian Memorial." These non-Indians wanted segregated all-Indian military units to carry forth the Native American "warrior" tradition of the nineteenth century.[1]

Enlistment Percentages

American Indians and Alaska Natives serve in the armed forces at five times the national average. Considering the population of the United States is approximately 1.4 percent Native and the military is 1.7 percent Native (not including those that did not disclose their identity), Native people have the highest per-capita involvement of any population to serve in the US military.

They also have a higher concentration of women service members than all other groups. Nearly 20 percent of American Indians and Alaska Natives service members were women, while 15.6 percent of all other servicemembers were women.

From the National Indian Council on Aging, Inc. *American Indian Veterans Have Highest Record of Service*. URL: https://www.nicoa.org/american-indian-veterans-have-highest-record-of-military-service.

In contrast, other influential non-Indians wanted Indians to be integrated with white soldiers. Cato Sells, commissioner of the BIA favored integration because this position supported the BIA's major policy of the period, which was assimilation and Americanization of Indians. Richard Pratt, former military officer of the Civil War, founder of the BIA off-reservation boarding school concept, and longtime superintendent of the Carlisle Indian School, also favored Indian integration in the military. Additionally, Arthur C. Parker (Seneca), corresponding secretary of the Society of American Indians (SAI), the first intertribal organization of the twentieth century, also favored integration. In the end, the integrationist position prevailed, and Indian soldiers of World War I (WWI) served in the various military branches in 1917 and 1918.[2]

Numbers vary regarding the number of Native Americans who served in the military during WWI. One number indicated that 17,060 served in all branches of the military. Of this overall number, approximately two-thirds enlisted or volunteered, whereas one-third were subject to the draft. There are several reasons why such a high number volunteered for the military. One factor was to escape economic poverty and federal government

Choctaw Telephone Squad

A little-known contribution of American Indians during WWI was the use of tribal languages to send coded messages. When most people think of the Indian "codetalkers," they are usually referring to the Indian veterans of WWII. However, it was a group of Choctaw soldiers in 1918 that presented the strategy of their language as a code.

"One Choctaw was placed at each of the Allied field camps to send and receive messages in the Choctaw language.... According to tribal records, nineteen Choctaw served in the communication corps as what became known as "codetalkers," though they've never been officially recognized for their contribution by the United Sates government."

From Robinson and Lucas. 2008. *From Warriors to Soldiers*, Bloomington, IN: iUniverse, 46–47.

"Choctaw Telephone Squad" 1919. (1962-08-6453)—Courtesy of the Wanamaker Collections, Indiana University

paternalism that existed on Indian reservations. On many reservations, tribal members had to secure daily passes from the BIA superintendent to shop off-reservation for a few hours. A second factor was to advance the "warrior tradition" of the nineteenth century and even earlier. Many young men of the early twentieth century had heard stories from their grandfathers who talked about military exploits that happened during the "Indian-white wars" of the nineteenth century. Going back even further in time, young men, based on the oral tradition, heard about "Indian-Indian" wars that preceded the coming of the Europeans. Being a warrior brought honor not only to an individual but also his family and clan and band. A third factor was American patriotism that was generated in the twenty-four off-reservation BIA boarding schools. Students were introduced to military regimentation and American patriotism, including the saluting of the American flag.[3] One Indian veteran, Andrew Black Hawk (Ho-Chunk) said the following about the flag: "I love my flag, so I went to the old world [Europe] to fight the Germans. If I had not loved the American flag it would not have come back, but now we are still using it."[4]

Some tribes went so far as to declare war against the Germans, including the Oneida of Wisconsin and the Onondaga of New York.[5] These tribes had a strong tradition of emphasizing sovereignty even before the arrival of the Europeans. After the formation of the United States, the tribes continued to assert an independent sovereignty status to varying degrees. Other tribes sided with the United States because they viewed the United States as "Indian Country" and that it needed to be protected from European enemies.

Thomas Yallup

"As Americans, in fact the original Americans, this war [WWII] really and truly means something to us. Our young men have gone forth to war and have been cited for bravery just as in 1918. Because we are Indians doesn't mean that we do not have as much at stake in the land as you do. Our stake may not mean so much in dollars, but in respect and feeling it means as much and probably more, because of our religion about the land and its resources."

From Yallup, Thomas. 2008. "Yakama." In *From Warriors to Soldiers*, ed. Robinson and Lucas, Bloomington, IN: iUniverse, 49.

On the other hand, a few tribes opposed Indian involvement in WWI. For example, on June 5, 1917, some Navajos ran out the BIA agent who was assigned to register them for the draft on the Navajo Reservation. And on the same day, a group of Utes on the Ute Mountain Reservation in Colorado refused to register for the draft. According to US Selective Service laws, reservation agents and superintendents were assigned to register Indians for the military. There was more than one reason why some Indians opposed the draft. Most Indians were not US citizens in 1917 when the draft process took place. In fact, Indians would not become US citizens until 1924. Other tribal individuals opposed the draft due to peace treaties that had been made with their ancestors in the nineteenth century. Still another reason was that a percentage of Indians harbored negative feelings toward the American government because of how they had been treated in the United States. At the time of WWI, the BIA was at its zenith in carrying out its assimilation and Americanization campaign against the Indian population in general, and placing young children in distant off-reservation boarding schools.

Perhaps the best example of Indian opposition to WWI came from a group of Goshutes from the Goshute Reservation that borders the Utah–Nevada state line. Seven Goshutes, three who were of eligible draft age (between twenty-one and thirty-one) and four elders much older than thirty-one, opposed the draft. In response to their protest, military officers from Fort Douglas, Utah, traveled to Goshute and arrested all seven. Very quickly the officers became aware that only three were eligible; four were not. Additionally, none of the Goshutes were US citizens. The Fort Douglas troops had no choice but to quickly release all seven protestors.[6]

When WWI ended, Native Americans across the nation were impacted by its legacy. For example, in 1920, a group of Indian veterans in Minneapolis created an organization called "American Indians of the War."[7] It became an intertribal and urban-based group that brought together Indian veterans after the war. In Oklahoma, the Comanche Nation recognized WWI veterans at powwow dances. Regarding this activity, Robert Coffey, a Comanche leader, said the following: "They were given a reception, honored with a dance for them. My brother-in-law was a [WWI] veteran and we went over to Indiahona where they were going to have a dance."[8] In 1928, the Comanche and other tribes of southwestern Oklahoma created the "All-Indian American Indian Legion" in Lawton, Oklahoma, to recognize WWI Indian veterans. Perhaps one of the biggest legacies of the post-WWI period was that all Indian veterans were granted US citizenship on November 6, 1919.

Some twenty-three years after the end of WWI, the United States became involved in World War II (1941–1945). Although the numbers vary, most authors agree that approximately 25,000 Indians fought in the various branches of the military, either in Europe or the Pacific Front. Additionally, some 40,000 other Indians, both men and women, left their respective reservations, moved to cities, and became involved in domestic wartime jobs.[9]

Although the BIA initially wanted Indians to serve in all-Indian divisions to preserve Native identity, the War Department opposed segregation for Indians. Thus, nearly all WWII Indian soldiers served in integrated military units. However, on occasion, a dark-skinned Indian ended up in segregated all-Black units.[10] This happened to Ben Hull, a full-blood Shoshone from the Duck Valley Reservation in Nevada. He was stationed in the South with Black troops for his military training.

Thousands of Indians, primarily men, enlisted in the armed forces for the same reasons they did in WWI. This included upholding the tribal "warrior tradition," escaping reservation economic poverty, upholding American patriotism taught in the BIA boarding schools, and seeking adventure in the larger world. In 1942, twenty-four high school students from the Stewart Indian School, near Carson City, Nevada, enlisted in the marines. This included my father, Earl Crum (Western Shoshone) from the Duck Valley Reservation. While stationed in the Pacific, he contracted malaria, and hospitalization saved his life.

Several Indians became military heroes during WWII. Jack Montgomery (Creek) received the Congressional Medal of Honor. In the Battle of Anzio in Italy, he killed eleven German soldiers and captured an additional thirty-two others.[11] Ira Hayes (Pima) from the Gila River Reservation in Arizona, became a hero after he and five other marines lifted the US flag on Mount Suribachi on the Japanese island of Iwo Jima in the spring of 1945. The flag photograph became a symbol of impending US military victory over Japan.

Louis Charlo and Montana HB 717

In the fierce battle for Iwo Jima, there were two flag raisings on the summit of Mount Suribachi. Private First Class Louis Charlo was with the patrol that first reached the summit. They descended to the base and returned as group of about forty and secured a small US flag to a pipe and raised it. A second flag raising later that day was captured in a photograph by Joe Rosenthal. Rosenthal's photograph became an iconic image of the war. Consequently, Louis Charlo and his patrol that raised the first flag have been lost in obscure history.

"In the last letter Charlo wrote to his parents, sometime during that following week, he wrote, 'I was part of the fracas atop Suribachi.' Louis Charlo died less than a week later, killed as he was attempting to rescue Private Ed McLaughlin, a wounded buddy stranded in an area of the Iwo Jima battlefield known as the Meat Grinder. Charlo was carrying McLaughlin on his back and both were killed just a few feet from safety, according to Ray Whelan, Charlo's platoon leader."

From McNeel, Jack. 2011. "American Indian Marine was Part of Iwo Jima, but Kept out of the Spotlight." Indian Country Today, Nov. 7, 2011.

The Veteran Warrior's Society on the Flathead Indian Reservation in Montana, home of the Confederated Salish and Kootenai Tribes, is working to see that Louis Charlo is granted the Congressional Medal of Honor posthumously. Montana senator Max Baucus was able to have Charlo's Bronze Medal elevated to a Silver Medal (Cajune Interview with Dan Jackson, 2016).

Charlo's deeds remain alive among the members of his community, and are now recorded on the tribal Veterans Memorial in Pablo, Montana. In 2019, the State of Montana honored and chronicled the military history of Louis Charlo with House Bill 717.

Confederated Salish and Kootenai Tribes' Veterans Memorial
by artist Corwin Clairmont—Courtesy of Amaru Bennett

Excerpt from Montana House Bill 717:

AN ACT ESTABLISHING THE LOUIS CHARLES CHARLO MEMORIAL HIGHWAY IN MISSOULA COUNTY…

WHEREAS, Louis Charles Charlo, a U.S. Marine from the Confederated Salish and Kootenai Tribes, served in crucial roles for the raising of the two U.S. flags on Mount Suribachi during the Battle of Iwo Jima;

…

WHEREAS, the Battle of Iwo Jima was a major battle in which the U.S. Marine Corps landed on and eventually captured the island of Iwo Jima from the Imperial Japanese Army during World War II;

and WHEREAS, Louis Charles Charlo ascended Mount Suribachi with three fellow Marines on the morning of February 23, 1945, to conduct route reconnaissance and determine enemy disposition on the summit prior to the first flag raising;

and WHEREAS, it is traditionally known that Louis Charles Charlo participated in the raising of the first U.S. flag, which came from aboard U.S.S. Missoula, on Mount Suribachi;

and WHEREAS, Louis Charles Charlo provided security on the summit of Mount Suribachi for the raising of the second U.S. flag, immortalized by Associated Press photographer Joseph Rosenthal;

and WHEREAS, Louis Charles Charlo was killed as he was attempting to rescue Private Ed McLaughlin, a wounded soldier stranded in an area of the Iwo Jima battlefield known as the Meat Grinder;

…

and WHEREAS, Louis Charles Charlo earned the Presidential Unit Citation Ribbon with one bronze star, the Asiatic-Pacific Campaign Ribbon with one bronze star, the World War II Victory Medal, and the Purple Heart; and

…

WHEREAS, the 66th Legislature of the State of Montana honors Louis Charles Charlo.

Perhaps the most famous group of WWII veterans were the Navajo Code Talkers. Although there were 420 total Code Talkers, what stood out was the so-called original twenty-nine. The government selected the first group on the Navajo Reservation. Once they left the reservation from Fort Wingate, they ended up at the Marine Corps Recruitment Center in San Diego in May 1942. While in training, the original group invented 220 terms over a period of months and then graduated from Camp Elliott in southern California. Once trained, the marine corps sent the Code Talkers to the Pacific Front to a number of islands, including Bougainville, Guadalcanal, Peleliu, and Guam. The Code Talkers remained on active duty until the Japanese government officially surrendered on August 14, 1945. None of their codes were ever broken by the Japanese.[12]

The Navajo Code Talkers did not forget their Native culture and history. For example, First Class Chester Nez (Dine), one of the original twenty-nine, gave vivid accounts of Navajo life while in the military and after. He learned English in a BIA boarding school. While on active duty, he kept a medicine bag that contained corn pollen. When the Code Talkers returned to the United States in 1945, they went through Navajo ceremonies, which included the "Bad Way" ceremony for cleansing purposes.[13]

Navajo Religion

"My Navajo religion is my religion that I'll never forget. They did a protection ceremony for me before I went overseas, and that's what brought me back. And when I got back, they did another one to purify my soul. This one medicine man did that for me."

From Foster, Harold. 2008. "Navajo Codetalker." In *From Warriors to Soldiers*, ed. Robinson and Lucas. Bloomington, IN: iUniverse, 73.

Navajos were not the only tribal Code Talkers who served the United States in WWII. Seven Lakota from South Dakota served as Code Talkers in Australia. A third group of Code Talkers were Comanche from Oklahoma. Seventeen were trained as Code Talkers and sent on active duty to Europe in June 1944. Several of them recall vivid accounts of European battles. Regarding the Normandy Invasion in 1944, Roderick Red Elk stated: "Everything was going fine until we hit the beach.... That's when I realized that this must be the real thing."[14] Once on the European mainland, Forrest Kassanavoid said: "I think it was in the Huertgen Forest … that forest over there is so thick … we were just getting into Germany."[15] When the Germans surrendered in May 1945, all the Comanche Code Talkers had survived and returned home.

Joseph Medicine Crow

Joseph Medicine Crow served as a private in the US Army, Company K, 411th Infantry, and 103rd Division during World War II. Upon his return from the war, he recalled his war experiences to Crow elders. Remarkably, he had completed the four requirements to become a Crow chief: (1) capture a well-guarded horse (from a group of about fifty of Hitler's SS officers who were on horseback), (2) take an enemy's weapon, (3) count coup (an honor earned by touching or striking an enemy during battle), and (4) lead a war party and return safely. Mr. Medicine Crow received the Bronze Star, the Legion d'Honneur, the highest French Order of Merit, both military and civilian. In 2009, Mr. Medicine Crow was awarded the Presidential Medal of Freedom.

From Medicine Crow and Viola. 2006. *Counting Coup: Becoming a Crow Chief on the Reservation and Beyond*. National Geographic.

Joseph Medicine Crow receives the Presidential Medal of Freedom from President Obama in 2009—Photographer Pete Souza

Besides Native men, some women also served the military during WWII. Jeradine Brown (Chickasaw) served in the Women's Auxiliary Corps in 1943. Before serving, she earned a bachelor's degree in education from Oklahoma A & M (today's Oklahoma State University). During the war, she worked in the Pentagon as a developer of military film. One of her jobs was to develop the film of the bombing of Japan in 1945. Regarding this experience, she wrote: "We were so used to seeing buildings knocked down, but what we saw there was just blocks and blocks of devastation. It was so much more intense."[16]

Like WWI, some Native Americans opposed involvement in WWII. Several Hopi traditionalists chose not to register for the draft, and a few were imprisoned during the duration of the war. One young Hopi, Thomas Jenkins (later known as Thomas Banyaca) spent two separate times behind bars. Jenkins said the following words in April 1944: "Today I stand before you a prisoner of the Federal Government … I have been called by some, a traitor, trouble maker, agitator and even been suspected of being a German spy.... I plead not guilty."[17] Another Hopi, Fred Pahongva, said in July 1944: "It has been the long belief of the Hopi that they should not participate in the present war.... This belief is based upon their religion and tradition."[18] But not all Hopi opposed US involvement in WWII. A few became Code Talkers and were honored by the government years later in 2012.[19]

After the end of WWII, Native Americans were recognized for their service in a number of ways. Francis Muncey (Western Shoshone) from Nevada died on the European front in early 1945. In recognition of Muncey, the residents of Battle Mountain, Nevada, changed the name of the local American Legion center from the Lander Post No. 15 to the Frances Muncey Post 15. In July 1946, some Western Shoshones held a Sun Dance near Wells, Nevada, to recognize the Shoshone veterans who returned home.[20]

Some five years after WWII ended, the United States became involved in the Korean War (1950–1953). During this war, Native Americans also made their presence known. But some interpreters view Indian veterans of the Korean War as the "forgotten warriors." One such solder was Woodrow Wilson "Woody" Keeble (Dakota) from the Sisseton-Wahpaton Reservation in South Dakota. He was a member of the G Company of the 19th Infantry Regiment of the 24th Division. In

Emory Rogers "Doogie" Swaney, WWII Veteran

Ellen Swaney said her dad didn't talk about the war. She remembers a single instance of him telling her what happened at Guadalcanal and Tarawa. He never spoke of it again to her. Emory Rogers "Doogie" Swaney graduated from Dixon High School in 1940. Dixon is a town of several hundred on the Flathead Indian Reservation in Montana. In November 1941, at the age of twenty, he enlisted in the US Marine Corps; he served in B Company, 1st Battalion, 8th Regiment, 2nd Marine Division.

Photo of Emory Rogers "Doogie" Swaney—Courtesy of Ellen Swaney

In November 1942, he was part of one of the first wave landings on Guadalcanal, in the Solomon Islands chain. He was wounded in this battle and was initially sent to Suva in the Fiji Islands and later to New Caledonia, New Zealand, for recuperation. In mid-1943 he was given the choice to remain in New Zealand or return to his outfit that was preparing for a major offensive landing on Tarawa Island in the Gilbert Islands. He chose to return to his outfit. During one of the first wave landings, he was badly wounded. He likely would not have survived had another soldier not rescued him.

He described to Ellen being picked up out of the water by another soldier, who looked at him and said "Doogie?" The soldier was Oliver Strombo, a classmate of Doogie's from the small town of Dixon, Montana, a world away. Oliver was also a relative of Doogie's future wife. For his service at Guadalcanal and Tarawa, he received a Presidential Unit Citation and two Purple Hearts. These experiences forever changed him, and he was a staunch and loyal friend of those with whom he served.

1982, Keeble died. He would not receive recognition until 2006 when Congress awarded him the Medal of Honor for eliminating various Korean gunnery locations around Kumson, North Korea, in 1951. Senator Tim Johnson of South Dakota said: "This brave soldier clearly distinguished himself through his courageous actions. The Army and our nation are forever grateful for his heroic service."[21]

Then, eleven years after the Korean War ended, the United States became involved in the Vietnam War. US involvement in Vietnam continued until it withdrew the last troops in 1975, after which South Vietnam fell to the communists, and Vietnam became a single nation. Around 58,000 US troops died in the war. As for Native Americans, 42,500 participated: 10,829 in the army, 24,004 in the navy, 2,540 in the marines, and 5,237 in the air force. Approximately 90 percent enlisted.[22]

One Native American who fought in Vietnam was Woody Kipp (Blackfeet) from Montana. He enlisted in the marines in 1964 and reported to Camp Pendleton for training until 1965. Kipp was in Vietnam until 1968; while there, he made many comments about his war experiences. He points out that other US soldiers called him "Chief," a popular name given to Indians by whites who did not understand the significance of the word. Kipp also noted the Indian "physical resemblance to the Vietnamese people."[23] Besides the physical, he also noted the cultural and social parallels when he wrote, "I began to understand my connections to the Vietnamese through their understanding of nature and family, animist beliefs...." Kipp further noted: "I ... felt [a] bond with the Vietnamese people."[24]

Other Indians who fought in Vietnam had varied experiences. One Umatilla soldier was drafted into the army in June 1969. Soon after, he went AWOL and was arrested. In his statement for walking away from participation in the Vietnam War, he stated: "I wish to remain loyal to the people of the Umatilla Walla Walla Nations.... It (the war) is against the things I have been taught by my family, my tribal elders and other spiritual leaders throughout this land."[25] The outcome of his court martial is not known.

Once the Vietnam War ended in 1975, veterans received a mixed reception due to the controversy of the war, although Native communities continued to honor their veterans. In 1981, Indian veterans in Oklahoma established the American Inter-Tribal Association of Vietnam Veterans.

One of its functions is to provide counseling to veterans who dealt with Postwar Traumatic Stress Syndrome.[26] On January 24, 1988, South Dakota Public Television showed a film called *Warriors*. Produced by Prairie Public TV in Fargo, North Dakota, the film took a serious look at the Indians who fought in the Vietnam War. Vietnam Veterans interviewed gave different views about their war experiences. Bob St. John (Sisseton-Wahpeton) said: "The saying is everyone knew Chief but nobody knows his name."[27] Myron Williams, also from Sisseton, said: "While I was sitting out there, I think what really dawned on me was that what they did to my people 100 years ago."[28] The documentary depicted a number of perspectives. But by way of conclusion, the producers noted that "Indian people hold veterans in high-esteem and deep respect, just as they did the warriors of old."[29]

In early 1991, the United States declared war against Iraq for invading Kuwait. The data shows that 2,975 Native Americans fought in this war called Operation Desert Storm. As in previous wars, Indians were subject to racist slurs. One comment came from Marine Brigadier General Richard Neal who referred to Iraqi-controlled areas as "Indian Country."[30] Like the nineteenth-century "Indian-white" wars of the American West, enemy lands were deemed "Indian Country."

Ten years later, in 2001, the United States once again became involved in the Mideast, in both Iraq and nearby Afghanistan. In what became known as Operation Iraqi Freedom (2003–2010), Native Americans once again became involved in this military campaign. Of the 4,411 American troops who lost their lives, 43 were Native American.[31] One of them was Lori Piestewa (Hopi) who was captured in a convoy and lost her life in 2003. She has been honored in different ways over the years, including the name of Piestewa Peak in Arizona in 2013–2014. One Native soldier who survived the Iraqi War was Jimmy Langley (Cherokee). In reflecting on his war experience, he said in March 2014: "Before I deployed in 2003 … some friends … gave me a Cherokee Braves Flag.... I brought that flag in because it belongs to all the Cherokee people. It flew over Iraq from 2003 through 2010."[32] Langley turned the flag over to the newly established Cherokee Veterans Center.

Native American veterans continue to receive recognition for their military service. In 2013, a new book, *Under the Eagle*, became the thirteenth book written about Navajo Code Talkers.[33] On November 20, 2013, the US government honored more than two hundred Native American Code

Talkers of different tribes. Besides Navajo, individuals from other tribal nations received recognition: Hopi, White Mountain Apache, and Tonto Apache. In December 2013, President Barack Obama signed the Native American Veterans' Memorial Amendments Act of 2012. The new act amends an earlier act of 1994, calling for the construction of a statue on the National Mall to acknowledge all the past accomplishments of Native American veterans. On November 11, 2020, the new National Native American Veterans Memorial, located adjacent to the National Museum of the American Indian, opened to the public. It was designed by Harvey Pratt (Cheyenne-Arapahoe), a veteran of the Vietnam War.[34]

Continuing to Serve

Native Americans continue to serve their people and country through military service. Lisette Wells enlisted in the national guard at the age of twenty-one. Her family proudly attended her swearing-in. She comes from a long tradition of military service. Her grandfather, Dwight William Billedeaux, served in the US Air Force during the Vietnam War. Looking back to WWII, her great-great-uncle Isaac Francis Matt, served as a private in the US Army and was killed in the Ardennes in Belgium. Another great-great-uncle, Ernest Moses Matt served in the US Army Corps and Army during WWII and the Korean War.

Lisette is Salish and Blackfeet, with a strong sense of family identity and cultural tradition. She spent several months in Texas qualifying for weapons, fieldwork, and navigation and preparing for an intense climate. She was deployed to Kuwait in January 2022 for a nine-month assignment. When asked why she enlisted, Lisette responded that she wanted to challenge herself and that she has a dream of becoming a pilot.

Lisette Wells, US Army National Guard—Photo by Amaru Bennett

Isaac Frances Matt, US Army—Courtesy of Duretta Billedeaux

Ernest Moses Matt, US Army Air Corps and Army—
Courtesy of Duretta Billedeaux

PART III

Arise

INTRODUCTION

The sovereignty of self, language, education, culture, land, economy, family, and even the burials of our relatives are human rights explored within these narratives, along with the actions of Native people and nations to reclaim and restore them. With strength and honesty, we see the challenge, but so, too, the hope.

> *The line where my grandmother ends, and I begin is no line at all. I am a child that once lived inside her, that was carried inside the builders of the mounds, the cells of mourners along the Trail of Tears. From them I still remember to honor life, mystery, and this incomparable ongoing creation.*
>
> *And living at the secret heart of this creation, I am the grandmother now, traveling among those who cannot see or know me, learning the healing of plants, caring for children, struggling against the madness called progress, and believing the sun's old ways. I know this land is charged with life. I know what has happened to it, and to us. And I know our survival.*
>
> —*Linda Hogan,*
> *"Seeing, Knowing, Remembering"*[a]

CHAPTER 17

US American Indian Policy and Civil Rights

Donald Grinde, Jr.

The phrase "civil rights" means protection from laws and policies that restrict freedom and equality. With the beginning of white contact, Native Americans have been systematically dispossessed, killed, harassed, and subjugated by colonial, local, state, and federal policies and officials. These oppressive policies were aimed at whole American Indian nations as well as individuals within those nations. To many Native Americans, it seems paradoxical to study the historical subject of American Indian civil rights. But American Indians have become citizens of the United States and residents of their respective states while maintaining their rights as citizens of American Indian nations. Like other oppressed groups, American Indians have endured the repeated deprivation of their rights by local, state, and federal governments. Throughout American history, Native American people sought to exercise religious, treaty, and cultural rights that conflicted with state and federal laws that did not accommodate such practices; when such conflicts occurred, American Indians were often denied basic civil rights.

Since the creation of the United States, Native Americans, like other peoples of color, have experienced private and governmental prejudice. However, American Indians' perceptions of their rights under US law are different from the expectations of most other racial groups. Most Native American rights involve a broad range of preferences, prerogatives, and immunities that are based not on their status as members of a "minority" group but rather on their treaty rights as citizens of American Indian nations. Thus, American Indian people are treated, in the law, as both a "group" with contractual rights (treaties) with the US government and as individuals of color existing in the broader American society. These two confusing and often conflicting legal statuses have often worked against Native Americans in the legal system.

To comprehend the civil rights of American Indian people, it is important to examine its legal concepts in two separate spheres. The first category includes those issues associated with civil rights (freedom of religion and speech, due process, voting rights, and freedom from racial discrimination). But it is important to recognize that the rights in this category engage not only constitutional limitations on federal and state governments but also limitations on the prerogatives of Native American governments. The second factor relating to Native American civil rights includes the rights and disabilities of Native peoples as citizens of Native American communities. Because of this duality under the law, the United States has created immunities, disabilities, and legal preferences that apply to American Indian individuals as well as immunities and rights that are a product of the American Indian governmental system. In each of these areas, it is citizenship in a Native American group that institutes an immunity or a right.

By the end of the nineteenth century, the federal government had decided how it would conduct its affairs with Native American nations. At the conquest period, the remaining American Indian nations were located on reservations that represented only a small portion of their original lands. In order to give the US House of Representatives more say in Indian affairs, Congress passed on March 3, 1871, the Indian Appropriations Act, which terminated treaty making between the

American Indian nations and the federal government. After 1871, Indian affairs would be carried out through legislation approved in both houses rather than through treaties ratified only in the Senate. In addition, this new law denied noncitizen Indians and Indian nations the power to make contracts that involved the payment of money for services involving Indian lands or claims against the federal government, unless the contracts were approved by the secretary of the interior and the commissioner of Indian affairs. Since many Indian grievances were against the secretary of the interior and the commissioner of Indian affairs, this statute denied Native Americans one of the basic rights in the common law—the right of free choice of counsel for the redress of injuries; these restrictions were further hindered by the Act of May 21, 1872.

With this legislation, the capacity of American Indian nations to stop federal encroachment into the conduct of tribal affairs was extinguished, and the use of federal power in American Indian affairs became arbitrary. Basically, tribal-federal relations changed from treaties negotiated between sovereign nations to an oppressive guardianship over a powerless ward. In the early part of the nineteenth century, Chief Justice John Marshall asserted that federal–Indian relations resembled the status of a guardian and a ward.[1] In the late nineteenth century, Congress and the courts used Marshall's words to sanction this radical transformation in Indian policy.

Consequently, the federal government justified its interference with intratribal affairs by stating that Indian nations were to be sheltered by the federal government from malevolent local populations. In *United States v. Kagama*, the Supreme Court upheld the validity of the 1885 Indian Major Crimes Act, which imposed certain federal criminal laws on Indians living in federal reservations. The court held:

> *[T]hey are spoken of as "wards of the nation," "pupils," as local dependent communities. In this spirit the United States has conducted its relations to them from its organization to this time....*[2]
>
> *These Indian tribes are wards of the nation. They are communities dependent on the United States.... From their very weakness and*

> *helplessness, so largely due to the dealing of the Federal Government with them, and its treaties in which it has been promised, there arises the duty of protection, and with it the power.*[3]
>
> *The power of the General Government over these remnants of a race once powerful, now weak and diminished in numbers, is necessary to their protection, as well as the safety of those among whom they dwell.*[4]

In other words, federal policy could justify negating treaty rights and stipulations.

A disastrous policy for American Indian rights was the allotment of reservation lands to adult members of their Indian nation and then selling the "surplus" lands to non-Indians. On February 8, 1887, the US government passed the General Allotment Act, which set up a commission to survey and allot reservations in order to distribute lands to individual tribal members.[5]

Most American Indian nations vigorously resisted allotment policies, but the federal government decided to implement the policy over their protest. Although the Bureau of Indian Affairs and the Allotment Commission conducted supposed "negotiations" with Native American governments, the results were debased by coercion, fraud, forgery, and duress.

Allotment on the Flathead Reservation

The first round of allotment on the Flathead Indian Reservation assigned 228,434 acres to individual members of the Confederated Salish and Kootenai Tribes. Unassigned lands were declared surplus and opened to homesteading in 1910. Two lotteries and a public sale resulted in the loss of more than 400,000 reservation acres. By the end of the allotment era, the Confederated Salish and Kootenai Tribes held less than 40 percent of their reservation land. The Tribes waged an aggressive and costly land recovery campaign, buying back thousands of acres, resulting in ownership of 64 percent of their reservation lands.

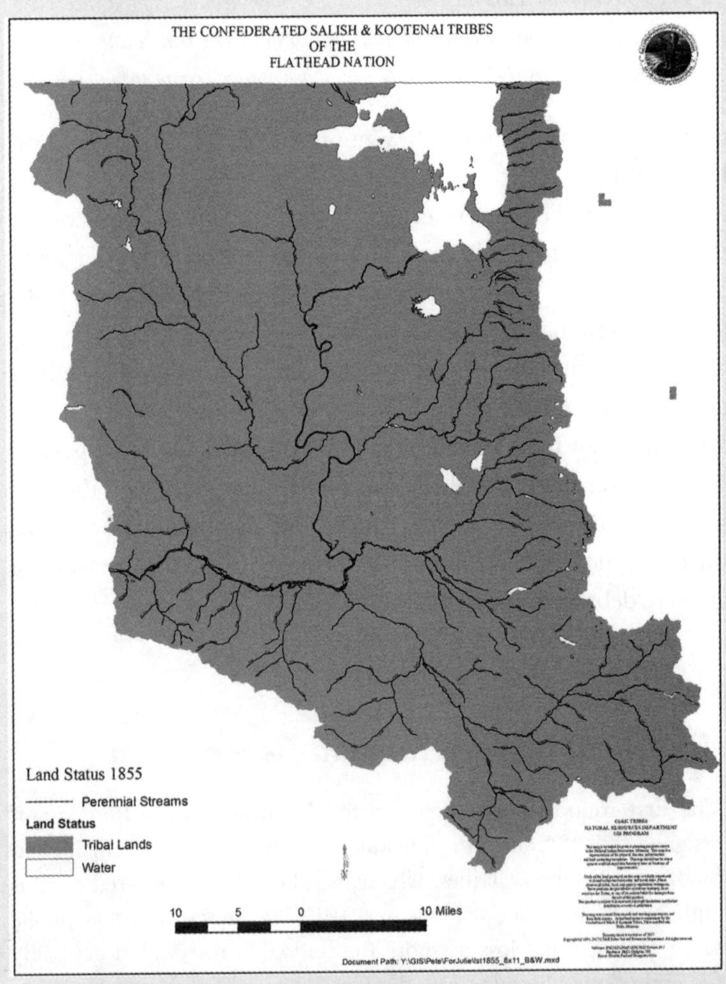

Flathead Reservation Land Status 1855 map—
Courtesy of the Confederated Salish and Kootenai Tribes

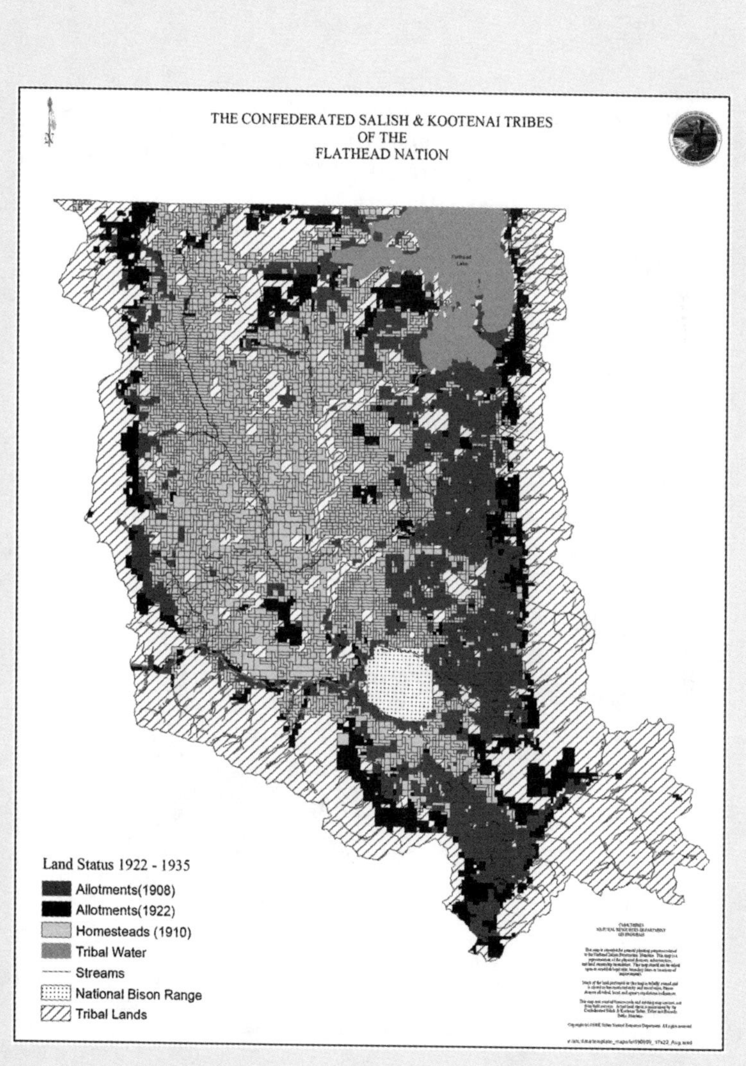

Flathead Reservation Land Status 1922–1935 map—
Courtesy of the Confederated Salish and Kootenai Tribes

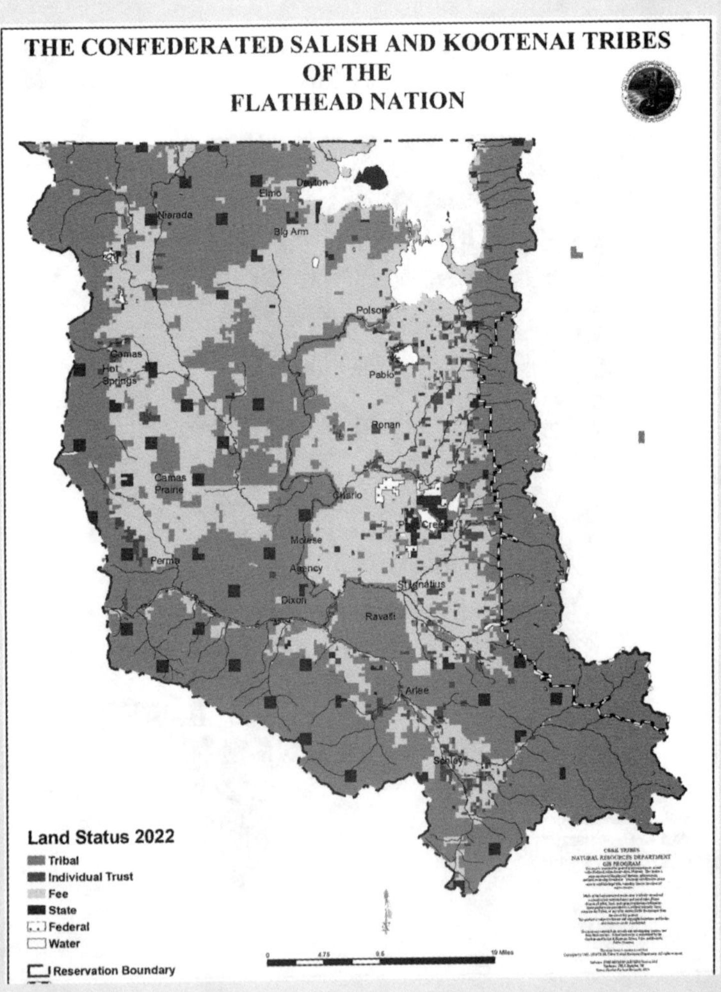

Flathead Reservation Land Status 2022 map—
Courtesy of the Confederated Salish and Kootenai Tribes

In *Lone Wolf v. Hitchcock*, Kiowa chief Lone Wolf sought to negate the validity of the "allotment agreement" that sold Comanche, Kiowa, and Kiowa Apache lands to non-Indians. Under the Treaty of Medicine Lodge (1867), no part of the Kiowa-Comanche Reservation could be sold to the federal government without the approval of three-fourths of the adult male Indians. Under the General Allotment Act, Congress allotted the reservation and then sold the "surplus" without obtaining the three-fourths approval as stipulated in the 1867 treaty. In upholding the actions of the government, the Supreme Court stated:

> *The power exists to abrogate the provisions of an Indian treaty, though presumably such power will be exercised only when circumstances arise which not only justify the government in disregarding the stipulations of the treaty, but may demand, in the interest of the country and the Indians themselves, that it should do so.*[6]
>
> *In view of the legislative power possessed by Congress over treaties with the Indians, and Indian tribal property, we may not specially consider [the allegations of fraud], since all these matters, in any event, were solely within the domain within the legislative authority and its action is conclusive upon the courts.*[7]

The judges described this as "plenary authority over the tribal relations of the Indians," and deemed the exercise of these "plenary" powers as being beyond judicial review. Theoretically, Congress could only utilize such powers for the good of Native American nations, but the court would not second guess Congress as to what was good for Indian nations. Hence, congressional power under the *Lone Wolf* decision was basically unlimited.

The attack on American Indian people in the late nineteenth century was much broader than subverting the traditional landholding patterns. The government actively suppressed tribal religious rituals and beliefs in direct violation of the Bill of Rights. The government encouraged and subsidized Christian missionaries to proselytize within tribal communities. Zealous missionaries and Indian agents legally prohibited American Indian religious rituals and dances because they believed in the sanctity of their efforts to convert Indians to Christianity.

Rules Governing the Indian Court of Offenses

Department of the Interior
Office of Indian Affairs
Washington, March 30, 1883

1st. There shall be established at each Indian agency, except the agency for the five civilized tribes in the Indian territory, a tribunal, consisting of three Indians, to be known as "the Court of Indian Offenses."

2nd. The Court of Indian Offenses shall hold at least two regular sessions in each and every month....

4th. The "sun-dance," the "scalp-dance," the "war-dance," and all other so-called feasts assimilating thereto, shall be considered "Indian offenses," and any Indian found guilty of being a participant....

5th. The usual practices of so-called "medicine-men," shall be considered "Indian offenses" cognizable by the Court of Indian Offenses,... upon conviction ... shall be confined in the agency prison for a term not less than ten days, or until such time as he shall produce evidence satisfactory to the court ... that he will forever abandon all practices styled Indian offenses under this rule.

From National Archives, Records of the Bureau of Indian Affairs (BIA), Record Group 75. http://www.archives.gov/research/guide-fed-records/groups/075.html.

After World War I, some enlightened individuals decided to reform these oppressive "assimilation" policies with new legislation. Although many American Indians had become US citizens through "competency commissions" and treaties, Congress unilaterally granted citizenship to all American Indians in 1924. However, many Indians were wary of being declared citizens through "competency" as it often meant that their federal land allotments were no longer protected and thus subject to sale. A significant amount of the tribal estate was taken from Native Americans through fraud and state tax sales. In fact, thousands of newly created Native American citizens saw their lands removed from federal protection and sold out from under them.

Many Native American leaders asserted that the American Indian Citizenship Act of 1924 was a mischief-maker in American Indian policy. They did not like the way it was imposed without consultation and consent from American Indian communities.

Although the 1924 American Indian Citizenship Act granted citizenship unilaterally, it did not end federal protection of Indian lands and governmental entities. Hence, American Indians acquired a new status as American citizens while maintaining their privileges and rights as members of distinct Native American political units. However, Indian policy makers in 1924 assumed that tribal governments would wither away when American Indians became US citizens. But most tribal governments did not disappear as anticipated, and today American Indians enjoy a special dual citizenship.

Poverty, poor education, and ill health characterized the existence of most Native Americans in the 1920s. When American Indian lands were allotted, the federal government assured communities that they would be supported during the transition from communal ways to the individualistic mores of Euro-American society. But government promises were not kept, and many American Indians continued to reject American individualism and cling to traditional values. In some cases, American Indian communities were devoured by their more greedy and competitive neighbors. By the end of the 1920s, many reformers and American Indian leaders understood that instilling private property through allotment and Christianity through missionization had wreaked havoc in Indian Country.

In 1928, the federal government commissioned a study of Indian policy, and the resulting Meriam Report catalogued the woeful conditions of American Indians. In health care, Native Americans were found to be without even rudimentary services. Infant mortality rates were twice the national average. American Indians were also seven times more likely to die of tuberculosis than the general population. Sanitary conditions were bad, and many Indians were disease ridden. The Meriam Report criticized Indian boarding schools as "grossly inadequate." From 1800 to 1926, the Bureau of Indian Affairs separated Indian children from their parents in a cruel attempt to Christianize and civilize them. The Meriam Report pointed out the harsh discipline heaped on Indian children. Basically, the boarding schools forbade Native American children to speak their own languages, practice their religions, or wear traditional clothes. Violators of these rules were subject to physical abuse. Male American Indian survivors of this period joked that upon arriving at boarding schools a missionary/teacher would point to a picture of Jesus Christ on the wall with long, flowing hair and state that they were to become like this man and then order that the boys' long hair be cut. Most boarding schools relied on Native American child labor to keep them going. The Meriam Report characterized boarding schools as overcrowded and staffed with unqualified personnel that provided poor medical care and an unhealthy diet. Under these harsh conditions, Indian literacy rates remained low.

Furthermore, no economic or legal structure appeared to be in place to protect the rights of Native Americans. The Meriam Report found that only 2 percent of all American Indians earned in excess of $500 per annum and that 96 percent of all Native Americans made less than $200 per year. Almost half of all Native Americans had lost their land because unscrupulous people were manipulating the law to take advantage of allotted Native American lands. Legal authorities were unsure who heard cases involving Indian and Non-Indians as defendants and victims, on reservations or off reservations. Often, when such cases were adjudicated, justice was not often the result.

Having diagnosed this staggering array of problems, the Meriam Report recommended an infusion of funds to correct the ills of the system. It called for a new office in the Bureau of Indian Affairs to institute new programs and monitor existing ones. The report also stated that the government and especially the Bureau of Indian Affairs had exhibited an extremely hostile attitude toward Indian families and Indian culture. The allotment system, a cornerstone of Indian policy since 1887, was found to be the major cause of American Indian poverty. Basically, the Meriam Report documented a national scandal, and the deplorable conditions on reservations were a byproduct of governmental policies and neglect. By the 1930s, American Indian policy was taken out of the hands of missionaries and transferred to social scientists. American Indian leaders also knew that the persistence of American Indian ways depended on maintaining the land base and traditional identity, and they looked to the Bill of Rights for the legal machinery to facilitate this survival process.

The reform community was responsible for these excesses as they had backed the discredited allotment policies and the Indian Citizenship Act. The resulting reforms that emerged in the 1930s were built on the idea that American Indian culture and nations had a place in twentieth-century America. President Franklin D. Roosevelt's new commissioner of Indian affairs, John Collier, instituted a policy to restore the vitality of Native American governments through the Indian Reorganization Act (IRA) of 1934. The IRA encouraged tribes to promulgate their own constitutions and renounce the old allotment policies. In addition, American Indian governments were recognized as the basic way to foster federal Indian policies. For the first time in fifty years, the right of Native Americans to maintain distinct tribal communities was sustained. The idea that tribes would eventually disappear was no longer the underlying assumption behind US Indian policy.

Paradoxically, federal officials during the 1930s often pursued goals of American Indian autonomy with an enthusiasm that limited the American Indians' rights of choice. In the zeal for social change, Collier pushed for the adoption of Native American constitutions that reflected bureaucratic opinions as to how older tribal structures could be converted to contemporary constitutional structures. As a result, IRA constitutions were forced upon many tribes that clearly opposed such measures. During the 1930s, most Native Americans continued to be suspicious of governmental programs to aid them.

Despite these fears by Indian people, the reforms of the 1930s continued. Tribal governments were revitalized, and their authority over reservation life was reinvigorated. Gradually, American Indians started to recover from the devastations of the allotment policy, and health and education programs improved. But these reforms were short-lived.

As the Great Depression ended and World War II began, the United States turned away from Native American issues. The budget for the Bureau of Indians Affairs was cut, and conservative politicians attacked Collier's policies of empowering Native American societies. Racism played an important role in this backlash as did non-Indian businessmen who had lost their ability to plunder the American Indian resources and lands. The cost of reforming the administration of Indian affairs was also a source of friction. These ideological critiques paved the way for another attack on American Indian societies in the late 1940s and early 1950s.

In the late 1940s, the new federal policy was called "liquidation," and for many Native Americans it conjured up images of the Nazi final solution for the Jews during World War II. In response to these fears, the name for the new US policy was changed to "termination." Because it stressed the abrogation of treaty rights, this policy demanded the dismantling of Indian governments, the distribution of the tribal estate to tribal members, and the termination of federal services to individual Indians.

Termination policy espoused an end to the federal government's treaty obligations. In order to establish these goals, termination legislation was implemented in four distinct areas: (1) federal trust responsibilities and treaty relations were to be ended with specified American Indian nations, (2) legislation that set Native Americans apart from other citizens was to be repealed, (3) supervision over certain individual American Indians and restrictions relating to federal guardianship were to be removed, and (4) services historically provided by the Bureau of Indian Affairs would be shifted to other local, state, or federal agencies, or to Native American governments.

In August of 1953, the cornerstone of termination policies, House Concurrent Resolution 108, was passed. It asserted:

> *It is the policy of Congress, as rapidly as possible, to make the Indians within the territorial limits of the United States subject to the same laws and entitled to the same privileges and responsibilities as are applicable to other citizens of the United States, to end their status as wards of the United States, to grant them all the rights and prerogatives pertaining to American citizenship.*[8]

In addition, the resolution provided that certain Native Americans "be freed from federal supervision and control and from all disabilities and limitations specifically applicable to Indians."

Federal responsibilities and tribal power were further eroded by the passage of Public Law 280, a statute that shifted federal, civil, and criminal jurisdiction in Indian country to certain states. Other states were offered the option of taking jurisdiction over federal Indian reservations when they felt the need. Slowly, education and health programs were shifted to the states through subsequent legislation. In the Truman and Eisenhower administrations, 109 American Indian groups lost their status as federally recognized tribes. In human terms, 13,263 individuals owning 1,365,801 acres of land were unilaterally denied their treaty rights as Native Americans.

During this era of termination, the doctrine of plenary powers was used to condemn thousands of acres of American Indian lands protected by treaty. With judicial acquiescence, Congress permitted

Termination

Congress passed the Klamath Termination Act in 1954. The tribe lost all federal services, their claim to the headwaters of the Klamath River, and a million acres of forest. Enrolled members of the tribe received $43,000 dollars from the federal government, paid out in 1954 and to the remaining tribal members in 1974. Tribal member Edison Chiloquin refused his payment. He lit a Sacred Fire near the town of Chiloquin; the fire burned for five and a half years. In 1980, President Jimmy Carter signed the Chiloquin Act, which gave Edison and his descendants title to 580 acres. On August 28, 1986, the Klamath Tribe was restored, but received no land base.

Lee Juillerat, *Oregon Encyclopedia,* oregonencyclopedia.org

the Army Corps of Engineers and/or the Bureau of Reclamation in the Interior Department to seize significant portions of the Colorado River, Chemehuevi, Fort Mohave, and the Yuma and Gila Bend Reservations in Arizona to manage the power and watershed of the Colorado River basin. The Pick-Sloan Plan for the Missouri River basin condemned tribal lands in Montana, Wyoming, and North and South Dakota. All of this land was flooded when the Oahe, Fort Randal, and Big Bend dams were completed. In western New York, the US government built the Kinzua Dam, which violated the Pickering Treaty of 1794; flooded more than 9,000 acres of excellent farmland; ruined the Cold Spring Longhouse, the spiritual center of the Allegany Seneca Reservation; and caused the removal of 130 families from the rural area adjacent to the dam and relocation to suburban style housing several miles away at Steamboat and Jimersontown. In the ensuing legal battles, government attorneys argued that in *Lone Wolf v. Hitchcock* and other cases "treaty rights do not forbid the taking, by the United States, of lands within the Allegany Reservation." In all of these land confiscations, the federal government exercised its plenary powers over Native Americans by uprooting them from their homelands, disturbing sacred sites, and significantly altering the ecology of the region.

Essentially, the federal government's flood control projects showed little concern for the treaty and civil rights of American Indians during the 1940s and 1950s. Without a doubt, the federal government was seeking to abrogate its treaty responsibilities during the 1950s with a vengeance, but it was doing it for reasons other than civil rights.

George Gillette, Chairman of the Three Affiliated Tribes weeps as the Garrison Dam Agreement of 1948 is signed. The tribes were pressured into the agreement that flooded 152,360 acres, most of the prime agricultural lands on the Fort Berthold Reservation. The flooding caused the relocation of 80 percent of the tribal members. From Lawson Michael 2009. *Dammed Indians: The Pick Sloan and Missouri River Sioux*. Pierre: South Dakota Historical Society Press, 52—Courtesy of the National Archives (1948) Department of the Interior. Bureau of Indian Affairs, Aberdeen Area Office, Fort Berthold Agency, Record Group 75; National Archives and Records Administration–Kansas City; National Archives Identifier 45641547

When the civil rights movement gained momentum in the 1960s, American Indian activists joined the struggle. Although the Native American agenda was similar to other minorities in terms of citizenship rights, American Indian people also wanted to protect other rights (including treaty rights) that were fundamentally different from other groups. American Indians wanted not only to assert their constitutional rights as members of the American political system but also to preserve their special and separate cultural and political communities—their sovereignty.

Although many mainstream Americans failed to appreciate the diverse aspirations of Native Americans in the 1960s, American Indians did regain some civil rights and group rights. In the civil rights arena, the legislation and judicial decisions of the 1960s and early 1970s routinely made American Indians a part of the Voting Rights Act, the Fair Housing Act, and the Equal Employment Opportunity Act. For instance, the Voting Rights Act not only bans discrimination against American Indians but also gives them special protection as a people since their primary language may not be English.

ACLU Voting Rights and Carol Juneau

While the Voting Rights Act of 1965 was paramount, it did not resolve all of the challenges facing Indian voters. Reservations that are checkerboarded due to allotment and homesteading experience a political quagmire where tribal government and individual tribal members have to engage with white elected officials as school board members, county commissioners, sheriffs, and judges. Getting an Indian elected into any of these positions has proved daunting on many reservations. State elections mirror similar difficulties. This has often been the result of unfair districting. An ACLU Report in 2009 quoted Carol Juneau, Former Montana state legislator and citizen of the Three Affiliated Tribes. "Indian people are far from equitably represented in county government systems, school boards, city governments and all those other policy making bodies that make decisions that impact all people in the state, including tribal communities."

From Voting Rights in Indian Country. September 2009. ACLU Voting Rights Project, 16.

Social legislation passed in the 1960s also acknowledged Indian tribes as unique and distinct political communities. Many Great Society programs (e.g., Headstart, Community Action programs, The Comprehensive Older Americans Act, and the Elementary and Secondary Act) during this time allowed Indian tribal governments to participate. The civil rights movement had an enormous impact on American Indian people and their governments. Oddly enough, one major area of civil rights for American Indians continued to be neglected until the late 1970s—religious freedom. In 1978, Congress passed the American Indian Religious Freedom Act; it declared that the federal government would seek to preserve and protect the exercise of spiritual practices. This act gave American Indians access to sacred sites on federal lands for religious ritual purposes. In the past, the courts had not been sympathetic to American Indian site-based religious rituals. Unfortunately, the law proved to be very ineffective and did not give the tribes any judicial redress for arbitrary federal actions. A decade after its passage, the Supreme Court struck down the heart of the law in *Lyng v. Northwest Indian Cemetery Protective Association*, 485 U.S. 439 (1988). Basically, the Supreme Court found that the National Forest Service could construct a road through sacred Indian sites even when such a road clearly destroyed Native Americans' ability to conduct important rituals that they had practiced in the area from time immemorial. Justice Sandra Day O'Connor, in the majority opinion, admitted that:

> *The government does not dispute, and we have no reason to doubt, that the logging and road-building projects at issue in this case could have devastating effects on traditional Indian religious practices.*[9]

A majority of the court stated that government activities could not be disrupted by the religious claims of its citizens as there was a wide array of religious beliefs in American society. O'Connor stated that a "sudden revelation" of sacredness to an individual at the Lincoln Memorial ought not to constrain visitation to this federal landmark, as if such a far-fetched possibility were comparable to continuing religious practices of three groups of Indians that extended back thousands of years. Essentially, O'Connor and the majority of the court sought to destroy the notion of American Indian religious freedom with their "sudden revelation" argument so that American Indians could be denied their rights to practice traditional tribal spirituality.

During the 1980s, the issue of the reburial of American Indian human remains deposited in federal agencies was debated. After a thorough investigation in academic circles, it was asserted that the federal government "had a firm policy which encouraged the acquisition and retention of these remains." Many American Indians opposed the retention of Native American remains in places like the Smithsonian Institution. Indeed, Native American spiritual leaders argued that American Indian human remains should be placed back in Mother Earth. Since no other ethnic groups were submitted to such practices with regard to burials, many Native American leaders termed this practice "conquest archaeology." After a concerted effort by Native American rights organizations, Congress enacted the Native American Graves Protection and Repatriation Act (NAGPRA) of 1990.

Essentially, the law enacted four things: (1) federal agencies and private museums holding federal grants must inventory their collections of Native American human remains and funerary objects associated with them, and tribal governments must be notified by the agencies that the remains and objects may be returned to them upon request; (2) cultural artifacts and human remains excavated and/or found on federal and tribal lands belong to the respective tribes; (3) the trafficking in Native American cultural objects and human remains acquired in violation of NAGPRA is banned; and (4) private museums receiving federal monies and federal agencies must prepare an itemized catalogue of other Native American sacred and funerary artifacts and return the objects to Native American communities where the right of possession can be determined. Legal scholars have characterized this law as "the single most important piece of human rights legislation for Indian people which has been enacted by the Congress since the passage of the American Indian Freedom of Religion Act of 1978."

After much deliberation, Congress passed the Indian Civil Rights Act in 1968. Essentially, the act orders tribal governments to give people under its authority the basic civil rights that they enjoy under the US Constitution. However, the legislation was flexible with regard to tribal prerogatives. For instance, the free exercise of religion was incorporated but not the restrictions on the establishment of a state religion. As some tribal governments are theocracies, the legislation sought to protect them. The act also differed from the Bill of Rights on the right to counsel in criminal cases. The Supreme Court, by 1968, had mandated state and federal governments to pay for counsel in proceedings involving poor criminal defendants. However, tribal governments did not have the funds for such a right, so the law stated that in tribal courts defendants had a right to counsel, but only if they paid for it.

Unlike the US Constitution, the Indian Civil Rights Act of 1968 set limits on punishments issued by tribal courts. The maximum punishment allowed in criminal sentences in tribal courts was $500 and six months in jail. Under the Major Crimes Act of 1883, the federal government held the power to prosecute almost all felonies on Indian reservations.

This provision has caused many problems because federal officials are slow to act on reservation crimes, so tribal judges must mete out minimal sentences for serious crimes. Furthermore, the act did not address tribal concerns about the possibility of an abundance of federal lawsuits lodged against tribal officials. The act was ambiguous about which suits might be appropriate, and for more than a decade, the federal courts heard a wide array of cases arising from this dilemma. Essentially, federal courts overruled tribal claims of sovereign immunity as well as challenges to jurisdiction of tribal courts. Until 1978, federal courts had unchallenged jurisdiction over suits against tribes.

In 1978, the Supreme Court reexamined the right of federal courts to hear cases under the Indian Civil Rights Act in *Santa Clara Pueblo v. Martinez*. In a seven-to-one decision, the high court found that since the act did not surrender the tribal governments' sovereign immunity, Native American nations were immune to suits under the law. Tribal officials were also protected by the act because the court held that it did not grant tribal members the right to file suit. In effect, the court struck down ten years of suits against tribal governments.

The *Martinez* Case basically denied federal judicial redress to persons who could sue Native American nations under the Indian Civil Rights Act. The court held out one exception to its ruling: it continued to uphold the right of habeas corpus to those persons held in tribal custody. As a result of the *Martinez* case, students of Native American law and civil libertarians expressed concerns about the absence of federal judicial review of tribal court decisions. Knowledgeable people asked who would defend American Indians from caprice by their own tribal governments? In response, the high court stated that tribal governments or tribal courts would protect Native American civil rights under the Indian Civil Rights Act. It was a deliberate but tentative step forward for American Indian self-determination.

In the wake of the *Martinez* decision, tribal courts have performed a critical judicial role in the lives of American Indian people. Initially, many people were skeptical that the tribal courts would uphold Native American civil rights. However, a recent survey of the situation after the *Martinez* case indicated that such misapprehensions were unfounded.

Judges in tribal courts created a national association in 1970 to further judicial education programs for its members. Basically, tribal courts have steadily enhanced their abilities to deal with civil rights issues on their reservations. Some of the larger Native American nations have created courts of appeal, while smaller tribes have set up intertribal courts.

Although the tribal courts have their critics, the Supreme Court continues to uphold the jurisdiction of such courts. In *National Farmers Union Insurance Company v. Crow Tribe*, and *Iowa Mutual Insurance Company v. LaPlante*, the high court affirmed the right of tribal courts to adjudicate personal injury cases involving non-Indians. Both decisions found that federal courts could not take jurisdiction in personal injury cases until the tribal courts had a chance to hear the cases initially and had determined its own jurisdiction in such cases. By the 1990s, tribal courts had become an integral part of tribal government.

Tribal Courts

The Navajo Nation is a sovereign, self-governing society that has been in existence since the Holy People gave the Navajo the land between the Four Sacred Mountains for their use and occupancy. Long before Europeans arrived as newcomers, the Navajo people were living according to the laws, the rules, and the prayers taught to them by the Holy People, laws that brought order, beauty, peace, and harmony to the People and their world.

From Becker, Navajo Nation, Bidtah N. (1995) "Profile of the Law of the Navajo Nation." *Tribal Law Journal* 0(1), 2. https://digitalrepository.unm.edu/tlj/vol0/iss1/2.

"By the early 1980s, members of the Navajo Nation Council, judges and the Navajo People sought to revive traditional Navajo justice methods, and the judges began to apply traditional Navajo legal principles in their decisions."

From Navajo Nation, Hashkééjí Nahat'á = Judicial Branch. courts.navajo-nsn.gov.

Navajo Peacemaker Courts were established in 1982, followed by the Judicial Reform Act in 1985, "which encouraged use of Navajo common law in tribal court decisions and established the Navajo Supreme Court."

From Wilkins, David. 2003. *The Navajo Political Experience*, Lanham, MD; Boulder, CO; New York; Oxford, UK: Rowman & Littlefield Publishers, Inc., 139.

The Yruok Tribal Courts

The Yurok Tribal Court (YTC) seeks to develop judicial practices that are consistent with the values of the Yurok people who have continued to face difficult circumstances following the invasion of their homeland. In 1974, the YTC was established to assist with the regulation of fishing on the Klamath River; it has expanded to additional regulatory areas, particularly family law (the Tribe operates the only Tribally controlled Child Support program in California); wellness courts (family, juvenile, adult, and veteran); juvenile and adult guardianships; and a civil access center for members with tribal, federal, or state court legal or administrative needs, or who need assistance in responding to Yurok ordinance violations or wish to initiate civil litigation. The majority of hearings held in YTC are family law, including child custody, dissolution of marriage, domestic violence restraining orders, and child support cases. The number of court-appointed guardianship cases involving tribal children has recently increased, due to an extremely high rate of substance use and high opioid addiction rates. In 2018, the YTC established the first-ever joint jurisdiction juvenile dependency court with Humboldt County, with a second joint jurisdiction dependency court established in March 2019 in Del Norte County. The court offers advocates (modeled on the cultural roles of aunts and uncles) to assist those enrolled in court programs. Compared to state or federal systems, the court's programs operate with lower caseloads and higher involvement across each individual case.

Submitted by: Abby Abinanti, Jessica Carter, and Blythe George

As the civil rights struggles of the 1960s subsided, Native Americans started a new rights movement that would carry them beyond the gains of the 1960s. With their individual rights as American citizens formally codified in law (although not always affirmed in fact), American Indians continued to assert their rights as tribal citizens. These rights were inherent in American Indian nations' status as "domestic" nations. Hundreds of treaties upheld these rights as well. Treaty rights and self-determination became the focus of Native American efforts when the fervor of the civil rights movement waned.

Native American fishing rights guaranteed through treaties were one of the primary battlegrounds for Native American civil rights. The Native

American right to fish on the Nisqually River in Washington State was one of the early focal points of the struggle. The Treaty of Point Elliott, signed by Native American nations and ratified by the United States Senate in the 1850s, stated that American Indians could reserve the right to take "fish at usual and accustomed grounds … in common with all citizens of the territory." Native Americans in Washington State utilized this right for more than a hundred years before the State of Washington began to infringe on them. Although a 1963 federal court decision upheld the fishing rights of American Indians, Washington state courts continued to forbid Native Americans from net fishing. In a series of protests, Native American fishermen were cited, arrested, and incarcerated for violating state fishing laws. In response, American Indians also lodged complaints of police brutality, but to no avail. In spite of their victories in federal court, Native American fishermen were mistreated, threatened, and, in one instance, shot by non-Indian vigilantes. In this case, victories came slowly.

Undaunted by the odds they were up against, the Indians of Washington State persisted in their struggle until 1974 when Judge George H. Boldt, in *United States v. Washington*,[10] found that American Indians were entitled to almost one-half of the salmon catch in Washington State. Although many non-Indians were infuriated, the decision was sustained through judicial review and was reaffirmed by the Supreme Court in *United States v. Washington*. American Indians had succeeded in the fight to keep their century-old treaty rights to fish, and they demonstrated that treaty rights do not alter with the passage of time.

Eastern American Indians began to claim their rights as well. Tribal attorneys in the eastern part of the United States discovered that many of the treaties that took lands from Native American nations were not ratified by Congress, even though the Indian Trade and Intercourse Acts enacted at the end of the eighteenth and early nineteenth centuries required it. These eastern Indian land cases challenged the United States' commitment to the rule of law. With claims almost two hundred years old, the ancient rules of law enacted two centuries ago would result in court victories for many eastern American Indian nations. Despite intense pressure from state governments and residents, federal courts ruled favorably on Indian claims cases in the East. Also, many cases were settled out of court (the settlements were subsequently approved by Congress). However, some cases wound up in the courts. In 1985, the Supreme Court, in *County of Oneida v. Oneida*

Fishing Rights

"Billy Frank was fishing with his father in an area restricted by the State of Washington when at the age of 14 he was first arrested by state officials. The opponents of tribal fishers held that tribal members were subject to state regulations while fishing off their reservations, and that the treaties signed in the mid-1800s were invalid.... Over the years, Billy was arrested more than 50 times. His family endured repeated persecutions: raids, beatings, fines and jail."

From *Great Tribal Leaders of Modern Times*. 2004. Institute for Tribal Government, Portland State University, 108–109.

Billy Frank, Jr. 1973—Courtesy of Northwest Indian Fisheries Commission

Indian Nation, upheld Oneida Indian land claims and found that abuses done two centuries ago could be redressed in the courts, and the rights of American Indian could be upheld.

Rights to self-government were also regained through congressional acts. Termination policies were formally forsaken when the Menominee Tribe of Wisconsin recovered its tribal status in 1973. In 1975, the Indian

Self-Determination Act granted tribes the right to administer federal assistance programs. Thus, it ended the control of such programs by non-Indian administrators who had dominated reservation life for more than a century. In 1978, the Indian Child Welfare Act put the welfare of American Indian children firmly in the hands of the tribes and curtailed the powers of the states in this crucial area. In the past, American Indian children had been taken arbitrarily from their tribal setting and placed in non-Indian environments. The Indian Child Welfare Act tried to curb the power of non-Indians in the affairs of American Indian families. In 1978, the American Indian Religious Freedom Act sought to honor and nurture traditional Native American religious rituals and practices.

American Indian leaders, lawyers, and activists expanded upon their victories by capitalizing on the gains secured during the 1960s. The broader civil rights movement sustained the rights of American Indians as individuals, but only Native Americans could regain tribal rights. American Indian rights as sovereign nations have remained largely misunderstood by the non-Indian population, and this is a continuing dilemma for American Indian people and their governments. It also is a challenge to non-Indians and the court system.

Although it is difficult to analyze the impact of militant groups like the American Indian Movement (AIM) on the political landscape, the frustrations and aspirations of AIM did echo much of the anger and despair that many Native Americans had with governmental policies. With the occupation of Alcatraz Island in 1969, the seizure of the Bureau of Indian Affairs headquarters in 1972, and the confrontations at Wounded Knee, South Dakota, in 1973, the injustices in contemporary American Indian life were dramatically depicted in the media. Young American Indian militants took action in the late 1960s and early 1970s because they assumed that the system was incapable of reforming itself. AIM was adroit at focusing media attention on the deplorable conditions that Native Americans lived under. Often, the agenda of AIM differed from the objectives of tribal governments. Tensions were also heightened between Indians and non-Indians. AIM's activities on the Pine Ridge Reservation in South Dakota were met with excessive force by federal authorities that created a climate of systematic abuse of civil rights of Native Americans both affiliated and not affiliated with AIM. In the final analysis, the impact of AIM was mostly positive because it coalesced the determination of Native Americans to advance their rights and confirmed the lengths that some people were prepared to go if justice was not served. Since the 1970s, the influence and power of AIM has decreased because of federal harassment by the Federal Bureau of Investigation and its COINTELPRO programs and other systematic campaigns to defame its membership and purposes.

John Trudell, AIM

"They waged war against us. They hunted us down. They killed, jailed, destroyed, by any means necessary. They saw that magical thing that happened with Alcatraz ... all of a sudden all this spirit is popping up and gaining momentum through A.I.M., and this is why the spirit-hunters, those who hunt free thought, came after us."

From johntrudell.com/biography.

John Trudell speaking to the press, 1971—Photographer Ilka Hartmann

The notion of civil rights is many things to many people, and the Bill of Rights is often regarded as the foundation of individual freedom and liberty in the United States. History has shown us that individuals and groups may hold basic, fundamental rights that they may use to check the caprice of government. Certainly, liberty and freedom involve the balancing of coercive state power against collective and individual rights guaranteed in the Bill of Rights. Essentially, the Bill of Rights does not grant protection for Native Americans from the abuses of tribal, local, state, and federal governments. Hence, Native Americans are denied the basic rights that other inhabitants of the United States take for granted. In contemporary legal decisions, American Indian sovereignty has not been deemed compatible with the Bill of Rights. Hence, only the US Congress can end the denial of American Indian rights by the non-Indians.

Without a doubt, American Indians suffer injustices that are a product of historically discriminatory policies toward them as individuals and as members of tribal political entities. The sensitivity or insensitivity in different historical periods to the rights of American Indians marks the ebb and flow of America's faith in democratic principles. Indeed, Felix Cohen once characterized the rights of American Indians in our society as the "miner's canary," holding that if American Indian legal rights suffered, then the fundamental freedoms in American democracy are endangered for everyone. Every generation of American Indians wonders if the dominant society will continue to acknowledge the special rights of American Indians granted by previous generations. In the final analysis, the solution to this rights dilemma will demand significant progress in comprehending and adapting the legal systems of the larger American society so that Native American demands for the recognition and nurturing of their treaty rights and civil rights can be accommodated.

CHAPTER 18

They Had Everything

AN INTERVIEW WITH BILLY FRANK, JR.

An excerpt of a 2001 interview with Portland State University's Institute for Tribal Government, from Great Tribal Leaders of Modern Times

You know this place was a magical place. My dad and grandpa always talked about how they never wished for anything. They had everything.

They asked my dad about a social security number, and he never had one. He always said he never needed one. He had everything. He had all the fish and all the food. We had the vegetables up on the prairie and the medicines. We had shellfish down here and clean water and clean air.

Every year on the watershed we had our lodges up in the mountains where we picked huckleberries and all our berries that we gathered up on our mountain. With our canoes we went down and out into the Peugeot Sound. We gathered and dried all of our shellfish. We caught a lot of flounders and different foods that we would put up for winter. It was always a cycle. The first salmon that would come in springtime—that would start our ceremonies. That cycle would just keep going and winter would be over. From that day on we would start preparing for the next winter.

We had our flutes and our drums. We made our own music. We knew our own songs. We had our dances. Our society was intact.

All of a sudden, the laws started to be written. Here comes the State of Washington. They had a legislature that started writing laws. They wrote laws against us, against Indian people for fishing not on the reservation. Our reservation was only two miles long along the watershed. That's what brought about the *United States v. Washington*. It was a continual fight with the State of Washington. Even the US Army was on the State of Washington's side. They were across the river at the time and the State of Washington used their property to get to us.

Nisqually River—Photographer Jeanette Dorner, Nisqually Land Trust

I'd take my canoe and go up the river. You can't do that now there are so many people along that watershed. You can't even hide your canoe. But I could hide my canoe along the river. I could go up the trail, dark time, no light or anything and get my canoe, come down, pick up my net and come on home. I'd just pick one or two nets up, depending on what I had, and I'd just float on down. No one would ever hear me or see me. But if they were laying for you they could catch you and they were laying for me. They caught me on that side of the river. You find a bar—a sand bar or gravel bar—and put your net out, park your canoe and get your fish. That's when these guys caught me the first time and a whole hell of a lot of times after that. They wouldn't take my canoe at that time. They wouldn't confiscate all of your things. They'd take maybe one net or something, but then they started taking everything.

I fished all the time you know—sneaking out and fishing. I fished right in front of the house. You know our house was right on the river. But they continued to arrest me right up until 1950. It was '54 when I got out of the marine corps and when I got out then we started to fish and going back to jail again. The 50's wasn't a good time for Indian people. They were taking away our reservations in other parts of the country. Termination was going on strong throughout the country. There was a lot of things going on.

Eisenhower was president at the time. They started relocation of Indians. Sending them to Los Angeles, New York, Chicago, Seattle, and everywhere. So all of those things were going on in our time.

We were involved in all of this—fighting termination. But we were still fishing on the river and not even dreaming that we were going to be a part of a big movement. The civil rights movement had started happening in the '60s.

They pretty well had us just on the reservation. That's what brought about the *United States v. State of Washington*. It was a continual fight with the State of Washington. I continued to go to jail, along with a whole bunch of us. We continued to fight the State of Washington. Other tribes also continued to do that. We protested.

The fight never ends. The fight is going on today. It's just a war between a culture and them.

There were people that didn't like what the State of Washington and the United States government was doing, what the dams were doing, and what was going on with just the environment. There were coalitions all over. There were people at the universities, and there were doctors, and people in just every profession thinking of getting involved. Certainly, we would never have made it without them. You can't—with all your power, and all your community and everything staying together—you can't fight the battle alone.

It's an ongoing fight, a continual ongoing fight. Even in the year 2000. David, my partner, my friend, I went over to testify for him, over in Yakima. You know they killed David. The United States people killed David Sohappy. One of our own people that just wanted to be left alone, to just be able to harvest salmon down the Columbia River.

What the hell is that? That is not a big thing! Two or three or four or five thousand salmon a year, or whatever, for this community? You know, what is so big about that? They made such a big thing and they put him in prison.

David Sohappy

Sohappy v. Smith in 1969 led to Judge Belloni's ruling of a "fair and equitable" share of fish for tribes, which influenced later debates on allocations. Years after the ruling, David Sohappy Sr. served a sentence in federal prison for selling fish out of season. Sohappy suffered several strokes in prison.

From Sohappy v. Smith, 302 F. Supp. 899, 1969.

Way back in the 1800s they talked about trade and commerce for the Indian people. We had it then. We had it way before Lewis and Clark ever came. We had trade with big baskets of salmon—trading with these big ships and everything. Here in 1968 and up until our time, every time that we had anything to do with the economy, they didn't want us to be part of it. Even blaming us for killing the salmon—even though we had judges on the Columbia River as well as in our district that ruled for us and continue to rule for us. Thank them, but we never win anything.

The allocation can't work if we go back to the turn of the century because there were lots of fish, twenty or thirty million salmon in the Columbia River. Now there are three million—very little fish. They looked at the tribes and said the tribes have to have an allocation, and they looked at the non-Indian and cut him way down.

So out of all of that fighting and law and winning, something good comes out of that. But you look at it and we are still fighting, and they are still raping the water. They want potatoes. They want grapes. That's more important than salmon. They use the water for irrigation. Eighty percent is going to the guys for potatoes and whatever they grow. Irrigation. What goes for the fish? They've completely sold this fish out, the United States, the states, and the political people.

Survival. Survival is what we are talking about—of us Indian people, of our salmon, and our food chain out there, and our whales, and our eagles, and all of our fur-bearing animals. We are talking about all of those things—our mountains and our trees. That's what we are talking about.

I'll never quit doing what I do. You know, everybody says have you got a retirement? Hell, no, I don't have a retirement. I live right here. If things go to hell, I can go right down and dig clams and catch fish, flounders. They are still here. That's what I do. That's being an Indian.

When I'm gone and all of the people that we have, my age or over and young people—they'll take our place. We will still have the treaty, we'll still have fighting to bring our salmon back now that they are gone, and clean water, and the principles of life, and the food chain that sustains all of us. This is what it's all about.

> *"Because the right of each treaty tribe to take anadromous fish arises from a treaty with the United States, that right is reserved and protected under the supreme law of the land, does not depend on state law, is distinct from rights or privileges held by others, and may not be qualified by any action of the state."*
>
> United States v. Washington, 384 F. Supp. 312 (W.D. Wash. Feb. 12,1974) (Boldt, J.)

Billy Frank, Jr.—Photographer Ann Yow-Dyson, *Seattle Times*

CHAPTER 19

The Intergenerational Battle for the Bodies of Our Ancestors

Clayton Dumont

At 10:20 in the morning our war leaders were dropped from the gallows. Captain Jack and Black Jim seemed to die quickly, but Boston Charlie and Sconchin suffered mightily, repeatedly lifting their legs as they writhed in agony. It was October 3, 1873, and Fort Klamath was crowded with soldiers, reporters, the families of the condemned Modocs, and the entire Klamath Nation made to witness the execution.[1] At 10:28 the four men were pronounced dead, and people cut away pieces of rope and clothing for souvenirs. Soldiers then decapitated their bodies, burying the headless remains in graves near the scaffold.

The leaders' heads became war trophies, then objects of curiosity for the white public, and finally scientific data—shipped to Washington, D.C., in a barrel labeled simply "natural history specimens." Upon arrival, Jack's head was reportedly pickled and jarred before ultimately becoming "catalog #225,070" of the Army Medical Museum's "craniological collection." All four skulls would remain there, thousands of miles from their graves, for the next 111 years.

Grisly scenes like this were common in nineteenth-century Indian Country. At least four thousand Natives from tribes across the continent had their heads severed and shipped to what would become the nation's most prestigious museum, the Smithsonian—often directly from battlefields. In 1868, the surgeon general of the United States issued an order to troops "stationed in Indian Country or in the vicinity of ancient mounds or cemeteries" to rob Indian graves. Although the total number of stolen dead remains unknown, more than 175,000 deceased ancestors of today's Native Americans and Native Hawaiians were mutilated on battlefields or ripped from their graves only to be stockpiled in the boxes, drawers, and closets of American museums and universities.[2] More than half of these known dead remain trapped in US institutions, despite the passage in 1990 of the Native American Graves Protection and Repatriation Act.[3]

NAGPRA is Indian law. Literally located in United States Code under Title 25 "Indians," it is as Senator Daniel Inouye remarked before its passage, "human rights" legislation designed for "Indians to recover the skeletal remains of their ancestors."[4] It covers not only Indigenous dead "collected" by generations of American scientists and hobbyists but also "inadvertent discoveries," meaning graves uncovered unintentionally or intentionally by development. This is important because prior to 1990, when Native dead were uncovered they were treated differently from the dead of other peoples. While white folks were sent for reburial, deceased Indians routinely went to museums and universities. The law also includes language requiring the return of funerary objects placed into graves at the time of burial. And because generations of anthropologists coveted not only the bodies of our ancestors but also our sacred objects and other items important to our cultural identities, the statute also calls for the return of "sacred objects" and "objects of cultural patrimony." But perhaps most important of all, the law explicitly recognizes Indian oral histories ("folkloric" and "oral traditional") as forms of evidence equal to those produced by scientists, when disputes over ownership of human remains and objects arise.

Our elders fought hard for NAGPRA.[5] Large and powerful scientific organizations, including the Society for American Archaeology (SAA), The American Association of Physical Anthropologists, and the American Association of Museums (AAM), fiercely opposed the legislation. Despite weeks of jarring, unanimous testimony from Indians and

Red Sleep's Dress

The family of Red Sleep requested to view her dress held in an ethnographic collection at a state higher education institution. The family was given a single sheet of paper with a short list of artifacts in the collection. The dress was not on the list. At that time, it was discovered there was no proper inventory of what was in the ethnographic or archaeological collection. It was also revealed that the archaeological collection held human remains. It took five years to gain access to view the dress and other family items. Through the five-year dialogue, a committed graduate student properly inventoried and curated the ethnographic collection that had for decades been kept in abhorrent condition.

Red Sleep's Dress—Photographer Jake Wallis, Cajune Family Collection

Native Hawaiians before congressional committees—given over forty-one months from 1987 to 1990—leaders of the scientific community maintained that they had a long history of working cooperatively with Native peoples and that no law was necessary.[6]

Unfortunately, serious resistance continues. Many tribes, including my own, remain frustrated by the inability of too many American museums and universities to implement the law responsibly. For example, in 2000 the same Army Medical Museum that received the heads of our war leaders, now renamed the National Museum of Health and Medicine, said it could not identify a lineal descendant of an individual they had labeled "brother of Sconchin."[7] They referred to the battlefield where his remains were recovered as "an unknown area in Oregon or California referred to as 'the Lava Beds.'"[8]

Other institutions are openly defiant, simply refusing to implement NAGPRA in good faith. For example, the University of California at Berkeley continues to refer to eighty-one of our ancestors as "culturally unidentifiable" despite clear evidence, published by them, indicating where these dead belong. One of these individuals has an accompanying document labeling her "Klamath Falls Indian." (Klamath Falls is the nearest town of any size to our reservation, is part of our traditional land, and is where most of us have been born since the closing of the Klamath Indian Agency more than fifty years ago.) The university is also holding thirteen of our ancestors documented as coming from "the Lava Beds" in "Modoc County" and two more from "a Modoc grave."

In the remainder of this chapter I tell the story of how this came to be, of how dead Natives from Alaska to Florida and Maine to Hawaii became white scientists' "prehistoric skeletal materials,"[9] "the archaeological record,"[10] and "a unique irreplaceable archive of bio-cultural data."[11] I then explain some of the strategy used by too many of these scientists as they continue to resist the law. Finally, I will outline the difficult road ahead, should the courts decide the future of NAGPRA, as now appears near certain.

SCIENTIFIC RACISM

Eighteenth- and nineteenth-century scientists were sure that separate "races" of humanity existed and that they were unequal in development and ability.[12] Although they agreed that white men were superior, debates about why this was so raged among the learned classes. American scientists of the early nineteenth century inherited the eighteenth-century European debate over whether humanity was part of a single Biblical Creation or whether "the races" were outcomes of separate and distinct Creations. The "monogenists," those suggesting all humans were part of a single Creation, argued that as a "degenerate life form" American Indians should be explained as the product of an inferior New World environment.[13] Europeans, they claimed, evolved more quickly than Native Americans because the European continent was environmentally superior.

One of the most strident rebuttals to this charge came from Thomas Jefferson.[14] To fuel his debate with European scholars bent on disparaging the North American continent, Jefferson opened thousands of Indian graves for study, including a mass burial mound on what had become his property. He did so knowing full well that the former inhabitants would not approve, having observed Natives who were probably descendants of the buried dead quietly and solemnly visiting the graves.[15] Although an early desecration of Indian burials, Jefferson's was certainly not the first. We know for example that as early as 1620 Puritans opened the grave of a Native child "making off with sundry of the prettiest things" and recording the event in their diaries.[16]

Dr. Samuel Morton was an equally vociferous critic of the monogenists. An ardent defender of the theory of polygenism (the claim that "the races" were physiologically distinct and derived of multiple Creations), Morton asserted that the inferiority of dark-skinned peoples was original and not the outcome of inferior lands outside Europe. To prove his racist claims, Morton needed the bodies of those he deemed inferior. By the time he published *Crania Americana* in 1839 he had the largest collection of dead Indians in the world, particularly severed heads. As a wealthy Philadelphia physician, Morton could afford to pay ghouls to steal Indian bodies. He wasn't alone. The practice was widespread and continued throughout the nineteenth century.

One of Morton's paid grave robbers wrote to him in the fall of 1835:

> *It is rather a perilous business to procure Indians' skulls in this country—The natives are so jealous of you that they watch you very closely while you are wandering near their mausoleums and instant and sanguinary [bloody] vengeance would fall upon the luckless—*

> *who would presume to interfere with the sacred relics.... There is an epidemic raging among them which carries them off so fast that the cemeteries will soon lack watchers—I don't rejoice in the prospects of death of the poor creatures certainly, but then you know it will be very convenient for my purposes.*[17]

As the tribes were defeated militarily, removed westward, and decimated by European diseases, their cemeteries were desecrated, often by US military personnel, and dead family members were sent to Morton. Ultimately, he claimed to prove the inferiority of Indians by stuffing our ancestors' skulls with mustard seeds, maintaining the practice revealed that Indian brains were smaller than those of whites.[18]

The behaviors of the later nineteenth and early twentieth century fathers of modern American anthropology were no less disturbing. In his 1895 inauguration address, titled "The Aims of Anthropology," the president of the American Association for the Advancement of Science bragged: "We rifle their graves, measure their skulls, and analyze their bones; we carry to our museums the utensils and weapons, the gods and jewels, which sad and loving hands laid beside them; we dig up the foundations of their houses and cart off the monuments which their proud kings set up. Nothing is sacred to us."[19] Franz Boas is often referred to as the father of American anthropology, and by the mid-1920s his students chaired every academic anthropology department in the United States.[20] He was also among the most prolific of grave thieves. Native dead from his "collection expeditions" were sent to some of the world's largest and most prestigious museums, including the American Museum of Natural History, the Field Museum of Chicago, and the Berlin Museum. Boas and his paid agents engaged in a competitive rivalry with collectors from other institutions to see who could accumulate the greatest number of dead Indians and cultural objects.[21] He was particularly infamous among the Northwest coast peoples, where he falsified shipping invoices to illegally transport the contents of their ancestors' graves. He also instructed one of his agents to be sure he was seen leaving town only to return after tribal members left for seasonal work at a cannery and steal the contents of a large mausoleum.[22]

In 1888, while "collecting" in British Columbia, Boas wrote the following in his notebook:

> *It is most unpleasant work to steal bones from a grave, but what is the use, someone has to do it. I have carefully locked the skeleton into my trunk until I can pack it away. I hope to get a great deal of anthropological material here. Yesterday I wrote the Museum in Washington asking whether they would consider buying skulls this winter for $600; if they will, I shall collect assiduously.*[23]

George Dorsey was a rival of Boas, was awarded Harvard's first PhD in anthropology, and became curator of the Chicago Field Museum. He also spent part of 1897 searching for and violating the graves of Tlingit and Haida spiritual leaders. He then authored a tale of his "adventure" in their country for *Popular Science Monthly*, complete with a grisly picture of a Native woman's corpse and the funerary objects she was buried with.[24] Later in the same year he was arrested for robbing Indian cemeteries on the Oregon side of the Columbia River.

A colleague of Boas and Dorsey, Aleš Hrdlička, was perhaps the most horrendous of the professional anthropological body snatchers. He was the first president of the American Association of Physical Anthropology, chair of the Anthropology Department at the Smithsonian Institution, and president of the Washington Academy of Sciences. He was awarded the Huxley Memorial Medal of the Royal Institute of Anthropology of Great Britain and Ireland, had an American World War II Liberty Ship commissioned in his name, and had his picture placed with a skull and bones on a Czechoslovakian postage stamp.

To deserve these accolades, he, too, violated burial grounds and stole bodies, sometimes from cemeteries still in use.[25] In one particularly horrible instance, he held a fake funeral to convince a young Inuit boy that his father—who had been living at the Smithsonian as Hrdlička's guest when he died of tuberculosis—was being buried according to Inuit custom. Once he was sure the boy was satisfied, he had the elder Inuit man macerated (stripped of flesh) and boiled. The son only learned of his father's true fate when he saw his bones on display in the museum years later.[26] He also published detailed "how to" instructions for "miners, prospectors, and surveyors and engineers of railroads; men engaged in trades that take them into virgin regions; and travelers of means and leisure," or anyone who might stumble across an "ancient burial place or cemetery."[27]

But Hrdlička's instructions make it clear that while "ancient dead" were valuable, the newly deceased were preferred. As he instructed: "The fresher the product the better."[28] Particularly prized were dead Native babies, or as he narrated, "embryological and infant material."[29] This, he explained, was because "it is this material alone from which may be learned racial differences or similarities in early phases of development."[30] He also made a special request for Native brains, concluding with instructions for how his ghouls should conceal their work by carefully combing the hair of the deceased over the marks left from splitting open his or her skull.

THE POLITICAL STRUGGLE FOR GRAVES PROTECTION AND REPATRIATION LEGISLATION

Although Natives have always fought to protect our dead, Indian activism in the late 1960s and 1970s succeeded in forcing the scientific community to take the issue seriously. For example, in December 1970 a group of approximately one hundred Indians from several tribes occupied the Southwest Museum in Los Angeles. Twelve were arrested. There to protest displays of Native burials, some had used chains to lock themselves in the museum auditorium.[31] Then in 1971, American Indian Movement (AIM) activists interrupted archaeologists near Welch, Minnesota, as they were teaching members of a local Talented Youth Group to desecrate Native graves. The AIM members physically removed shovels from hands, filled in the opened graves, and burned the archaeologists' field notes.[32]

But many archaeologists remained undeterred. In 1972 the State Museum of Pennsylvania violated the final resting places of eighty-six Native people, removing not only their bodies but also snuffboxes, mouth harps, perfume bottles, cuff links, spectacles, coins, mirrors, thimbles, pieces of shoes, a vanity box, and even a crucifix from the graves. The Nevada State Museum admitted in 2001 that when they "excavated" a Native woman they had also taken the ring she wore to her funeral, her shoes and clothing, and even the kitchen knife placed with her in the grave. In Mesa Verde National Park in Colorado, archaeologists dug up the burials of an entire Native community, removing more than 1,500 dead and more than 4,800 funerary objects in disinterments that continued until NAGPRA became law in 1990.[33] In Kansas, it wasn't until 1989 that the Pawnee were able to close a roadside tourist attraction selling views of their dead ancestors still lying in open graves.[34]

In part, these difficulties came to pass because in 1979 archaeologists and physical anthropologists had succeeded in lobbying for passage of the Archaeological Resources Protection Act (ARPA). Although the law for the first time placed Indian graves that were less than one hundred years old off limits, it also enshrined scientists' beliefs and claims on our dead as the law of the land.

The term "archaeological resource" means any material remains of past human life or activities that are of archaeological interest. "Such determination shall include, but not be limited to: pottery, basketry, bottles, weapons, projectiles, tools, structures or portions of structures, pit houses, rock paintings, rock carvings, intaglios [engraved objects such as grave markers or jewelry], graves, human skeletal materials, or any portion or piece of any of the forgoing items."[35]

However, by the late 1980s, Congress was increasingly interested in the battle between Native peoples and members of the scientific community. By the time House Resolution 5237 became law in November 1990 as the Native American Graves Protection and Repatriation Act, twenty-six separate bills dealing with the protection of Native dead and cultural objects had been introduced or proposed.[36] Between 1987 and 1990, five congressional hearings were held on seven of those bills.

During these proceedings, more than forty scientific leaders representing more than ten professional institutions fought first to kill and then to weaken the proposed legislation. They were confronted by equally united Indian and Native Hawaiian representatives who provided blunt, direct testimony about the desperate need for a law to protect Native dead from archaeologists, physical anthropologists, and museums. Approximately forty representatives of approximately twenty tribes and nations and fifteen Indian and Native Hawaiian organizations testified before the congressional committees.

Michael S. Haney, chairman of the Repatriation Committee of the United Indian Nations of Oklahoma, called the scientists thieves: "You know, they call it scientific research. They call it educational opportunity.

But if it happened to any other people, it would be called grand larceny."[37] Susan Shown Harjo asked the congressional committee to help "take Indians out of anthropology, take Indians out of archaeology," insisting that "Indian people are living today and have a future." "We as Indian people," she continued, "have an objection to being among the flora and fauna of the natural history museum … as things past and things not quite human."[38] Walter Echo-Hawk testified that NAGPRA was necessary because the "feelings of Native people have simply been ignored and disregarded as federal, state and private parties have worked historically and presently to disturb and remove as many Indian burials as possible." He went on to characterize "all the national organizations of professional anthropologists and archaeologists" as "impotent sources for leadership."[39]

Despite the unanimous reports of Native leaders that archaeologists and physical anthropologists could not be trusted do the right thing unless compelled by a new law, representatives of the scientific community testified that they had a long history of cooperative relationships with the tribes and that the proposed legislation would jeopardize this ongoing and mutually respectful collaboration. However, the statements of these scientific leaders quickly revealed that they had little understanding of the Native peoples whom they claimed to work with so closely.

For example, the secretary of the Smithsonian Institution, Robert McCormick Adams asserted:

> *Inclusion of artifacts in graves, by itself, does not mean that such objects were considered sacred by those that buried them, if we can judge this issue by comparison to most historically documented Indian burial practices.... In only a very few cases can the sacredness of grave goods be established even in recent Indian burials; determination of this status in ancient graves has to be based largely on speculation and personal, rather than scientific, judgment.*[40]

Having asserted that "documented Indian burial practices" reveal that Indians do not hold the graves of either our "recent" or "ancient" ancestors as sacred, Secretary Adams also compared our dead relatives to library books.

Just as no thoughtful researcher would think of discarding a library reference book after one examination, as if it had served its purpose, so too, archaeological reference materials are reexamined time and time again as research orientation, techniques of investigation, and specific scientific questions change. Thus, the North American Archaeological Collection of the National Museum of Natural History can be compared to the Library of Congress or to the National Archives. The collections are available for loan to museums and other institutions for both research and public display. They are also used in traveling exhibitions and for illustrating a wide variety of educational publication, films, and even postage stamps.[41]

Suggesting that dead Indians are "the North American Archaeological Collection" and available for public display, traveling exhibitions, and for illustrating postage stamps was an ignorant and racist gesture. Yet leaders of the scientific community argued against the passage of NAGPRA by making many such statements, narrations that Ponca elder and participant in the fight for NAGPRA Roger Buffalohead has called "stunning".[42] Time and again they claimed to have long and deeply respectful relationships with Indians, only to make stunningly uninformed statements about us and our responsibilities to our deceased ancestors, often with their next breath.

Fortunately, Congress was not fooled by the scientists' "happy talk" strategy. Montana senator John Melcher's summary of his feelings about the testimonies of representatives from the Smithsonian, the AAM, and the SAA in 1988 is representative of those voiced by other committee members.

> *I just think that the testimony of all three of you on what should be done with the remains defies logic.... I think it's repugnant to all Americans to think that we would tolerate the museums' refusal to return skeletal remains to families or tribes when requested. I think your testimony demonstrates that we'd better have a legal procedure.*[43]

LABELING OUR ANCESTORS "CULTURALLY UNIDENTIFIABLE"

Once it became clear that Congress was going to pass a law, the opposing scientists changed strategies—working instead to limit the range and strength of the pending legislation. To do so, they focused on weakening Native communities' ability to establish cultural affiliation with our ancestors. Ignoring Congress's explicit acknowledgment of "oral traditional" Indigenous ways of knowing as a form of evidence equal to those of the scientists, opponents claimed that dead taken from our traditional lands need not be affiliated with living Natives. The SAA representative articulated the strategy on July 17, 1990, less than four months before final passage of NAGPRA.

Even more problematic in the H.R. 5237 definition is the presumption of affiliation between a group and human remains or objects from their aboriginal lands. The development of modern tribal groups has taken place over such a long time that it is not possible to make a reasonable or unique assignment of modern tribal groups to atemporal lands.[44]

In other words, the largest professional organization of American archaeologists asserted that the dead buried on our traditional lands were not necessarily related to living Natives because they were too different from the Indians that Europeans came to know. Indeed, the SAA suggested that Natives who lived, died, and were buried before Europeans arrived are outside of interpretable history.[45]

This claim is wrong, as well as insulting, on several fronts. First, it assumes that Natives don't know our own histories. It assumes that we don't know about how we intermarried, fought, and mixed culturally with other Native peoples, about where and when we migrated or how long we have been in one area.[46] Rather it assumes that European and European American knowledge of the past is the only legitimate history. If knowledge of the past is not in terms that they understand and accept, then those times are deemed "atemporal" or "prehistoric."

Second, it suggests that Native peoples are culturally static. If we evolve and change too much or too quickly then we forfeit the right to protect our ancestors, who lived differently than the Indians that European American scientists recognize. Indeed, court cases brought by scientists since the passage of NAGPRA have shown just how bizarre this expectation has become. Were contemporary European Americans forced in court to use the same criteria required of Indians to document their affiliation with their American ancestors, they would be unable to "prove" their cultural relationship to George Washington.[47]

Third, "modern tribal groups" are often more creations of earlier generations of anthropologists and US government officials than ideas that precontact Native peoples used to organize themselves. For example, I sometimes wonder how my great-, great-, great-grandfather, who made his mark on our treaty in 1864, would understand concepts like tribe and blood quantum. Or given our specific concern here with the future of NAGPRA, how would he make sense of the label "culturally unidentifiable" or the legal requirement to establish "a relationship of shared group identity which can be reasonably traced historically or prehistorically"?

Kilo'kaga,[48] or "Kellogue," as his identity was recorded on the treaty, probably voiced responses to mid-nineteenth-century American cultural constructs. But these were no doubt fashioned not in the ways of what the United States called "the tribe," but of his s?aaMaks (relations). He and many of his relations lived at a specific place on ?ews (Upper Klamath Lake), and they were distinct from ma'klaks (other—now "Indian"—people) who lived elsewhere on the lake, on ya'aga (lower Williamson River), and from the e'ukshi ma'klaks (Klamath Marsh people). But he and all the distinct communities that became the federally recognized Klamath Tribes had to learn to see themselves in ways that mattered to the United States.

In one example of this double standard, scientists refuse to return ancestors of the Fallon Paiute-Shoshone people because of "evidence of discontinuity in material culture, settlement patterns, and subsistence strategies" over thousands of years (Barker, Ellis, and Damadio 2007: 97). Yet when George Washington died (comparatively recently) in 1799, more than 90 percent of the American population was rural ("settlement patterns") compared to about 16 percent today; 90 percent farmed for a living ("subsistence strategies") compared to about 2 percent today; and they wore powdered wigs and possessed nothing made of nylon or plastic ("material culture").

From Fallon Paiute-Shoshone Tribe v. United States Bureau of Land Management, U.S. District Court for the District of Nevada (2006); Bonnichsen Robson et al. v. United States of America and the Confederated Tribes of the Colville Reservation et al. (2004); and Simic, Andre, and Harry G. Custred Jr., Motion for Leave to File Brief of Amicus Curiae, Bonnichsen et al.

Scientists fighting to weaken NAGPRA, then, continue to insist that modern Natives are not related to our precontact ancestors if we cannot prove that anthropological concepts that their own ancestors created ("modern tribal groups") existed among Native peoples before anthropologists arrived.

Said another way, earlier generations of anthropologists and government officials grouped and organized Native peoples in ways that were politically expedient for the United States. Justifying the theft of lands, signing treaties, assigning reservations, creating tribal rolls, dissolving reservations with land allotments, and tribal terminations all required that the United States be able to claim to know about and deal honestly with Native political entities. Although now inseparable from modern Indian life, federally recognized tribes, tribal governments, and tribal constitutions were created for that purpose. For scientists to insist that Native dead who lived before the United States existed must now be proven to have been of "modern-day tribes," then, is compounded foolishness.

In the decades since the passage of NAGPRA, scientists have upped the ante on this strategy. They now claim that when Congress created the law it intended to make a bizarre distinction between being Native American and being "Native American within the meaning of NAGPRA." While the dead buried in our traditional homelands before Europeans arrived may be Natives, they say, they are not Indians under the law. To push this tortured logic, they insist on a ridiculously literal and inventive reading of the definition of "Native American" from the statute.

In section 2, "Definitions," NAGPRA says: "'Native American' means of, or relating to, a tribe, people, or culture that is indigenous to the United States." In the lawsuits they have filed, the scientists claim that the word "is," here, means that Native communities that existed before the United States became a nation—but no longer existed *at the time* it came into existence—*are not* "Native American within the meaning of NAGPRA."[49] Living Native peoples, the scientists assert, must prove that our ancestors who lived before the creation of the United States were members of "tribes" recognized by the United States since its inception. Otherwise, they say, these ancestors are not legally Native Americans, and NAGPRA does not apply to them. And if NAGPRA does not apply, then the oral history clause in NAGPRA is also meaningless. If there is no longer a legal requirement that our oral histories be considered in our attempts to recover the bodies of our ancestors, then we are right back where we started—before NAGPRA was passed.

Should the scientists succeed with this strategy—and so far, the courts have supported them—Indians will once again be placed in the dubious position of needing hostile scientists to protect us from hostile scientists.

NAGPRA will only apply if these scientists, using science, conclude that our dead belong under our care and protection. Again, this is exactly the unchecked colonialism that necessitated the passage of NAGPRA in the first place.

In 2005, Walter Echo-Hawk asked the US Senate Committee on Indian Affairs to recognize just how dishonorably creative the scientists opposing NAGPRA had become. In his testimony he referenced the Ninth Circuit Court, which ruled in favor of scientists who sued to stop the return of the Columbia River tribes' ancestor, whom they call "the Ancient One" and the scientists call "Kennewick Man."

> *It is telling that no legislative history is cited to support the Ninth Circuit's restrictive interpretation of NAGPRA's definition of "Native American." ... Indeed, there is not legislative history concerning that definition because it was not considered controversial. Everyone who worked on the bill, including myself, logically assumed that all pre-Columbian remains indigenous to the United States are "Native American" and would be covered by the Act.*[50]

While it is certainly the case that Native leaders fighting for the passage of NAGPRA did not anticipate this particular tactic of interpretation gymnastics, the legislative history clearly shows that they distrusted the motivations of the scientists opposing them. At the same congressional hearing where the SAA began questioning "the presumption of affiliation" between living Native peoples and "human remains or objects from their aboriginal lands,"[51] Native American Rights Fund attorney Henry Sockbeson (Penobscott) warned the congressional committee not to trust the leaders of the scientific organizations whose testimony was to follow his own.

> *I would ask that the committee ... really just consider what the museums are attempting to accomplish here. They are simply attempting to maintain control over these collections.... I believe that the committee should be on guard against recalcitrance [stubborn resistance] on the part of these museums.... They're going to do everything possible to retard the return of these remains.*[52]

In retrospect, it appears that at least some of the scientists fighting to prevent and then weaken the law knew in the months leading up to passage exactly what they were planning. Why, unless they had thought carefully about their current strategy of contesting the definition of "Native American," would they have challenged (prior to passage of the law) "the presumption of affiliation between a group and human remains or objects from their aboriginal lands"? If they had not quietly planned to hold hundreds of thousands of our ancestors, why would the same group of archaeologists insist, again before passage, that "the difficult and contentious provisions concerning unaffiliated remains should be deleted," only agreeing to a final version of the law "after elimination of the provisions determining disposition of unidentifiable remains."[53]

Again, it appears that once scientific leaders opposing graves protection realized that a law was inevitable, they concocted a highly inventive strategy for undercutting the new law's purpose. First, they argued that living Natives are unaffiliated with our precontact ancestors; then they insisted that, "provisions concerning unaffiliated remains should be deleted" from the final version of NAGPRA; and to seal the deal, they pressured the committee to remove language about what would become of ("disposition") our ancestors labeled, *by scientists*, as "unidentifiable."

In conclusion, twenty-two years after NAGPRA became law, at least 120,000 of our dead relatives continue to be held and labeled by archaeologists, physical anthropologists, and museum professionals as "culturally unidentifiable." Many of these universities and museums have declared 100 percent, or nearly 100 percent to be "culturally unidentifiable."[54] In addition, the total number of Indian dead held by federal and state agencies remains unknown because they have yet to even complete accurate "inventories," as required by NAGPRA. As their success in resisting the law thus far proves, these scientists are smart and powerful. But as Natives, our responsibility to our ancestors connects every generation to the one that follows. Thus, we will prevail.

CHAPTER 20

Blood Quantum

DENYING ANCESTRY AND FRAGMENTING LĀHUI

Jonathan Osorio

The Hawaiian sovereignty movement is often traced to the creation of Ka Lāhui Hawai'i in 1987, a native initiative for self-government that drafted a constitution, created a government, and registered more than twenty thousand citizens over the following three years. Ka Lāhui laid claim to the so-called Ceded Lands, approximately two million acres of Hawaiian Kingdom Crown and government lands that had been turned over to the United States in 1898 by the American assisted Republic of Hawai'i. The republic, which "owed its entire existence"[1] to the United States' interference in January 1893 when the queen was forced to leave the throne of Hawai'i, had lobbied for annexation from its inception, and represented about four thousand mostly white citizens in a country made up of forty thousand Kanaka and one hundred thousand mostly Asian residents.

Ka Lāhui emerged in part because of the failure of American education to fully eradicate a distinct Hawaiian identity, in part because of the massive contradictions between American ideologies and actual political practices in the Islands since the takeover, and also in part because of the impoverishment and dispossession of our own Native people, largely in the twenthieth century. Ka Lāhui's constitution framed a nation-within-a-nation, called for recognition of our status as a Native people within the United States, and laid claim to the "Ceded Lands."

Since 1993, however, vigorous scholarship has asserted that Hawaiʻi's actual status is not an American state that houses a native American population but rather an independent nation-state occupied by American military forces for more than a century and unlawfully dispossessed of its government and its dominion over its own lands.[2] While the Native American notion faces mounting challenges from a growing number of independence adherents in Hawaiʻi, it is fairly clear that a majority of Kanaka, perhaps an overwhelming majority, favor some kind of self-government and restoration of our traditional resources. In fact in 1993, an apology resolution engineered by two of Hawaiʻi's senators was signed by President Bill Clinton, which acknowledged the United States' role in the overthrow of our independent government and the subsequent taking of our lands.

In 1989, I became a citizen of Ka Lāhui Hawaiʻi and registered the names of my two sons as well. It was about the same time that I had begun researching the Hawaiian Kingdom's constitutions and legislatures that would eventually produce a history of the kingdom entitled *Dismembering Lāhui*, and associating with incredible scholars, patriots, and leaders such as Haunani Kay and Mililani Trask, Kekuni Blaisdell, Coochie Cayan, Sam Kealoha, Clara Kakalia, Lilikalā, Soli Niheu, Kanalu Young, and others too numerous to name. I knew that my life from that point on would always be connected and committed to this nation. Well before the American president and his Congress signed the apology bill I knew that America had taken the kingdom's and our queen's lands along with our nation's government in 1893. Like Kawaipuna Prejean, I knew that there was only one word for a country that would do this: "thief." When in 1993 the US Congress issued a lengthy apology to the Hawaiian people, acknowledging that we had never relinquished either our claim to our lands[3] or our inherent sovereignty, my reaction, like many others' was, "Good. Now, when are you going to give our country back to us?"

In 1994, I joined three other plaintiffs to sue the state and prevent it from selling any more of these lands to which neither it nor the US government was entitled. I knew by then that our nation's claim to the land was not just moral, it was legal, and I believed then that we had law and justice on our side, and I believed that I was acting for the whole āhui—not Ka Lāhui, but all of us who were descended from the kingdom subjects; all of us, whether Native born or naturalized, all of us, who felt that we were not Americans, that we would live and die as Hawaiians.

My name is Jonathan Kay Kamakawiwoʻole Osorio. My names are the surnames of three grandparents. Kay is from my German American grandfather from Ohio, Kamakawiwoʻole from my ʻŌiwi grandmother, and Osorio from the Portuguese laborer who came to Hilo as a child more than a century ago. My mother's mother, Nani Akiona, is the only grandparent whose name I do not carry. She is also the only grandparent I never knew.

I was born in Hilo, Hawaiʻi. I knew none of my sixteen great-grandparents, half of whom were ʻŌiwi wale (of only native ancestry) and of the others, only my Chinese great-grandfather, Akiona, even came to Hawaiʻi. I am, like the vast majority of Kanaka Maoli living in the world today, the grateful descendant of many ethnicities. I am also related to every single Kanaka Maoli (Native person) because of my ancestry. It is that relationship to Kanaka Maoli that I want to speak of in this story.

Our people, our lāhui, have always been quite conscious of the importance of genealogy. Among our Aliʻi (chiefs), the choice of mates, particularly the one who would raise their status and advance their rank through their children, was a significant part of their role. It was said that makaʻāinana (people of the land—not chiefs) did not really know their moʻokūʻauhau (genealogies), and that was all that separated them from aliʻi, since everyone knew that all Kanaka came from the same original ancestors. But makaʻāinana also knew the significance of moʻokūʻauha because the aliʻi personified that knowledge in the power they wielded and the status the society granted them.

Even after the aliʻi were no longer our chiefs, no longer ruled over the ʻāina (land), no longer held the House of Nobles, and no longer reigned over the Kingdom of Kamehameha,[4] we Kanaka continued to cherish ancestry. We continued to uphold the relationships we had with one another, although by the twentieth century we were increasingly related to people of other nationalities as well. What did those other relationships with different ancestries—German, Portuguese, Chinese, Japanese, Korean, Ilocano, mean? I'm certain that each relationship meant different things to different families, and even to individuals within each different family. For instance, what did it mean to be part Chinese? In some ʻohana, it was a source of pride; in some, like ours, it meant little. As a teacher I have read so many essays written by students who have said that their families were ashamed of their Hawaiian ancestry, and they clung to their Chinese side or Japanese or haole (Caucasian) side. Some students wrote that a large part of their own maturity was their claiming of their Kanaka ancestry despite their own families' prejudices.

This reminds me of a novel that I read once set in modern China and the agony experienced by a so-called half-breed who experienced nothing but isolation from his Chinese relatives and racist contempt from the white community in Hong Kong. I remember thinking how fortunate we were to be Hawaiians, accepting of everyone—in fact, even to the point where some of our ʻohana thought that we had been fortunate to marry above ourselves—into a Japanese family, or a haole family. Then it occurred to me that such "fortune" often accompanied a contempt for our own Hawaiianness.

And that is when I realized what a horrible legacy racism has left for us here in our own country. For even as we have willingly embraced and married into virtually every ethnicity that exists, even as we have never adopted the policies of racial discrimination so favored by our haole ancestors in America, we have been infected by the belief that race—not ancestry—matters.

There is such a difference between the two. Ancestry acknowledges your ancestors. It knows them. It understands that some ancestors were more capable, skilled, and perhaps more worth knowing than others. It recognizes that some ancestors are more relevant to you as an individual than others. It even recognizes that such relevance is relative, so that when you travel to Portugal and meet the cousins and brothers and nephews of your grandfather for the first time, they are for that week or month, the most important people on earth. Ancestry connects you to the myriad human beings who have walked this planet before you and allows you to connect with the unseen billions who may follow you.

Racism is the belief that human beings are really the product of different races and that there are powerful differences in intelligence, alertness, creativity—even honesty and trustworthiness—that only a kind of blood-rinsing can erase. Racism at its height, in the last century, supposed a hierarchy of ethnicities with Haole at the top, Blacks at the Bottom, and Browns and Yellows in between. In the peculiar science of racism, capacity and destiny were color coded, and the white society that dreamed up this little science imagined that over generations of intermarriage, one's undesirable traits, like one's color, could be washed away.

That is the genesis of the blood quantum rule in the Hawaiian Homes Act. Most of us understand that the rule was engineered by members of the US Congress and some of the territorial leaders in order to minimize the numbers of Kanaka who would qualify for homesteads. Thanks to the scholarship of J. Kēhaulani Kauanui in her book, *Hawaiian Blood*, we know that the blood quantum idea was surprising and upsetting to Kanaka members of the Ahahui Puʻuhonua who were lobbying for Hawaiian Homesteads in Congress in 1920, and that when asked by a US congressman about what blood quantum should qualify, Kanaka John Wise replied that perhaps one had to be at least 1/32 Hawaiian to be considered Hawaiian. It was really another way of saying that blood quantum didn't matter—that we were all Hawaiians and should all qualify.[5]

Congress's deliberations were the cruelest kind of cynicism, knowing that within as little as a single generation, the families of some awardees would no longer qualify, and the land would return to the colonial government. Yet I doubt that the return of the land was the foremost thing on Congress's mind. American leaders also believed that the Homestead Act was about assisting a struggling minority—struggling not because our national government and lands had been stolen from us, but struggling because we were lazy and not very bright, generous perhaps, but also somewhat brutal and prone to alcoholism. As our minority intermarried into more *reliable* races, the need for free land would gradually disappear. It was bad enough that people could conceive of such a thing about us. It was worse that so many of our people believed it.

Racism continued to define Hawaiians right up to the end of the twentieth century when the US Supreme Court decided that Office of Hawaiian Affairs (OHA) Trustees could not be elected in state elections by Hawaiian beneficiaries. A fourth-generation Caucasian landowner on

Applying for Hawaiian Home Lands
Loa'a Ka 'Āina Ho'opulapula

Aloha Kākou!

Welcome to the Hawaiian Home Lands program. The program has its roots in the Hawaiian Homes Commission Act of 1920, as amended. It provides native Hawaiians with several benefits that we hope will assist you and your 'ohana for generations to come.... In the course of applying for a homestead, you may find yourself embarking on a journey of discovery into your family's history. While it often takes time, for most people it is a process well worth the effort.

Eligibility Requirements:

To be eligible to apply for a Hawaiian Home Lands homestead lease, you must meet two requirements:

- You must be at least 18 years of age; and
- You must be a native Hawaiian, defined as "any descendant of not less than one-half part of the blood of the races inhabiting the Hawaiian Islands previous to 1778." This means you must have a blood quantum of at least 50 percent Hawaiian. This requirement remains unchanged since the HHCA's passage in 1921.

From https://dhhl.hawaii.gov/applications/applying-for-hawaiian-home-lands

Hawai'i named Harold Rice claimed that his being barred from voting in an OHA election was racial discrimination and a violation of the Fourteenth and Fifteenth Amendments to the US Constitution. In the majority opinion of *Rice v Cayetano*, Justice Anthony Kennedy declared that Hawaiian ancestry was really no different from race, and that our practices were a violation of American civil rights laws and practices. The irony of the American high court idealistically rooting out racism in Hawai'i, while its blood quantum practices remain inviolate throughout the country, is almost too painful to acknowledge. Just a decade after *Rice v Cayetano*, the Hawai'i state attorney general summoned the blood quantum argument in order to prevent me from remaining as the lone plaintiff in a lawsuit that had gone to the US Supreme Court. A handful of us, including the Office of Hawaiian Affairs, had been coplaintiffs in a suit to stop the state's sale of lands belonging to the Hawaiian Kingdom government and our former queen. After we obtained a substantially favorable ruling by the Hawai'i Supreme Court, the Hawai'i governor Linda Lingle appealed to the US Supreme Court in 2009.

Some Hawaiian people were fearful of what the strongly conservative federal court might decide. When the Supreme Court made a fairly narrow ruling, overruling (vacating) the state's decision and remanding it back to our court, our attorneys, and, no doubt, the Office of Hawaiian Affairs, were greatly relieved. The US Supreme Court justices could have, after all, decided that Hawaiians had no claims at all to the lands. Instead, the federals insisted that the state supreme court could make any decisions about the lands it wished, but it could not use as a foundation or justification the 1993 Apology Resolution passed by Congress and signed by President Clinton. The court clarified that the apology could not create any obligation on the state of Hawai'i and reaffirmed the state's ultimate authority over the lands.

In their great relief that the decision was not worse than it could have been, our plaintiffs, including the Office of Hawaiian Affairs, leaped at an offer from the state legislature to require a two-thirds majority vote in the state legislature to authorize a sale of Ceded Lands in return for all of the plaintiffs withdrawing from the lawsuit. However, the very same law made it equally difficult to prevent the state from exchanging Ceded Lands with private landowners, and in that decade thousands of acres of Ceded Lands had been exchanged for less than three acres of urban lands in Honolulu.

When I refused to withdraw, the state attorney general played the blood quantum card, asserting to the state court that I should be denied standing case because I am not a 50 percent blood quantum Native. It was an astonishing argument: I had no legal standing to sue to protect my nation's lands because I did not meet the blood quantum requirement set by a racist Congress in 1921. The attorney general's strategy, in fact, created an immediate problem for the Office of Hawaiian Affairs, which had agreed to support his attempt to get this case dismissed. But his attack on my standing was also an attack on hundreds of thousands of Hawaiians of less than 50 percent blood quantum who are also OHA's beneficiaries. OHA found itself in an impossible position. In fact, one trustee blamed me for the situation, and the agency seemed to be at a loss to understand why I didn't simply withdraw from the fight with the rest of them.

In the end, the Hawai'i Supreme Court denied our petition to continue the case on the basis of ripeness. Because the legislature had made the sale of ceded lands more difficult, the court did not believe that there was an urgency requiring their intervention, and they dismissed the case without prejudice. But not before proclaiming that I, and therefore every Kanaka of Hawaiian ancestry, has standing before the court with regard to our land claims.

There are things worth fighting for, even if the fight may be lost. I believe that the Crown and Government Lands of the Hawaiian Kingdom do not belong to the United States and that the state should not have power over them. In fact, I believe that the descendants of maka'āinana have undivided tenant interests in every square inch of the lands of Hawai'i, not just Crown and Government lands. These are rights that have been provided by Hawaiian Kingdom laws since 1839 and clarified by the Kuleana Act in 1850. Finally, I believe that the Hawaiian Homes Act of 1921 not only disguised the theft of our national lands by pretending that the two hundred thousand acres *granted* by Congress was a generous act to help our people but also saddled us with a blood quantum requirement that encouraged us to believe that the more Hawaiian we are, the less capable, the less responsible, the less legitimate we are.

The issue of blood quantum is not only about the law. Blood quantum, race, and ancestry are also about politics. And neither the attorney general and governor, nor the Hawai'i and US Supreme Court, control the politics of blood quantum. We Kanaka Maoli do. In this case, the attorney general's strategy and the court's response forces us to do what has always been in our power to do, and that is denounce quantum as the racist policy that it is and call for its repeal. So I call on all the Hawaiian organizations, even the Homestead Associations, to denounce blood quantum as a racist law and validate what John Wise in 1920 knew: that we are all Hawaiians, we are related. We are the lāhui. This is our country, and the United States still has our lands.

I understand how difficult this is for some of our poʻe Hawaiʻi. There are, I am sure, some who think there is some legitimacy to the notion that the more Hawaiian blood you have the more Hawaiian you are. But wherever we look, we find that there is no evidence and no rational basis for the idea that having ancestors other than Kanaka Maoli lessens your Hawaiian qualities—whatever we think they are—rather than simply enhancing our qualities with other genetic traits and even genetic memories.

Still, I am sure that anyone who has spent thirty-five years on that bloody waiting list is not going to leap at the chance of adding another two or three hundred thousand beneficiaries to it. Regulations could be adopted by the Hawaiian Homes Department that no new beneficiary can be awarded before those who are currently on waiting lists. But if we continue to allow blood quantum to define us, we are significantly smaller than the 200,000 that live in Hawaiʻi, and within a generation or two, we will be practically gone. I say to you that the theft of our lands is temporary, and that so long as we never stop our claims to them our nation will once again secure them. To do this we have to be a nation, one lāhui, and we need everyone, every voice, to fight for each other.

I began this by speaking of the aliʻi and how they consciously mated with other Aliʻi in order to preserve or enhance their rank. Some of our own people today think that we could do the same thing—Hawaiians marry only Hawaiians, 50 percenters marry only 50 percenters, and keep the blood quantum high in your family, or even keep the race "pure." But Aliʻi rarely limited their love interests to those who could benefit their rank and careers. They had numerous liaisons with one another, so that rank was only one criterion for pursuing a mate. Once they chose to limit their marriages to monogamy, we see more instances of chiefs marrying for reasons that had nothing to do with rank. In the process, I think we have all discovered that it isn't easy to control your children's marriage and sexual preferences. In some ways, that kind of control would be as oppressive as racism—not just to non-Hawaiians but to our own children.

I think we need to be as courageous as those Aliʻi and maka'āinana were, who came to grips with the host of bewildering changes that came with the exposure of Hawaiʻi to the wide world. They accepted foreigners into the aupuni, into their families, into their hearts—haole, pake, kepani, pāʻele, everyone—and still kept their ʻŌiwi ancestral heritages alive so that we today can reclaim what they never surrendered: our kinship, and more importantly, pride in who we are—a people of different colors and origins but bound together by a common moʻokuʻauhau. But we must also continue the legal fight for the lands. The ʻāina is a part of our genealogy, the elder sibling of our ancient stories that cares and nurtures the lāhui. We have a kuleana to protect our kuaʻana, the land, and it is a kuleana that extends to all of us who share this Kanaka Maoli genealogy. It is that genealogy and the responsibility that goes with it that sets us apart from the American and other settlers, not some ridiculous calculation of blood percentages.

It is not only the law that matters now. It matters what we do. The governor and the state have handed the initiative to us, and they don't even know it. We have said we are a lāhui. Let us act like one.

CHAPTER 21

We Almost Forgot Who We Are

ONE FAMILY'S JOURNEY SURVIVING COLONIALISM

Joseph Whittle

DAD

We almost forgot who we are. When it's too painful to remember, that's what happens. It's a predictable response. Pain and trauma are pen and ink rewriting life's trajectory, blotting out the past in exchange for a hastily scribbled edit meant to replace chapters in the book of life. Pain and trauma can weave the narratives of human history, describing war after war through the annals of time; from the wars we fight with each other to occupy physical space, to the wars we fight within ourselves. Pain and trauma are essential tools of the colonizer.

My father never knew his father. He barely knew his Caddo/Delaware mother, who died in our tribal territory near Anadarko, Oklahoma, when he was a toddler. Long before the passage of the Indian Child Welfare Act, which reversed federal policy of preferentially choosing white families as guardians of Indian orphans, my father found himself an Indian orphan. The Whittles were a white family whose mother lived in the apartment downstairs from my grandmother, father, and his two brothers. When my grandmother died, they agreed to adopt my father.

The Whittles—Courtesy of Joseph Whittle

I'm not sure if Grandma Lavera wanted Dad adopted by a white family and taken away from Anadarko, or if it just happened that way. I do know that it broke my great-aunt Florence Halfmoon's heart when her sister's boy, Tommy, was taken from Indian Country, and that she didn't get to raise him as her own. Auntie Florence was the closest thing Dad had to an Indian mother after Grandma died. Symbolically, in the "Indian way" of relation, she was his mother. It wasn't her first time as a surrogate mother, either. Florence helped raise my grandma Lavera when their parents died, leaving Grandma orphaned at about six years old (only slightly older than my father was when she left him an orphan). Florence was much older than Lavera, and already an adult and a mother herself when my great-grandparents Harris (an original Delaware Nation allottee) and Nora (an original Caddo Nation allottee) died one year apart from each other. Years later, sitting in the shade on her porch during a hot Oklahoma summer afternoon, Auntie Florence would tell my brother, "Tommy is my boy…," with love and sadness in her eyes as she watched him walk across the lawn. She'd hoped to adopt my dad when Lavera died. Florence and her husband, Edgar, lived in Oklahoma City. By the time she found out Lavera had died, and they arrived in Anadarko to check on Dad and his two brothers, the adoption paperwork was done. My dad, born Tommy Lee Allenbaugh (Conner), had become Thomas Claude Whittle.

Grandma Florence—
Courtesy of Joseph Whittle

Grandma Lavera—
Courtesy of Joseph Whittle

I don't know much about my grandma Lavera. I know that my dad was not her husband's son. I know that her estranged husband would not care for my illegitimate father when she died, but that he took Dad's two older brothers, who were his sons. I know that Grandma liked to drink, much like my dad did most of his life. I know that my dad told my mom that Grandma used to tie him to his crib when he was a toddler so she could go to work. I know that my dad speculated to my mom that Grandma had been a "working girl" to support herself and her children, and that may have had something to do with her death. I know that my dad never wanted to know who his birth father was—or so he told himself. He told me once that Auntie Florence told him she knew who his father was, but Dad told her he didn't want to know. I know that I wish he had wanted to know, because I do.

One thing that I'll never know is all of the myriad and devastating ways in which losing his mother, and being removed from his Native family, affected my father. Certainly the results of his removal from Indian Country weren't all bad, however. It did lead to the existence of his children, who were a profound joy in his life (despite his long physical and emotional absences from our lives). Not to mention that the love the Whittles gave him—in particular that of his adopted mother—Mary Ellen, was a saving grace to him given the circumstances he was thrust into as a child. Sadly, he lost his second mother, Mary Ellen Whittle, to brain cancer when he was sixteen years old. I don't know how a person recovers from losing one mother as a child, let alone two. I don't think my dad ever did recover from losing his mommas.

The love of Auntie Florence, his adopted mother, Mary Ellen, and his children and wives, was likely the reason my dad survived this world for sixty-eight years. Auntie Florence, the last Caddo/Delaware matriarch and Elder of my immediate Native family, kept his connection to his tribes and blood alive—tenuous and weak though it was. My stepmother, Lillian, led him away from his alcohol addiction, no doubt adding years to his life. My mother made sure that, regardless of the failure of their marriage, or even his failures as a father, his children were able to maintain our connection to him as much as possible. His self-medication with alcohol and unhealthy responses to the trauma of his life interfered dramatically with his role as a parent and a husband. Yet despite the pain his failures as a parent caused my siblings and me, I've often wondered if the scars from his parental downfalls weren't deeper in him than they are in me. Because it was clear he carried not only the pain of it but the guilt of it as well. For me, no matter his absence, I never doubted the deep love he had for us. I certainly felt and was traumatized by his lack of presence in my life, but I never consciously doubted his love.

One of the last things my dad said to me, as I showed him a photo of Grandma Lavera he'd given me years before, which I'd saved on my phone, was, "That's my momma?" His fading eyes lit up, tears welling as he reached for the phone. He gazed intently for a long time at the photo, as if lost in another world. I saw the warmth that only a momma can provide wash over him, and he sank contentedly back onto his pillow. Before he drifted off to sleep he said with a smile on his face, "Son, you know what I want to do? Let's all go back to Oklahoma together again...." Two days later, cancer took him to join his mommas.

OKLAHOMA AND DAD

There are many reasons Dad lacked a strong connection to his cultural identity as a Caddo and Delaware man. The era into which he was born was not the least of them. Indeed, that era played a major role in his removal from Indian Country, given the willful preference of adopting Native children to white families for assimilation purposes. Dad was born on October 26, 1945, during a period I call the "John Wayne Era": the crowning moment for Manifest Destiny, cultural genocide, and the forced assimilation of American Indians. By that time, two generations of Indian boarding school victims, having had (or survived the attempt to have) the Indianness beaten and whipped—or even raped—out of them, were churned back into the world with the philosophy "kill the Indian, save the man" tattooed onto their psyches. Self-loathing to the point of complete identity abandonment was colonialism's ultimate goal for Indian children.

The assimilation era began in earnest with the passage of the Dawes Severalty Act of 1887 and the implementation of lawful child kidnapping via Indian boarding schools, which continued in an official capacity until the civil rights movement. The 1940s and 1950s were the ultimate height of success for what began with the Indian Wars and was intended to end with forced assimilation for Native American people. At that time, society was wholeheartedly deluded by the illusion of American exceptionalism and inherent righteousness. The US economy was booming after the end of World War II, and so were the resource extraction and military industries that grew from it. Those industries are still largely sustained by resources taken from Native lands with little benefit and high costs (such as black lung disease and cancer) to Native communities. John Wayne was killing Indians every weekend on the silver screen, reinforcing the right of American might and the wrongness of Indianness. Government and industry were hard at work making sure the public never questioned where the wealth powering that "exceptionalism" came from or who was paying the highest share of the cost for American "greatness." (America seems yet eager to fall prey to the fallacy of exceptionalism, given the "Make America Great Again" slogan of its former president—which hearkens back to that John Wayne Era).

Dad was born at the same time Indian Termination Policy was being put into place. Termination was a series of laws enacted with the intent of assimilating Native Americans into mainstream society in the belief that Indigenous people should abandon their traditional lives and become "civilized." Assimilation efforts had been in place for centuries through multiple governments; however, laws that enforced without consent the termination of tribal existence were a new development at the time of Dad's birth. The premise was that tribal structure and culture must be completely terminated and Indigenous identity dissolved into American society. Congress set about ending the relationship between tribes and the federal government and enacting policies to force or push assimilation. Policies such as the Indian Relocation Act of 1956, which facilitated and encouraged Indian people to relocate from reservations to urban areas and abandon cultural ties to take up living as "productive modern Americans."

As is the Indigenous way with hardship, assimilation policy became a story of resilience for Indigenous people. But not before it had devastating effects on my father's identity and relationship with his Native cultures. He, too, was an urban Indian, who grew up on the mean streets of Richmond, California. Having become an urban Indian by adoption, however, my father had no tribal connections in his home or social life. Most people just assumed he was Mexican. He had more connection with Latinx culture throughout his life than he did with Native culture. In fact, my stepmother, Lillian, is from an Indigenous Mexican immigrant family.

Shortly after Dad's adoption, the Whittles, like many poor "Okies" before them, packed up and moved to California in search of better opportunity. Luckily, Dad was able to enjoy occasional summer visits back to Oklahoma with the Whittles to see their family, which also meant he would visit his Auntie Florence and two brothers. His loving mother, Mary Ellen, made sure that Dad would stay connected with his Native family. He was able to grow up making fond memories of summer adventures with his brothers, and receiving motherly love from Auntie Florence. That was basically his connection to his Native family, history, and culture in its entirety. It was just enough … just enough to keep us alive as Hasinai and Lenape people. As an adult, he would return occasionally to Oklahoma to visit his Native family and look after our family's tribal land.

Mary Ellen and Auntie Florence also made sure Dad remained an enrolled tribal member and the inheritor of my great-grandma Nora's land allotment in Anadarko, which sits just across the Washita River from the Riverside School. Founded in 1871, the Riverside School is the oldest federally operated Indian boarding school still in existence. Generations of my family went there. Today it is run by Native staff and has become a sought-after education opportunity for Native people, offering traditional and cultural engagement. Its history, however, remains that of institutional whitewashing and assimilation. Both my uncles went there, my grandmother, and possibly my great-grandparents, though I am not sure.

The Conners—Top, left to right: Great Grandpa Harris Conner (Grandson of John Conner) Great Grandma Nora Conner, Great Uncle Wilbur Conner, Unknown Uncle; Bottom, left to right: Great Uncle Sammy Connor, Grandmother Lavera Conner, Great Aunt Florence (Conner) Halfmoon, Cousin Irene Halfmoon (baby)— Photo taken on family's tribal allotment in Oklahoma—Courtesy of Joseph Whittle

Dad's visits to Oklahoma kept him connected to his family, but they didn't do much to keep him connected to his cultures. It was hard enough for residents of the reservation at that time in history to remain connected to their cultures. Pan-Indianism was prevalent among many tribes, wherein generalized tribal customs and practices were being adopted by some tribal members, and often were represented to a public that expected a stereotypical and pictorialized version of Native Americans—a version that would have America wistfully remember with romanticized fondness a "vanished race" that had become no more than a mythical display for consumption and entertainment; real-life "wooden Indians." The effects of assimilation were amalgamating Native cultures into one easily packaged representation that could be brought out and displayed when it was useful or entertaining, then put away out of sight when it was inconvenient.

The assimilation programming Native people endured over decades of cultural assault allowed us at times to participate in our own erasure. I remember my dad recounting with fondness watching John Wayne movies with his brothers at the Redskin Theater in downtown Anadarko. A giant sign hangs from its facade in all capitals proclaiming, "REDSKIN"; a term rooted in bounties for our bloody scalps, and a not-so-subtle reminder of the value colonialism applies to Native people and identity. I do recall Dad saying he always rooted for the Indians in those movies. Of course, any time a "good Indian" was depicted, it was actually a white actor in redface. When Native actors were hired, they typically played extras and villains. It was almost always a white man who would play an Indian with redeeming characteristics—programming the idea that an Indian must look to the white man to best interpret what was redeeming about Indigenous people. The redeeming part, of course, required whiteness.

Technically, Anadarko is not on "reservation" land. It is in "tribal jurisdiction." The reason for that lies in the Dawes Act of 1887, which surveyed tribal land and divided it into allotments for individual Indians. The intent was to promote assimilation and transfer lands to white settlers. It also drove tribes to accept individual rather than communal ownership of land, forcing an end to cyclical and nomadic subsistence hunting and gathering practices upon which all Indigenous cultures are built. (Even tribes with agrarian practice as a part of their cultures required cyclical and communal land base to truly sustain those practices on a community level.) The act provided that the government would classify as "excess" Indian lands remaining after allotments and sell them on the open market. Senator Henry M. Teller of Colorado, an opponent of the act, said it would "despoil the Indians of their lands and to make them vagabonds on the face of the earth." Teller also said, "The real aim is to get at the Indian lands and open them up to settlement. The provisions for the apparent benefit of the Indians are but the pretext to get at his lands and occupy them.... If this were done in the name of Greed, it would be bad enough; but to do it in the name of Humanity ... is infinitely worse."[1]

The effect of the Dawes Act was profound in Oklahoma Indian Territory, given that Oklahoma territory was initially intended serve as one giant reservation/conglomeration of reservations for tribes from across the land. The Dawes Act ended the reservation system in Oklahoma, fractionalizing and dividing up communal lands into allotments and Bureau of Indian Affairs jurisdictions. Tribes would hold both individual and tribal lands, but they were not defined by a reservation or community border and could be sold off. Some Oklahoma tribes still refer to their communities as "reservations," but they have been culturally integrated at a much higher extent than actual reservation lands. The act allowed for the state of Oklahoma to come into being and resulted in the Oklahoma Land Rush, a frenzied rush by settlers to seize Indian land on a first-come, first-claim basis. (I imagine it must have looked something like Black Friday at Wal-Mart, except with wagons and horses and colonial conquest and genocide.)

Grandma Lavera was born toward the end of the Dawes Era and just before the beginning of the John Wayne Era. Lavera and her younger brother Sammy were the youngest of five children, the rest of whom were grown when their parents Harris and Nora Conner died in 1929 and 1930, respectively. I can only imagine how difficult life may have been for Grandma Lavera as an Indian orphan of the Great Depression/ Dust Bowl. I know nothing of her childhood experiences.

Great-Grandpa and Grandma Harris and Nora were of the first Indian boarding school generation whose families were forced to abandon the traditional way of life. They were born just before the passage of the Dawes Act. At that time the last holdouts of the Indian Wars, final western frontier tribes such as the Nez Perce and Lakota, were newly facing displacement, the reservation system, and nearly complete loss of homeland. Tribes like mine, the Caddo and Delaware, had been facing waves of colonialism since the early 1600s. Before the passage of the Dawes Act, however, we had managed to maintain most of our traditional way of life despite displacement, war, forced exodus, diaspora migration, and multiple treaties that had been violated over the preceding two centuries.

Nora's father, Willie Edwards, had survived the Trail of Tears, having left our traditional Caddo homelands in Louisiana as a child and joined the devastating march with his mother, Mary Lafitte Edwards. His younger brother died on the Trail and was buried beside it during their forced exodus to Oklahoma Indian Territory. At that time there was no Caddo reservation, so they lived among the Chickasaw and Choctaw after settling in Oklahoma.

About twenty years after the Trail of Tears, the last Caddo bands living in our homelands in East Texas were forced to flee for their lives to Oklahoma as well. The Texans encroaching on Caddo homelands, including the infamous Texas Rangers, had begun murderous rampages in our territory in an effort to eradicate us. (The name "Texas" comes from the Caddo word "teysha," which means "friend" in our language. The Spanish pronounced it "tejas" and used the word to refer to our homeland. Eventually the Americans changed it to Texas.)

To this day the Caddo honor the Indian agent Robert S. Neighbors for calling in federal troops to escort us safely to the reservation in Oklahoma in 1859, because the Texans were intent on killing every last Indian in that region. The Texans were so angry with Neighbors for doing this that when he returned to Texas after safely escorting us to the reservation and releasing the troops, he was ambushed and shot in the back by settlers for letting us live. Little had been done by the Caddo to elicit such hatred, other than refuse to willingly give up our last bit of homeland. (We had already ceded millions of acres to Spain, Mexico, and eventually the United States, who kept violating and rewriting our treaties.)

The Indian agent who took over for Neighbors was named Matthew Leeper. He wrote of our removal from Texas to Oklahoma and the treatment of my tribes by the Texans:

They are a most patient people—they have met with the cruelest reverses I ever knew. After many years of strife and the shedding of blood in Texas, they in good faith entered into treaty stipulations, [and] quietly settled upon the land allotted to them.... Evil minded and designing men commenced their work of desolation upon them, outrages and monstrosities were committed, difficult to realize in an enlightened age. Their property was destroyed, some of their women and children killed, and the remainder threatened to be hunted down; until finally they were forced to abandon Texas and settle here; they did so under promises of peace, protection and ample supplies, until such time as they could learn to become a self-sustaining people; but they appear still to be pursued and threatened by the Texans.[2]

DELAWARE HISTORY AND MY FAMILY

Living among the Caddos in our Texas homelands were a band of Lenni Lenape (Delaware) people known as the "Absentee Delaware." In our language they are "Eheliwsikakw Lenapeyok." The Absentee Delawares had left the main body of Lenni Lenape in the Eastern Woodlands during the late 1700s, as they wished to escape the encroaching settlement of the Americans. (Delaware was the name assigned to our tribe by English colonists, as they had named the Delaware River along which we lived after Virginia governor Thomas West, Third Baron de la Warr. It is the name Lenape people use in our political and sovereign relationship with the colonial world.) On the Delaware side of my family I descend from the Absentee band as well as the main band of Delawares. Over the years I have come to learn more about the Delaware side of my Native family history than the Caddo side, but I have much yet to learn, and probably much I will never have the opportunity to learn, about both sides. Particularly lacking (as my daughter frequently points out) are accounts of the women in our Native family. History has recorded notable men in my Native lineage because many of the men in my family were political leaders for our tribe who signed and/or negotiated treaties. This gave me the opportunity to learn about them sans oral tradition from my elders. In its typically misogynistic fashion, however, "history" recorded very little about the women of my tribes, despite the fact that both tribes are matriarchal cultures. No one among our communities holds more esteem than our grandmothers and aunties.

Harris Conner's parents were Charlie Delaware and Nin-Yun. They were among the Caddos and Absentee Delawares who left Texas for the Oklahoma reservation. Charlie was of main band Delaware descent, and Nin-Yun was Caddo and possibly Absentee Delaware. I don't know who Charlie's mother was for certain. His father was known as

Harris Conner (left) with his friend James Hunter (Delaware), taken in the early 1900s—Courtesy of Joseph Whittle

Captain John Conner. "Captain" was a term given to Delaware war leaders and chieftains; John Conner was the principal chief of the main band of Delawares in Kansas during their final move to Oklahoma. Prior to that he was a leader among the Absentee Delawares in Texas and had accompanied them to Anadarko. How he came to live among the Absentees, after leaving the main band of Delawares earlier in his life, became a significant part of the legacy of American history on the western frontier.

Historian Timothy Crumrin writes of John Conner, "Conner's life was varied, exciting, and played out across much of the American West. So well regarded was Conner that famed frontiersman Richard Dodge wrote that he was 'renowned as having a more minute and extensive knowledge of the North American Continent' than anyone in America. In some ways his life was a mini-series waiting to be filmed." Crumrin goes on to tell of Conner's decision to split from the main group of Delaware as a young man, after the tribe had been required to remove from their promised resettlement lands in Indiana by the 1818 Treaty of St. Mary's.

After a harrowing journey that saw them harassed by whites and many of their goods stolen, the Delaware made it to Kaskaskia, Illinois. It was there that John Conner's path diverged from the Delaware. While their journey was to take them to Missouri, then Kansas, and finally to Oklahoma, John Conner set out on his own. Later recounting the incident Conner said he was stirred by a 'most intense desire' to see an ocean. He knew there were two oceans. Since to go east meant traveling through white man's country, he headed west. Traveling mainly on foot and alone, he made his way to the mouth of the Columbia River in the Pacific Northwest. Turning south, he trekked along the Pacific coast, eventually making his way into Mexico. "Liking the residents of Durango, he lived with them for three years, learning their language and customs."[3]

Eventually Captain Conner grew weary of city life in Durango and decided to return to his people. On his way through Texas he met up with the Absentee Delawares living there with the Caddos and other Eastern Woodland tribes who'd settled in the region. The Absentee Delawares had accepted an invitation from the Spanish to settle in modern Texas and Arkansas during the 1790s. The Spanish government, fearing American encroachment on Spanish territory, invited various Indian nations to settle and act as a buffer against encroaching whites. The Absentee Delawares, many having been disillusioned by American treachery and betrayal, wanted to move west to escape encroachment themselves and to keep living a traditional Indian way of life. The agreement served both parties well for the time being. Throughout the turmoil of changing colonial control of Texas from Spain to Mexico to the Republic of Texas, and finally to the United States, the role of the Delaware as a buffer continued, albeit going from protection of Spanish territory against American encroachment to protection of Texans and Americans from warring Plains Tribes such as the Kiowa and Comanche.

The Delaware had long served a role as peacemakers among Indian nations. We continued that role with the Americans in order to try and serve our own tribal interest as well as that of other Indian nations in securing peace treaties and land grants.

Kerry Holton, my cousin and the current chief of the Delaware Nation (which the federally recognized Absentee Delawares are now known as), shared an account of how the Lenni Lenape came to be widely regarded and respected as peacemakers among other Indian nations. Lenape and Delaware are not the only names we have been known by. We were also known as the "The Grandfathers" by neighboring tribes, as we had been the first to settle in that region. Archaeologists trace consistent occupation of Lenapehoking by Lenape ancestors for at least thirteen thousand years. Many tribes around us were related to or were offshoots of the original Algonquin-speaking Lenape people.

Five hundred years of violent and monumental efforts to force assimilation and erasure throughout generations, and tribal people still refuse to forget who they are. I think that at least in part, this is the context that led John Conner to leave the main band of Delaware (who were once again being displaced and resettled among increasingly more "civilized" and populous surroundings) and set out into the wilderness to live in the way of his ancestors. That path would lead him back to his people, however, as he was unable to abandon their plight for a life of solitude wandering the wilds of Turtle Island. Eventually, he would take on a political and hereditary role as a peacemaker and a leader among the Lenni Lenape.

By the time we found ourselves on the frontier of the Great Plains, many tribal members refused to remain on shrinking and failing farm allotments and simply wandered farther and farther into the West, practicing nomadic subsistence hunting and supplying the tribal community when they could. But the community and cultural structure were beginning to suffer as the ability to subsist/survive on the land shrank. The total loss of homeland for subsistence meant that the Delaware religion known as the "Big House" was lost as well. A longhouse religion unique to the Delaware people, it required that our medicine people find spiritual Power and vision from the land and its spirits—deep within the ability of humankind to exist as a part of this planet with full access to all of its elemental forces and medicine. As that connection was severed, our visionary people lost their true Power, and so the Big House was laid to rest by the Elder Culture Bearers of the Lenape. We still honor and respect that religion and those powers. But we accept and honor that our existence as a people has changed. That doesn't mean we lose our power as a culture and people. But we have changed. We survived that change through the guidance of those spiritual leaders and Culture Bearers, and we trust their vision yet.

A HOMECOMING FOR MY FAMILY

The first memory I have of being aware of my Indigenous identity was when I was about three years old. I had just learned what the term "Indian giver" meant. I knew that I was "Indian," but I didn't really know what that meant. I remember it being explained that an "Indian giver" was a dishonest person who took back promises they had made. I didn't want to be that. I didn't want to be known as that. Later on, when I began white Christian elementary school, I thought that being Indian meant I could receive an "Indian sunburn" without flinching. An "Indian sunburn" is when someone twists the skin on your arm in opposite directions until you make them stop because of the pain. The term has its origins in colonial tales of so-called merciless savages (as the Declaration of Independence calls Native Americans) who were said to persecute and torture innocent settlers they had kidnapped. I didn't know the term's history, but I was proud of the fact that I had taught myself to withstand anyone's efforts to get me to flinch during that process, and I used to show it off to my classmates. By the time I had reached high school, the mascot for the sports teams of my public school was the "Savage," depicted by the same leering, stereotypical big-nosed and stupid-looking cartoon Indian used by the baseball team the Cleveland Indians. The school had chosen that name in "honor" of Chief Joseph (Hinmatóowyalahtq'it) and the Wallowa Band of Nez Perce who had been removed from the (now predominantly white) region in northeast Oregon where I grew up. At every pep assembly two white students from the school would dress up in fake feathers and war paint and dance around the gymnasium "war whooping," clapping their hands over their mouths, and waving around plastic tomahawks.

If there is anything left of the frontier "Wild West" in the lower forty-eight states, it can be found in Wallowa County, Oregon. Tucked away in the remote northeastern corner, it is one of the state's largest counties, with a total population of roughly seven thousand people. Within it are millions of acres of rugged, wild land and Oregon's largest designated wilderness area. Of course, the term "wilderness" is relative. What colonial governments have always called "wilderness," Native people have always called "home." For Native people there is no separation between natural and human history; we are one and the same. My traditions do not say Native people grew into being "on" Turtle Island, they say we grew "from" it. We are part of it. Even the Christian Bible says that humans were created from the "dust of the Earth." That connection was tragically attacked for the Wellamotkin (Wallowa Band Nez Perce) people who had cared for their homeland since time immemorial—much like the tale of so many other tribes, such as the Caddo and Delaware.

My parents arrived in Wallowa County separately in the early 1970s. My dad met my mother, who hailed from an Irish/English family descended from some of the first colonial settlers, when they were in high school together in Richmond, California. They married and had my three older siblings at an early age. When the 1960s hippie movement kicked into full swing, they "turned on, tuned in, and dropped out." My dad, trauma survivor that he was, responded more to the drug, alcohol, and party life aspects of the hippie movement; my mom to the "peace and love" counterculture. It wasn't long before my dad's drinking and anger began to cause a rift between them, eventually leading him to hit the road and drift the country with his hippie buddies. He lived on the beach in Hawaii, worked at a fish cannery in Alaska, and hopped a train from Alaska with a friend and rode the rails hobo-style across Canada. (They separated in Montreal after railroad cops caught his friend and beat him senseless with nightsticks while my dad escaped to another train.) He finally ended up in New York City—our Lenapehoking homeland. I'm not sure how long he was in New York or what he did there—or if he even thought about the fact that he was standing on the ancient homeland of his ancestors. The Dutch, who were the first to colonize what is now New York City, thought they had swindled us out of the Island of Manhattan by trading us a few trinkets and beads. In reality it had been a ceremonial exchange wherein the Lenni Lenape who are the thirteen-thousand-year caretakers of that land, not its "owners," had simply given them permission to access its life cycle as we and other tribes had done sustainably for thousands of years. Those Dutch colonists eventually built a wall around their settlement on the island to keep us off of it, which they decorated with our heads as a reminder. Today it is marked and remembered in the name "Wall Street."

As my dad drifted around the country, my mom took her own journey with my siblings in search of peace and love. They lived in communes and traveled around the West Coast. That led her to the "back to Earth" movement within the hippie community (much inspired by a changing view among the younger generation of the Indian relationship with nature), which in turn through the invitation of a friend led them to the wild landscape of Wallowa County. It wasn't long before my parents decided to give their marriage another try, and my dad joined his family once again. Not long after that, I was born at home on February 19, 1975, in the small town of Enterprise, Oregon. My dad wanted my name to be Joseph in honor of the Nez Perce leader whose homeland he had just arrived in.

At that time, not a whole lot beyond technology had changed about Wallowa County from the early days of its settlement. Society at large was slowly beginning to change for Native Americans, however. The American Indian Movement (AIM), founded by urban Indians like my dad, was in full swing, having occupied the island of Alcatraz. After that, AIM occupied the site of the Wounded Knee Massacre, and more Americans began to pay attention to the voices of Indigenous people.

When I was four years old, alcohol and anger once again drove my parents apart, and my dad went back to California, where he was to live the rest of his life. After that I lived with him for a summer when I was nine, for the last half of my sixth grade year, and for the first half of my junior year in high school. Aside from those brief periods, I saw my dad on some holidays and a few random visits. Our relationship consisted mostly of occasional phone calls, late birthday cards or presents, and a lot of "spoiling" when I would see him. On visits with my dad I would eat whatever I wanted, and toys I liked were purchased for me. I felt loved, because even at a young age I understood why that was happening. I understood the guilt he felt over his absence, and I forgave him for it. That meant so much more to me than the plastic robot with flashing lights that made annoying sounds he bought for me at an Oakland flea market in 1984.

Nonetheless, by the time I reached high school, I was angry. I don't think I ever felt consciously angry at my dad. I was angry at society, and I didn't connect the two. I was angry at the frameworks that were being put around my life, but perhaps in part because they were frameworks not of my own choosing. I was angry at the idea that my fate seemed out of my control. I couldn't simply choose to have a father in my life or the sense of wholeness that I craved. That's not to say that anger defined me, and I'd wager that classmates' and friends' memories of me would more likely be characterized in terms of "happy-go-lucky." I think people probably remember my dad that way as well, outside of his violent moments.

My dad did very little in my life to connect me to my Indigenous identity. I do remember that during Chief Joseph Days he would go out partying and often bring home groups of Nez Perce tribal members from the bar late at night to continue partying and eventually crash out on our floor. This was actually an exciting occasion for us kids, as it was a rare moment that we were able to connect with our fellow Indigenous people. Dad grew up an inner-city street fighter who came out on top. The local "tough guys" of Wallowa County soon learned that my father was not to be trifled with. Some even learned this after being hospitalized for "trifling" with him. He used the space that he had carved for himself in the community to offer solidarity to the Nez Perce tribal members he met during Chief Joseph Days, who on many occasions had to physically fight for their own right to be in the town of Joseph (which had been named for their famous leader—as was the rodeo they came for). Seventy years before my dad arrived, on one of Chief Joseph's visits back Wallowa County to plead for a small parcel of land for his people, Joseph was told in no uncertain terms that any tribal members who showed up in the county would be killed.

When I was in Christian elementary school, I was taught that things like alcohol addiction and drug use were the "ravages of sin." It wouldn't be long until I would outright reject the idea that my father wasn't present in my life because he was a "sinner." It would be decades, however, before I truly understood that his alcoholism and drug use were not the ravages of "sin" but instead the ravages of colonialism. The colonial and missionary view of the suffering among American Indian communities as being the result of their own "sin" easily allowed the colonizers to dismiss the trauma and damage that they themselves were delivering to Native people.

I think there is an alternate path where I could have actually been a drug dealer, or met who knows what other dead-end societal fate. There are a few essential things that kept me from that path, though. Along with the love of my family and friends, and the birth of my daughter when I was twenty-one, is my connection to nature. That's what eventually led me back to the path of my Indigenous ancestors. It was my mother, not my urban Native father, however, who connected me to the natural world. That connection played as large a role as any in leading me back to my Indigenous roots. My mother had embraced the philosophy of the "Jesus Freaks," the hippies who'd turned to Christianity for the message of peace and love that Jesus spoke of in the Bible, and she joined the Seventh-Day Adventist Church. It appealed because of the holistic and natural health practices their doctrines promoted, and the strong connection to nature and "back to the Earth" living that many church members practiced. It was her best friend, whom she was converting to Adventism with, who introduced her to the people who introduced our family to Wallowa County. That family's father was a pilot and an Alaskan homesteader. He brought my mother and siblings to Wallowa County for their first time. Looking down as they flew over the sprawling Eagle Cap Wilderness, it was seeing the shining peaks of the Wallowa Mountains jutting from it, the azure alpine lakes scattered between them, the deep canyons and rivers running from them, and finally the flowing green grasses of the Wallowa Valley turning to distant prairie and forest that made her realize this would be our home.

By the time I was six years old I had climbed my first nine-thousand-foot peak and backpacked into the Wallowa Mountains to spend multiple nights in the wilderness with my mom and brother. On that journey my brother, twelve years old at the time, seriously sprained his ankle sliding down a snowfield. My mother tried to carry him but didn't make it far before she decided the best thing was to leave us and go get help by fast-hiking out in the dark. We spent most of the night huddled together at an eight-thousand-foot elevation on the side of a mountain waiting for help to arrive. Sometime shortly before dawn, we heard a gunshot on the darkened slopes above us and started shouting, "We're down here! Help!" It was a group of hearty local outdoorsmen, mostly from our church, who'd hiked up those mountains in the dark to retrieve us. (Six years later one of them would become my stepdad, and he would teach me much about living with the land.) After that night on the cold, dark mountainside, the wild land of this continent became a home for me, and I've been returning ever since.

I was the youngest sibling by six years, which basically meant I grew up an only child. I spent countless hours wandering the hills near our house alone with my dog, trying to make friends with the wildlife I encountered and pondering what mysteries blew in the breeze or were hidden just over the next hilltop. My father left when I was four years old, and not long after I began to have night terrors. I would wake up frozen in the middle of the night envisioning a little green man at the end of my bed or right next to my pillow staring at me. Soon I found that the way I could prevent these night terrors was to drift into a fantasy realm every night when I went to bed. I would imagine various fantastic scenarios, such as living in my own zoo where all the animals were tame, and I had a pet lion I could ride around. Sometimes I would lie awake for what seemed like hours imagining whatever reality I was currently longing for. In every one of those fantasies, the searing hole left in me by the absence of my father was filled. Nothing was lacking; instead, fantastical realities were the reward for my longing. When I began to wander the hills and fields as a child, I found a place in the real world where that empty space, that longing, seemed to fill with something good, something healthy, something that was supposed to be a part of me, something that was attainable.

I never stopped wandering the wild. When I was twelve years old, I went on my first solo camping trip for three days, accompanied only by my dog and my horse, and unwittingly emulating a timeless coming-of-age tradition among many tribes, including my own. Every night a large coyote would arrive and perch on a rock directly above camp and watch us until the sun began to set, at which point he would disappear into the tall grass to join his pack, yowling and yipping at the arriving darkness. Much later I would learn that Coyote played an essential role in the creation stories of both the Caddo and the Nez Perce people. When I was fourteen, I climbed my first ten-thousand-foot mountain alone. Over the years, my love of wandering and exploring the wilderness—finding not only adventure but fulfillment for the yearnings of my soul—led me to learn many of the land-based skills and understandings that were practiced by my own and others' Indigenous ancestors. Learning to "survive" in the wilderness turned to learning to thrive in the wilderness. An essential part of that is striving to understand the myriad life cycles that are interconnected to the greater life cycle of the planet, of which humanity is an equivalent part. We are neither greater nor less than any of the other parts and are equally connected to all when we are in a healthy symbiotic state. It was access to those life cycles and that great circle, or "hoop," of spiritual and physical subsistence that my ancestors sought to sustain in all their struggles to maintain land for our tribes and cultures. That was why the most essential part of every treaty we signed was the promise that we would have a land and water base from which to practice our subsistence and existence. Few tribes, especially among those who were completely extirpated from their homelands, have been able to wholly maintain that connection.

Eventually I became a backcountry wilderness ranger for the US Forest Service (USFS). I would patrol hundreds of miles by foot every summer across the Eagle Cap and Hells Canyon Wilderness Areas, which possess the deepest canyon in North America and more peaks over nine thousand feet high than any other mountain range in Oregon. That job entailed backpacking and camping for nine days at a time to care for wilderness lands and the people who recreate there. I also worked as a biology aide for the Oregon Department of Fish and Wildlife, inventorying wild steelhead trout spawning grounds in remote streams in northeast Oregon. Finally, I took the position of USFS field patrol ranger in the greater Hells Canyon National Recreation Area. Part of that job entails interpreting the natural and human history of the region for the public. That means trying to connect thousands of years of human history written in the land to what visitors see and feel today, in hopes of bringing the American "wilderness" alive with a sense of living history.

Beyond simply interpreting and caring for wildlands and the people who use them, an important part of my field ranger job is to uphold the treaty obligations the federal government owes the Nez Perce Tribe based on their 1855 and 1863 treaties. Like all treaties, the government still cherry-picks which parts of them it will honor and which parts it will ignore. The 1855 treaty, which was never abrogated by the Wallowa Band Nez Perce, promises the lands that are now in Wallowa County to the tribe forever. It also promises perpetual access to all of the fish, wildlife, roots, and berries that sustained their people from time immemorial. Today, the federal government still honors the promise of sovereign treaty subsistence access on all federal lands (except national parks—which ban hunting regardless of treaty rights). They do not honor the 1855 right of the Nez Perce to occupy lands in the Wallowa country, however, despite the fact that all federal employees and elected representatives swear an oath to defend the Constitution, which designates all treaties as the "supreme law of the land."

In many ways I strive to make the work I do as a USFS field ranger pay homage to my own ancestors, such as John Conner, who not only understood the sacred relationship human beings must have with the land and all its life but also dedicated their own lives to protecting that relationship for our people. Captain Conner served as a peacemaker and bridge between the Indigenous and colonial worlds. I hope that I can serve to honor that mission, and in doing so honor my ancestors and their legacy. I also hope to pay respect and homage to the ancestors of the land I live and work in, and thank them as well as their living descendants for welcoming me to their homeland.

I am not the first Lenape among the Nimiipuu. Many of those Lenape westward wanderers of the fur-trade era ended up among the Nez Perce. In fact, the son of a Delaware man named Tom Hill who scouted for John C. Fremont (along with my three uncle ancestors) and later married a Nez Perce woman, interpreted for Chief Joseph's surrender. He and his brother lived much of their lives among the Nez Perce and have many descendants among them today. Delaware people have played a role before in helping navigate between the colonial and Nez Perce worlds. Given that Eastern Woodland and coastal tribes such as the Delaware had been dealing with colonists for two hundred years before Lewis and Clark, that role makes sense in more ways than one.

My walk in the world of outdoor adventure and recreation also led me to understand that my access to those things came from my access to whiteness. It was my white mother and her white friends with an airplane who brought us to Wallowa County, and our white Christian church friends who introduced us to things like backpacking and hunting and fishing. It was not my displaced-by-assimilation-and-relocation-urban Indian father who introduced me to those things. After his brief stint in Oregon and the painful failure of his marriage to my mother, he retreated back to the closest thing he ever had to a homeland: the urban sprawl of the San Francisco Bay Area. Dad always loved the ocean, though, and growing up in urban California, it was about the only connection to nature he ever had. It wasn't until late in his life that he learned his great-great-grandpa John Conner had shared the same passion for the ocean and walked halfway across the continent to see one. My dad rarely had access to nature and thus not much of a conscious desire to seek it or to understand the roots of his longing for the rhythmic sound of wave after wave crashing on the shores of Turtle Island.

My father did pass on to me one central gift and connection to what it means to be Indigenous: a passion for artistic and creative storytelling. My dad was an incredibly talented artist. Strong graphic images that told a story seemed to effortlessly flow from his pencil or brush. He carried forward a long tradition of artistic craftsmanship and storytelling among Indigenous people. Our cultures, our spirit, and our way of life are sustained by our stories. I knew at an early age that I would be an artist like my dad. Eventually frustration with not being able to put to paper or canvas the stories I envisioned in my mind to my satisfaction led me to pick up a camera instead of a brush. At fifteen, I decided I would become a photojournalist, and I've been following that path ever since. My work as a ranger (not to mention years of waiting tables, tending bar, and various customer service and manual labor jobs) has been to support that dream. Early on in my journey as a storyteller I made a conscious decision to use my photography and writing to connect to my own indigeneity, as well as serve other Indigenous people and cultures.

When my dad called to tell me he'd been diagnosed with stage 4 lung cancer from a lifetime of smoking cigarettes, and that he'd been given a positive prognosis of two years to live, it was one of the hardest things he'd ever done. I heard in his voice a profoundly remorseful apology for all of the moments of my life he had missed. He didn't say as much, but before we got off the phone I told him I forgave him for it anyway. I told him that I was not angry with him; that I had never been angry with him. He was quiet for a moment, and in a soft, breaking voice said, "Thank you, son."

He explained how he'd immediately decided he was going to "take the high road" when his doctor gave him the news. There was no sense of desperation to make up for lost time in his voice; no anger or fear. There was sadness for what he knew his family would go through in losing him, and that seemed to be the most traumatizing part for him. It had taken him almost a month to tell my stepmother and several months to tell his kids. He hadn't wanted to ruin the upcoming holidays. By the time he told me the news, he had gone through a significant amount of soul-searching. It was clear that the main emotional hurdle he had left to face was coming to terms with how the loss was going to affect his loved ones. There was a sense of relief in his voice after he told me. He went on to enthusiastically explain the many plans he was making to do some very special things with his children and grandchildren, not in a panic to make up for anything but rather simply out of a sense of excitement about the moments we were going to enjoy together. I truly understood what he meant by "taking the high road," and I was excited to join him on it. I knew I was already connecting with my father on a level of profundity I had never experienced, and in some ways I'd been longing for that moment my whole life. It was perhaps the most real moment I had ever shared with him, which was profound because in some ways my father had not seemed very real to me throughout my life.

Dad told me how he was going to take all of us kids to Oklahoma to visit our tribal lands and family allotment together for the first time, once he recovered from his first round of chemotherapy. My brother, Larry, had visited Oklahoma with Dad before and met Auntie Florence and her daughter, Irene (who was much older than Dad), as well as our uncles who had both passed away by that time. But my sisters and I had never been there. I was very excited to take that journey. We got off the phone with a sense of hopefulness for the moments to come and where that "high road" would lead. I wasn't sure how I was going to settle into this new reality, but I told Dad I loved him with a sense of earnestness I'd never felt before. He did the same for me. I hung up the phone and went back inside my mother's house where I had been when I received the call and hugged her for a long time. Then I got in my car with my dog and drove out to the Zumwalt Prairie to run to the top of a high butte called Meexum Heepey by the Cayuse people (meaning "middle mountain"). I topped the summit as silent blue dusk settled across the land, and I wept and prayed as I never had before. I released a lot into that evening sky, looking up at those cobalt prairie clouds with tears streaming down. Then I ran back down that mountain in the dark with a new sense of purpose. That "high road" Dad spoke of was going to ensure my family would never forget where we came from.

Our visit to Oklahoma would change the trajectory of my family's relationship with its Indigenous history. I think it may have even changed it for my dad during the short time he had left with us. A sense of childlike joy sparkled from the eyes of my sixty-five-year-old recovering-from-chemotherapy father as he climbed over the steel gate leading to our allotment land. The exhaustion his physique bore from the battle his body was facing seemed to wash away, and he came alive with purposeful enthusiasm. A contented happiness exuded from him in relishing that moment with all his children together, standing in the footprints of our ancestors, and being present with us in his childhood memories of Oklahoma summers spent with Auntie Florence and his brothers and extended Caddo/Delaware relatives.

We walked together across the land that had borne generations of my family since the Allotment Act, soaking up the palpable love and hope for the future written in the Earth and passed down through countless millennia right to that moment between an elder Indian father and his children. Dad recounted memories of family members he'd spent time with or things he did with his brothers. As we were walking back to the car, he seemed to recall in passing, almost as an afterthought, that he'd once visited our family burial grounds hidden in an oak grove somewhere across the property on the next allotment, which had long ago been sold off to a local white farmer. He pointed at a distant line of trees and recounted how back in the early 1970s before the land had been as fractionalized as it was now, an auntie who lived there had shown him and his brothers where their mother, and Harris and Nora, and several other family members had been buried in an ancient and sacred oak grove. Since then, further fractionalization had taken place, and the neighboring lands that had once belonged to various members of our family had been sold off. Dad motioned vaguely toward the general direction where he thought it was, describing old wooden markers fading into the grass by the time he visited there. There was no way he would have the energy to walk out there and find it.

Those four days we spent together in Oklahoma flew by far too fast, yet they will resonate through generations of our family to come. Dad and my stepmom and three siblings returned together, but I chose to stay several more days and began to do some family research. My brother told a story afterward of how on their flight home my dad and he had a brief conflict when my brother referred to him as a "tribal elder." Dad sort of bristled at the mention, and said he wasn't an "elder" (as in the term of cultural respect and honor) and not to call him that. Not long after, my brother was reading the tribal newsletter that he'd picked up when we visited the tribal offices, and in it there was an announcement honoring the tribal elders whose birthdays were that month. He was taken by surprise when he saw our father's name listed among them. When he showed my dad that the tribal newsletter had included his name under the heading, "Honoring Our Tribal Elders," Dad seemed almost stunned. Clearly, even nearing the end of his life, he didn't think of himself or define himself in terms of his tribal identity—even though his own tribe did. I like to think that perhaps that began a change in him before it was too late. A couple years later when I shared with him the stories of John Conner I had learned, his eyes seemed to light up with a sort of disbelief and wonder, and a sense of pride and contentment, not in the fantastic tales of Captain Conner's adventures, but that his son was sharing these things with him.

The additional time I spent on that trip to Oklahoma seven years ago opened the door to almost all of the historical accounts I've shared here. With the help and kindness of people like the director of the Caddo Tribal History Museum and the enrollment officer of the tribe (who ended up being related to me), my first trip to visit my tribal lands began to follow a thread that now has led me all the way back to the first Indian treaty the United States ever signed (forged and signed by my Lenape Delaware great-grandfather times six—Chief White Eyes), and beyond. One of the most important things I intended to do during the time I spent in Oklahoma was to try to find that family burial ground. I didn't care if I had to "trespass" to do it. So I made my way back to our allotment one evening to do just that. I found the gate to the property, which we didn't have the key to, open. I assumed it must be the local farmer who leased the land from my dad. His name was B. W. Hammert, and Dad had never actually met the man in person but had spoken to him on the phone a few times over the decades. (While individual allotments were often not viable to make a living from for their Native owners, local white farmers would buy them up at below market prices and add them to larger holdings that were viable. Or, lease the allotments cheaply to add to their crop production.)

As I walked down the old two-track leading onto the land, someone in a white pickup truck came driving across the primary field toward me. It pulled up abruptly and a white-haired elderly farmer in a large set of overalls and a stern countenance peered suspiciously out the window at me. I stuck out my hand and asked him if he was B. W. Hammert, at which he seemed to stiffen even more, perhaps wondering who this stranger was on "his" farmland asking questions of him. I told him my name and that my father was Tom Whittle. The moment he heard my dad's name he immediately relaxed his posture and began to actually listen to what I was saying. I explained exactly what was happening (including my dad's cancer), and that I was looking for my grandmother's burial ground. His suspicious posture had transformed to a warm invitation. He smiled and said, "Hop in," with just the slow southern drawl you'd expect from an eighty-year-old Oklahoma farmer in overalls, and he began to clear a place for me to sit in that dusty old farm truck.

He drove us back across the field. As he did, he explained how he'd been coming out in the evenings to try and shoot wild hogs that had been rooting up his soybean crops, and that's what he was doing there. As he pulled up to the fence line at the far end of the property, he stopped the truck and pointed to a specific stand of oaks across the neighboring allotment. "That's what you're looking for," he said matter-of-factly. He told me how he and the fellow who now owned that allotment had put up a fence around the burial ground years before to keep their cows out of it, knowing what it was and wanting to respect and protect it. I was sort of dumbfounded. What were the odds I would come out much later than I intended and happen to catch Mr. Hammert, who had leased this land since before my dad took over ownership, to have him share that story with me? I was particularly grateful as it was not where I had intended to look. I was also grateful that he had shown that respect. He said the neighbor wouldn't mind, and if I encountered him to tell him who I was and what I was doing. He would also be the one to later explain to me that even though the land had been sold, my family retained an easement because of that burial ground, and we actually didn't need permission from anyone to access it.

The moon was full and just beginning to rise as I approached the grove. I recognized it by the fence the farmers had built. I stopped for a long time before entering, with my hand on a giant monarch of an oak just outside the fence, praying in the glowing dusk as moonlight brightened the blue Oklahoma sky glowing behind green oak tops. Finally, I climbed over the fence and set my foot down onto that sacred ground. I was home. I felt the warmth of a grandmother's love flood through every fiber of my being. I felt thousands of ancestors reaching out with strength and love and support for every dream I ever dreamt, for every longing of my heart and every hope for the future, for my daughter's future, for her children's future, and theirs. I felt the strength that held my family aloft through countless trials and tribulations of the ages, and the ceaseless eternal love that fueled that strength. I felt my family represented in the roots and growing tops of those mighty oaks that had been nourished by the life of my ancestors and represented a living connection to them. I touched every one of those sentinel family trees, including two that had fallen to become the nourishment of the Earth that had nourished them. I prayed next to the one that called to me the strongest and stared up at the moonlight fluttering through its leaves, trying to comprehend the dreams of my ancestors. Darkness fell across the fields and groves to a chorus of cicadas, and I lingered and lingered among those sacred trees. The wooden markers Dad had described had long ago rotted into the ground, another indication of how blessed I'd been to have had the location pointed out to me.

As I walked back across the fields to our allotment, I felt that my ancestors were walking with me. I felt the joy they would feel at knowing their children had found them, and that we were not lost, and neither were they. I felt the plans of a thousand generations for our family and people to not only survive but thrive on Turtle Island. I knew those plans of love were still unfolding, and that I had a role to play. I was determined to do just that, and I felt empowered to do so.

One of the last things I did before leaving Anadarko on that trip was visit the National Indian Hall of Fame, a museum featuring bronze busts of renowned American Indians. One of them was of a Caddo/Kiowa artist named T. C. Cannon, whose paintings remind me of my dad's artwork. Upon the bust was inscribed a poem he had written, which read:

> *I have a strong bond with Heaven and its angels that grows more and more available. Nothing can deter my many routes to the heart of God.... Let's shine on the world for a long time even if we are beyond the voice and ear of those that proclaim us the dreamers of*

> *some dismissed religion.... I refuse to shed tears for my shortcomings anymore. I am comfortable and sane and smiling, running towards the arms of God this evening.*

Just over three years later, and almost two years longer than the doctor had given him, I would read that poem at Dad's funeral. He was cremated to be able to rest with his wife, Lillian, one day in Lodi, California. But a small part of his ashes were kept by me to be ceremonially interred in our family burial grounds. (Cremation is not the traditional Caddo way, but my stepmother is Catholic, and my father wished to honor her Mexican/Catholic traditions. He converted so that he could receive his last rites and leave her with peace of mind and heart.) I am still learning and connecting with the appropriate way to go about the ceremonial process of bringing him to our burial ground, and the timing will work out as it is supposed to. But one thing is certain: we will be able to honor that wish he made for us to "all go back to Oklahoma together again." His family will gather in that sacred oak grove and ceremonially return my father to the warm loving arms of his mama, and all of his children will be there with him when we do.

My dad would be so proud to see where his children and grandchildren are today as Indigenous people. When my daughter was born in 1996, Google didn't exist, and I didn't know a single word in the Caddo or Lenape languages. Her mother and I had purchased a baby name book during the pregnancy, and I began to look for Native American names in it. I knew that I wanted something in her name to be an homage to our Native heritage, much like my father had wanted the same for me. And much like my father had done, I selected a name that was not a reference to my own tribes, because I had no access to our tribal languages or cultures. I found the name "Nataneh" listed in the name book as a Plains Indian word meaning "daughter." To this day I honestly don't know if that's accurate, or what specific tribe it was purported to have come from. At birth we gave her the first name Mia but wanted to wait until we had a better sense of who she was to give her the rest of her name. When she was one year old we decided her true name would mean "River" during a ceremony we held in the Wallowa Mountains. It was in honor of the sacred River of Life that unites all living things past and present. Her full name became Mia Nataneh River—representing the meaning, "My Daughter River." (Years later I would learn how sacred to Lenape culture rivers are.)

When Mia was sixteen we attended her first Indigenous protest action. We joined the hereditary chief of the Walla Walla Tribe, elder Carl Sampson, and his family and many of his fellow Walla Walla, Umatilla, Cayuse, and Nez Perce tribal members, on a cold December night beside a highway near Pendleton, Oregon. We were there to protest the movement of tar sands mega-load equipment through confederated treaty territory. Chief Sampson asked me to speak to the group about my recent experiences documenting a devastating tar sands pipeline spill on Lubicon Cree First Nations land in Alberta, Canada. The protests of the local tribes in northeast Oregon were in solidarity with Canadian First Nations who had suffered terrible effects from tar sands mining in their territories. Plateau Tribes had long had relations with northern First Nations before the drawing of colonial borders, and many northern tribes offered refuge to tribes like the Nez Perce and Lakota who were fleeing US persecution.

Interestingly, my own Delaware family also had historical connections with Chief Carl Sampson's family. His traditional name, Peo Peo Mox Mox, was given to him in a ceremony wherein he took on the name of an ancestor named Peo Peo Mox Mox, who was the chief of the Walla Wallas during the signing of the Treaty of 1855. Peo Peo Mox Mox was eventually murdered by white settlers who then cut off his head to keep him from going to the afterlife according to his tribal tradition. When Chief Sampson assumed his ancestor's name he was also assuming his spirit and will carry that on to the next life when he takes his final walk, bringing his ancestor to a long-awaited rest. Peo Peo Mox Mox, the original, had joined the Delaware scout Tom Hill and traveled to California with warriors from his tribe and others, and he fought in the Mexican-American War under Colonel Fremont. There he would fight alongside three of my own ancestor uncles, who had been scouts and guides for Fremont. These histories show us not only how complicated colonial versus tribal histories are, but also how interwoven and complicated tribal relations are, even on an intra-continental scale.

When Mia and I made our first journey to Oklahoma just over two years after my father had passed, digital tools led us back to long-lost family. Through Instagram I had connected with some Caddo/Delaware cousins in Oklahoma descended from a Delaware chief named Black Beaver, who was John Conner's second cousin. Tracy and her daughters Alaina and Kira (both very close to Mia's age) are expert Caddo regalia makers and often make regalia for Caddo dances and ceremonies on commission for other tribal members. Mia and Alaina are the same age and look like sisters. Alaina and her younger sister, Kira, are both former Caddo Nation Princesses. As such, and being regalia makers, they both had extra regalia that they offered to let Mia wear, and they invited her to dance with them in an annual Caddo dance called the Clara Brown Memorial Dance. Our original mission had been simply to honor my father and take Mia to our family burial grounds and introduce her to our tribal territory and allotment for the first time. I'd no idea that trip would lead both of us to participate in our traditional Caddo culture for the first time, together. After that gracious and life-changing invitation by our long-lost cousins, we planned our trip around that dance. We've since connected with even more Oklahoma family.

Mia Whittle in regalia with her cousin—Courtesy of Joseph Whittle

Our cousins Tracy, Alaina, Kira, and Philip welcomed us into their home and arms as the long-lost family we were. It was a fitting and perfect example of the ancient Caddo and Lenape hospitality, tribal communion, love, and support that my family had been absent from in a cultural and community sense for too long. I cannot describe what it meant for us to be welcomed back with loving arms that way. Nor can I describe the profound and overwhelming joy, relief, beauty, and pride I felt seeing Mia walk into that Oklahoma sunshine decked out in full regalia for the first time. It brought tears to all our eyes, especially her new auntie Tracy and myself. Tracy had immediately assumed that traditional tribal "auntie" role with Mia, and to this day dotes on her in the most loving way. It was just what our family needed.

I wish my father had been alive to see that moment, but it in a way he felt more alive to me than he ever had before. The love and pride that would have glowed from him to look upon his granddaughter decked in the culture of his mother seemed to emanate from the ribbons flowing gently in the summer breeze on the hairpiece she wore. The comforting strength and love he'd given his grandchildren was present in the shawl draped across her arms. My father's adoration for his children was sewn into the patterns of Mia's dress, and his mother's loving comfort was woven into the fibers of her apron. The smile that was written across Mia's face was an echo of her grandfather's beaming Native grin.

That had followed a profound ceremony we'd held to honor my father and our Indigenous cultures the week before, which we'd performed high in the most remote mountain basin within Oregon's largest wilderness. Two years after his passing, I was finding that my father's Indigenous presence in my life was growing stronger, not weaker. How could this be? I was beginning to understand Indigenous survivance. I was beginning to understand how Indigenous people can still be here after five hundred years of continued assault on our very existence. I was beginning to understand why at any given moment my father could flash that warm, happy grin that welcomed all to join in his deep humor and appreciation for life—no matter how difficult things had been for him. Nothing can break the power and strength of Indigenous love, culture, and tribal bond. This is how we have sustained on Turtle Island since time immemorial.

It gave me a profound sense of joy when Mia told me on Father's Day this spring that she'd commissioned her cousin Alaina to make my first traditional ribbon shirt, and that the next time we dance ancient footsteps together on the sacred red earth of Caddo country, I, too, will be wearing traditional Caddo regalia. It gave me a profound sense of joy when I wore that ribbon shirt ceremonially for the first time last week, with my daughter present, at the dedication of the first Nez Perce Longhouse to be consecrated in the Wallowa Band Nez Perce homeland since before their tragic exodus in 1877. I imagine that my ancestors would have been proud to see us represent our people and cultures with respect to our gracious hosts in such a way, at such a momentous occasion. I imagine that seeing that would give my father a profound sense of joy as well. I hope that he knows we did not forget who we are.

CHAPTER 22

Selling Hawai'i

Lia O'Neill Keawe

THE BEST SALES PITCH EVER: PARADISE

In 2019, tourism brought 10,386,673 travelers[1] to Hawai'i. In its sales pitch the tourism industry actively seeks to persuade visitors to come to Hawai'i—*Paradise*. This statement is confirmed by Mike McCartney, CEO of the Hawai'i Tourism Authority who said, "The tourism authority worked very hard to tell travel agents about what Hawai'i has to offer ... our people, our place and our culture—as a destination providing a unique experience to our guests."[2] As an extension of its marketing strategies the industry relies heavily on specific images to "Sell Hawai'i." One particular image used includes that of the Kanaka Maoli[3] female image, the *Hula Girl*.[4] For decades now, this image has been successfully used to sell everything from Spam[5] to feather dusters and everything in between! You might say this visual image has become the everyday backdrop to life in Hawai'i.

The oversaturation of the *Hula Girl* image is part of a process known as rhetorical tropes. The term "rhetorical" comes from the word "rhetoric."

Within the context of this conversation, rhetoric deals with the use of language as a means to persuade. A trope is a figure of speech. There are many different types of tropes, and when used well, they can become powerful tools. Tropes are often used in advertising and are usually used with cultural or social norms. A metaphor is a well-known example of a figure of speech where "a word or phrase literally denoting one kind of object or idea [or even an image] is used in place of another to suggest a likeness or analogy between them."[6]

Picture this—images of a canoe with paddlers in the foreground of a magnificent golden sunset; breathtaking images of the Pacific Ocean detailed in multilayered hues of blue and green; pristine, white sandy beaches and endless coconut trees swaying in the balmy breeze. All of these visual images are examples of rhetorical tropes for Hawai'i. Also, in this rhetorical trope of Hawai'i is the *Hula Girl* with her long, dark hair, dressed in her coconut bra, grass skirt, and wearing lei. These images are so powerful that even without mentioning the word "Hawai'i," they can be used to create visual messages—advertisements about Hawai'i—*Paradise.*

This chapter explores, examines, and analyzes the observations of images, culture, identity, and capitalism in Hawai'i. It is part of a larger research project that closely studies these observations through a semiotic reading of various textures that include images and advertisements. Semiotics can be understood as the process of how meaning is constructed and then understood. Perhaps for now, it might be useful to think of semiotics as a kind of language or a means of communication. It's a kind of language or communication that includes words, images, gestures, tastes, textures, and sounds used as signs or codes to convey messages. With this approach, we will examine how the *Hula Girl* image has been commodified, appropriated, misrepresented, and expropriated.

PAYING ATTENTION TO THE SIGNS AND CODES SURROUNDING US

On a visit to my department's administrative office, I saw a sign peering out from a window located near the entrance of the office. The dimensions of the sign resembled that of a bumper sticker. The sign had a black background and in bold white lettering said, "Hawaiian Culture Not For Sale." Reflecting on this sign that had just greeted me, I was reminded of an experience I had with a colleague, Kekailoa. He had just returned from a conference on "the continent."[7] Shortly after his return, we met up in the department mailroom where he announced, "Eh, I got something for you. I was visiting a bookstore and saw something that reminded me of your research. I'll leave it in your mailbox," as after which he headed off to teach his class.

Later, I returned to find an envelope waiting for me in my mailbox. Excited, I quickly grabbed it and returned to my office. Still excited, I opened the envelope and found a white box. It was approximately five inches long, two and half inches wide and one and a quarter inch in depth. Upon careful examination, I realized a book was attached to the white box. The size of the book perfectly mirrored the white box that accompanied it. The book was bound by three vertical holes on the left side. Paper made from what looked like a brown paper bag that was fashioned into strips and twisted to resemble raffia[8] was used to connect the book to the box. These strands of paper were threaded through metal grommets covering the vertical holes of the book's front and back covers as well as the left side spine of the box.

On the cover of the book was an image of a *Hula Girl* dressed in the stereotypical elements of the image itself-the long, flowing brunette hair adorned with a lei poʻo.[9] On her body lay a floral garden. Around her neck was a flower lei and a lush band of flowers and leaves fashioned like a belt for her kīkala[10] and kūpeʻe[11] around her wrists and ankles.

The Art of Hula Dancing was the book's title. A caption below the title read, "Sway Your Way to a Sexier You!" The presentation of this caption was cleverly designed to mimic the swaying hips, from left to right, with the *Hula Girl* image in the background. More printing on the book's front cover informed readers of the following:

> *Includes: Colorful Hawaiian leis, ʻiliʻili (or lava stones), a 64-page guide to teach you essential hula moves, plus, a bonus CD with mood-setting Hawaiian music.*[12]

At that very moment, I opened the box and saw everything that was stated above. Suddenly a rush of anger and sadness moved through my body. I was angry because this was proof that Hawaiian culture was indeed for sale. I was also sad because products like this are acts of culture violence and are harmful and injurious for the Kanaka

The Art of Hula Dancing—Courtesy of Lia O'Neill Keawe

Maoli community and for Indigenous peoples around the world. My mind quickly reverted back to the sign in the office window. Instantly I thought, "Oh, no, Hawaiian culture IS for sale! The example is right here." As disappointed as I was, I continued the journey of exploration. While hurriedly flipping through the sixty-four-page guide, I encountered what looked like illustrations of tourists dressed up in hula attire posing with their bodies and limbs in hula gestures.[13] Immediately, I turned back to the table of contents where my concerns continued to intensify. I went straight to the book's introduction and began reading,

> *Say the word "hula," and we are immediately transported to the islands of Hawaii. We think of palm trees, moonlit beaches, and soft guitars. Even if we have never been to Hawaii before, we can easily imagine the Hula Girl. Usually dressed in a sarong or grass skirt, a flower in her hair and a lei around her neck, she stands*

> *poised with swaying hips and graceful hands that tell a story. No other dance conjures up the same images and certainly no other dance can take us on a virtual Hawaiian vacation like hula can."*[14]

Let's pause and analyze what is being said here because it is an example of a rhetorical trope. Through our initial discussion about the rhetorical tropes of Hawaiʻi and the *Hula Girl*, we understand that these types of tropes are repeating images. Assisting in clarifying our knowledge of tropes, we were provided with visual examples of rhetorical tropes through images (a canoe with paddlers; a magnificent golden sunset; pristine, white sandy beaches and coconut trees swaying in the balmy breeze). As we examine the statement from the introduction above, let's apply a semiotic reading to this trope. In doing so, we see its delivery is made through written text (words) as compared to our previous discussion of images. Upon closer examination of the passage, we also notice subtle changes in the descriptions of the landscape and the *Hula Girl's* attire. In our initial discussion, she was dressed in a coconut bra and a grass skirt. In the trope created by the authors, she's now dressed in a sarong and a grass skirt. Nevertheless, the text successfully captures and reinforces the rhetorical trope of the image itself. At this point it might be useful and important to employ a critical reading of the text because it allows the reader to examine its claims and any bias in the framing and selection of the information presented.

Our first probe begins with identifying the general topic being discussed. It involves textual images of hula, Hawaiʻi, and the *Hula Girl*. Next, we investigate if there is any bias in its claims or in the framing and selection of the information presented. Because we now have a working understanding of rhetorical tropes, we should already be cautious. From this vantage point let's consider further what the text is saying. From the start, the term "hula" situates readers to a specific geographic location—Hawaiʻi. From this position the framing and selection of information, "palm trees, moonlit beaches, and soft guitars" allows the text to reinforce the idyllic imaging of Hawaiʻi—*Paradise*. Next, the rhetorical trope continues in its introduction of the *Hula Girl*. From there we return to the single term with which this statement began, "hula." By using a semiotic reading the tropes reveal a kind of language, a means of communication that was created. In this presentation of tropes, the form of communication included words, images, and gestures used to convey messages. The message promotes a Hawaiian vacation—*Paradise*.

Now that we've explained what the text is saying, let's take a look at the descriptions of the text and see what it does with such remarks. Is it fact or interpretation? Hawai'i does have magnificent scenic landscapes, this is true! Often times practitioners of hula will be dressed similarly to descriptions provided in the statement. Their poised bodies, with "swaying hips and graceful hands" are certainly part of an engaging story that is told through hula. Furthermore, there is no doubt that hula is special. For Kanaka Maoli, hula is sacred. It is our national dance and an expression of our culture. Here, there was clearly a gross misunderstanding of hula and its spiritual connection to Kanaka Maoli and culture. In this statement hula is being understood merely as a form of entertainment "on a virtual Hawaiian vacation." Statements like this serve as an example of how hula is stripped of its spiritual and cultural markers.

As a critical reader of this text, I am deeply concerned by the danger that lurks in the meaning of this text—its interpretation. As I interrogate how the text portrays the subject matter, I return to the beginning of this article and reflect on the quote made by Mike McCartney and question the narrative told to "travel agents about what Hawai'i has to offer … our people, our place and our culture—as a destination providing a unique experience to our guests."[15] As a member of the Kanaka Maoli community, I can challenge this interpretation because I know what is presented is not fact but rather an interpretation of these events. However, for people who never travel to Hawai'i, these texts and statements act like windows into the world. What these people see, hear, or even read is taken to be the truth. The ultimate danger of the rhetorical trope is its continued presentation, over and over, which gives way to myth making. And when myths are repeated over time, they become truths.

As I read on, I encountered this alarming statement:

> *Hula celebrates a woman's body and will make you feel beautiful. With Sexy movements and playful glances it encourages women of all ages, shapes and sizes to enjoy their sensuality.*[16]

This statement is concerning because it simply is not true and serves as an example of misrepresenting and appropriating culture. While hula can make you feel beautiful, its purpose, function, and meaning are clearly not to celebrate women's bodies. The narrative is further complicated because men engage in hula as well. In hula there is no gender bias. Yet from this statement it appears that only women dance hula. As I have stated, hula is the national dance of Kanaka Maoli and an expression of culture. Clearly these authors offer an outsider's interpretation of hula that reveals their limited understanding of Kanaka Maoli culture and hula.

The misinformation continues. In a section entitled the "History of Hula," the authors walk readers through a general survey of hula history where claims are made without any supporting references. Here is an example:

> *At first, the dance was vigorous, gymnastic, and masculine. As women were allowed to learn the hula, the movements became more graceful and fluid.*[17]

As I read these remarks, my critical thinking skills were already at work. Immediately, I wanted to know who said this. Okay, I could accept the opening sentence to be someone's opinion or interpretation. However, the next sentence was problematic, and I wanted there to be a source responsible for this claim. Not just any source but a valid source, from someone who has the kuleana[18] to make such a claim, like a kumu hula.[19] To be recognized as a kumu hula involves protocol and entails years of study as a hula practitioner under the close supervision of a kumu hula who has studied in the same manner and has earned the right to use that distinguished title and be the keeper of such knowledge. Curious, I conducted an internet search relating to these credentials about the authors but could not find any evidence that would warrant such recognition. Therefore, from a Kanaka Maoli perspective, to make such a claim is highly inappropriate and a display of bad behavior that would not be welcomed. The danger of this example is that it doesn't encourage readers to question the material presented but rather to accept it as truth.

Let's look at another statement made in this section:

> *When the missionaries came to Hawaii in the early 1820s, they were shocked at the sensual and suggestive nature of hula, viewing it as lewd and pagan.*[20]

Given my own knowledge about these missionaries, I would have to agree with the authors here. This probably was the reaction from the conservative missionary mind upon seeing the hula. What is concerning for me about this statement is that no mention is made of the missionaries' lack of understanding of what hula was in the first place. Their negative attitudes toward hula intensified, leading to their appropriation of it and later resulting in a total ban of hula in Hawai'i.[21] Imagine that, at one point in Hawai'i's history, hula, the national dance of Kanaka Maoli, was banned. And yet the very descendants of these missionaries, responsible for the demise of hula, would later embrace it, via tourism, allowing them to gain tremendous power and wealth in Hawai'i. This is another example of the cultural violence endured by our kūpuna.[22]

It appears that the authors have mimicked the missionaries' actions and behaviors by their own appropriation of hula. "Hula celebrates a woman's body" is the first evidence of appropriation. And then to say that hula, "with sexy movements and playful glances . . . encourages women of all ages, shapes and sizes to enjoy their sensuality" is the next evidence of appropriation.

An important aspect of examining the *Hula Girl* rhetorical trope is to understand that it is often viewed through the lens of entertainment. When viewed this way, the imaging that comprises the trope masks and conceals the colonial structures that lie "hidden in plain sight." In other words, the dynamic of looking through the lens of entertainment disallows the reader/audience to comprehend other messages being communicated. In this way western perspectives about sexuality have been attached to this imaging, relegating the *Hula Girl* to the realm of exotic, hypersexualized image. The danger of this imaging is that it constructs the *Hula Girl* image as the basis for a fictional, fantasy-driven culture.

Revisiting the authors' remark about sensuality results in the mis-re-presentation of a traditional and customary practice such as hula. In this way, the cultural and spiritual markers of hula are permanently stripped away. Hula, once regarded as something sacred, now moves into the arena of pop culture. It is commodified as something to be consumed. Further, it is appropriated and treated like a fashion accessory worn with a hip outfit, creating a new identity. These actions are harmful to Kanaka Maoli because this is how our culture and identity have been expropriated.[23]

In a section entitled "A Mind and Body Workout," the benefits of hula are discussed as recreational exercise. Let me first say that there are partial truths captured in this section. For example, if you engage in hula, it is highly likely that you will engage in physical movement. This is true. Equally, I agree that hula is a great way to exercise and stay in shape. What is absent, however, from this section is a reminder to readers that hula remains a national dance of Kanaka Maoli and is an expression of culture that has deep connections to spirituality.

My next concern is the approach used to talk about hula in comparison to something similar from another culture. In an example the authors say, "Some have compared hula to Tai Chi"[24] or another type of meditation movement. Overall, hula should not be promoted as some kind of exercise or fitness workout routine. Similarly, statements like this are concerning:

> *As with most aerobic exercise, hula is an effective way to maintain bone strength. Any weight bearing exercise, especially dance, put stress on the bone, and that stress helps maintain or even increase bone strength. These hula steps strengthen the muscles in the hips and thighs. As they "pull" on the bone the muscles are constantly being contracted which creates a good stimulus for renewal of bone growth. Done regularly, hula can help prevent brittle bones.*[25]

What?—Really?—According to whom? There is no source given for this statement or any of the information presented in this section. Now, in case you are wondering if any scientific study was conducted regarding the benefits of hula, the answer is yes. In 2012, a first-time study was conducted showing that hula was "found to be a promising cardiovascular therapy."[26]

After exploring this text, I conclude that what is offered in this book is simply an outsider's interpretation to the "Art of Hula Dancing." None of the information in the book is substantiated with references. As such, there is always a concern that hula will lose its cultural purpose, function, and true meaning as promoted through products like this book. The detriment of such actions perpetuates the continual appropriation, commodification, mis-re-presentation, and expropriation of Indigenous cultures.

CONSUMING CULTURE: PUT A LITTLE HULA GIRL IN YOUR POCKET

While writing this chapter my concerns about the *Hula Girl* image being consumed were confirmed. Taking a quick break, I stopped in at my neighborhood Starbucks to get a beverage. After ordering, I walked away from the counter and quickly glanced over the items near the register and was surprised to see the latest Starbucks gift cards. Much to my horror, I saw a 2012 Starbucks *Hula Girl* card. In 2004, Starbucks stores in Hawai'i debuted their first *Hula Girl* gift card.

2012 Starbucks *Hula Girl* card—Courtesy of Julie Cajune

According to an article at Honolulu Advertiser.com,[27] it was decorated with a retro hula dancer scene and was issued only in Hawai'i. After its debut, customers quickly began hawking Hawai'i versions of the rechargeable cards as "rare" collectors' items worth more than their cash value. Soon after "mainland customers and card dealers also called Hawai'i stores asking if they could order the 'hula girl' card."[28] It seems that even Starbucks is following the marketing strategy of the tourist industry to sell coffee by using the *Hula Girl* image.

INHALING CULTURE AND EXHALING POLITICS IN HAWAI'I

So far, our conversation has been focused mainly around rhetorical tropes of Hawai'i and the *Hula Girl*. But there are other ways in which Kanaka Maoli culture is being consumed. Amidst a heightened sense of political awareness, appropriation, commodification, mis-re-presentation, and expropriation of Kanaka identity and culture continues.

In Hawai'i, an interesting site to observe this activity on grand scale is Disney's Aulani resort and spa[29] located on the west side of the island of O'ahu. In creating its only resort and spa in Hawai'i, this site serves up a fine example of how a multinational corporation like Disney has engaged in the ultimate consumption of Kanaka Maoli culture and identity.

This is not Disney's first attempt to consume Kanaka Maoli culture. In fact, it's their second. The first came in 2002 via the movie entitled *Lilo & Stitch*.[30] To capitalize on Kanaka Maoli culture, Disney hired several cultural consultants. One consultant was a Kumu Hula. Remember now, we already talked about hula and its relationship to protocol. So, the fact that a Kumu Hula was hired to capitalize on Kanaka Maoli culture sparked a huge controversy within the hula community and also within the greater Kanaka Maoli community. One of the movie's most egregious offenses was the cultural appropriation and misrepresentation of a 130-year-old name chant for one of our beloved monarchs, which was appropriated into a new stylized hip-hop form of hula. Even after all this time, the controversy has not been settled, lingering to this day.

In Disney's current attempt to consume Kanaka Maoli culture, it hired several Kanaka Maoli artists to again capitalize on the culture. I invite you to visit "Inside the Magic," Disney's official website covering its news and theme park events. There, you can read, hear, and see for yourself the events on Aulani's opening day.[31] Of particular note on this site is a video interview[32] with several Disney "Imagineers,"[33] who talk about the creation of the Aulani Resort & Spa. In the interview, these Disney executive representatives tell how they created "an immersive environment, about story" through art created by Kanaka Maoli artists. It is evident that art is how Kanaka Maoli culture has been incorporated into Disney magic. I will admit it is beautiful! However, don't be fooled by the allure of its "palace of art,"—it's still consuming culture.

When asked how Disney fits into Hawai'i, these Imagineers acknowledge that "there's this image of Hawai'i that's kind of grass shacky, beachy thing. That's actually not very Hawaiian. The culture of Hawai'i is tremendously elegant and has this deep sense of tradition. We want that to be the impression."[34] In this response, these "Imagineers" appear to understand Kanaka Maoli culture and the challenge of Hawai'i's rhetorical imaging. But the clarity of their supposed understanding is contradicted when they share how they have managed to *distill* the depth and breadth of Kanaka Maoli culture into just three specific elements: mo'olelo,[35] 'ohana,[36] and magic. Therefore, the totality of Disney's actions causes great concern for me.

In the interview, one of the "Imagineers" says, "Someone once told me, 'Look twice, think three times'—that's the Hawaiian culture."[37] I challenge this statement because it is simply not true! Again, it is an example of someone's interpretation of Hawaiian culture. However, the idea of looking closely and thinking critically was the impetus for an art exhibit that occurred earlier this year. As part of the Maoli Arts Festival, an exhibit entitled "'a' mini retort" opened at The ARTS at Marks Garage, located in downtown Honolulu. The exhibit, curated by Professor April A. H. Drexel, was an opportunity to bring much needed public awareness to the consumption of Kanaka Maoli culture.[38] As a scholar and artist herself, Drexel deeply understands the critical importance of educating the public, including Kanaka Maoli artists, about this topical arena. Her sentiments are articulated in the exhibit gallery statement she composed:

> *"a" mini retort-encourages and positions "critical dialogue" as a place to stand, move, and thoughtfully consider how/when/why/where creative textualities can simultaneously and/or subsequently contribute, complete, and perhaps, distort understanding.*
>
> *Existing implications and nuances associated with "imaging" and "imagined" constructs plus socio-economic/political/historical predicaments initiate a particular conversation from whence "a" retort has space and voice."*[39]

Each invited artist presented diverse expressions on the topic of cultural consumption. The exhibit was successful in its attempt to educate through a critical reading of sites and methods where this is occurring in Hawai'i. The knowledge resulting from this exhibit can and should be applied to Indigenous peoples around the world.

The goal of this chapter was to engage in a conversation and discuss the ways in which Indigenous cultures are being consumed. From this conversation, I hope readers have become more knowledgeable and aware of the dangers that threaten to harm Indigenous Peoples. I remain hopeful that readers will be inspired by this conversation and share the information presented here in their own Indigenous communities to achieve social justice and well-being.

"Using Pocahontas as a sex symbol is incredibly hurtful considering the high rates of sexual harassment, sexual assault, abuse, murder, and rape of Indigenous women, which is made worse by the toleration of fetishization of Indigenous women and other women of colour....

This issue ... will continue ... if we don't question the media and overall world around us. One step at a time, we can all learn about the issues that persist for any woman of colour, and make a safer world for our women. But when will that be?...

Our women give life, and we continue the existence of our people.

We are strong, we are resilient, we are courageous, we are intelligent.

We don't exist to feed your fantasies."

Neegahnii Madeline Chakasim, from "Sexualization of Indigenous Women through Cultural Appropriation and Media." The Indigenous Foundation (source: https://www.theindigenousfoundation.org/articles/sexualization-of-indigenous-women).

CHAPTER 23

History of Kodiak Alutiiq Education and Impacts on Families Today

Alisha Drabek

Since the mid-1700s, Alaska Native peoples have experienced the process familiar worldwide of Indigenous conquest and assimilation, resulting in consequences still felt today. The history of western influence is overwhelming for Alaskan communities, causing embitterment and a fractured sense of well-being on many levels. The rapid cultural changes Alaska Native peoples have survived during the past two hundred years are but a blink of an eye compared to the millennia our ancestors successfully adapted to their changing environment, as well as in trade or conflict with other tribes, all the while maintaining autonomy. The difference during the past two hundred years is the devastating loss of self-determination, only now being regained.

Knowing the history behind the modern Alaska Native experience and understanding the chain of effects still influencing us today can allow a healing process to grow and solutions to surface. Such an exploration ultimately serves as a means to develop a healthier and more community-empowering education process. With a deeper understanding of the historical trauma that has radically changed Alaska Native families and communities over the past two centuries, there is hope to reverse the cycle of loss without succumbing to further assimilation or leaving behind traditional knowledge and lifeways that sustained Alaska Natives in prior generations.

Alaska Native Cultural Groups—Courtesy of Alicia Drabek

The greater Alutiiq Nation (also known as Sugpiaq) reaches from the Alaska Peninsula to Prince William Sound, the Lower Cook Inlet, and the Kodiak Archipelago in the Gulf of Alaska. The Alutiiq are closely related to the Central Yup'ik linguistically and culturally and share many common traditions with the Unangan or Aleut as island maritime peoples, yet they are their own distinct culture. This chapter explores the history of education for the Alutiiq and its impacts on families today. Reflecting on the experiences of the nearly 2,500 Alutiiq people in the Kodiak Archipelago today, or 17.6 percent of the island's population of 13,900,[1] there is now a growing sense of cultural empowerment within families due to efforts by Elders and leaders to regain autonomy since the passage of the Alaska Native Claims Settlement Act (ANCSA) in 1971. The colonial history of the Kodiak Alutiiq people is similar to the experiences of other Indigenous communities worldwide who have survived conquest and assimilation, struggling to hold on to a worldview and traditional knowledge that is misunderstood or threatening to the mainstream society. As we look at next steps to ensure a more empowering educational processes for future generations, we must maintain a balanced local and global perspective, considering past events and how history influences educational content and practices today.

TRADITIONAL ALUTIIQ EDUCATION (PRECOLONIZATION) (8,000 BP–1784)

Prior to colonization, the Kodiak Alutiiq people had lived in the Kodiak Archipelago for more than seventy-five hundred years in approximately sixty-five villages and seasonal traditional harvest camps, according to archaeological evidence.[2] Education within Alutiiq culture, as in other Indigenous cultures, was integrated into daily life, as opposed to a detached classroom experience, so that children were raised not just in a culturally appropriate manner in their homes but were also trained by their Elders in life skills to help them thrive within the tribal economy and society. Some lessons learned were gender specific, based on the efficiency of living as a self-sufficient family and community, passing on subsistence, child-rearing, and household care traditions. Most lessons were taught through apprenticeship, where watching and practicing alongside a technical expert built skills, or as one Alutiiq Elder said, "learn[ing] by watching what is done and by doing what they are told to do."[3] Other lessons were taught via immersion and personal experience, as real-life situations and curiosities motivated young people to make new sense of their world and ways of life.[4] Regardless of the context, Indigenous peoples, including the Alutiiq, maintained an intricate educational and traditional knowledge system supported through the oral tradition.

Indigenous methods of education encompassed practical, experiential learning in the context of seasonal life cycles; competency was determined by performance in lived situations. Oral tradition was the main means for passing on knowledge and values essential for survival and success in life. Like other Indigenous peoples, Alutiiq ancestors were fluent in their language, but many were also fluent in the languages of neighboring tribes through trade, marriage, or extended expeditions outside the region. The Alutiiq were far from isolated prior to Russian invasion, as there are many stories of water voyages between the mainland and the archipelago, including forays to the Aleutian Chain, Cook Inlet, and southeast Alaska. Multilingualism was vital for trade and intermarriage, as families traditionally incorporated cultural diversity and a blending of cultural knowledge from neighboring tribes, as indicated in stories, tools, and arts.

In fact, prior to colonization, Alutiiq culture and way of life passed through at least three major societal evolutions.[5] Starting seventy-five hundred years ago, from 5500 BC to 1800 BC, the period known as Ocean Bay was characterized by nomadic tent living in pursuit of traditional harvest foods at multiple campsites throughout the year, which was followed by development of small, single-family sod dwellings about five thousand years ago. Then thirty-eight hundred years ago, from 1800 BC to 1400 AD, the Kachemak period brought development of larger multiroom sod houses, or ciqlluat, allowing for extended family living in seasonal communities as people began developing fishing nets and processing tools to fish in new ways. Then eight hundred years ago, from 1400 AD to 1784, the Koniag period was marked by climate change and increased trade with other tribes, leading to the creation of a complex class system and more elaborate ceremonies and arts. These economic and societal shifts within the Alutiiq precontact history contributed to development of traditional values and education practices still evident today. Knowledge of cultural phases in Alutiiq history informs us about trade, traditional harvest practices, and concepts of wealth, which were the foundation of the Alutiiq economy prior to Russian conquest.

Now more widely recognized due to efforts by Alutiiq organizations, the Kodiak Alutiiq knew a great deal about their environment, as passed down via stories and traditional practices. Elders today are still keepers of much of this traditional knowledge, having experienced some traditional education processes as young people. As Kawagley[6] describes of our cousins the Yup'ik, there exists a rich, complex knowledge base within each Indigenous culture, as knowledge about their homeland has accumulated over millennia, continually refined and distilled as new generations acquired it to survive in their specific area of the planet.

As a coastal maritime people, the Alutiiq possessed an awareness of surrounding areas and a complex knowledge about ocean navigation, including methods of reading the stars, currents, tides, winds, and animal behaviors.[7] This close awareness of their environment also included knowledge of weather and natural catastrophic event predictions, including ways to contend with their often harsh environment. They understood and perfected engineering methods that enabled them to develop tools specifically suited to their environment. The kayak and kayak paddle design indigenous to the Alutiiq region are excellent examples of their ancestral ingenuity, as these were made specifically for the types of currents and weather of the Kodiak Archipelago.[8] Each hunter learned the techniques and skills for building and maintaining their kayak and paddle; they knew how to produce waterproof clothing specifically custom-made for each person, all built to fit their exact body measurements for optimal maneuverability. Like other Indigenous peoples, the Alutiiq used a mathematical measurement system based on individual body measurement lengths to ensure an exact fit. All of this and other examples of ingenuity show the complex scientific and mathematical concepts that influenced precontact Alutiiq communities.

To subsist and thrive in the Kodiak Archipelago, the Alutiiq acquired hunting expertise, including knowledge of animal behaviors and relationships, and developed appropriate hunting techniques like snares, traps, and weapons, as well as herding as practiced by Alutiiq whalers. Elders also tell of traditional subsistence resource management practices that established protocols for requesting permission to hunt and instilled respect for territorial boundaries, including the proper allocation of resources to hunters within each territory.[9] These protocols were monitored by specific Elders acknowledged as the area's chiefs or resource managers, maintaining an effective resource management system based on respect and spiritual influence. This was before America acquired Alaska and created the Alaska Department of Fish and Game, which stripped the Alutiiq of their right to manage their homeland's harvest resources and pass these practices on to future generations.

As the Kodiak Archipelago is home to a vast variety of plants and is the northernmost point of the Pacific Northwest rain forest, the Alutiiq developed medicinal expertise in plant lore and healing techniques that sustained them in good health for millennia, before western conquerors brought devastating epidemics that upset the natural processes. Some of this knowledge still exists today with our Elders; and some is recorded in publications on plant uses, medicines and poisons.[10] However, a large body of knowledge is believed lost as traditional healers were killed or disempowered during Russian conquest and later assimilation during American colonization.[11]

EDUCATION UNDER RUSSIAN COLONIZATION (1784–1867)

While the Russian explorers, or promyshlennki (Russian fur hunters), began to map Kodiak in 1769, it wasn't until 1784 that Gregory Shelikhov established their first outpost in Alaska at Three Saints Bay,[12] near the present village of Old Harbor. Alutiiq stories and Russian accounts tell of occasional trading and frequent battles, leading up to the massacre and conquest of the Alutiiq people on August 14, 1784, by Shelikhov at Awa'uq (literally translated as Numb), or Refuge Rock as it is commonly known today.[13] This slaughter and the subsequent hostage taking began a dark era for the Alutiiq as Russian invaders enslaved men and boys to hunt sea otters year-round, while women and children were held captive.[14] In later years, half of all Alutiiq men between the ages of eighteen and fifty were forced to hunt sea otter to maintain Russian American Company (RAC) production.

Russian-led Alutiiq hunting parties traveled as far as California, two thousand miles away by sailboat and kayak, with many Alutiiq men never to return. One Alutiiq song, "Ukut Skuunat—These Schooners," tells the sad story of Alutiiq men taken away from their women to hunt. Akhiok Elder Mary Peterson narrates an introduction and history of the song's story about when men from Akhiok were enslaved to hunt sea otter and later abandoned near Unalaska.[15] With the men away for much of the year, or never to return, women and children struggled to survive on their own due to starvation from insufficient winter stores of food.[16] This tragic era suddenly interrupted the transmission of knowledge and forever changed family and social dynamics, introducing new, devastating traditions of alcoholism, depression, domestic violence, sexual abuse, and suicide.

Believing that formalized education would further control the Alutiiq people, in 1786, Shelikhov established the first school in Alaska at Three Saints Bay, nearby the current day village of Old Harbor, thus beginning western colonial control of Alaska Native education. In a 1786 letter to chief manager Konstantin Samoilov, Shelikhov wrote of the Alutiiq, "When they know a better way of living, they will understand and will take part in the work that enlightened people are doing."[17] Shelikhov's motivation to develop the school revolved around the RAC philosophy of assimilation for economic gain. He describes his plan to send young Alutiiq prisoners back to Russian for schooling, when he writes:

> *Education is useful and necessary. Only literate people can be good and accurate interpreters, so needed in this country.... For this purpose I am taking with me about forty Americans (Kodiak Alutiiq), male and female, both children and adults, some of their own free will and some as war prisoners. After they see Russia, our buildings and customs, I will reward one third of them and send them back. The other third I will attempt to present to the Imperial Court and the remaining third, the children, we are going to educate in Okhotsk or Irkutsk, and after their education is completed, if they wish it, we will return them here. From them their relatives and countrymen will learn about the law, order, and prosperity in Russia and will want to improve conditions here.*[18]

In a later reference to Shelikhov's efforts to educate the Natives, contained within a collection of Spanish documents dealing with Russian presence in California and housed within the Frank A. Golder Papers collection at Stanford University, an 1818 notation describes the results of Shelikhov's schooling efforts:

> *[The Russian American] Company has schools for Creoles and natives, has spent 37,000 rubles. In 1787 Shelikhov took 12 Creoles to Irkulsk. Half died in Siberia. Remaining returned good musicians. R. A. Co. recently brought eight to Kronstadt. Half died. Of other four 3 navigation, 1 ship building, and have returned to Alaska. Four girl creoles taken to Okhotsk. About seven years ago—one survived.*[19]

Shelikhov extended his plans for assimilation by requesting a mission of Russian Orthodox monks come to Kodiak, and they arrived on September 24, 1794.[20] The missionary group included seven monks, two novices, and ten Natives whom Shelikhov had sent to Russia for schooling in 1786. Prior to baptism, Alaska Natives had no rights in the eyes of their Russian conquerors. In fact, only those baptized and who agreed to assimilate were granted citizenship and its related rights. However, the missionary monks were not as cooperative as Shelikhov had hoped in helping subjugate the Alutiiq. While they taught at the church and school built in Kodiak, converting Natives to Orthodoxy, rather than supporting Shelikhov they instead tried to intervene against the acts of slavery and oppression they saw.[21] After witnessing the abuses suffered, the monks stood up for the Alutiiq captives, and were themselves arrested and abused. A monk called Father Herman survived the other monks, who were either martyred, died of natural causes, or returned to Russia.

The period from 1784 to 1818 has been described as the "darkest period" in the lives of Kodiak Island's Native people.[22] Life for the Alutiiq began to change for the positive when Father Herman fled Kodiak in 1817 to establish a school on nearby Spruce Island, relatively free from Russian American Company rule. After nearly two decades of persecution by RAC leadership, he was successful in providing intercession and offering education outside company objectives. Herman felt it was his duty to protect the Natives from exploitation and lived his life as their guardian.[23] This was the start of what is known as the Golden Age for the Alutiiq people. Father Herman, canonized in 1970 as Saint Herman (the first saint of America), built a school, orphanage, and garden at Anwik, now known as Monk's Lagoon. He remained there for twenty years until his repose in 1837.

As other churches were built around the island, so too were schools started and run by the clergy. The influence of the church and schools was pervasive; as Lydia Black describes, "Gideon established the first 'Russian-American' school at Kodiak in 1805 and by the time of his departure in 1807 at least two creoles and possibly one native were teaching in the school."[24]

In Kodiak, Hieromonk Gideon had nearly a hundred students in his school. Dauenhauer observes that "bilingual schools were paralleling the bilingualism that was the norm for the homes on Kodiak."[25] However, Davydov describes the stability of the school as fluctuating during its early years when he writes,

> *Only those Koniags who are brought up by the priests from childhood have learnt to read and write and receive the necessary understanding of Christian morality from daily example. A school has been re-established to take one hundred boys and could of course help to spread the Faith were the means available for the upkeep of this establishment. But in 1805 many children there died of hunger and scurvy and this will almost certainly happen again.*[26]

One of the most significant contributions to Alutiiq education during this time was efforts toward literacy by Russian Orthodox clergy and Alutiiq converts. They translated biblical texts into Sugt'stun (the Alutiiq language) and prepared various primers for reading and writing Sugt'stun using a church Slavonic cyrillic writing system. "Gideon envisioned the translation of Church and secular textbook literature into the languages of the native people, and he himself translated the Lord's Prayer into the Konyag language."[27] "In 1804, Hieromonk Gideon compiled a Kodiak Aleut [or Sugt'stun] grammar with the assistance of Creole Paraman Chumovits."[28] Il'via Tyzhonov (aka Elias Tishnoff) first published the *Sacred Catechism and Church History* in Sugt'stun in 1847, developing literate bilingualism with support by Russian Orthodox church leaders such as Bishop Innocent Veniaminov.[29] In 1848, Tyzhonov published a primer for Sugt'stun and a translation of the Gospel According to Matthew for use in Kodiak church services.[30] Between 1855 and 1867, Constantine Larionov wrote a *Primer and Prayerbook in Kodiak-Alutiiq* as well.[31] These publications indicate the positive perspective on bilingualism that Russian Orthodox clergy held.

Richard Dauenhauer describes in his book *Conflicting Visions in Alaskan Education* that "the Orthodox tradition maintains great respect for the language and culture of the individual."[32] He asserts that "for the Orthodox … one does not have to abandon or change his or her culture or language to become a Christian."[33] Within Russian colonial efforts, "There [was] no attack on a person's language. Rather the Church sought to instill a sense of pride in the Native language and foster popular literacy in it. Because competency in two languages was stressed, it should come as no surprise that Aleuts had the first bilingual schools in Alaska."[34] Ultimately, Saint Herman and the 1794 missionaries played a major role in Alutiiq education. Dauenhauer describes that "an unbroken history of Orthodox bilingual education existed on Kodiak Island from the 1790s into the 1960s" due to their efforts.[35]

Despite strides in literacy, atrocities and disease again decimated the Alutiiq population beyond the earlier period of conquest, enslavement, and starvation. Ships brought epidemics to Kodiak in 1804, 1819–1820, 1827–1828, and 1852, further subduing Alutiiq resistance to Russian empirical forces.[36] The smallpox epidemic of 1837–1840 was particularly destructive, killing huge numbers, leading to forced consolidation of the Kodiak Alutiiq people. Survivors of the sixty-five villages in the Kodiak Archipelago were evacuated by the Russians and relocated into seven communities.[37]

Similarly, Harold Napoleon[38] describes how the Yup'ik and other Alaska Native peoples suffered a series of deadly epidemics when foreigners entered their regions, exposing them to new illnesses they were not physically adapted to survive. The Great Death, as Napoleon calls it, left every family in a state of grief for their dead as whole generations were lost. The survivors awoke to a new reality without leaders or trust in the spiritual healing practices that had sustained them. In essence, their "resistance collapsed because of mass death."[39] Survival after so much loss explains why Alaska Natives appear to have so easily left behind cherished traditions to adopt new lifeways, and why generations later families still experience apathy or historical trauma that manifests as substance abuse, domestic violence, suicide, and chronic health issues. As Napoleon argues, "No people anywhere will voluntarily discard their culture, beliefs, customs and traditions unless they are under a great deal of stress, physically, psychologically or spiritually."[40]

The experience of the Great Death left Alaska Native peoples in a state of desperation and depression, allowing new spiritual traditions brought by missionaries to be melded with elements of their ancestral worldview, and older practices denounced as evil, resulting in an epistemological metamorphosis that severed connections to a large portion of ancestral knowledge.[41] These early acquiescences left an opening for western authority figures to influence greater assimilative changes during the century following.

As sea otter populations declined with the profitability of the Russian territory, the Russian tsar sold the Russian American Company (with implied rights to Alaska) to the United States in 1867.[42] The Alaska Commercial Company assumed holdings of the RAC, and although the Treaty of Cession recognized the Alaska Native claim to land, it was not until 1971 that the United States agreed to honor these claims with the Alaska Native Claims Settlement Act (ANCSA). Unfortunately, from the date of transfer until the passage of ANCSA, education and the Native way of life again entered a period of decline under new assimilative forces when the Russian colonizers withdrew. Supportive bilingualism did not last for the Alutiiq, as the transition to American colonization buried translated texts and suppressed both Alutiiq and Russian languages through "English Only" policies that encouraged corporal punishment, transforming the one high point of Russian colonial education into what is known as the period of "Forgotten Literacy."[43]

EDUCATION UNDER AMERICAN COLONIZATION (1867–1971)

One of the most noticeable changes that western assimilation under American colonization brought was near linguistic annihilation as Americans tried to silence Alaska Natives languages.[44] In just one hundred years, the Kodiak Alutiiq moved from trilingualism to monolingualism. During the 1700s and 1800s, Alutiiq families commonly spoke Sugt'stun, Russian, and English, and most were also fluent in other Alaska Native and Scandinavian languages. Then, after the 1900s when America took control of Alaska, they were left with only basic monolingualism: English. Today, there are only approximately thirty-three Sugt'stun first-language speakers left on Kodiak[45]—a tragic indictment of the power of educational assimilation.

After the United States acquired Alaska from Russia, the propagation of the American education system's "English Only" policy through the Bureau of Indian Affairs' (BIA) takeover of missionary schools, as well as through boarding schools, Native languages were effectively devalued. By limiting language transmission and creating communication barriers within families, both cultural transmission and emotional well-being were further impacted.[46] On Kodiak there were only three villages that had schools run through the US Indian Service Department in 1947: Afognak, Old Harbor, and Ouzinkie.[47] Children from the other villages had to travel to these villages or Kodiak in order to attend school, or attend boarding school elsewhere in Alaska or the lower forty-eight.

Countless Elders from throughout Kodiak tell the same story of how their Native language was forbidden in school as they suffered cruel punishment and ridicule by their teachers for speaking it.[48] Hirshberg and Sharp documented stories about Alaskan schools where "children were forbidden to speak their native languages and were even beaten for speaking them."[49] Ironically, the American education system instituted this policy believing that Native students would then more easily assimilate to become productive citizens in the new Alaskan society. However, their social engineering efforts instead left students with limited language proficiency and a debilitating lack of self-esteem as they lost their connection to Elders and their culture, and subsequently with themselves.[50]

As Gamble discusses, human language and thinking are interlinked.[51] While Gamble describes the communication disconnect experienced between western and Indigenous peoples, it is equally true within Indigenous societies where the younger generation grows up without a linguistic relationship to others in their own families. The continuing communication barriers between western and Native peoples, as well as among assimilated Native peoples, has resulted in many negative influences, ranging from misguided social service implementation to emotionally and environmentally damaging research and regulations. Gamble argues that a lack of effective communication across generations and cultures is almost ensured "unless their linguistic backgrounds are similar or can in some way be calibrated … [as interactions between cultures] often leads to fundamental differences in perceptions of what is true, what is right, and what conduces to public needs and welfare."[52] Joanne Mulcahy points out the paradox of the American welfare system for Alaska Natives when she says:

> *Ironically, as the material well-being of Native people grew with the antipoverty programs of the 1960s and '70s, their psychic and spiritual health eroded with dependence on Western ways of life.*

> *Handed down generation after generation the "infection of the soul" ultimately manifested itself in the suicide, domestic violence, and alcoholism that pervades Native villages.*[53]

Well-meaning individuals, including educators, from outside Native communities are notorious for making assumptions that the fundamentals of right and wrong and core values are much the same across cultures, or should be. One of the most common and tragic mistakes is in the prioritization of values. For example, Gamble explains that in western culture often "the only things that count are the things that can be counted."[54] This is arguably one of the main flaws within the western educational system, as educators are forced to place heavier priority on testing and quantitative measures of student performance than on more intrinsic values, which are deeply embedded in the practical and real-life application learning process important within traditional Indigenous cultures.

Consequently, as western education and government gained control within Alaska Native communities, it greatly diminished traditional harvest or subsistence lifeways, prioritizing academic learning over essential cultural knowledge necessary to make a living. The development of a cash economy, wage labor, the American education system's curricula, extinguishment of land claims through ANCSA (1971), the Alaska National Interest Lands Conservation Act (ANILCA) (1980), and the introduction of new technologies have all led to a disconnection in the lives of many modern Alaska Natives from their traditional interdependencies with the natural world. The loss of these life skills and spiritual ties has further contributed to health and social dysfunction as families have moved into cities or begun to rely on imported foods that must be purchased from a store. This has considerably limited their contact with the natural world and the application of traditional harvest knowledge. In turn, their radical diet change has resulted in new illnesses, such as diabetes and heart disease.[55] Further, many Alaska Native communities have experienced increased pollution as they have become more detached from their environment and the proper right relationships with it in order to sustain balance.[56]

And, as the subsistence way of life diminished, the American welfare system permeated Alaskan Native communities. Qualifying as poverty stricken in the American perspective, many Native families in their crises turned to welfare and government-assisted programs for housing, food, energy, and other social and health services. These resources have both positive and negative influences. One significant cultural transformation that many families have experienced is a growing sense of entitlement, which greatly impacts self-worth and retention of survival knowledge. The American welfare system has enabled many Native families to continue unhealthy lifeways, becoming increasingly dependent and dysfunctional—all of which greatly impacts the children growing up in homes reliant on this system. In turn, this impacts their success within the education system, as evidenced by high numbers of "special needs" designated students. Native students in Alaska are 50 percent more likely to be placed in special education programs for general learning disabilities compared to other students.[57]

In addition to the US government's welfare system, the Baptist Church in the 1900s began providing social services for orphans due to the epidemics and high numbers of orphans in need of homes.[58] They operated four mission houses, including Ouzinkie, Larsen Bay, and a Baptist Industrial School on Woody Island, which was later moved to establish the Kodiak Mission after a fire. From 1938 to 1958, the Ouzinkie Mission supported children under five and during World War II it made an effort to keep the younger children in a rural location in case of invasion into the more populated areas. The Baptist Mission provided homes for orphaned children who lost their parents or whose parents were unable to care for them. While the missions provided homes, they also pushed an "English Only" policy and a focus on acculturation, which further orphaned the children they tried to help.

Another significant occurrence that altered Alutiiq community communication and traditional education practices during the American period was the requirement to send children to boarding schools. As Hirshberg and Sharp explain,

> *The history of formal schooling for Alaska Natives, from the time of the U.S. acquisition of Alaska in 1867 to the present, is a troubled one. The initial goals of formal education in the North were to Christianize and "civilize" Alaska Natives.... Over time, the federal, territorial, and state governments established a boarding school system to accomplish these goals. For the first three quarters of the 20th century Alaska Native children were sent to boarding schools or boarding homes either inside or outside Alaska.*[59]

Children at Ouzinkie Baptist Mission Church during World War II—Courtesy of Alutiiq Museum

Students from Kodiak went to several different boarding schools, including Mount Edgecumbe Boarding School (an accredited high school) near Sitka, Alaska; Wrangell Institute (a middle ungraded school) in Wrangell, Alaska; Chemawa Indian School in Salem, Oregon; and Chilocco Indian School in Chilocco, Oklahoma. Mount Edgecumbe has since transitioned into a modern boarding school favored today by rural families. Wrangell Institute was built in 1932 by the BIA and served as a boarding school until the 1970s. Chemawa offered industrial training for boys and girls. The occupational training focus of these schools was perhaps the most effective at assimilating students to western social expectations and wage economics. The shift in values away from a subsistence lifestyle and the disconnection from family and community was devastating for most. However, there were those who appreciated the new opportunities the boarding schools offered, but they, too, were forever changed.

Regardless of whether boarding school was an individually positive or negative experience, the boarding schools inevitably resulted in loss of language and traditions, loss of access to community role models, shifts in sense of identity, and were successful at assimilating a whole generation of Alaska Natives.[60] For the many students who suffered abuse as well, these losses were further exacerbated.[61] Elders and family histories tell many stories of painful experiences associated with being forced to live away from home to attend American boarding schools.[62]

In fact, from 1969 to 1972, Kodiak attempted to address the ongoing rural exodus of high school students to boarding schools both in Alaska and the lower forty-eight by establishing a local dormitory complex at the Kodiak Aleutian Regional High School in the city of Kodiak. This local boarding school offered rural students from Kodiak's six villages an opportunity to attend high school alongside town-based students. The school served 113 boarded students in 1969—its first year of operation—followed by 120 in 1970, 152 in 1972,[63] and 73 in 1973.[64] This regional boarding school experienced significant issues, including cases of abuse by guardians and other students. It was ultimately abandoned as an ineffective strategy for serving rural high school students. This school within a school was short-lived due to a host of negative impacts, and ultimately closed in 1973.

As Hirshberg and Sharp report, "[Boarding school] cost many students not only the loss of their language, but also their culture and identity."[65] They interviewed sixty-one Alaska Natives about their experiences and the long-term effects of attending boarding school between the 1940s and the early 1980s. Interviewees agreed that the school policies were effective at assimilating them to the dominant culture, but with this assimilation came lasting scars. They write,

> *These practices had lasting effects on individual students, their families, and communities. Those we interviewed told of finding it difficult to return home and be accepted. They felt that by being sent to boarding school they had missed out on learning important traditional skills and had a harder time raising their own children. For communities, the loss of children to boarding schools created a tremendous void, one that interviewees said was filled by alcohol and a breakdown in society. Drugs, alcohol, and suicide are some of the effects interviewees spoke of as coming from boarding home experiences and the loss of cultural identity and family.*[66]

Despite this legacy, many rural community members today still support the reestablishment of a boarding school on Kodiak Island. The common solution offered to circumvent past failures with this and other boarding schools is to place the school in one of the six rural villages rather than the city of Kodiak. But this solution assumes that only urban temptations were the factor, which was not the case.

In the case of Afognak village, the BIA took over authority of the village school, and many biracial families chose to leave the village and move to nearby Kodiak after complaining about the school.[67] In this way, the BIA school became a major factor in rural out-migration. Some interpreted the move as a denial of Native ethnicity and elitism. Today, the inequitable quality of education in Kodiak's rural schools has also led families to leave their village communities in order to provide their children with more educational opportunities. Ultimately, the issue of schooling has been, and continues to be, a major factor influencing out-migration.

After one hundred years as a territory, in 1959 Alaska became a state and changed from a federal BIA education system to a state education system. The full transition took several years, as outlined in the 1963 *Overall Education Plan for Rural Alaska* published by Alaska governor William A. Egan's office. The plan provided for "the orderly transfer of Bureau schools to non-federal operation under the principle of mutual readiness on the part of the community, the State, and the Bureau."[68] It established Advisory School Boards, which allowed rural communities a greater voice in their local schools. The Kodiak Island Borough School District (KIBSD) formed to manage Kodiak's transition to a state-run system.

Then in 1976, the Alaska state lawsuit, "Molly Hootch" (*Tobeluk v. Lind*), settled with a commitment by the state to provide local schools for Native communities as it had in predominately white communities.[69] This resulted in construction of new K–12 schools in all six rural villages on Kodiak and implementation of high schools within each community. With rural schools available, families had the opportunity to keep their kids home, rather than send them to boarding schools or opt for them not to complete high school.

Since 1976, KIBSD has undergone significant changes in the services provided to Alutiiq students. In rural schools, they continue to struggle with high teacher turnover, but they have softened their previous "no local hires" philosophy and are working with the Native community to develop teacher orientation programs that address culture shock and better prepare teachers to work and live in rural communities. Rural schools still struggle with high travel and shipping costs. The budget constraints and challenges inherent in small school operations contribute to a perception of reduced quality or equity. Ultimately, there is room for continued reform to improve continuity and applicability of education in rural schools. Further, efforts to make district curriculum more place-based continue to progress as KIBSD is more open to change than ever before.

The Kodiak Island Borough School District has obtained several Department of Education Alaska Native Education federal grants to help mitigate issues of high teacher turnover, low student assessment performance, and high dropout rates. KIBSD serves approximately twenty-five hundred students in fourteen schools, including five hundred, or 19 percent, Alaska Native. However, as more than 90 percent of KIBSD teachers are white, and only 3.8 percent Native, it is difficult for Native students or parents to relate to the non-Native teachers unfamiliar with how Alutiiq traditional knowledge should be integrated into all levels of school for place-based learning.[70] Currently, KIBSD offers a standardized curriculum with limited inclusion of traditional Alutiiq knowledge, but curriculum revision efforts continue to increase inclusion.

Kodiak has been fortunate as a small Alaskan community to have higher educational opportunities available locally. In 1969, Kodiak College was founded, and it is now a two-year satellite campus of the University of Alaska–Anchorage system, with approximately sixteen hundred students served annually.[71] During the past decade, they have extended support to the Alutiiq community by offering courses in Alutiiq Studies and cosponsoring the Kodiak Rural Forum to address rural out-migration, education, and community issues, including access to additional training and exposure to best practices. In 2011, Kodiak College received a five-year Department of Education, Alaska Native Education grant to develop an Alutiiq Studies Program and support Alutiiq language revitalization.[72] This program promises to train teachers in culturally responsive practices, traditions, and Alutiiq language.

The St. Herman's Theological Seminary, established in 1972, today offers statewide opportunities for training to become Russian Orthodox clergy.[73] The seminary has brought many Yup'ik families to study and live in the Kodiak community. Their interest in the Alutiiq language has increased usage of the language in church services, raising attention to the revitalization movement. Members of the seminary also meet regularly now with several Alutiiq Elders, exploring the Alutiiq church texts in the prior Cyrillic orthography.

ALUTIIQ RENAISSANCE: AN EDUCATIONAL COUNTERMOVEMENT (1971–PRESENT)

Following an international wave of Indigenous decolonization efforts, the Kodiak Alutiiq began an educational countermovement, often described as the Alutiiq Renaissance. Just prior to and following the passage of ANCSA in 1971, Kodiak Alutiiq peoples began to unite their efforts in protecting and sharing traditional ways of life and knowledge as they regained autonomy. There were a number of early efforts by Alutiiq leaders to revitalize the Alutiiq language in the 1980s and 1990s, including creation of a high-school and college-level Alutiiq Language class, developed and taught by Philomena Knecht and Alutiiq speaker Florence Pestrikoff in a 1993 pilot class.[74] Their efforts and others grew from an increased interest and pride in Alutiiq heritage after ANCSA and the new availability of the Alutiiq language in a written form, made possible with Jeff Leer's research and publication of an Alutiiq dictionary in 1978 and a grammar book in 1990. While the Knecht and Pestrikoff class pilot was ultimately not sustained, the unpublished lesson booklet they produced has been used to develop current language learning resources.[75] It is likely that all the cultural revitalization efforts had not yet gained enough momentum to influence students' commitment to learn the language.[76] In January 2011, the community launched a second pilot of an Alutiiq language class at Kodiak High School. As of 2013, the course was in its third year with twelve students in Level I and six in Level II.

Through a combined Alutiiq community effort, with funding from the Exxon Valdez Oil Spill Trust, the Alutiiq Museum and Archaeological Repository through the Alutiiq Heritage Foundation was founded in 1995. The museum has significantly influenced cultural education and helped reestablish a positive sense of identity and unity for the Alutiiq people by having a regional focus for Alutiiq cultural and historical research, offering a home for artifacts and gathered cultural knowledge, and providing educational materials and workshops to help carry on traditional knowledge among each new generation. Through the museum, Alutiiq leaders and educators have been able to teach mask carving, bentwood bowl and hat construction, kayak building, and the Alutiiq language. The museum—and its staff—have won a number of awards, and it continues to be a community focal point as we use it to support educational efforts within the Kodiak Alutiiq community as well as educate visitors and other community members about the traditional practices and lifeways of our people throughout time and into the present.

One of the most significant education programs the Alutiiq Museum manages is the Kodiak Alutiiq Language Revitalization Program. Through this program, an Elders council called the New Words Council, or Nuta'at Niugnelistet, is working to empower Alutiiq people with the creation of terms for modern scientific, technological, and medical items, helping bring the language into the twenty-first century. As a collaborative effort between grassroots language revitalization leaders, the community is developing curriculum to expand instruction and help sustain Kodiak Alutiiq as a living language. This movement is continuing to gain momentum.

Perhaps less known outside the Kodiak Alutiiq community are a number of Native education programs quietly supporting Kodiak Alutiiq students and families. In 1966, the Kodiak Area Native Association was established. Through their education department they provide job training, scholarships, and preschools in three of the largest villages:

Old Harbor, Ouzinkie, and Port Lions. A number of tribal councils around the island also offer Alutiiq dance training programs and other after-school programs. The Kodiak Island Housing Authority (KIHA) provides a series of education programs and an after-school family center for residents of their Woody Way complex as well as funding support for Native educational programs throughout the region. As a result of the ANCSA, and our regional corporation Koniag, Inc., the Koniag Education Foundation was founded in 1993 to provide higher education scholarships, mentorship, internships, and job training.

A significant influence on Alaska Native education statewide was the development of the Alaska Rural Systemic Initiative (AKRSI) through combined support by the Alaska Federation of Natives and the University of Alaska–Fairbanks, with leadership by Ray Barnhardt, PhD, Angayuqaq Oscar Kawagley, PhD, and Frank Hill.[77] A number of grassroots efforts were put into action through their influence, including the AKRSI series of *Guidelines for Cultural-Responsive Schools*.[78]

As a graduate of the University of Alaska–Fairbanks Education Department, with its strong emphasis in cross-cultural studies, Alutiiq educator Teresa Schneider took on a role as Alutiiq studies coordinator at the Kodiak Island Borough School District through AKRSI efforts and funding. In 1999, she and a group of Alutiiq Elders and educators established a regional Native education association called the Native Educators of the Alutiiq Region (NEAR). NEAR and the educators in its network have supported development of several curriculum units, such as a Kodiak Alutiiq Spring Plants curriculum, and new teacher orientation sessions that began to make a difference in the level of involvement the Alutiiq community had in schools. Perhaps one of the most significant publications to promote culturally relevant education practices was their collaboration with Alutiiq Elders to produce an Alutiiq Values poster, publishing fourteen core value statements that help show how Alutiiq traditional practices and worldview today are part of a continuous knowledge stream and provide the framework for Alutiiq education.[79]

Since 1995, various organizations have sponsored culture-based summer camps around the island, which have significantly impacted Kodiak Alutiiq youth by building positive exposure to Alutiiq culture and ways of life through intergenerational learning environments aligned to traditional Alutiiq education practices. Through summer camps like these the community has produced new curriculum and publications such as the *Red Cedar of Afognak*, a Native science children's book, which won an Honoring Alaska's Indigenous Literature Award and an American Book Award by the Before Columbus Foundation.[80]

Since 2000, the Kodiak Native community has cosponsored a regional gathering called Esgarlluku Taquka'aq, or Awakening Bear, which for several years featured an annual education summit. Later, through KIHA efforts, community empowerment and leadership in education and other areas were further extended with the creation of a Rural Leadership Forum, which meets three times a year. Through their education sessions, the Kodiak rural villages have been able to build a stronger relationship with Kodiak Island Borough School District and Kodiak College and developed *Advisory School Boards Best Practices.*

Combined, there are many Alutiiq organizations and leaders working together to develop new ways to support respect for the Alutiiq worldview and traditional knowledge. They are well aware that it is through education that we can transform our communities back into empowered, self-sufficient communities, rooted within our Alutiiq values. These efforts require collaboration, creative solutions, and learning from other Indigenous communities who are proving they can establish successful Indigenous place-based education systems.[81]

Dance Workshop at Alutiiq Museum—Courtesy of Alutiiq Museum

HISTORICAL TRAUMA IMPLICATIONS WITHIN EDUCATION

Despite all of the many strides to improve education, specifically within the lives of Alaska Native children, their daily experience within school continues to have many assimilative impacts, particularly when they are not being taught their history, or are bombarded with conflicting messages of what is true and valued between school and home. Within the Alaskan K–12 schooling environment, if educators do not engage students in culturally relevant experiential learning, nor embrace Alaska Native cultural beliefs, values, and traditions every day in the classroom, then they are perpetrating assimilative forces that result in students becoming increasingly detached from their community and environment, and subsequently themselves.

The process of engaging in western education is a cross-cultural journey that, without an understanding of why and how the new experience is foreign, can make students susceptible to perpetuate assimilative forces themselves. Alaska Native families and communities need to be more aware of the history of western influences on their lives and in their communities. How we learn and in what environment we learn are major factors in our state of well-being and subsequent ways of life. If learning within school continues to lack relevancy and applicability to daily life and the traditions of our ancestors, it will continue to erode values and community traditional knowledge. Western influences will not stop, but if Alaska Natives truly regain self-determination in all aspects of their lives, including education, they will be better able to reconcile their cultural knowledge with western knowledge, taking the best from both worlds.

Within the Kodiak Archipelago, the Alaska Native community has been marginalized for more than two hundred years. Still today the Native community is viewed by many in power as incapable of effective self-governance. Honor and respect appear only to be paid to those few Natives who have assimilated and achieved higher education credentials and positions of power. This further makes their role uncomfortable, as it is believed that since they succeeded within western higher education and employment, they must share the same dominant, prejudiced view about Natives who have not attained their levels of educational achievement. This condescension that our Native community struggles with is disempowering and frustrating for all who recognize its reality, as we continue to watch each new generation taught outdated, irrelevant, or misconceived information about our community; worse yet, they are encouraged to look outside for their hope of a better future—as if we have nothing to offer them.

The reality is that some in power in our education system do not believe that Kodiak Alaska Natives are capable of providing their youth with a "complete" education, arguing that if we could, we would have done so already. However, what they neglect to recognize is that because "schools" are established power structures that have inculcated generations it is challenging to awaken to how much the American education system has impacted us and continues to influence us today, or how the system should be working for, and not against us.

Ultimately, it is not acceptable to consider western educational achievement as superior to our traditional knowledge systems. We must be able to give our children an awareness of these realities and the options to pursue education in whatever realm calls them, whether it be to maintain a traditional subsistence lifestyle within their own community, or to pursue cross-cultural leadership to benefit their community by building bridges between the two distinct worldviews. We deserve the right to determine what and how our children learn in a manner relevant to our own community. Education is the source of power to maintain self-governance, and so it is essential that Alaska Native communities take this power back.

While much of Alaska Native educational history tells stories about what has been taken away, there is much to celebrate. Despite near extinction of our Indigenous languages, despite attempted elimination of our Native villages and lifeways, despite dysfunctional dynamics within our families due to generations of social engineering and a paternalistic education, we are strong survivors who have held onto our values and ways of looking at the world. We are finding our own ways toward positive change as we learn to bridge these worlds. Educators today need to consider the current implications of this educational history for Native students. Educators who come to teach in our communities need to know the history of the place they enter and the experiences of its children through their grandparents, and they need to love them for it without taking ownership of it; rather, they must share the power they wield with the community. As author Thomas King writes, "The truth about stories is that's all we are."[82] We are the sum of our and our ancestors' experiences. These experiences shape how we see, communicate, and react to the world around us. Educators beyond any other humans on earth must come from a place of understanding that there is no global or universal "us." Their students start from the place they're from and will always return to it, even if it is limping. Efforts to shape or mold young minds will perpetuate generations of harm in the name of "education," but teaching from place, identity, and cultural knowledge gives students the power to become lifelong learners.

CHAPTER 24

We Can Play Too

A NEW ERA

Ron Solis

WE CAN PLAY TOO

"We can play too? What does that mean?" someone may ask. There are a few reasons for this title. At first reading, the statement "We can play too" may seem childlike. What is wrong with that? Well, it all depends on the child. In our culture, we have stories of children who have an abundance of knowledge, and the consequences of adults who do not realize these children have knowledge or do not heed their knowledge is death. Therefore, I hope you will find this title thought-provoking. Through the concept We Can Play Too, I am suggesting a few meanings, most of which are historically driven. Historically driven meaning that due to circumstances in Kanaka Maoli history, we, the descendants, may not be as confident as our ancestors in terms of cultural knowledge, language, and perhaps our identity as Indigenous People. There were key events that led to where we are now.

A NEW ERA

It seems that each new generation deals with a new era, a whole new game. It is not easy. There are differences, from a few to many, from minor to devastating. How does one deal with a new era? Nānā i ke kumu (Look to the source). Our kūpuna (ancestors) and their legacy is our source. How did they deal with a new era? There have been several eras, but let me share a historical example from a recent era. One of the most devastating in our history was the arrival of Captain Cook. This is a key event, not because Captain Cook *discovered* us, but because the result of his landing was the introduction of western material culture, like guns, cannons, and nails to Hawai'i. The men of his crew also exposed our kūpuna to many contagious foreign diseases like syphilis and gonorrhea. These diseases were fatal to a population who had no immunity to them, and a great number of the population of Kanaka Maoli was decimated as a result. This is tragic not only for the great numbers who died, but also for the great amount of knowledge that was lost due to their passing. Our kūpuna were playing the game of life as they were used to; however, with the introduction of new and never before heard of pieces to the game, the game of life changed. The next historical event was the arrival of the missionaries. Shortly after this, the Native religion was out, and the new religion, Christianity, was in.

How did our kūpuna deal with the many challenges, new technologies and cultures, and so forth? We are still in the process of finding out. We are blessed to have many of our stories passed down to us in this current time. This transference of knowledge, their legacy, continues through a variety of ways. And because our kūpuna played the game so well, when the missionaries introduced the printing press and newspapers to them, they grasped that knowledge and took it to a new level. Oral tradition is still ongoing; we also have printed and written texts (manuscripts, newspapers, books, songs, etc.), artifacts, voice and video recordings, and instinctual and spiritual knowledge. The more we search, the more we nānā i ke kumu, look to the source, the more we find, and the more we learn and know about how our kūpuna dealt with a new era. Many times, we find different stories from what is typically said in the colonizers' history books, which is usually void of our kūpunas' voices and is commonly from someone else's perspective. That is why it is important to nānā i ke kumu, to look to the source. Let me be clear, our ancestors didn't actually say, "We can play too," they just *played*. They lived it. They showed that they can play too.

By the 1860s, we see how English versus Hawaiian becomes a big issue being discussed in Hawaiʻi. Some Kanaka Maoli supported English schools and some Kanaka Maoli supported Hawaiian schools. Well, English influence won, and by the time my parents were born, Hawaiian was no longer the language of intergenerational knowledge transfer in most families. Both my grandmothers—my maternal grandmother and my paternal grandmother—spoke Hawaiian, but never passed it on to their children; that is, my parents, uncles, and aunties. Because intergenerational transfer of language stopped in the majority of our ʻohana (families), a lot of traditional knowledge also stopped being passed on to the younger generations.

Why did Hawaiian language not continue to be the medium in our families? Well, as I said earlier, some Kanaka Maoli felt that English was the way to assimilate and be successful, especially for the success of their children in the future. They made a choice and acted upon it and made their voices heard. They did not make their choices for themselves. They believed that their choice would enable their children, grandchildren, and so on to be successful in a new era. Here is an example where a grandmother tells her grandchild to learn English well in 1917. The grandmother tells her grandchild, Sarah Keliʻilolena Nākoa,

> *Ke hele nei lā ʻoe i ke kula. E hoʻomanawanui i ka naʻauao. E paʻa pono i ka ʻōlelo a ka Haole. Mai kālele i kā kākou ʻōlelo. ʻAʻohe he pono i laila. Aia ke ola o ka noho ʻana ma kēia mua aku i ka ʻike pono i ka ʻōlelo a ka poʻe Haole. No laila, e hoʻoikaika.*
>
> *You are going to school. Persevere in education. Learn well the language of the white foreigner. Don't depend on our language. There is no benefit there. Success in life in the future lies in knowing the language of the white foreigner well. Therefore, work hard [in learning English].*

And this is probably how it was in most families who supported English—the main issue was for the child to be successful in life.

The example above was in Hawaiian and translated for this text. This is one example that proves there were still families using their mother tongue, the Hawaiian language, as the language of home. Why didn't this continue? One reason is the way Hawaiian children were treated in school for either using their ʻōlelo makuahine (mother tongue), not being able to speak English, or not being able to understand English. They were abused. Sarah Nākoa, from the story above, shares her story:

> *And the teacher called my name. However, I had no idea because that was the first time I heard my name called out, and here it was that I had an English name. I only knew of my Hawaiian name. And because I didn't respond to her she slapped my face.*

No problem, right? Just a slap. Not so! In our culture, the head is sacred. It is the area where our kūpuna reside. "The head was considered the dwelling place of one's own spirit and the temporary home for aumākua (ancestor gods) and other good spirits."[1] This idea is so strong that "the tradition-observing Hawaiian does not even pat a child's head in affection."[2]

Rose Manu, another kūpuna, also shares her story about going to school and the abuse she received:

> *Hele wau i ke kula aole maopopo wau i ka olelo haole. Olelo mai ke kumu iau e kakau ko'u inoa. Aole hiki iau. Mamake au e hele hoopau pilikia, aole hiki iau ke namu. No laila, hoi a uumi au a hoi i ka hale. Pulu loa ka lole.*[3]

> *When I went to school I didn't know English. The teacher told me to write my name. I wasn't able to. I wanted to use the bathroom, but I wasn't able to speak English. So, I went back (to my seat) and held it, until I went home. But my clothes got soiled.*

Who would want their children to receive the same type of inhumane treatment? Would you want your child or grandchild … or *any* child to receive such treatment? Children are so impressionable. The kūpuna, who experienced such abuse or other types of abuse during their childhood, made the conscious choice not to pass the language on to their children probably with the idea that they, their children, would not receive such abuse for speaking Hawaiian or not understanding English. The life experiences of our kūpuna influenced their choices. Although the kūpuna were making their own choices, it is what Ngũgĩ wa Thiongo refers to as the cultural bomb, an "annihilation of the people's belief in their names, their language, in their environment, in their heritage of struggle in their unity, in their capacities and ultimately in themselves." The damage of being subjected to this continued process is so severe that the colonized assimilate to the ways of the colonizer. They no longer see themselves as Indigenous. I have heard many people from my parents' generation call themselves Americans. When I began learning Hawaiian, a few asked me, "Why are you learning Hawaiian?" Some parents whose children are in the Hawaiian Immersion Program have also said that they have been asked, "Why are you putting your child in Hawaiian immersion?"

Before we go on, I would like to share my reflections on looking back at our history. I believe that history is there for us to learn from. It is not there for us to point to and find fault. One of my friends, upon finding an old newspaper article from the 1860s written by one of his ancestors, became somewhat ashamed to see that his ancestor was pro-English. My thoughts were that we shouldn't be embarrassed. Our kūpuna were fighting to live in a brand-new culture. They experienced so many new things and also so many misfortunes in such a short time. They had to react. Ngũgĩ's concept of the cultural bomb is definitely credible; however, there are also other variables that affected the choices of our kūpuna. The end of one's lineage is very important. Our kūpuna had to take that into consideration. To look back now and say or think, "The kūpuna should have done this," is a disgrace. Is it that easy, really? Our kūpuna played the game to the best of their ability. We can play too.

We can play too means that we are ready and able to be *at the table*. That is, we are not just going to be spectators to our destiny. We are active participants. We can play too means we want to be *in the game*, not just sitting back and watching. Letting people speak for us and about us.

We can play too also means that we have the kuleana (responsibility) to *play*. We have the right to make decisions for ourselves as a Lāhui (nation, peoples), and as individual Kanaka Maoli. And not have to follow what others say about us.

Another reason I chose the phrase "We can play too" as the title of this chapter is because it has meaning and relevancy for each new generation. It does not stop at my generation. It can relate to all future generations.

The final reason for the title "We Can Play Too" is related to the way our kūpuna played on/with words and their meanings, using ʻōlelo noʻeau (wise sayings, proverbs), riddles, and so forth. We should strive to do the same. In *Decolonising the Mind*, Kenyan novelist and theorist of postcolonial literature Ngũgĩ wa Thiong'o educates us about the importance of valuing one's native language.[4] He says, "Language, any language has a dual character: it is both a means of communication and a carrier of culture: culture is a means of communication. Language carries culture, and culture carries, particularly through orature and literature, the entire body of values by which we come to perceive ourselves and our place in the world."[5] Throughout that publication he shares many experiences of being raised in his native language and further claims that language has a suggestive power well beyond the immediate and lexical meaning: the suggestive magical power of language was reinforced by the games we played with words through riddles, proverbs, transpositions of syllables, or through nonsensical but musically arranged words … so we learnt the music of our language on top of the content … the language, through images and symbols, gave us a view of the world but it had a beauty of its own."[6]

As a practitioner of ʻōlelo Hawaiʻi[7] (Hawaiian language), I was immediately struck by the similarity of this understanding to that of Hawaiian language. For example, in our culture we have, as I mentioned, something called ʻōlelo noʻeau—wise sayings or proverbs. It's one type of traditional knowledge from our kūpuna that was perpetuated and passed down to each subsequent generation through language. ʻŌlelo noʻeau are not merely wise sayings; they also serve as examples of kūpuna wisdom, illustrating imagery, metaphor, and symbols that help us understand a Kanaka Maoli worldview. The beauty of their wisdom is demonstrated by the complex intricacies found within them. For Kanaka, the magical power of language that Ngũgĩ speaks of also appears in other forms like nane (riddles). In these ways, our kūpuna, like Ngũgĩ, were raised in their Native tongue and were grounded in the depth and breadth of their worldview and, most importantly, their identity through language.[8]

LET US PLAY!

"Let us play" is a statement, a suggestion, a command to let us do what we want to do in the revitalization of our language, our culture, and our people. The main thing is we do our research and we do it for the benefit of our children, of future generations. When we say, "Let us play," it means we don't want to do things the colonized way, we want to do them the way our kūpuna did them. So if what we do does not conform to the colonized way; we don't care—no matter what anyone tells us.

Let's look at an example of a person who tries to influence Kanaka Maoli or tries to tell us that we are creating "revisionist history," whenever we "re-right" or "re-write" history by uncovering history that was hidden, that was silenced. I will share a story of my exchange of ideas with this person.

I mua, e nā pōkiʻi, a inu i ka wai ʻawaʻawa ("Forward, my younger brothers, until you drink the bitter water)."[9] This wise saying is from a story about one of our Aliʻi (kings), Kamehameha I. Without knowing the story, one might guess the "bitter water" to be a variety of things—actual bitter water; "awa, a narcotic drink … used in ceremonies";[10] or any liquid substance that is considered bitter. Metaphorically, the "bitter water" could also be an unpleasant or tragic experience.[11] You may also have thought of a couple of other possibilities. However, Kamehameha's words to his soldiers are referring to battle and its possible negative consequences, injuries, and death. Here I will tell you this story in English, but please know the original story happened in ʻōlelo Hawaiʻi.

> *One day after a battle, one of Kamehameha's soldiers was walking along boasting out loud that he was Kamehameha's own brother. Just so happens, one of Kamehameha's war leaders overheard this boasting and became furious: "Who told you that you are related to the Heavenly One? You are lying!"*
>
> *"No. I am telling the truth. I am his younger brother, and he is the first born."*
>
> *When the war leader heard this, he got even more enraged and said, "Kamehameha only has one younger brother, Keliʻimaikaʻi. Not you, you mahaʻoi."*
>
> *And with those words the war leader rushed off and went before the Aliʻi, Kamehameha, and told him everything the soldier said. When Kamehameha heard this, he immediately ordered some men, "Go get this perpetrator and bring him before me." And he told some other of his men to prepare the imu (underground oven), "If this man is guilty, he will be cooked in the imu."*
>
> *When the soldier arrived, he crawled before Kamehameha. Kamehameha stood and asked him, "Is this story I heard true? That you said I am your older brother?"*
>
> *"Yes. It is true, my chief."*
> *"Who said such a thing to you?"*
> *"It was you who told me."*
> *"When did I say such a thing?" replied Kamehameha.*

> *"When we went to battle on O'ahu, you turned to us and said, 'Go forth my pōki'i (younger siblings), and drink the bitter waters!' and it is because of these wonderful words of the chief that I am saying that I am a younger sibling of yours! And we went forth and drank the bitter waters."*
>
> *When Kamehameha heard these wise words, he laughed and ordered his people to prepare a feast for his new younger sibling.*

As we see here, our kūpuna played with words. Kamehameha wasn't the older sibling of all his men, but he used the term "pōki'i" (younger siblings) to show solidarity with his warriors. And one of the warriors played with this to show Kamehameha that if he used the term "pōki'i" during a time of war, the relation remains after the war. And Kamehameha also played on the term "wai 'awa'awa." He was not going to give his soldiers bitter water to drink. In the story above, the bitter water that Kamehameha speaks of is battle.

One day, I wrote a newspaper column about drinking and driving entitled, "I mua e nā pōki'i a inu i ka wai 'awa'awa." I was obviously playing on the meaning of "wai 'awa'awa" in the title of this story, which I used in the column. However, someone posted the following comment on the column's website:

> *Wow! It never occurred to me that "ka wai 'awa'awa" might be a metaphorical name for beer. So, does this mean that at the Battle Kepaniwai, when Kamehameha The Great shouted "I mua, e nā pōki'i, e inu i ka wai 'awa'awa," he [Kamehameha] was actually telling his warriors to go forward and drink beer? Gosh, I never knew about that! Or maybe he was revving them up for battle by telling them that after they win the battle then they can go out drinking.*
>
> *Putting both parts of Kamehameha's exhortation together, and using the metaphorical interpretation, Kamehameha's famous two-sentence battle cry is sending an important message to his "little brothers" in modern times: Hey guys, if you go out and drink too much booz [sic], you might never come back. So thanks to Kekeha Solis for giving us this history lesson today—a new piece of historical revisionism explaining the true meaning of Kamehameha's famous Kepaniwai battle cry.*[12]

One important issue here is that it "never occurred" to the commenter that "ka wai 'awa'awa" might also be a name or metaphor for beer/liquor. The commenter seems to suggest that metaphorical names were thought about; however, beer/liquor never made the list. The commenter also portrays or suggests having authority on the subject. This is interesting, because if the commenter read more or talked more with our kūpuna, he would know that the term "wai 'awa'awa" was used for liquor in the nineteenth century by people who spoke Hawaiian as their mother tongue. Okay, I really don't want to pull the race card here, but, I must. The commenter is not Kanaka Maoli, or a native speaker of Hawaiian. And the problem here is that this commenter is an outspoken member of the larger community in Hawai'i and is especially outspoken on issues about Kanaka Maoli, though it is usually in opposition to our causes. Because this person is outspoken and claims to be an "authoritative figure" on Kanaka Maoli issues, some Kanaka Maoli students are hesitant to publish in the Hawaiian language column.

Another important issue is that the comment suggests there is another interpretation for Kamehameha's command to his warriors. Hinting that because I used the saying in a different and perhaps more modern context than the usual story, the actual meaning of Kamehameha's command is not concerning going to battle. The commenter somehow insinuates that a contemporary author—me—is rewriting history. I can personally say that if such a thing were possible I would not have chosen that particular piece of history to rewrite. I digress. Due to history, as discussed briefly above, many of us are not native speakers of our own language, and may not know the intricacies of language used by our kūpuna. And this makes many of us hesitant to use the language. But, let us play, especially if you don't know how to play.

Dr. Laiana Wong, an 'ōlelo Hawai'i practitioner, provides this popular explanation on worldview. He says, "Pua doesn't equal flower." This phrase helps us understand the intricacies of our language, and perhaps any language that uses metaphor. Wong helps us understand that although pua equals flower sometimes, pua has other possible meanings and therefore does not only mean flower. An example in a speech published in the newspaper *Ka Nupepa Kuokoa* helps us understand Wong's idea:

> *E nihi ka hele mai hoopa i na pua rose o ka aina … he nui wale na pua rose i mohala maikai i ke kakahiaka,… a ina i ike aku oe i ka*

> *nani oia mau pua la a hookapilipili aku oe, laka aku la oe ma ko ia la aoao, me he ia la ua make i ka auhuhu.*
>
> *Tread lightly and don't touch the rose flowers of the land ... there are a lot of rose flowers that have developed beautifully in the morning,... and if you saw the beauty of those flowers and attached yourself to one, you would be in a daze of infatuation on her side, like a fish that was dazed by the ʻauhuhu plant.*[13]

In the above passage, it is evident that Kahinu is not referring to actual roses. The hidden meaning of pua rose (roses) is women. If he were referring to actual roses, it would be a very strange situation. And our kūpuna might have to worry about a possible end in the genealogical line. Pua is a single word. Is this possible with wise sayings? Not if we believe the comment by the poster. Well, instead I would rather follow our kūpuna. And if our kūpuna used metaphor for something introduced from the western society, such as "ka wai ʻawaʻawa" for liquor, we, their ancestors, should be able to do the same. And if we use it for some other type of water that is bitter, that is fine too. Do not tell us what we can and cannot do. We can play too.

WHOSE RULES?

We can play too. But whose rules do we play by? It all depends. Sometimes, there is just no getting around it, and we must play by the government's rules, laws, policies, and so forth. But usually those rules don't benefit Indigenous people. So, when possible, we need to create the rules. When I write in Hawaiian, I try to emulate the way our kūpuna wrote in the Hawaiian-language newspapers. Those are the rules I play by; that is, the way they wrote is the way I try to write.

In one of the stories that I wrote for Kauakūkalahale, the Hawaiian-language column published weekly in the daily newspaper, I Hawaiianized the name Metta World Peace, a professional basketball player formerly known as Ron Artest. The Hawaiianized name became Maluhia Honua Meka. Maluhia and Honua are conceptual translations. "Maluhia" means peace, and "honua" means world. Meka is a transliteration of Metta. This set off a big discussion, with criticism from the same commenter. However, all the criticisms were rules the commenter was imposing on me. Here is a list of this commenter's points: (1) "It is fundamentally disrespectful to a person to change his name unnecessarily, without good reason and without permission"; (2) "The insistence on Hawaiianizing names is a political act"; (3) "It's no longer necessary for Hawaiians to do that (transliterations, conceptual translations, descriptions of what the person looked like or what actions he performed) to be able to pronounce an English name or to understand any conceptual meaning it might have"; (4) "Citing a foreign-language name by translating its conceptual meaning into one's own language is not the normal way of citing names in any other language with which I am familiar (German, Russian, Spanish, French, Italian in that order of familiarity)."

My response to the points above are as follows: (1) First, Hawaiianizing the names is not unnecessary and without good reason. It is important toward revitalization of our language. It is related to Ngũgĩ's idea that language has a "suggestive power well beyond the immediate and lexical meaning." My saying a person's name in my language will bring more power to the person's name versus my saying that person's name in that person's language with wrong pronunciation or not fully knowing the meaning of the person's name. Therefore, this is not a disrespectful act. I am a Kanaka Maoli in my homeland and speaking the language of my kūpuna. I do not feel that I need his permission to Hawaiianize his name. I do not go around asking people in the continental United States for permission every time they pronounce "Hawaiʻi" incorrectly, which is a totally different name most of the time. I let them pronounce it the way they want to. (2) Of course, it's a political act. I want Hawaiian language to be of equal status to English or higher. In order for Hawaiian language to be revitalized and once again the main language of these islands, we have a lot of work to do. English is such an overpowering language, we need to go above and beyond in bringing back Hawaiian so that it is on the lips of everyone living here—or, if not everyone, at least all Kanaka Maoli. (3) This is related to Ngũgĩ's idea concerning "the suggestive magical power of language" being "reinforced by the games we played with words through riddles, proverbs, transpositions of syllables, or through nonsensical but musically arranged words." We need to learn all of these and all of those actions (transliterations, conceptual translations, descriptions of what the person looked like or what actions he/she performed) are a part of what we need to do to again have our people fluent in our language and to know that "suggestive magical power of language." And (4) the commenter is trying to prove or show that he has authority on this subject. His problem here is that he is trying to say that all those languages, which are mostly European languages, are the norm. Our kūpuna did transliterations, conceptual translations, and descriptions, and sometimes left the name in English. And as I said earlier, I try to emulate them; therefore, I do all of the above. Sometimes I leave the name in English because I do not know what the Hawaiian would be. But, I am going to keep on playing and every time it is possible, I will use my rules that will usually follow that of my kūpuna.

THE GAME IS NOT OVER

Aloha mai. This chapter is coming to a close, but the game is not over. Let's play. Let's continue in the footsteps of our ancestors. We use their actions as guides, not to find fault. Don't let others dictate what we can and cannot do. We can play too. Our kids can play too, and so on.

Kanaka ʻŌiwi

April A. H. Drexel, Lia O'Neill M. A. Keawe, Pōhai Kūkea-Shultz, Annette Kuʻuipolani Wong, Jonathan K. Osorio, R. Kekeha Solis, W. Kekailoa Perry, K. A. Kapāʻanaokalāokeola Oliveira, Kaiwipuni Lipe, and Nā Kupuna

ʻO Wākea noho iā Papahānaumoku
Hānau ʻo Hawaiʻi, he moku
Hānau ʻo Māui, he moku
Hoʻi hou ʻo Wākea noho iā Hoʻohōkūkalani
Hānau ʻo Molokaʻi, he moku
Hānau ʻo Lānaʻikāula, he moku
Liliʻōpū punalua ʻo Papa iā Hoʻohōkūkalani

Hoʻi hou ʻo Papa noho iā Wākea
Hānau ʻo Oʻahu, he moku
Hānau ʻo Kauaʻi, he moku
Hānau ʻo Niʻihau, he moku
He ʻula ʻo Kahoʻolawe

Intense, profound moments
Born are our kūpuna (ancestors)...
A special kuaʻana (elder sibling) ʻĀina—"land ... that which feeds"
Providing stability, sustenance, and protection

Hāloanakalaukapalili—emerges
Placed in the nurturing care of ʻĀina
Surrounded and invigorated by fresh waters
Encouraging growth, strength, and stability

Reaching toward the sun
Strutting purposefully in broad, defined spaces
With a distinct, cultivated swagger
Skills exhilarate—heightened by the moon

Maturity deliberately evolves
Ancestral knowledge perpetually rooted
Savored harvest to feed
Energize our kaikaina (younger siblings)

Acknowledgments

I must extend love and gratitude to all of the contributors to this book. Thank you for your kindness and generosity. Thank you for your trust. Thank you for bearing witness.

To my copy editor and thought partner, Sarah Bennett, I offer deep appreciation for your value of this work. That was my encouragement.

To Beth Hauer, thank you for technical assistance along the way.

In Remembrance

When this book project began, the first person I thought of asking to contribute was Oscar Kawagley. Meeting Oscar and reading his work inspired my own efforts as a Native educator. Unfortunately, at the time of this project, Oscar was quite ill. A shared colleague provided me with an essay he had written. That writing is included. Oscar is greatly missed.

Notes and Bibliographies

PART I

Chapter 3

Bibliography

Grinde, Donald A. Lifetime conversations with Bernice Woodrum Grinde.

Howard, James H. 1959. "Altamaha Cherokee Folklore and Customs," *Journal of American Folklore*, 72(2): 134–138.

———. 1960. "The Yamasees: A Supposedly Extinct Southeastern Tribe Rediscovered." *American Anthropologist*, 62(4): 681–683.

Shaffer, James, and James H. Howard. 1962. "Medicine and Medicine Headdresses of the Yamasees," *American Indian Tradition*, 8(3): 125–126.

Chapter 4

Notes

1 The word "otiianer" refers to the female heirs to the chieftainship titles of the League, the forty-eight authorized names for the chiefs of the Iroquois, passed through the female side of the otiianer. The otiianer women selected one of the men within their group to fill a vacated seat in the League. Two or more otiianers usually comprised a clan.

2 Hertzberg, *The Great Tree and the Longhouse*, 55–60.

3 Schoolcraft, *Notes on the Iroquois*, 80.

4 Canfield, *The Legends of the Iroquois*; and Severance, *Publications of the Buffalo Historical Society*, 415–416.

5 Schoolcraft, *Notes on the Iroquois*, 76–79; and Wallace, *The White Roots of Peace*, 12–13.

6 Wallace, *The White Roots of Peace*, 16–17; and Hertzberg, *The Great Tree*, 88–89.

7 Wallace, *The White Roots of Peace*, 20; and Converse, *Myths and Legends of the New York State Iroquois*, 117–118.

8 Canfield, *Legends of the Iroquois*, 137–148.

9 Wallace, *The White Roots of Peace*, 5.

10 Tehanetorens, *Wampum Belts*, 6–7.

11 Wallace, *The White Roots of Peace*, 7.

12 Tehanetorens, *Wampum Belts*, 6–7; and Jacobs, "Wampum, the Protocol of Indian Diplomacy": 596–604.

13 Wilson, *Apologies to the Iroquois*; and Josephy, *The Patriot Chiefs*, 21–22.

14 Tehanetorens, *Wampum Belts*, 7; and Josephy, *Patriot Chiefs*, 22.

15 Ka-Hon-Hes, *Kaianerekowa hotinonsionne*.

16 Ibid.

17 Ibid.

18 Hewitt, "Review of Parker's Constitution of the Five Nations": 432–433; and Morgan, *League of the Ho-De-No-Sau-Nee or Iroquois*, 5–6.

19 Ka-Hon-Hes, *Kaianerekowa hotinonsionne*, 12–19.

20 Morgan, *League of the Iroquois*, 64–70.

21 Ka-Hon-Hes, *Kaianerekowa hotinonsionne*, 14.

22 Hertzberg, *Great Tree*, 104–105.

23 Tehanetorens, *Wampum Belts*, 5–6; and Elm, "The Hodinonshonni": 4.

24 Ibid.

25 Canfield, *Legends of the Iroquois*, 137–148.

26 Josephy, *Patriot Chiefs*, 26.

27 Wallace, *The White Roots of Peace*, 4–5.

28 Tuck, "The Howlett Hill Site," 78.

29 Ibid.

30 Graymont, *The Iroquois in the American Revolution*, 10.

31 Tooker, "An Ethnography of the Huron Indians, 1615–1619": 13.

32 Graymont, Iroquois, 10–11.

33 Ibid.

34 Graymont, *Iroquois*, 11–2.

35 Morgan, *League of the Iroquois*, 141–216.

36 Wissler, *Indians of the United States*, 136–137.

37 Ka-Hon-Hes, *Kaianerekowa hotinonsionne*, 34.

38 Josephy, *Patriot Chiefs*, 27.

39 Graymont, Iroquois, 20.

40 Ibid., 21.

Bibliography

Canfield, William W. 1902. *The Legends of the Iroquois: Told by "The Cornplanter."* Port Washington, NY: A. Wessels Company.

Elm, Lloyd M., Sr. 1976. "The Hodinonshonni." *The Conservationist*, 30(4) (January–February): 3–5.

Converse, Harriet Maxwell. 1908. *Myths and Legends of the New York State Iroquois*. Albany, NY: New York State Education Department.

Fenton, William N. 1962. "This Island the World of the Turtle's Back," *Journal of American Folklore*, LXXV, 298 (October–December): 283–300.

Graymont, Barbara. 1967. *The Iroquois in the American Revolution*. Syracuse, NY: Syracuse University Press.

Grinde, Donald A., Jr. 1973. "A Historical Sketch of the Eriez Indians," *Journal of Erie Studies*, II, 2 (Fall): 25–27.

Hertzberg, Hazel W. 1966. *The Great Tree and the Longhouse: The Culture of the Iroquois*. New York: Macmillan.

Hewitt, J. N. B. 1917. "Review of Parker's Constitution of the Five Nations." *American Anthropologist*, XIX, 3 (July–September), 432–433.

———. 1907. "Hiawatha." In *Handbook of American Indians North of Mexico*, ed. F. W. Hodge. BAE Bulletin 30, I. Washington, DC.

———. 1907. "Deganawidah." In *Handbook of American Indians North of Mexico*, ed. F. W. Hodge. BAE Bulletin 30, I. Washington, DC.

Jacobs, Wilbur R. 1949. "Wampum, the Protocol of Indian Diplomacy." *William and Mary Quarterly*, Third Series, IV (October): 596–604.

Josephy, Alvin. 1972. *The Patriot Chiefs: A Chronicle of American Indian Resistance*. New York: Viking Press.

Ka–Hon–Hes. 1971. *Kaianerekowa hotinonsionne = The Great Law of Peace of the Longhouse People*. Rooseveltown, NY: White Roots of Peace.

Morgan, Lewis Henry. 1901. *League of the Ho–De–No–Sau–Nee or Iroquois*. A new ed., with additional matter. Ed. and annotated by Herbert M. Lloyd. New York: Dodd, Mead, and Company.

Parker, Arthur C. 1916. *The Constitution of the Five Nations*, Albany, NY: The University of the State of New York.

Schoolcraft, Henry R. 1975. *Notes on the Iroquois*. Millwood, NY: Applewood.

Severance, Frank H., ed. 1903. *Publications of the Buffalo Historical Society*, VI. Buffalo, NY: Buffalo Historical Society.

Tehanetorens. N.d. *Wampum Belts*. Onchiota, NY: Six Nations.

Tooker, Elisabeth. 1964. *An Ethnography of the Huron Indians, 1615–1619*. BAE Bulletin 190. Washington, DC.

Tuck, James A. 1967. "The Howlett Hill Site: An Early Iroquois Village in Central New York." In *Iroquois Culture, History and Prehistory*, ed. Elisabeth Tooker, Albany, NY: The University of the State of New York, The State Education Dept., New York State Education and Science Service, 78.

Wallace, Paul A. W. 1946. *The White Roots of Peace*. Philadelphia: University of Pennsylvania Press.

Wilson, Edmund. 1960. *Apologies to the Iroquois*. Syracuse, NY: Syracuse University Press.

Wissler, Clark. 1967. *Indians of the United States*. Garden City, NY: Doubleday.

Chapter 5

Notes

1 This excerpt of A. O. Kawagley, 1999, "Alaska Native Education: History and Adaption in the New Millennium," *Journal of American Indian Education*, 39(1): 31–51, has been reprinted with the permission of JAIE. Note: The text has not intentionally been changed from the original.

2 Oquilluk, *People of Kauwerak*, 119–122.

3 Robinson, *Nature Power.*

4 Grof and Bennett, *The Holotropic Mind, 147–150.*

5 Ibid.

Bibliography

Campbell, Joseph. 1969. *The Flight of the Wild Gander: Explorations in the Mythological Dimension*. Washington, DC: Regnery Gateway.

Grof, Stanislav, and Hal Zina Bennett. 1993. *The Holotropic Mind: The Three Levels of Human Consciousness and How They Shape Our Lives.* New York: HarperCollins.

Kawagley, A. Oscar. 1995. *A Yupiaq Worldview: A Pathway to Ecology and Spirit*, Prospect Heights, IL: Waveland Press.

Oquilluk, William. 1981. *People of Kauwerak: Legends of the Eskimo.* Anchorage: Alaska Methodist University.

Robinson, Harry and Wendy Wickwire. 1993. *Nature Power: In the Spirit of an Okanagan Storyteller*. Seattle: University of Washington Press.

Chapter 6

Notes

1 David Katzeek (Elder, clan leader of the Shangukeidi, and founding president of Sealaska Heritage Institute), personal communication.

2 When you dream your mother passes away, you are going to kill a moose (that's what Mom said 02/19/12).

3 Mombourquette, personal communication, February 18, 2012.

4 Mom and I went to University of Alaska, Southeast, 2010, to learn how to read and speak Tlingit. We were introduced to many Tlingit language learning tools. Mom and I have decided that we would support coastal spellings in our own work. (Taff, Belarde, Scott, et al., Unedited Tlingit Language Proficiency Scope and Sequence [Levels 1–4].

5 For as long as I can remember, all I ever heard is that we were members of the K̲ook̲hittaan clan. I first read we were members of the G̲aanax̲.ádi in 2008.

6 Battiste, "Research Ethics for Protecting Indigenous Knowledge and Heritage": 111–132; Brayboy, "Toward a Tribal Critical Race Theory in Education": 425–446; Barnhardt and Kawagley, "Indigenous Knowledge Systems/Alaska Native Ways of Knowing"; and Thornton, *Haa Léelk'w Hás Aaní Saax'u/Our Grandparents' Names on the Land.*

7 Archibald, *Indigenous Storywork*; Crippon, "Reviews Unpublished Jeff Leer Document"; Dauenhauer and Dauenhauer, *Haa Shuká, Our Ancestors.*

8 E. Shorty, G. Johnston, P. Keenan, J. Johnson, S. Johnson, J. Smarch, M. Vanheel, personal communication, lifelong learning.

9 Thornton, *Klondike Gold Rush National and Historical Park*, 7–8.

10 Jim Fox talked with his offspring and their decedents about his migration inland circa 1700s due to Russian invasions. Jim Fox is old Yanyeidí (McClellan, "My Old People's Stories": 595) and has DNA connections to Kwaday Dan Sinchi (Wolf Clan), long ago man found in the ice, at the Ruby Mountain Range, British Columbia. This range falls onto the Chilkat trail, which

was controlled by the Chilkats of Lyn Canal (D. Henry, personal communication, 2011).

11 P. Keenan, personal communication, March 15, 2012.

12 Tlingit people abide by the clan system, and some stories are clan stories (Dauenhauer and Dauenhauer, *Haa Shuká*, p. x).

13 The policy was to do away with the "Indian"—so there would be no Indian Affairs (D. Scott, Superintendent Indian Affairs, 1920; National Archives of Canada, Record Group 10).

14 Writing down our culture stories is exacerbated by clan restrictions and laws on clan stories, objects, and symbols (Dauenhauer and Dauenhauer, *Haa Shuká*, 24).

15 P. Keenan, E. Shorty, J. Johnson, personal communication, March 15, 2012.

16 Ibid.

17 I work with Teslin elders on a social justice file, developing curriculum together. I am the scribe, and the one who applies the formal school lens (learning outcomes, objectives…). The curriculum focus is working, living, and learning among us—this course is intended for frontline social justice workers. The curriculum development project is funded by the School of Social Justice, Yukon College.

18 An Indian is defined as someone who is registered as an Indian under the Indian Act of Canada. (Coates, *Best Left as Indians*, 128; Council of Yukon First Nations, *Together Today for Our Children Tomorrow*, 19; and Minister of Indian Affairs and Northern Development, "Statement of the Government of Canada on Indian Policy," 7).

19 P. Keenan, J. Johnston, E. Shorty, and M. Vanheel, personal communication, lifelong learning.

20 Crippon, "Reviews Unpublished"; Henry, *Timeline Rhetorical History of Chilkoot*; Dauenhauer and Dauenhauer, *Haa Shuká*.

21 As legislated in 1920 by Canada's Department of Indian Affairs, the assimilation of Canada's Indians was to occur through the children (Coates, Best Left as Indians, abstract). The vehicle for assimilation was the mission schools.

22 Coates, *Best Left as Indians*, 126; and Thornton, *Klondike Gold Rush*, 7.

23 The more I bring Mom's clan or community stories forward, the more she remembers what her great-grandmother and others

told her at a young age. Mom says the knowledge was right here (behind ear) all along, and as she rehears, she recollects what her mom and grandmom told her.

24 Mom spent small portions of her formative years with her community. She and others did return home from time to time.

25 E. Shorty, personal communication, ferry ride, 2011, from Skagway to Juneau.

26 I was shrouded in cloth at a headstone potlatch—the pile went just over my head. I walked around with Mom and Auntie Gladys, and they gave this cloth out to opposite clan members. While the reasons may have been explained to me, I don't remember clearly why this is done in the Teslin region. Based on experiences, this cloth giveaway is done to pay those who witness your name giving.

27 My master's project, 2003, attempted to enact legislation toward an immersion school. My project attempted to coordinate the Minister of Education, Elijah Smith school principal, Elijah Smith School Council, and Kwanlin Dun First Nation toward the implementation of a Southern Tutchone Immersion School (a school within a school). What I found was that even with the nation's extreme desire to preserve Indigenous languages, including Government of Yukon legislation on language immersion, no action whatsoever was taken.

28 From Professor Margaret Maaka, a Māori professor of Curriculum Studies at the University of Hawaii–Mānoa, 2002.

29 The progress of articulating Indigenous education has been very slow. As shown in the Office of the Auditor General of Canada's report, "Public Schools and Advanced Education," all Yukon people have very little autonomy in the area of public education.

30 Print, audio and visual, websites, posters.

31 Teslin Tlingit elders concur (I. Freeman, personal communication, June 2012).

32 L. Smith, 1999; M. Maaka, July 2000; Shawn Wilson, 2009; and Bryon Brayboy, 2006; personal communications.

33 Kawagley, *A Yupiaq Worldview*; Crippon, "Reviews Unpublished Jeff Leer document"; Thornton, *Haa Léelk'w Hás Aaní Saax'u.*

34 Leonard, *Deg Xinag Oral Traditions*, 121

35 Wilson, *Research as Ceremony*; and Smith, *Decolonizing Methodologies.*

36 Crippon, "Reviews Unpublished Jeff Leer document," see first paragraph.

37 Harris, *Schwatka's Last Search*, 32

38 Chief Andy Carville, Carcross Tagish First Nation, as quoted in Thornton, *Klondike Gold Rush*, XIII.

39 E. Shorty, J. Smarch, J. Johnson, S. Johnson, B. and B. Coolie, P. Keenan, G. Sidney, M. Vanheel, M. Jackson, and H. Jacobs; personal communication, lifelong learning.

40 Dauenhauer and Dauenhauer, *Haa Shuká*; Dauenhauer and Taff, Nora Marks Dauenhauer Tape Collection; Crippon, "Reviews Unpublished Jeff Leer document;" McClellan, "The Inland Tlingit," "The Interrelations of Social Structure with Northern Tlingit Ceremonialism," "Avoidance between Siblings of the Same Sex in Northwestern North America," *My Old People Say*, "My Old People's Stories"; Jack et. al, Participants at Tlingit Literacy Workshop in Jeff Leer's, tlingit literacy workshop [sic]; Nyman and Leer, "Trails," Gágiwduł.àt; Harris, Schwatka's *Last Search*.

41 Greer, Field Report of Activities and Preliminary Results Teslin Lake Heritage Inventory.

42 As written in Harris's book, *Schwatka*, Schwatka walked inland via the T'aak̲u River trail, 1891, and notes how Tlingit tie trees together to mark the way and/or claim territory. Due to Schwatka's journal entry on trees I have determined that you need to know what you are looking for.

43 Lunáat', Chilkoot Chief as quoted in Thornton, *Klondike Gold Rush*, x.

44 Davidson, "Explanation of an Indian Map of the Rivers, Lakes, Trails and Mountains," 75–82.

45 de Laguna, *Under Mount St Elias*; Emmons, *The Tlingit Indians*; and Dauenhauer, Dauenhauer, and Black, *Russians in Tlingit America*.

46 In 1852, the Tlingit from Klukwan burned down the Hudson Bay Trading Post in Fort Selkirk (Henry, Timeline Rhetorical History) because Hudson's Bay was infringing upon Tlingit trade territory.

47 These are the headwaters to the Yukon River tributaries.

48 The Inland Tlingit in Teslin fought a war with the Tahltan for the land the Teslin people possess today (see Shorty, 2020,

Appendix One: *The Tahltan–Tlingit War: An Oral History*). The Tlingit do not like to discuss this war or refer to it. I struggle about including it, but I feel I need to include this in my research because it happened that way.

49 M. Vanheel, personal communication, February 23, 2012.

50 K̲wáan means "people from that place" (Edwards, *Dictionary of Tlingit*).

51 Thornton, *Haa Léelk'w Hás Aaní Saax'u*, 68.

52 On November 25, 2012, Mom just told me about the boat called Seenáa in Teslin. This boat was Pete Fox's, Grandma Fox's son.

53 Thornton *Haa Léelk'w Hás Aaní Saax'u*, 68; Emmons, *The Tlingit Indians*.

54 McClellan, *My Old People Say*; Emmons, *The Tlingit Indians*; Swanton, "Social, Condition, Beliefs, and Linguistic Relationship of the Tlingit Indians": 399–403; and de Laguna, *Under Mount Saint Elias*, 131–137.

55 McClellan, *My Old People Say*, 53.

56 Ibid.

57 These stories still exist among the Teslin Yanyeidí (D. Aucoin, personal communication, 2009).

58 McClellan's question mark, *My Old People Say*, 51.

59 Crippon ("Reviews Unpublished Jeff Leer Document") reports that nothing is known about this clan other than that it is listed by Andrew Hope in Traditional Tlingit Country Map.

60 See Kohklux Map (Davidson, "Explanation of an Indian Map"). This story is about Tlingit ownership of the Klukwan to Fort Selkirk trail.

61 Harris, *Schwatka's Last Search*.

62 Ibid., 31.

63 Ibid., 13.

64 H. Jacobs, personal communication July 16, 2012.

65 Oral histories: Flood stories and the Year of No Summer 1816.

66 Dauenhauer and Taff, Nora Marks Dauenhauer Tape Collection.

67 Henry, *Across the Shaman's River*.

68 In Teslin, there are no actual "houses"—these "houses" are non-tangible property. I have heard Mrs. Jane Smarch (my mother's true first cousin) talk about a "raven" house that people could rent for special events like weddings. It did not sound like a clan house but instead a house that belonged to someone from one of the Raven clans (personal communication, spring 2011).

69 Emmons in McClellan, "My Old People's Stories," 51, states that the K̲ook̲hittaan are an unimportant sib among the coastal T'aak̲u Kwaan.

70 This kind of opposite clan and unsolicited information is sometimes called validation.

71 It is said this discussion took place in Teslin at Lilly Smith's house. Mom said Lilly was the eldest G̲aanax̲.ádi (or was it K̲ook̲hittaan?).

72 There are details of Tlingit and Athabaskan and Tahltan peoples in the Tagish region (McClellan, *My Old People Say*, 36).

73 McClellan, "The Inland Tlingit," 47–52.

74 There was a bitter fight over a wolf headdress, and some elders do remember this time as well as how the argument was resolved; story has it that my mother's father was instrumental in its resolution. Mom's dad, John Sidney, was Dakl'aweidí. Also see McClellan, *My Old People Say*.

75 D. Aucoin, personal communication, October 21, 2012.

76 McClellan, *My Old People Say*, 53.

77 Contrary to Emmons's statement about raven clans in coastal T'aak̲u Kwaan.

78 McClellan, "The Inland Tlingit," 47.

79 McClellan, *My Old People Say*, 55

80 Edgar Sidney was mom's father's stepfather. Edgar is from Juneau and is G̲aanax̲.ádi (McClellan, *My Old People's Stories*, 729).

81 This metadata was collected with the support of National Science Foundation/National Endowment for the Humanities Documenting Endangered Languages award #0651787 to the University of Alaska Southeast under the direction of principal investigators Richard L. Dauenhauer and Alice Taff. Work took place from 2008 to 2011.

82 March 15, 2012.

83 The land that was warred over with the Tahltan is now the Teslin graveyard (oral history).

84 It was said to me that Aat.oow is not a word used among Teslin Tlingit (Jane Smarch). McClellan notes differences between coastal and inland Tlingit language ("The Inland Tlingit," 48.)

85 As seen in Wikipedia, *Delgamuukw vs. the Queen*, the Gitksan and Witsuwit'en used their oral histories as principal evidence in the case of ownership over land.

86 Thornton, *Klondike Gold Rush.*

87 P. Keenan, personal communication, November 26, 2012; and A. Taff, personal communication, November 25, 2011.

88 The Yukon Ministry of Education has poor research showings. We do not appear to have an electronic bank of scholarly and Indigenous research. Many Yukon First Nations have published ethnohistories on or about themselves.

89 Smith, *Decolonizing Methodologies.*

90 R. Dauenhauer and A. Taff, personal communication, November 24, 2011.

91 N. Dauenhauer, personal communication, 2009.

Bibliography

Archibald, J. 2008. Indigenous Storywork: *Educating the Heart, Mind, Body, and Spirit.* Vancouver, BC: UBC Press.

Barnhardt, R., and Kawagley O. 2006. "Indigenous Knowledge Systems/Alaska Native Ways of Knowing." August 17. http://ankn.uaf.edu/Curriculum/Articles/BarnhardtKawagley/Indigenous_Knowledge.html.

Battiste, M. 2007. "Research Ethics for Protecting Indigenous Knowledge and Heritage: Institutional and Research Responsibilities." In *Ethical Futures in Qualitative Research: Decolonizing the Politics of Knowledge*, ed. Norman Denzin and Michael D. Giardina, Walnut Creek, CA: Left Coast Press, 111–132.

Brayboy, B. 2006. "Toward a Tribal Critical Race Theory in Education." *The Urban Review*, 37(5) (December 2005): 425–446. DOI: 10.1007/s11256–005–0018–y.

Coates, S. K. 1984. "Best Left as Indians: Native–White Relations in the Yukon Territory, 1840–1950." Unpublished PhD diss. Vancouver, BC: The University of British Columbia.

Council of Yukon First Nations. 1973. *Together Today for Our Children Tomorrow: A Statement of Grievances and an Approach to Settlement by the Yukon Indian People*. Whitehorse, Yukon: Council for Yukon Indians.

Crippon, J. 2011. "Reviews Unpublished Jeff Leer Document, 1985, Tlingit Tribe, Clan, and House Group Names." Tlingit Kwáan, Clan, and House List. http://www.drangle.com/~james/tlingit/clan–list.html#ishkeetaan.

Daniel, P. 2011. "Residential Schools Twentieth Century Education for Native Americans." We Were Not the Savages: First Nation History blog. November 19. http://www.danielnpaul.com/

Dauenhauer, N., and R. Dauenhauer. 1987. *Haa Shuká, Our Ancestors: Tlingit Oral Narratives*. Seattle: University of Washington Press; Juneau, AK: Sealaska Heritage Foundation.

Dauenhauer, R., and A. Taff. 2008–2011. *Nora Marks Dauenhauer Tape Collection* (National Science Foundation/National Endowment for the Humanities Documenting Endangered Languages). Digitizing Tapes (Award #0651787). University of Alaska Southeast.

Dauenhauer, N., R. Dauenhauer, and L. Black. 2008. *Russians in Tlingit America*. Seattle: University of Washington Press.

Davidson, G. 1901. Explanation of an Indian Map of the Rivers, Lakes, Trails and Mountains from the Chilkaht to the Yukon Drawn by the Chilkaht Chief, Kohklux, in 1896. Mazama, April, 75–82.

de Laguna, F. 1972. "Under Mount Saint Elias: The History and Culture of the Yakutat Tlingit: Part Two." Washington, DC: Smithsonian Institution Press. In *Smithsonian Contributions to Anthropology*, 7 (2). https://doi.org/10.5479/si.00810223.7.2.

Edwards, K. 2009. *Dictionary of Tlingit*. Juneau, AK: Sealaska Heritage Institute.

Emmons, G. 1991. *The Tlingit Indians*. New York: American Museum of Natural History.

First Nations Centre. 2007. *Considerations and Templates for Ethical Research Practices*. Ottawa: National Aboriginal Health Organization. http://www.naho.ca/documents/fnc/english/FNC_ConsiderationsandTemplatesInformationResource.pdf.

Gotthardt, R. 1986. *Study of Culture and Land Use for the Little Salmon Indian Band* (Final Report, February 20). Private collection of Norma Shorty, Department of Anthropology, University of Toronto.

Greer, S. 2004. *Field Report of Activities and Preliminary Results, Teslin Lake*

Heritage Inventory (Permit #03–4ASR, 2004). Teslin Tlingit Council and Yukon Heritage Resources Unit.

Harris, A. S. 1996. *Schwatka's Last Search: The New York Ledger Expedition Through Unknown Alaska and British America*. Fairbanks: University of Alaska Press.

Henry, D. 2012. "Timeline Rhetorical History of Chilkoot, Chilkat Non Native Interface." Incomplete, not for public draft paper.

———. 2017. *Across the Shaman's River: John Muir, the Tlingit Stronghold, and the Opening of the North*. Fairbanks: University of Alaska Press.

Hope, Andrew. 2006. Traditional Tlingit Country Map. http://www.ankn.uaf.edu/ANCR/Southeast/TlingitMap/Taaku.html.

Jack, E., G. Jackson, G. Johnston, J. Leer, E. Nyman, C. Pettigrew, J. Ritter, C. Schinkel, G. Tom, D. Wedge, M. Wedge, M. Whelan, M. Workman, and L. Wren. 1985. Participants at Tlingit Literacy Workshop in Jeff Leer's, Tlingit Literacy Workshop. Workshop conducted by the Yukon Native Language Center: Whitehorse, Yukon.

Kawagley, A. O. 1995. *A Yupiaq Worldview: A Pathway to Ecology and Spirit*. Prospect Heights, IL: Waveland Press Inc.

Leonard, B. 2007. "Deg Xinag Oral Traditions: Reconnecting Indigenous Language and Education through Traditional Narratives." PhD diss., Fairbanks: University of Alaska. http://hdl.handle.net/11122/8930.

McClellan, C. 1953. "The Inland Tlingit." *Memoirs of the Society for American Archaeology*, No. 9, Asia and North America: Transpacific Contacts, 47–52.

———. 1954. "The Interrelations of Social Structure with Northern Tlingit Ceremonialism." *Southwestern Journal of Anthropology*, 10(1) (Spring 1954): 75–96.

———. 1961. "Avoidance between Siblings of the Same Sex in Northwestern North America." *Southwestern Journal of Anthropology*, 17(2) (Summer 1961): 103–123.

———. 2001. *My Old People Say: An Ethnographic Survey of Southern Yukon Territory*. Quebec, Canada: Canadian Museum of Civilization.

———. 2010. "My Old People's Stories: A Legacy for Yukon First Nations Part III: Inland Tlingit Narrators." *Occasional Papers in Yukon History* 5(3). Yukon Cultural Services Branch, Government of Yukon.

Minister of Indian Affairs and Northern Development. 1969. "Statement of the Government of Canada on Indian Policy." http://www.aadnc–aandc.gc.ca/eng/1100100010189/1100100010191.

National Archives of Canada, Record Group 10, vol. 6810, file 470–2–3, vol. 7, 55 (L–3) and 63 (N–3).

Nyman, E., and J. Leer. 1993. *Gágiwdul.àt: Brought Forth to Reconfirm: The Legacy of a Taku River Tlingit Clan*. Whitehorse, Yukon: Yukon Native Language Centre and Alaska Native Language Centre.

Office of the Auditor General of Canada. 2009. "Public Schools and Advanced Education." Yukon Department of Education (January). http://www.education.gov.yk.ca/pdf/auditor_general_report_yukon_education.pdf.

Palmater, P. 2011. *Beyond Blood, Rethinking Indigenous Identity*. Saskatoon, SA: Houghton Boston Printers and Lithographers.

Richards, M. et al. 2007. "Radiocarbon Dating and Dietary Stable Isotope Analysis of Kwaday Dan Ts'inchi." *American Antiquity* 72(4): 719–733. Society for American Archeology.

Shorty, E. N.d. *How Emma Got Her Indian Name*. Whitehorse, Yukon: Council for Yukon Indians Curriculum Development.

Shorty, N. 2004. "Immersion Classrooms: A Tool Towards the Realization of Jurisdiction in the Yukon Territory." Unpublished master's thesis. Education Foundations, Honolulu, HI: University of Hawaii at Manoa.

———. 2020. "Inland Tlingit of Teslin, Yukon: G̲aanax̲.ádi and K̲ook̲hittaan Clan Origin stories for the immediate and clan family of Emma Joanne Shorty (nee Sidney)." Doctoral thesis. Fairbanks, AK: University of Alaska.

Smith, G. H. 2000. "Protecting and Respecting Indigenous Knowledge." In *Reclaiming Indigenous Voice and Vision*, ed. M. Battiste, Vancouver: UBC Press, 209–224.

Smith, L. T. 1999. Decolonizing Methodologies: Research and Indigenous Peoples. London: Zed Books.

Swanton, J. 1908. "Social, Condition, Beliefs, and Linguistic Relationship of the Tlingit Indians." http://archive.org/details/socialconditions00swanrich.

Taff, A., L. Belarde, J. Scott, J. Chester, N. Douglas, Y. Vaara, D. Dauenhauer, N. Dauenhauer, and K. Edwards. 2008. Unedited

Tlingit Language Proficiency Scope and Sequence (Levels 1–4). Juneau, Alaska. University of Alaska Southeast, Juneau School District, Sealaska Heritage Institute.

Teslin Tlingit Council. 2012. "Teslin Tlingit Council." http://www.ttc-teslin.com/.

Thornton, T. 2004. Klondike Gold Rush National and Historical Park: Ethnographic Overview and Assessment. Skagway, AK: Klondike Gold Rush National and Historical Parks.

Thornton, T., ed. 2012. *Haa Léelk'w Hás Aaní Saax'u/Our Grandparents' Names on the Land*. Sealaska Heritage Institute. Seattle: University of Washington Press.

Wilson, S. 2009. *Research as Ceremony: Indigenous Research Methods*. Halifax, NS: Fernwood Publishing.

PART II

[a]Cook-Lynn, Elizabeth. 2007. *Notebooks of Elizabeth Cook-Lynn*. Tucson, AZ: University of Arizona, 14.

Chapter 8

Notes

1 This is an English translation of *Romanus Pontifex*, as published in Davenport and Paullin, European Treaties, 20–26. The original text in Latin is in the same volume, 13–20.

2 English translation published in Davenport, *European Treaties*, 72–75.

3 See R. J. Miller, *Native America, Discovered and Conquered*, 3–53, for a discussion of the Doctrine of Discovery, how it became American law, how it was defined in *Johnson v. M'Intosh*, and how it is applied today.

4 Ibid., 61–135.

5 Johnson, 21 U.S., 563.

6 Ibid., 567–868.

7 Ibid., 571–572.

8 Ibid., 572.

9 Ibid.

10 Ibid., 574.

11 Ibid., 582, 584.

12 Johnson, 21 U.S., 576–577.

13 Ibid., 588.

14 Ibid., 584–585.

15 Ibid., 573.

16 Ibid., 574.

17 Ibid., 604.

18 Ibid., 604–605.

19 Johnson, 21 U.S., 573–575, 584–585.

20 Ibid., 579, 584, 587–588.

21 Ibid., 587.

22 Ibid., 574.

23 Echo-Hawk, *In the Courts of the Conqueror*, 16–17.

24 Miller, *Native America, Discovered and Conquered*, 3–5.

Bibliography

Davenport, Frances G., and Charles Oscar Paullin. 1917. *European Treaties Bearing on the History of the United States and Its Dependencies*. Washington, DC: Carnegie Institution of Washington.

Echo-Hawk, Walter R. 2010. *In the Courts of the Conqueror*. Wheat Ridge, CO: Fulcrum Publishing.

Johnson v. M'Intosh, 21 U.S. (8 Wheat.) 543, 1823.

Miller, Robert J. 2008. *Native America, Discovered and Conquered: Thomas Jefferson, Lewis and Clark, and Manifest Destiny*. Lincoln: University of Nebraska Press.

Chapter 9

Notes

1 Beck and Walters, *The Sacred*, 67–70; Simmons, *Spirit of the New England Tribes*, 45–46; and Crosby, "The Algonkian Spiritual Landscape," 35–41.

2 Black Hawk, *Black Hawk: Life of Ma–Ka–Tai–Me–She–Kia–Kiak or Black Hawk*, 88; Snyderman, "Concepts of Land Ownership," 13–34; Calloway, *New Worlds for All*, 181; Axtell, *Natives and Newcomers*, 240; and Springer, "American Indians and the Law of Real Property in Colonial New England," 38, n. 58, 42, 44, and 48. Besides the cultural evidence, the numerous early colonial period English accounts of Native Americans "tresspassing" upon lands that they "sold" or "ceded" under English law, and seeming to completely disregard those laws and legal documents, could be interpreted as evidence that the American Indians simply did not comprehend the English legal notions regarding land.

3 Axtell, *Natives and Newcomers*, 240.

4 Salisbury, *Manitou and Providence*, 200–201; and Calloway, *New Worlds for All*, 22–23.

5 Jennings, *The Invasion of America*, 137.

6 Salisbury, *Manitou and Providence*, 193–194.

7 Jennings, *The Invasion of America*, 199–201.

8 Winthrop, "Generall Considerations for the Plantation in New England," 118; Nash, *Red, White, and Black*, 39; and Bridenbaugh, *Vexed and Troubled Englishmen*, 13

9 Jennings, *The Invasion of America*, 144–145; Axtell, *Natives and Newcomers*, 252; and Anderson, "King Phillip's Herds," 606–620.

10 Emery, *The History of the Church of North Middleborough*, 7; Taylor, "Indian Artifacts of Titicut," 5; Mitchell, *History of the Early Settlement of Bridgewater*, 21–22; and Peirce, *History of Middleboro*, 944.

11 Taylor, "Indian Artifacts of Titicut," 6.

12 Salisbury, "Red Puritans," 27–54.

13 Winthrop, "Generall Considerations for the Plantation in New England."

14 Mandell, *Behind the Frontier*, 90.

15 Ibid., 147–149; and Konig et al., vol. 1, 33–35, 339–343; vol. 8, 309–312; vol. 10, 539–542; and vol. 21, 79–81.

16 A "bloomery" is defined as "the first forge through which iron passes after it is melted from the ore into a *bloom*, a mass of wrought iron." Lederer, *Colonial American English*, 32.

17 Abbott, *History of King Philip*, 309–310.

18 Peirce, *Indian History, Biography and Genealogy*, 246.

19 Mandell, *Behind the Frontier*, 136. Note: Ahauton was the grandson of Leah Shantum, one of the tribal elders who signed Easton's land deed, and his signature (misspelled) was added to the deed as a later witness.

20 Massachusetts State Archives, v. 32, 489–492 and 527–528.

21 Ibid., v. 32, 419–421.

22 Leonard was not just a gentleman lawyer who savored the title, "Esquire," but the Plymouth Court records show that he was a practicing, frequently working lawyer, beginning in the 1720s, possibly beginning at the young age of 18 years (Plymouth County Court of Common Pleas, vol. 1, 277–282). He represented a variety of clients, usually other gentlemen who were seeking satisfaction from debtors, but on at least two occasions he even represented local Indians (Konig et al., v. 1, 339–343; and v. 6, 20–23).

23 Plymouth County, Massachusetts, Land Deeds, bk 43: 39, Doc. 320. Stephen David and Elkanah Leonard, December 26, 1754; Plymouth County Registry of Deeds, Plymouth, MA. (http://titleview.org/plymouthdeeds/ImageViewerEx.aspx); and Konig et al., v. 11, 21–25.

24 Peirce, "History of Middleboro," 1030.

25 Massachusetts State Archives, vol. 32, 409–410 and 529–531.

26 Ibid., vol. 32, 532–534.

27 Ibid., vol. 32, 419–421.

28 The "Corporation" to which Simon refers, was most likely the Corporation for the Promotion of the Gospel in Foreign Lands, under which he was apparently ordained.

29 Ibid., vol. 32, 419–421.

30 Ibid.

31 Mandell, *Beyond the Frontier*, 173; and State of Massachusetts, House Report #68.

Bibliography

Abbott, John S. C. 1899. *History of King Philip, Sovereign Chief of the Wampanoags*. New York: Harper and Brothers.

Anderson, Virginia. 1994. "King Phillip's Herds: Indians, Colonists, and the Problem of Livestock in Early New England." *William and Mary Quarterly*, 51(3), 601–624.

Axtell, J. 2000. Natives and Newcomers: The Cultural Origins of North America. Oxford, UK: Oxford University Press.

Beck, Peggy V., and Anna Lee Walters. 1977. *The Sacred: Ways of Knowledge, Sources of Life*. Tsaile, AZ: Navajo Community College.

Black H., Patterson J. B., and State Historical Society of Iowa. 1932. *Life of Ma-Ka-Tai-Me-She-Kia-Kiak or Black Hawk*. Iowa City, IA: State Historical Society of Iowa.

Bridenbaugh, Carl. 1968. *Vexed and Troubled Englishmen, 1590–1642*, New York: Oxford University Press.

Calloway, Colin G. 1997. New Worlds for All: Indians, Europeans, and the Remaking of Early America. Baltimore: Johns Hopkins University Press.

Crosby, Constance A. 1993. "The Algonkian Spiritual Landscape." In *Algonkians of New England: Past and Present*, ed. Peter Benes. The Dublin Seminar for New England Folklore Annual Proceedings, Boston: Boston University.

Emery, S. Hopkins. 1876. *The History of the Church of North Middleborough, Massachusetts, in Six Discourses*, Preached by Its Acting Pastor, S. Hopkins Emery. Middleborough, MA: Harlow and Thatcher.

Gray, Robert. 1992. *"A Good Speed to Virginia."* London, 1609, a pamphlet quoted in, *Red, White, and Black: The Peoples of Early North America*, ed. Hoboken, New Jersey: Prentice Hall.

Jennings, Francis. 1976. *The Invasion of America: Indians, Colonialism, and the Cant of Conquest*. New York: W. W. Norton and Co.

Konig D. T., Nelson W. E. and The Pilgrim Society. 1981. Plymouth court records 1686–1859, Plymouth County Court of Common Pleas, Wilmington, DE: M. Glazier, v. 1–16.

Lederer, Jr., Richard M. 1985. *Colonial American English: A Glossary*. Essex, CT: Verbatim Books.

Massachusetts Plymouth County. 1754. Land Deed, Book 43. Plymouth County Registry of Deeds, Plymouth, MA.

Massachusetts State Archives Collection, Colonial Period, 1622–1788, v. 32. v. 113, and v.114.

Mandell, Daniel. 1996. Behind the Frontier: Indians in Eighteenth–Century Eastern Massachusetts. Lincoln: University of Nebraska Press.

Mitchell, Nahum. 1897. *History of the Early Settlement of Bridgewater, in Plymouth County, Massachusetts*. Boston: Bridgewater.

Nash Gary B. (2000) *Red, White, and Black: The Peoples of Early North America*. Hoboken, NJ: Prentice Hall.

Peirce, Ebenezer W. 1878. *Indian History, Biography and Genealogy: Pertaining to the Good Sachem Massasoit of the Wampanoag Tribe, and His Descendants*. North Abington, MA: Z.G. Mitchell.

———. 1884. "History of Middleboro." In *History of Plymouth County, Massachusetts, with Biographical Sketches of Many of Its Pioneers and Prominent Men*, comp. D. Hamilton Hurd, Philadelphia: J. W. Lewis and Co., 938–1055.

Price, George R. 2020. *The Eastons: Five Generations of Human Rights Activism, 1748–1935*. United States: Independently published.

Salisbury, Neal. 1974. "Red Puritans: The 'Praying Indians' of Massachusetts Bay and John Elliot." *The William and Mary Quarterly*, Third Series 31(1) (January): 27–54.

———. 1982. *Manitou and Providence: Indians, Europeans, and the Making of New England, 1500–1643*. New York: Oxford University Press.

Secretary of the Commonwealth of Massachusetts. 1902. Acts and Resolves, Public and Private, of the Province of the Massachusetts Bay, Vol. X, Appendix, Resolves, etc., 1720–1726. Boston: Wright & Potter Printing Co.

Simmons, William. 1986. *Spirit of the New England Tribes: Indian History and Folklore*. Hanover, NH: University Press of New England.

Snyderman, George S. 1951. "Concepts of Land Ownership Among the Iroquois and Their Neighbors." In *Symposium on Local Diversity in Iroquois Culture, Bureau of American Ethnology Bulletin 149*, ed. William N. Fenton. Washington, DC: US Government Printing Office, 13–34.

Springer, James W. 1986. "American Indians and the Law of Real

Property in Colonial New England," *American Journal of Legal History*, 30(1), January; 25–58, https://doi.org/10.2307/845938

State of Massachusetts, House Report #68.

Wanoo, Benjamin, and Joshua Stantum. 1715. *Petition of Benjamin Wanoo* [sic] *and Joshua Shantum, May 25, 1715*, Massachusetts State Archives, Vol. 31.

William B. Taylor. "Indian Artifacts of Titicut." *The Middleborough Antiquarian*, 11(2): 5.

Winthrop, John. 1629. "Generall Considerations for the Plantation in New England." London, in *The John Winthrop Papers*, ed. Allen B. Forbes. Boston: Massachusetts Historical Society, 1929–47, v. 2.

Chapter 10

Notes

1 "Tolowa" is used in this chapter, although there is no clear tribal consensus regarding what the Tolowa traditionally refer to ourselves as Huss or Dee-ni are also terms used meaning "the people." In precontact times, Tolowa people would have had more of an identity with the villages of their parents and family.

2 We both are fully aware that we are also citizens of our respective sovereign Nations of Smith River Rancheria and Duck Valley Reservation. I chose to use enrolled and member because I acknowledge the long hard fight that those before me fought to have our Smith River Rancheria recognized again in 1983 with the Tillie Hardwick case. In addition, being a member to me honors my family and those who are part of our community.

3 Crum, *Po'I Pentun Tammen Kimmappeh*, 1.

4 Tolowa world was embroiled in rapid societal change. Tolowa elders thus referred to the 1850s as "the time the world was turned upside down." Loren Bommelyn, interview by Reed, 1983.

5 Resolution 260 (III) A, Article 2.

6 Military Records, 1854–1856.

7 "The Smith River Reservation, 1866–1868."

8 Prucha, *The Great Father*, 179–242; and Gibson, *The American Indian*, 303–331.

9 Unknown, "A Bill," 2; and Wentworth to Dole, 471.

10 Nelson, *Our Home Forever*, 88.

11 Hill, *The Indians of Chico Rancheria*, 39–41.

12 Ibid.

13 Heintzleman, reported to Henley.

14 Note: One cannot "settle" a land that is occupied.

15 Strobridge, *Regulars in the Redwoods*, 154.

16 Crook to Mackall, October 21, 1857.

17 Ibid.

18 Ibid.

19 Gould, "Indian and White Versions of 'The Burnt Ranch Massacre,'" 33.

20 State of California Native American Heritage Commission.

21 Crook to Mackall, November 21, 1857.

22 Ibid.

23 Ibid.

24 Heintzleman, reported to Henley.

25 Loren Bommelyn, interviewed by Reed, 1991.

26 Hanson to Dole.

27 The term "they returned to their old haunts" was used repeatedly by Indian agents, local militia, and government officials regarding the Tolowa returning to their homeland.

28 Danziger, *Indians and Bureaucrats*, 190; and "Indian Reservation," 2.

29 "Indian Reservations," 2.

30 Hanson to Dole, September 22, 1862; Bryson to Hanson, November 20, 1862; and Wiley to Dole, September 1, 1864, 260–263.

31 Contis to Drum, October 10, 1862.

32 Whiting to Parker, August 1, 1869.

33 "Have to Go," 3.

34 "More Humbuggery in Indian Matters," 2.

35 Haynes to Kibbe, May 18, 1862.

36 Contis to Drum, September 15, 1862.

37 Captain Brien letter, September 3, 1863.

38 Captain Brien letter, October 30, 1863.

39 Hanson to Dole, July 18, 1863; Wiley to Dole, September 1, 1864, 261–263; Kingsbury to Maltby, September 9, 1866, 98–99; Orman to Taylor, May 31, 1868; and Orman to Whiting, July 31, 1868, 589.

40 "The Smith River Reservation, 1866–1868." Wright to Bryson, March 31, 1866.

41 "The Smith River Reservation, 1866–1868."

42 Kingsbury to Maltby, September 9, 1866, 98–99.

43 Whiting to Parker, August 15, 1869, 620.

44 Nelson, *Our Home Forever*, 89.

45 Orman to Taylor, December 31, 1868.

46 Whiting to Taylor, December 11, 1867.

47 Lowry to Commissioner of Indian Affairs, September 1, 1871, 747.

48 Tolowa Dee-ni' Nation, "About Us."

Bibliography

Bommelyn, Loren Me'-lash-ne. 1983 (January). Interview by Annette Reed, Crescent City, CA.

———. 1991 (August). Interview by Annette Reed, Crescent City, CA.

Brien, Captain. 1863. Letter, September 3, 1863, CLR, Record Group 393, National Archives and Records Administration.

———. 1863. Letter, October 30, 1863, CLR, Record Group 393, National Archives and Records Administration.

Bryson, W., to G. M. Hanson. November 20, 1862. Letters Received, War Department. Office of Indian Affairs. Record Group 75: Roll 39, National Archives and Records Administration.

Contis, Major James T., to Lieutenant R. C. Drum. September 15, 1862, Camp Lincoln Records (CLR), Record Group 393, National Archives and Records Administration.

———. October 10, 1862, Camp Lincoln Records (CLR), Record Group 393, National Archives and Records Administration.

Crook, George (Lt.), to Major Mackall. October 21, 1857. Returns from Military Post, Camp Lincoln, Record Group 393: M617–627.

———. November 21, 1857. Returns from Military Post, Camp Lincoln, Record Group 393:M617–627.

Crum, Steven J. 1994. *Po'I Pentun Tammen Kimmappeh/The Road on Which We Came: A History of the Western Shoshone*. Salt Lake City: University of Utah Press.

Danziger, Edmond Jefferson Jr. 1974. *Indians and Bureaucrats: Administering the Reservation Policy during the Civil War*. Urbana: University of Illinois Press.

Gibson, Arrell Morgan. 1980. *The American Indian: Prehistory to the Present*, Lexington, MA: D. C. Heath and Company.

Gould, Richard A. 1966. "Indian and White Versions of 'The Burnt Ranch Massacre': A Study in Comparative Ethnohistory." *Journal of the Folklore Institute*, 3(1): 30–42. https://doi.org/10.2307/3813952.

Hanson, George, Supt. Office of Indian Affairs, to William P. Dole, California Superintendency, 1849–1880; 1863–1864, War Department. Office of Indian Affairs, 1824–1849. Record Group 75: Roll 39, National Archives and Records Administration.

———. September 22, 1862. Letters Received, War Department. Office of Indian Affairs. Record Group 75: Roll 38, National Archives and Records Administration.

———. July 13, 1863. Letters Received, War Department. Office of Indian Affairs. 1824–1849. Record Group 75: Roll 38, National Archives and Records Administration.

———. July 18, 1863. Letters Received, War Department. Office of Indian Affairs. 1824–1849. Record Group 75: Roll 38, National Archives and Records Administration.

"Have to Go." *Weekly Humboldt Times* (Eureka, CA), September 13, 1862.

Haynes, I. T., to William C. Kibbe. May 18, 1862, Military Records, Crescent City Guards, 1861–64, California State Archives, Sacramento, CA.

Heintzleman, H. P., sub–Indian Agent, reported to Thomas J. Henley, Superintendent of Indian Affairs in San Francisco, July 1, 1858.

Annual Report of the Commissioner of Indian Affairs (ARCIA), Serial 997.

Hill, Dorothy. 1978. *The Indians of Chico Rancheria*, Sacramento: State of California Resources Agency, 39–41.

"Indian Reservation." *Weekly Humboldt Times* (Eureka, CA), January 25, 1862.

"Indian Reservations." *Weekly Humboldt Times* (Eureka, CA), February 8, 1862.

Kingsbury, G., to C. Maltby. September 9, 1866. Annual Report of the Commissioner of Indian Affairs, 1866, Serial 1284.

Lowry, D. H., to Commissioner of Indian Affairs. September 1, 1871, Annual Report of the Commissioner of Indian Affairs, 1871, Serial 1505.

Military Records, California State Archives, Sacramento, CA. 1854–1856.

"More Humbuggery in Indian Matters." *Weekly Humboldt Times* (Eureka, CA), November 8, 1862.

Nelson, Byron Jr. 1988. *Our Home Forever: The Hupa Indians of Northern California.* Salt Lake City: Howe Brothers.

Orman, Henry Jr., to A. G. Taylor. May 31, 1868. Letters Received, War Department. Office of Indian Affairs. Record Group 75: Roll 42, National Archives and Records Administration.

———. December 31, 1868. Letters Received, War Department. Office of Indian Affairs. Record Group 75: Roll 43, National Archives and Records Administration.

Orman, Henry Jr., to B. C. Whiting. July 31, 1868. Annual Report of the Commissioner of Indian Affairs, 1868, Serial 1366.

Prucha, Francis Paul. 1984. *The Great Father*, Vol. 1, Lincoln: University of Nebraska Press.

State of California Native American Heritage Commission, http://nahc.ca.gov/webmaster/atlas/evidence/i0772g.pdf (original source unknown).

Strobridge, William. 1994. *Regulars in the Redwoods: The U.S. Army in Northern California, 1852–1861*. Spokane, WA: The Arthur H. Clark Company.

"The Smith River Reservation, 1866–1868." Smith River Rancheria Archive Collection. Diary. Arcata, CA: Cal Poly Humboldt.

Tolowa Dee-ni' Nation. N.d. "About Us," https://www.tolowa-nsn.gov/35/About-Us.

United Nations General Assembly. 1948. Resolution 260 (III) A, at the Convention on the Prevention and Punishment of the Crime of Genocide, adopted on 9 December.

Unknown. 1862. "A Bill," *Visalia Weekly Delta* (Visalia, CA), June 5, 1862.

Wentworth, John P. H., to William P. Dole. August 30, 1862. Document no. 67 in "Report of the Commissioner of Indian Affairs," H. Exec. Docs., 37 Cong., 3 Sess., Vol. 2, Doc. 1, Pt. 2, 468–472 (1157).

Whiting, B. C., to N. G. Taylor. December 11, 1867. Letters Received, War Department. Office of Indian Affairs. Record Group 75: Roll 42, National Archives and Records Administration.

Whiting B. C., to E. S. Parker. August 1, 1869. Letters Received, War Department. Office of Indian Affairs. Record Group 75: Roll 43, National Archives and Records Administration.

———. August 15, 1869. Annual Report of the Commissioner of Indian Affairs, 1869, Serial 1414.

Wiley, Austin, to W. P. Dole. September 1, 1864. Superintendent of Indian Affairs in San Francisco. Annual Report of the Commissioner of Indian Affairs, Serial 12, 20.

Wright, Dr. F. M., to Bryson. March 31, 1866. Letters Received, War Department. Office of Indian Affairs. 1824–1849. Record Group 75: Roll 41, National Archives and Records Administration.

Chapter 12

Notes

1 Case and Voluck, *Alaska Natives and American Laws*, 61–68; and Mitchell, *Take My Land, Take My Life*.

2 Langdon, *Introduction to The Native People of Alaska*.

3 Case and Voluck, *Alaska Natives and American Laws*, 65–98.

4 Black, *Russians in Alaska* 1732–1867.

5 Jones, *Alaska Native Claims Settlement Act of 1971 (Public Law 92–203)*, 1.

6 Metcalfe, Central Council Historical Profile, 13–14.

7 Ibid., 6–7.

8 Dauenhauer and Dauenhauer, *Anooshi Lingit Aani Ka, Russians in Tlingit America*, 503–524; and Drucker, *The Native Brotherhoods.*

9 Mitchell, *Take My Land, Take My Life.*

10 Voice of Brotherhood, "Voices of the Brotherhood."

11 Voice of Brotherhood, "What Kind of Citizens Are We?"

12 Vaughan, *Towards a New and Better Life.*

13 Ibid., 245–247.

14 Ibid., 266.

15 Ibid., 269–271.

16 Case and Voluck, *Alaska Natives and American Laws*, 6.

17 Strickler, "*Tundra Times*, Howard Rock and ANOSA," 70–74.

18 McConnell, Spatz, and Templeton, ANCSA at 30.

19 Alaska Federation of Natives, "About."

20 Fischer, *Alaska's Constitutional Convention*, 138.

21 Arnold, *Alaska Native Land Claims.*

22 Ibid.

23 Ibid.

24 Alaska Native Claims Settlement Act Amendments of 1987.

25 Fast, "Alaska Native Language, Culture, and Identity," 4.

26 Thomas, "The Alaska Native Claims Settlement Act: An Update," 328–329.

27 Fast, "Alaska Native Language, Culture, and Identity," 4.

28 McClanahan, *Growing Up Native in Alaska.*

29 Ibid., 217.

30 Thomas, "The Alaska Native Claims Settlement Act: An Update," 328.

31 Case and Voluck, *Alaska Natives and American Laws*, 380–386.

32 Alaska v. Native Village of Venetie Tribal Government, 7–8.

33 Public Law 83–280, 18 U.S.C.A. § 1151 *et. seq.*; and Kimmel "Revisiting Governance in a Changing Arctic Environment," 13–14.

34 University of Alaska–Fairbanks, "Federal Recognition of Alaska Tribes and Relations with the State of Alaska."

35 McDowell v. State; and McBeath and Morehouse, *Alaska Politics and Government.*

36 Linxwiler, "The Alaska Native Claims Settlement Act at 35," 19–22; and Ongtooguk, "The Annotated ANCSA," 14.

37 Merculieff, "Another Response: ANCSA and Economic Development," 45.

38 Ongtooguk, "One Response: A Broad Perspective," 42.

39 Ibid., 40.

40 Brown, "A Third Response: Our Land, Our Decisions, Our Destiny," 52.

41 Ibid.; and Groh, *Oil, Money, Land and Power*, 16.

42 GAO, "Corporations 40 Years After Establishment and Future Conditions," 47.

43 Brown, "A Third Response: Our Land, Our Decisions, Our Destiny," 54–55.

Bibliography

Alaska Federation of Natives. 2021. "About." https://www.nativefederation.org/about-afn/.

Alaska Native Claims Settlement Act Amendments of 1987. 1988. Pub. L. No. 100–241, 101 Stat. 1788–1814.

Alaska v. Native Village of Venetie Tribal Government. 1998. 522 U.S. 520 (U.S. Supreme Court).

Arnold, Robert D. 1976. *Alaska Native Land Claims*. Anchorage: Alaska Native Foundation.

Black, Lydia T. 2004. *Russians in Alaska 1732–1867*. Fairbanks: University of Alaska Press.

Brown, Margie. 2010. "A Third Response: Our Land, Our Decisions, Our Destiny." In *Alaska Native Cultures and Issues*, ed. Libby Roderick. Anchorage: University of Alaska, 52–55.

Case, David S., and David A. Voluck. 2002. *Alaska Natives and American Laws*, 2nd ed. Fairbanks: University of Alaska Press.

Christianson, Susan Stark. 1995. *Historical Profile of Central Council of Tlingit and Haida Indian Tribes of Alaska*. Juneau: Central Council Tlingit and Haida.

Dauenhauer, Richard, and Nora Marks Dauenhauer. 1994. *Haa Kusteeyí, Our Culture*, vol. 3. Juneau, AK: Sealaska Heritage Foundation.

———. 2008. *Anooshi Lingit Aani Ka, Russians in Tlingit America: The Battles of Sitka, 1802–1804*. Seattle: University of Washington Press.

Drucker, Philip. 1958. *The Native Brotherhoods: Modern Intertribal Organizations on the Northwest Coast*. Vols. 85th Congress, no. 39. Washington, DC: U.S. G.P.O.

Fast, Phyllis. 2008. "Alaska Native Language, Culture, and Identity." Essay. Anchorage: University of Alaska.

Fischer, Victor. 1975. *Alaska's Constitutional Convention*. Fairbanks: University of Alaska Press.

GAO. 2012. "Corporations 40 Years After Establishment and Future Conditions." Regional Alaska Native Government. United States Government Accountability Office, 38–42. http://www.gao.gov/assets/660/650857.pdf.

Groh, Clifford J. 1976. *Oil, Money, Land and Power: The Passage of the Alaska Native Claims Settlement Act of 1971*. Juneau, AK: Independently published.

Jones, Richard S. 1981. *Alaska Native Claims Settlement Act of 1971 (Public Law 92–203): History and Analysis Together with Subsequent Amendments*. Congressional Research Service Reports, Washington, DC: Library of Congress. Congressional Research Service.

Kimmel, Mara. 2009. "Revisiting Governance in a Changing Arctic Environment: An Alaskan Case Study." White Paper. Anchorage: University of Alaska. http://www.earthsystemgovernance.org/ac2009/papers/AC2009–0116.pdf.

Langdon, Stephen J. 2002. *Introduction to the Native People of Alaska*, 4th ed. Anchorage: Greatland Graphics.

Linxwiler, James D. 2007. "The Alaska Native Claims Settlement Act at 35: Delivering on the Promise." 53rd Annual Rocky Mountain Mineral Law Institute, 19–22.

McBeath, Gerald A., and Thomas A. Morehouse. 1994. *Alaska Politics and*

Government. Lincoln: University of Nebraska Press.

McClanahan, Alexandra J. 2000. *Growing Up Native in Alaska*. Anchorage: The CIRI Foundation.

McConnell, Sharon, Ronald Spatz, and Willy Templeton. 2000. *ANCSA at 30*. Anchorage: University of Alaska. http://www.litsitealaska.org/index.cfm?section=History–and–Culture&page=ANCSA–at–30.

McDowell v. State. 2001. 807 So. 2d 413 (Supreme Court of Mississippi).

Merculieff, Ilarion. 2010. "Another Response: ANCSA and Economic Development." In *Alaska Native Cultures and Issues*, ed. Libby Roderick. Anchorage: University of Alaska Press, 44–50.

Metcalfe, Peter M. 1995. *Central Council Historical Profile: Tlingit and Haida Indian Tribes of Alaska*. Edited by Susan Stark Christianson. Juneau, AK: Central Council Tlingit and Haida.

Metcalfe, Peter M., and Kathy. K. Ruddy, 2014. *A Dangerous Idea: The Alaska Native Brotherhood and the Struggle for Indigenous Rights*. University Press of Colorado. http://www.jstor.org/stable/jj.1176819

Mitchell, Donald Craig. 2001. *Take My Land, Take My Life*. Fairbanks: University of Alaska Press.

Ongtooguk, Paul. 2010. "One Response: A Broad Perspective." In *Alaska Native Cultures and Issues*, ed. Libby Roderick. Anchorage: University of Alaska Press, 38–43.

———. 2012. "The Annotated ANCSA." Alaska Historical Society. https://alaskahistoricalsociety.org/wp–content/uploads/Annotated–ANCSA.pdf.

Public Law 83–280. 1953. State Jurisdiction over Offenses Committed by or Against Indians in the Indian Country. 18 U.S.C. § 1151 et. seq.

Strickler, Julie. 2011. "*Tundra Times*, Howard Rock and ANOSA: The Birth of Native Power in Alaska." *Alaska Business Monthly* 27(1): 70–74. EBSCO.

Thomas, Monica E. 1988. "The Alaska Native Claims Settlement Act: An Update." *Polar Record*. 24: 151, 328–329. Cambridge University. doi:10.1017/S0032247400009645.

University of Alaska–Fairbanks. 2022. "Federal Recognition of Alaska Tribes and Relations with the State of Alaska." https://www.uaf.edu/tribal/112/unit_4/federalrecognitionofalaskatribesandrelationswiththestateofalaska.php.

Vaughan, Daniel J. 1985. "Towards a New and Better Life: Two Hundred Years of Alaska Haida Cultural Change." PhD diss. Seattle: University of Washington.

Voice of Brotherhood. 1958. "Voices of the Brotherhood." June 4–5.

Voice of Brotherhood. 1959. "What Kind of Citizens Are We?" March 2–3, 44.

Chapter 13

Notes

1 Reyhner and Eder, *American Indian Education*; and Wilkins, *American Indian Politics and the American Political System.*

2 Adams, *Education for Extinction*, 57.

3 Reed, personal memory.

4 Norton, *Genocide in Northwestern California.*

5 Mitchell, interview by Reed, May 10, 1994.

6 Norton, *Genocide in Northwestern California*, 107; and Secrest, *When the Great Spirit Died.*

7 Norton, *Genocide in Northwestern California*, 107.

8 Smith and Ross, "Introduction: Native Women and State Violence," 1–7.

9 Reed, Interview with Mitchell, May 10, 1994.

10 Child, *Boarding School Seasons.*

11 Reed, Interview with Mitchell, May 12, 1994.

12 Ibid.

13 Ibid.

14 LaPena, "Native American Experience," September 1999.

15 Reed, Interview with Mitchell, October 1994.

16 Reed, Interview with Elder Native American woman, November 1986.

Bibliography

Adams, David Wallace. 1995. *Education for Extinction: American Indian Boarding School Experience, 1875–1928*. Lawrence: University Press of Kansas.

Child, Brenda. 2000. *Boarding School Seasons: American Indian Families, 1900–1940*, Lincoln: University of Nebraska Press.

LaPena, Frank. 1999. "Native American Experience." Classroom presentation.

Norton, Jack. 1979. *Genocide in Northwestern California: When Our Worlds Cried*. San Francisco: Indian Historian Press.

Reed, Annette. Personal memory.

———. May 10, 1994. Interview conducted with Genny Mitchell.

———. May 12, 1994. Interview conducted with Genny Mitchell

———. October 1994. Interview conducted with Genny Mitchell.

———. November 1986. Interview conducted with Elder Native American woman.

Reyhner, Jon, and Jeanne Eder. 2004. *American Indian Education: A History*. Norman: University of Oklahoma Press.

Secrest, William B. 2003. *When the Great Spirit Died: The Destruction of the California Indians, 1850–1860*. Sanger, CA: Word Dancer Press.

Smith, Andrea, and Luana Ross. 2004 "Introduction: Native Women and State Violence." *Social Justice* 31(4): 1–7.

Wilkins, David E. 2002. *American Indian Politics and the American Political System*. New York: Rowman & Littlefield Publishers, Inc.

Chapter 14

Notes

1 *Ali'i*—Chief, chiefess, officer, ruler, monarch, peer, headman, noble, aristocrat, king, queen, commander; royal, regal, aristocratic, kingly; to rule or act as a chief, govern, reign; to become a chief (Pukui and Elbert, *Hawaiian Dictionary*).

2 *Mele*—Song, anthem, or chant of any kind; poem, poetry; to sing, chant (Pukui and Elbert, *Hawaiian Dictionary*).

3 *Ali'i Nui*—high chief (Pukui and Elbert, *Hawaiian Dictionary*).

4 *Kanaka Maoli* a traditional Hawaiian ethnonym that can be translated as "true human being" or "real person" (Pukui and Elbert, *Hawaiian Dictionary*).

5 United States Senate, 1893, 1253.

6 Cleveland, message, 457.

7 Graff, *Grover Cleveland.*

8 Lili'uokalani, *Hawaii's Story by Hawaii's Queen*, 251.

9 There was nothing Hawaiian about the Hawaiian League, a political organization of haole (whites) that was working toward limiting monarchy and even American annexation.

10 The Bayonet constitution placed almost all of the real executive power in the cabinet ministry, and the monarch was required to execute whatever the ministry demanded. Meanwhile, the makeup of the cabinet was at the mercy of a fractious legislature, which by a simple majority could vote a cabinet out of power. Lili'u had to appoint nine cabinets in the two years of her reign.

11 Lili'uokalani, *Hawaii's Story by Hawaii's Queen*, 228–229.

Bibliography

Cleveland, G. 1893. "Message." House Ex. Doc. No. 47, Fifty–third Congress, second session Foreign Relations of the United States, 1894, Appendix II, Affairs in Hawaii.

Graff, Henry F. 2022. *Grover Cleveland: Domestic Affairs*. Charlottesville: Miller Center, University of Virginia. https://millercenter.org/president/cleveland/domestic–affairs.

Ho'omanawanui, Ku'ualoha. 2005. "He Lei Ho'oheno No Nā Kau a Kau: Language, Performance, and Form in Hawaiian Poetry." *Contemporary Pacific* 17 (1): 29–81. doi:10.1353/cp.2005.0008.

Lili'uokalani. 1898. *Hawaii's Story by Hawaii's Queen*. Boston: Lothrop, Lee & Shepard Co.

Pukui, M., and S. Elbert, eds. 2022. *Hawaiian Dictionary*. Honolulu: University of Hawai'i Press.

United States Senate. 1893. *Hawaiian Islands*. Report of the Committee on Foreign Relations, United States Senate, with accompanying testimony, and Executive documents transmitted to Congress from January 1, 1883, to March 10, 1894, 1253.

Chapter 15

Notes

1 Pfister, *The Yale Indian*; Messer, *Henry Roe Cloud*; Crum, "Henry Roe Cloud" 171–184; Warren, *The Quest for Citizenship*; Ramirez, "Henry Roe Cloud," 77–105; Ramirez, "From Henry Roe Cloud to Henry Cloud," 118–137; Ramirez, *Standing Up to Colonial Power*; and Goodwin, *Without Destroying Ourselves*.

2 Tezloff, *To Do Some Good Among the Indians*.

3 Treat, *Native and Christian*. He discusses how others view Native Christians as "assimilated," "inauthentic," and "heretical"; Hertzberg, *The Search for an American Indian Identity*; James, "American Indian Women," 311–345. She discusses "sell–outs."

4 Hoxie, *Talking Back to Civilization*, 1–28; Iverson, *Carlos Montezuma and the Changing World of American Indians*; and Porter, *To Be Indian*.

5 Comaroff and Comaroff, *Ethnicity, Inc.*; Povenelli, *The Cunning of Recognition*; and Jolly and Thomas, "Introduction: The Politics of Tradition in the Pacific": 241–248.

6 Cloud to Mary Roe, July 18, 1907.

7 Cloud North, "Informal Education in Winnebago Tribal Society with Implications for Formal Education."

8 Cloud, "Graduation Speech to Mount Edgecomb High School Students."

9 Cloud, "From Wigwam to Pulpit," 400–413.

10 Ibid.

11 Jacobs, *White Mother to the Dark Race*.

12 Lomawaima, *They Called It Prairie Light*.

13 Cloud, "Graduation Speech to Mount Edgecomb High School Students."

14 Ibid.

15 Ibid.

16 Denetdale, *Reclaiming Dine Histories.*

17 Cloud to Mary Roe, January 7, 1908.

18 Cloud, "From Wigwam to Pulpit."

19 Carrol, *American Masculinities*, 206.

20 Ramirez, "From Henry Roe Cloud to Henry Cloud"; Hokowhitu, "Maori Masculinity, Post–Structuralism, and the Emerging Self," 179–201; Tengan, *Native Men Remade*; Anthony, Clark, and Nagle, "'Indian' Manhood in Imagined Wests"; and Basso, McCall, and Garceau, *Across the Great Divide.*

21 Basso, McCall, and Garceau, *Across the Great Divide*, 1–2.

22 Ibid.

23 Culin, *Games of the North American Indians*, vol. 1 and 2; and Fletcher, *Indian Games and Dances with Native Songs.*

24 Cloud, "Graduation Speech to Mount Edgecomb High School Students."

25 Ibid.

26 Lincoln, informal interview, July 15, 2001.

27 Cloud, untitled document, August 11, 1911.

28 Rosaldo, *Culture and Truth.*

29 Good, *A History of American Education*; Tezloff, *To Do Some Good Among the Indians*, 90; and Ramirez, "Henry Roe Cloud."

30 Crum, "Henry Roe Cloud," 171–185.

31 Cloud Hughes, April 27, 1987, "Memoirs."

32 Pawnee Nation, Pawnee Council Meeting.

33 Cloud, "Graduation Speech to Mt. Edgecumbe High School Students."

34 Ibid.

35 Ibid.

36 Mitchell, *Take My Land, Take My Life*; Pritzker, *Native American Encyclopedia.*

Bibliography

Anthony, David, Tyeeme Clark, and Joane Nagle. 2001. "White Men, Red Masks: Appropriations of 'Indian' Manhood in Imagined Wests." In *Across the Great Divide: Culture of Manhood in the American West*, ed. Matthew Basso, Laura McCAll, and Dee Garceau. New York: Routledge, 108–130.

Basso, Mathew, Laura McCall, and Dee Garceau, eds. 2001. *Across the Great Divide: Culture of Manhood in the American West.* New York: Routledge.

Carrol, Bret E. 2003. *American Masculinities: A Historical Encyclopedia.* Thousand Oaks, CA: Sage Publications.

Cloud to Mary Roe, July 18, 1907, Box 67, Folder 1078, Yale Library, RFP.

———. January 7, 1908, Box 67, Folder 1082, Yale Library, RFP.

Cloud, Henry Roe. 1911. Untitled document, August 11, 1911. Woesha Cloud North files, in author's possession.

———. 1915. "From Wigwam to Pulpit." *Missionary Review of the World* (May): 400–413.

———. 1949. "Graduation Speech to Mount Edgecumbe High School Students." Woesha Cloud North's films, in author's possession.

Cloud Hughes, Elizabeth Marion. 1987. "Memoirs," April 27, 1987. Woesha Cloud North's files.

Cloud North, Woesha. 1978. "Informal Education in Winnebago Tribal Society with Implications for Formal Education." PhD diss. Lincoln: University of Nebraska.

Comaroff, John, and Jean Comaroff. 2009. *Ethnicity, Inc.* Chicago: University of Chicago Press.

Crum, Steven. 1988. "Henry Roe Cloud, A Winnebago Reformer: His Quest for American Indian Higher Education." *Kansas History* 11(3): 171–185.

Cuban, Larry. 1993. How Teachers Taught: Constancy and Change in American Classrooms, 1880–1990. New York: Teacher College Press.

Culin, Stewart. 1992. *Games of the North American Indians*, vol. 1 and 2. Lincoln: University of Nebraska Press.

Denetdale, Jennifer Nez. 2007. Reclaiming Dine Histories: The Legacies of Navajo Chief Manuelito and Juanita. Tucson: University of Arizona Press.

Fletcher, Alice. 1994. *Indian Games and Dances with Native Songs*. Lincoln: University of Nebraska Press.

Good, H. G. 1962. *A History of American Education*. New York: The Macmillan Co.

Goodwin, John. 2022. *Without Destroying Ourselves: A Century of Native Intellectual Activism for Higher Education*. Lincoln: University of Nebraska Press.

Hertzberg, Hazel. 1971. *The Search for an American Indian Identity: Modern Pan–Indian Movements*. Syracuse, NY: Syracuse University Press.

Hokowhitu, B. 2003. "Maori Masculinity, Post–Structuralism, and the Emerging Self." *New Zealand Sociology* 18(2): 179–201.

Hoxie, Frederick, ed. 2001. *Talking Back to Civilization: Indian Voices in the Progressive Era*. Boston: Bedford/Martin's.

Iverson, Peter. 1982. *Carlos Montezuma and the Changing World of American Indians*. Albuquerque: University of New Mexico Press.

Jacobs, Margaret. 2009. *White Mother to the Dark Race*. Lincoln: University of Nebraska Press.

James, M. Annette. 1999. "American Indian Women: At the Center of Indigenous Resistance in North America." In *The State of Native America: Genocide, Colonization, and Resistance*. Boston: South End Press, 311–345.

Jolly, Margaret, and Nicolas Thomas. "Introduction: The Politics of Tradition in the Pacific." Special Issue, *Oceania* 62: 241–248.

Lincoln, Helen. 2001. Informal interview, July 15, 2001.

Lomawaima, K. Tsianina. 1994. *They Called It Prairie Light: The Story of Chilocco Indian School*. Lincoln: University of Nebraska.

Messer, David. 2010. *Henry Roe Cloud: A Biography*. Lanham, MD: Hamilton Books.

Mitchell, Donald. 2001. *Take My Land, Take My Life: The Story of Congress's Historic Settlement of Alaska Native Claims, 1960–1971*. Fairbanks: University of Alaska Press.

Pawnee Nation. 1927. Pawnee Council Meeting, April 22, 1927. Woesha Cloud North's files.

Pfister, Joel. 2009. *The Yale Indian: The Education of Henry Roe Cloud.* Durham, NC: Duke University Press.

Porter, Joy. 2001. *To Be Indian: The Life of Iroquois-Seneca Arthur Caswell Parker*. Norman: University of Oklahoma Press.

Povenelli, Elizabeth. 2002. *The Cunning of Recognition: Indigenous Alterities and the Making of Australian Multiculturalism*. Durham, NC: Duke University Press.

Pritzker, Barry. 2000. *Native American Encyclopedia: History, Culture, and Peoples*. New York: Oxford University Press.

Ramirez, Renya. 2009. "Henry Roe Cloud: A Granddaughter's Native Feminist Biographical Account." *Wicazo Sa Review*, 24(2) 77–103.

———. 2012. "From Henry Roe Cloud to Henry Cloud: Ho–Chunk Strategies and Colonialism." *Settler Colonial Studied* 2 (2): 118–137.

———. 2018. *Standing Up to Colonial Power: The Lives of Henry Roe and Elizabeth Bender Cloud*. Lincoln: University of Nebraska Press.

Rosaldo, Renato. 1989. *Culture and Truth: The Remaking of Social Analysis*. Boston: Beacon Press.

Tengan, Ty Kawaka. 2008. *Native Men Remade: Gender and Nation in Contemporary Hawaii*. Durham, NC: Duke University Press.

Tezloff, Jason. 1996. "To Do Some Good Among the Indians: Henry Roe Cloud and Twentieth Century Advocacy." PhD diss. West Lafayette, IN: Purdue University.

Treat, James. 1996. *Native and Christian*. New York: Routledge.

Warren, Kim. 2010. *The Quest for Citizenship: African-Amercans and Native Americans in Education, 1880–1935*. Chapel Hill: University of North Carolina Press.

Chapter 16

Notes

1 Rosier, *Serving Their Country*, 46–47; and Britten, *American Indians in World War I*, 37–39.

2 Rosier, *Serving Their Country*, 46–47; and Britten, *American Indians in World War I*, 43–44.

3 Rosier, *Serving Their Country*, 47.

4 Quoted in Britten, *American Indians in World War I*, 150.

5 Britten, *American Indians in World War I*, 69; Rosier, *Serving Their Country*, 50.

6 Britten, *American Indians in World War I*, 67–68.

7 Ibid., 166.

8 Quoted in Morris W. Foster, *Being Comanche*, 125.

9 Rosier, *Serving Their Country*, 72, 227; Bernstein, *Towards a New Era in Indian Affairs*, 40, 68, 86.

10 Bernstein, *Towards a New Era in Indian Affairs*, 22, 40.

11 "Congressional Medal of Honor Winner Passes," B3.

12 Nez and Avila, *Code Talker*, 13, 89, 115.

13 Ibid., 7, 27–29, 38–39, 74–78, 223.

14 Quoted in Meadows, *The Comanche Code Talkers of World War II*, 143–144.

15 Ibid., 155.

16 Lance, "Chickasaw Elders' Life Reflects Continued Service to Others," 16–17.

17 Jenkins, Thomas, statement, April 24, 1944.

18 Pahongva to Vanarsdall, July 12, 1944.

19 "Hopi CodeTalkers Honored," 22.

20 "F. Muncey Dies of Wound in Nazi War," 1; "Francis Muncey Buried with Military Honors," 1; "Indian Sun Dance Held Near Wells," 1.

21 "'Under the Eagle' Eye Spiritual Side of War," C5; and "Woody Keeble: Finally a Medal of Honor," 9.

22 Holm, *Strong Hearts, Wounded Souls*, 103–128.

23 Kipp, *Viet Cong at Wound Knee*, 36.

24 Ibid., 41, 48.

25 Quoted in "Indian P.O.W. to Return," 2.

26 "Vietnam Vets Hope to Set Up Indian V.A.," 4.

27 "Film 'Warriors' Captures Spirit of Vietnam Tribal Veterans."

28 Ibid.

29 Ibid.

30 "Apology Sought for 'Indian Country' Remark," A3.

31 Harris and Hirsch, *Why We Serve*, 170.

32 "Items donated to Display at Cherokee Veterans Center," 14.

33 "'Under the Eagle' Eye Spiritual Side of War," C5; "Woody Keeble: Finally a Medal of Honor," 9.

34 "Statue to Be Erected in Honor of Native Vets," A7; Harris and Hirsch, Why We Serve, 177.

Bibliography

"Apology Sought for 'Indian Country' Remark." *Sacramento Bee*, February 23, 1991, A3.

Bernstein, Alison R. 1995. *Towards a New Era in Indian Affairs: American Indians and World War II*. Norman: University of Oklahoma Press.

Britten, Thomas A. 1997. *American Indians in World War I: At Home and at War*. Albuquerque: University of New Mexico Press.

"Congressional Medal of Honor Winner Passes." *Indian Country Today*, July 10, 2002, B3.

"Film 'Warriors' Captures Spirit of Vietnam Tribal Veterans." *Lakota Times*, February 3, 1988.

"F. Muncey Dies of Wound in Nazi War." *Battle Mountain Scout*, March 22, 1945, 1.

Foster, Morris W. 1991. *Being Comanche: A Social History of an American Indian Community*. Tucson: University of Arizona Press.

"Francis Muncey Buried with Military Honors." *Battle Mountain Scout*, May 13, 1948, 1.

Harris, Alexandra N., and Mark G. Hirsch. 2020. *Why We Serve: Native Americans in the United States Armed Forces*. Washington, D.C.: National Museum of the American Indian, 170.

Holm, Tom. 1996. *Strong Hearts, Wounded Souls: Native American Veterans of the Vietnam War*. Austin, TX: University of Texas Press.

"Hopi CodeTalkers Honored." *News From Indian Country*, May 2013, 22.

"Indian Sun Dance Held Near Wells." *Elko Daily Free Press*, July 1, 1946, 1.

"Items Donated to Display at Cherokee Veterans Center." *Cherokee Advocate*, March 2014, 14.

Jenkins, Thomas, statement. April 24, 1944. New Mexico Association of Indian Affairs, File "#111, Hopi Correspondence, 1941–54," New Mexico State Historical Society, Santa Fe, New Mexico.

Kipp, Woody. 2004. *Viet Cong at Wound Knee: The Trail of a Blackfeet Activist.* Lincoln: University of Nebraska Press.

Lance, Dana. "Chickasaw Elders' Life Reflects Continued Service to Others." *News from Indian Country*, 03, 2014, 16–17.

Meadows, William C. 2002. *The Comanche Code Talkers of World War II.* Austin: University of Texas Press.

Nez, Chester, and Judith Schiess Avila. 2011. *Code Talker: The First and Only Memoir by One of the Original Navajo Code Talkers of WWII.* New York: Berkeley Caliber.

Pahongva Fred A. to Karl E. Vanarsdall, July 12, 1944. File: "#Hopi Correspondence, 1941–54."

Rosier, Paul C. 2009. *Serving Their Country: American Indian Politics and Patriotism in the Twentieth Century*. Cambridge, MA: Harvard University Press.

"Statue to Be Erected in Honor of Native Vets." *Navajo Times*, January 2, 2014, A7.

"'Under the Eagle' Eye Spiritual Side of War." *Navajo Times*, October 10, 2013, C5.

"Vietnam Vets Hope to Set Up Indian V.A." *Lakota Times*, October 24, 1984, 4.

"Woody Keeble: Finally a Medal of Honor." *Indian Country Today*, June 28, 2006, 9.

PART III

[a]Hogan, Linda. 1999. "Seeing, Knowing, Remembering." In *Native American Literature: An Anthology*, ed. Lawana Trout, Chicago: National Textbook Company, 747–749.

Chapter 17

Notes

1 *Cherokee Nation v. Georgia*, 30 U.S. (5 Pet.) 1 (1831).

2 *United States v. Kagama*, 118 U.S. 375, 382.

3 Ibid., 383–384.

4 Ibid., 384.

5 US Statutes at Large, 24:388–91.

6 General Allotment Act, 566.

7 Ibid., 567.

8 House Concurrent Resolution 108 § 67, B132–2.

9 *Lyng v. Northwest Indian Cemetery Protective Association*, 485 U.S. 439 (1988), 439.

10 *United States v. Washington*, 384 F. Supp. 312 (W.D. Wash. 1974).

Bibliography

An Act to Provide for the Allotment of Lands in Severalty to Indians on the Various Reservations (General Allotment Act or Dawes Act). 1887. Statutes at Large 24, 388–91, NADP Document A1887.

Barsh, Russel Lawrence, and James Youngblood Henderson. 1980. *The Road: Indian Tribes and Political Liberty*. Berkeley: University of California Press.

Canby, William C. 1981. *American Indian Law*. St. Paul, MN: West Publishing.

Cherokee Nation v. Georgia, 30 U.S. (5 Pet.) 1 (1831).

Cohen, Felix S. 1982. *Felix Cohen's Handbook of Federal Indian Law*. Charlottesville, VA: Bobbs–Merrill.

Cornell, Stephen. 1988. *The Return of the Native: American Indian Political Resurgence*. New York: Oxford University Press.

County of Oneida v. Oneida Indian Nation, 470 U.S. 226, 1985.

Getches, David H., and Charles F. Wilkinson. 1986. *Federal Indian Law: Cases and Materials*. St. Paul, MN: West Publishing.

Iowa Mutual Insurance Company v. LaPlante, 480 U.S. 9, 1987.

Jaimes, M. Annette. 1992. *The State of Native America*. Boston: South End Press.

Lone Wolf v. Hitchcock, 187 U.S. 553, 1903.

Lyng v. Northwest Indian Cemetery Protective Association, 485 U.S. 439, 1988.

Lyons, Oren. 1992. *Exiled in the Land of the Free: Democracy, Indian Nations and the U.S. Constitution*. Santa Fe, NM: Clear Light Publishers.

National Farmers Union Insurance Company v. Crow Tribe, 471 U.S. 845, 1985.

Pevar, Stephen L. 1992. *The Rights of Indians and Tribes*. Carbondale and Edwardsville, IL: Southern Illinois University Press.

Price, Monroe E., and Robert Clinton. 1983. *Law and the American Indian*. Charlottesville, VA: Mitchie/Bobbs–Merrill.

Santa Clara Pueblo v. Martinez, 436 U.S. 49, 1978.

Shattuck, Petra H., and Jill Norgren. 1991. *Partial Justice: Federal Indian Law in a Liberal Constitutional System*. New York: Berg.

Treaty of Point Elliott. January 22, 1855. Treaty between the United States and the Dwámish, Suquámish, and Other Allied and Subordinate Tribes of Indians in Washington Territory. Ratified January 22, 1859: 927–932.

United States Commission on Civil Rights. 1980. *American Indian Civil Rights Handbook*. Washington, DC: US Government Printing Office.

United States v. Kagama, 118 U.S. 375, 1886.

United States v. Washington, 384 F. Supp. 312 (W.D. Wash.), 1974.

United States v. Washington, 443 U.S. 658, 1979.

US Congress. House Concurrent Resolution 108. Indians. 83rd Cong., 1st sess. Introduced in House on June 9, 1953. https://www.govinfo.gov/content/pkg/STATUTE-67/pdf/STATUTE-67-PgB132-2.pdf.

West, W. Richard, Jr., and Kevin Gover. 1998. "The Struggle for Indian Civil Rights." In *Indians in American History*, ed. Frederick E. Hoxie. Arlington Heights, IL: Harlan Davidson, 218–234.

Wunder, John R. 1994. *"Retained by the People": A History of American Indians and the Bill of Rights*. New York: Oxford University Press.

Zionitz, Alvin J. 1979. "After Martinez: Indian Civil Rights Under Tribal Government." *University of California, Davis Law Review* 12:1, 1–35.

Chapter 19

Notes

1 Following the treaty of 1864, the Klamath, Modoc, and Yahooskin Band of Snake Indians were placed on the same reservation in southern Oregon. Known today as the Klamath Tribes, many of us now trace our ancestry to more than one of the three.

2 Anishinaabe scholar and National Native American Graves and Repatriation Act (NAGPRA) Review Committee member Sonya Atalay (2012) has pointed out that this number is destined to be much higher as US federal and state agencies are forced into compliance with the law. Among other problems, federal agencies have housed and lost track of remains and objects in repositories all over the nation.

3 P.L. 101–601 NAGPRA, 25 U.S.C. 3001 et seq., 104 Stat. 3048.

4 Inouye, prepared statement, Committee on Indian Affairs, 1–2.

5 Suzan Shown Harjo (Cheyenne/Hodulgee Muscogee), Walter Echo-Hawk (Pawnee), and Henry Sockbeson (Penobscott) are prominent names in the legislative history. Other key advocates include Roger Buffalohead (Ponca) and Alan Parker (Chippewa/Cree).

6 Dumont, "Contesting Scientists' Narrations of NAGPRA's Legislative History," 8–9.

7 Sconchin remains a prominent name on our reservation.

8 The Lava Beds are now a national monument and the scene of the war that led to the executions of Captain Jack, Black Jim, Boston Charlie, and Sconchin, as described in the opening paragraph.

9 Weiss, Elizabeth, *Reburying the Past*, 80.

10 Mallouf, "Repatriation: An Interdisciplinary Dialogue," 206.

11 Adams, prepared statement, Senate Select Committee on Indian Affairs, 192.

12 The notion of "race" is a now discredited biological concept. There is simply no physiological basis for distinguishing where one "race" begins and another leaves off. Beyond superficial

differences in skin pigmentation, facial features, and hair (what scholars call "phenotype"), no real biological differences between so-called races exist. However, centuries of believing in this biological fiction have created an American nation where "race" remains a sociological reality, meaning, for example, that society remains plagued by institutionalized racial inequality.

13 Bieder, *Science Encounters the Indian*, 4–5.

14 Jefferson, *Notes on the State of Virginia*, 55–66.

15 Bieder *Science Encounters the Indian*, 167–170; Riding In, "Without Ethics or Morality," 15–17; and Thomas, *Skull Wars*, 30–35.

16 Thornton, "Who Owns Our Past?" 387.

17 Bieder, *Science Encounters the Indian*, 66.

18 Gould, *The Mismeasure of Man, 85–89.*

19 Brinton, "The Aims of Anthropology," 244.

20 Krupat, *Ethnocriticism*, 66.

21 Bieder, *A Brief Historical Survey of the Expropriation of American Indian Remains*, 23–34.

22 Cole, *Captured Heritage*, 120, 158–162.

23 Riding In, "Without Ethics or Morality," 22.

24 Dorsey, "A Cruise Among the Haida and Tlingit Villages About Dixon's Entrance."

25 Pullar, "The Qikertarmiut and the Scientist," 21–22.

26 Bieder, *A Brief Historical Survey of the Expropriation of American Indian Remains,* 48–50; *Harper, Give Me My Father's Body;* and *Preston, Skeletons in Our Museums Closets.*

27 Hrdlička, *Directions for Collecting Information and Specimens for Physical Anthropology*, 23.

28 Ibid., 17.

29 Ibid., 6–7.

30 Ibid., 17.

31 Johnson, *The Occupation of Alcatraz Island*, 230; and Watkins, *Indigenous Archaeology*, 11.

32 Deloria, *God Is Red*, 13–14.

33 Dumont, *The Promise of Poststructuralist Sociology*, 139.

34 Echo–Hawk and Echo–Hawk, *Battlefields and Burial Grounds*, 66–68.

35 16 U.S. Code 470aa–470mm.

36 McKeown and Hutt, "In the Smaller Scope of Conscience," 153.

37 Haney, prepared statement, House Committee on Interior and Insular Affairs, 110.

38 Harjo, prepared statement, Senate Select Committee on Indian Affairs and Senate Committee on Rules and Administration, 42.

39 Echo–Hawk, prepared statement, Senate Select Committee on Indian Affairs, 213–214.

40 Adams, prepared statement, Senate Select Committee on Indian Affairs, 187.

41 Ibid., 186.

42 Buffalohead, presentation at "Repatriation at Twenty."

43 Melcher, Senate Committee, Museum Claims Commission, 70.

44 "Atemporal" means "outside of time."

45 Dumont, "Contesting Scientists' Narrations," 5–6.

46 Riding In, *Graves Protection and Repatriation*, 39.

47 Dumont, "Navigating a Colonial Quagmire," 242–243. Translated as: "warrior of small stature" by the 1890 ethnographer Albert Gatschet.

48 Timothy White, Robert L. Bettinger, and Margaret Schoeninger v. The University of California, Superior Court of the State of California for the County of Alameda, 2012.

49 Echo–Hawk, Testimony Before the United States Senate Committee on Indian Affairs, 3.

50 Kintigh, prepared statement, House Committee, 137.

51 Sockbeson, Henry J. 1990. prepared statement, House Committee on Interior and Insular Affairs, 55.

52 Kintigh, prepared statement, House Committee, 138.

53 Miyamoto, "The Status of the NAGPRA Process Among Museums with the Largest Collections of Native American Human Remains," presentation.

54 Miyamoto, "The Status of the NAGPRA Process Among Museums with the Largest Collections of Native American Human Remains," presentation.

Bibliography

Adams, Robert M. 1987. Prepared statement, Senate Select Committee on Indian Affairs, Native American Cultural Preservation Act: Hearings on S. 187, 100th Cong., 1st session, 186–187.

Atalay, Sonya. 2012. "Enduring Responsibility to the Ancestors: Repatriation Strategies and Barriers on University Campuses." Presentation at Annual Meeting of the Native American and Indigenous Studies Association: Uncasville, CT.

Barker, Pat, Cynthia Ellis, and Stephanie Damadio. July 26, 2000. "Summary of the Determination of Cultural Affiliation of Ancient Remains From Spirit Cave, Nevada." Bureau of Land Management Nevada Office.

Bieder, Robert E. 1986. *Science Encounters the Indian, 1820–1880*, Norman: University of Oklahoma Press.

———. 1990. *A Brief Historical Survey of the Expropriation of American Indian Remains*. Native American Rights Fund.

Brinton, Daniel G. 1895. "The Aims of Anthropology." *Science*, 2(35): 241–252.

Buffalohead, Roger. January 29, 2010. Presentation at "Repatriation at Twenty: A Gathering on Native Self-Determination and Human Rights." Arizona State University, Tempe.

Cole, Douglas. 1985. *Captured Heritage*. Norman: University of Oklahoma Press.

Deloria, Vine. 1994. *God Is Red*. Golden, CO: Fulcrum Publishing.

Dorsey, George A. 1898. "A Cruise Among the Haida and Tlingit Villages About Dixon's Entrance." *Popular Science Monthly*, 53(13):160–174.

Dumont, Clayton W. 2008. *The Promise of Poststructuralist Sociology: Marginalized Peoples and the Problem of Knowledge*. New York: SUNY Press.

———. 2011. "Contesting Scientists' Narrations of NAGPRA's Legislative History: Rule 10.11 and the Recovery of 'Culturally Unidentifiable' Ancestors." *Wicazo Sa Review*, 1(26): 5–42.

———. 2013. "Navigating a Colonial Quagmire: Affirming Native Lives in the Struggle to Defend Our Dead." In Accomplishing NAGPRA: Perspectives on the Intent, Impact, and Future of the

Native American Graves Protection and Repatriation Act, 3d. Sangita Chari and Jaime M. N. Lavalle. Corvallis: Oregon State University Press, 239–264.

Echo–Hawk, Roger C., and Walter R. Echo–Hawk. 1994. *Battlefields and Burial Grounds: The Indian Struggle to Protect Ancestral Graves in the United States*. Minneapolis: Lerner Publications Company.

Echo–Hawk, Walter R. 1988. Prepared statement, Senate Select Committee on Indian Affairs, Native American Museum Claims Commission Act: Hearings on S. 187, 100th Cong., 2nd sess., 213–214.

———. July 28, 2005. "Testimony Before the United States Senate Committee on Indian Affairs." Available at http://www.narf.org/nagpra/echohawk.pdf.

GAO. 2010. Report to Congressional Requesters, Native American Graves Protection and Repatriation Act: After Almost 20 Years, Key Federal Agencies Still Have Not Complied with the Act.

Gould, Stephen J. 1997. *The Mismeasure of Man*. W. W. Norton & Company: New York.

Haney, Michael S. 1990. Prepared statement, House Committee on Interior and Insular Affairs, Protection of Native American Graves and the Repatriation of Human Remains and Sacred Objects: Hearings on H.R. 1381, H.R. 1646, and H.R. 5237, 101st Cong., 2nd sess., 110.

Harjo, Suzan. 1987. Prepared statement, Senate Select Committee on Indian Affairs and Senate Committee on Rules and Administration, National Museum of the American Indian Act (Part 1): Hearings on S. 1722 and S. 1723, 100th Cong., 1st sess., 42.

Harper, Ken. 1986. *Give Me My Father's Body: The Life of Minik, The New York Eskimo*. Frobisher Bay, NWT, Canada: Blacklead Books.

Hrdlička, Aleš. 1904. *Directions for Collecting Information and Specimens for Physical Anthropology*. Washington, DC: US Government Printing Office.

Inouye, Hon. Daniel K. 2002. Prepared Statement to the U.S. Senate Committee on Indian Affairs, June 11, 1–2.

Jefferson, Thomas. 1861/1964. *Notes on the State of Virginia*. New York: Harper and Row.

Johnson, Troy R. 1996. *The Occupation of Alcatraz Island: Indian Self Determination and the Rise of Indian Activism*. Champaign: University of Illinois Press.

Kintigh, Keith. 2005. Prepared statement, House Committee, Protection of Native American Graves. https://www.public.asu.edu/~kintigh/KintighOnNAGPRA.pdf

Krupat, Arnold. 1992. *Ethnocriticism*. Berkeley: University of California Press.

Makah Indian Tribe and NATHPO. 2008. Federal Agency Implementation of the Native American Graves Protection and Repatriation Act: A Report by the Makah Indian Tribe and the National Association of Tribal Historic Preservation Officers.

Mallouf, Robert J. 1996. "Repatriation: An Interdisciplinary Dialogue," *American Indian Quarterly*, 20(2), Special Issue (Spring): 197–208.

McKeown, Timothy, and Sherry Hutt. 2003. "In the Smaller Scope of Conscience: The Native American Graves Protection and Repatriation Act Twelve Years After." *UCLA Journal of Environmental Law and Policy*, 2(21):153.

Melcher, John. 1988. Senate Committee, Museum Claims Commission.

Miyamoto, Lauren. November 19, 2010. "The Status of the NAGPRA Process Among Museums with the Largest Collections of Native American Human Remains." Public presentation at NAGPRA Review Committee Meeting (copy on file with author).

Preston, Douglas J. 1989. "Skeletons in Our Museums' Closets: Native Americans Want Their Ancestors' Bones Back." *Harper's Magazine*, (278), 66–75.

Public Law 101–601. 1990. Native American Graves Protection and Repatriation Act (NAGPRA). 25 U.S.C. 3001 et seq., 104 Stat. 3048.

Pullar, Gordon. 1994. "The Qikertarmiut and the Scientist: Fifty Years of Clashing World Views." In *Reckoning with the Dead: The Larsen Bay Repatriation and the Smithsonian Institution*, ed. T. Killion and T. Bray. Washington, DC: Smithsonian Institution Press, 15–25.

Riding In, James. 1992. "Without Ethics or Morality: A Historical Overview of Imperial Archaeology and American Indians." *Arizona State Law Journal*, 24: 11–34.

———. 2008. "Graves Protection and Repatriation: An Unresolved Universal Human Rights Problem Affected by Institutional Racism." In *Human Rights in Global Light*, ed. Mariana Ferreira. San Francisco: Treganza Anthropology Museum Papers, 37–42.

Sockbeson, Henry J. 1990. Prepared statement, House Committee on Interior and Insular Affairs, Protection of Native American Graves and the Repatriation of Human Remains and Sacred Objects: Hearings on H.R. 1381, H.R. 1646, and H.R. 5237, 101st Cong., 2d sess., 59.

Thomas, David H. 2000. *Skull Wars*. New York: Basic Books.

Thornton, Russell. 1998. "Who Owns Our Past?" In *Studying Native America: Problems and Prospects*, ed. R. Thornton, Madison: University of Wisconsin Press, 385–415.

Watkins, Joe. 2000. *Indigenous Archaeology*. Walnut Creek, CA: Alta Mira Press.

Weiss, Elizabeth. 2008. *Reburying the Past: The Effects of Repatriation and Reburial on Scientific Inquiry*. New York: Nova Science Publishers, Incorporated.

Chapter 20

Notes

1 President Grover Cleveland, "Speech before Congress." 1894

2 See David Keanu Sai, 2011: *Ua Mau ke Ea*, Honolulu, University of Hawai'i Press; see also Jonathan Osorio, 2002, *Dismembering Lāhui*; and George Terry Kanalu Young, personal communication, lifelong learning.

3 The United States took possession of nearly 2 million acres of land belonging to the Hawaiian Kingdom and to the Queen, without compensation and thereafter treated those lands as federalized public lands. In 1959 when the US declared Hawai'i an American state, it transferred about 1.4 million acres to the new State of Hawai'i, keeping control of the military and park lands it had already developed. These "Ceded Lands" were the subject of our subsequent lawsuit.

4 Kamehameha Paiea was the Hawai'i island Ali'i nui (high chief) who took possession of all of the Hawaiian islands through invasion and diplomacy in the late 18th century. His unification led to the inauguration of constitutional government and private land ownership by one of his sons in the 1840s.

5 Kehaulani Kauanui. 2008: *Hawaiian Blood: Politics of Sovereignty and Indigeneity*. Durham, NC: Duke University Press.

Bibliography

Cleveland, Grover. 1894. Presidential speech before Congress.

Kauanui, Kehaulani. 2008. *Hawaiian Blood: Politics of Sovereignty and Indigeneity*. Durham, NC: Duke University Press.

Osorio, Jonathan Kay Kamakawiwo'ole. 2002. *Dismembering Lāhui: A History of the Hawaiian Nation to 1887*. Honolulu: University of Hawaii Press.

Sai, David Keanu. 2011. Ua Mau ke Ea *Sovereignty Endures: An Overview of the Political and Legal History of the Hawaiian Islands*. Honolulu, HI: Pua'a Foundation.

Young, George Terry Kanalu. Personal correspondence.

Chapter 21

Notes

1 Pommersheim, *Broken Landscape*, 128.

2 Hale, *Peacemakers on the Frontier*, 72.

3 Crumrin, *Captain John Conner and the Lenape*.

Bibliography

Crumrin, Timothy. 2021. *Captain John Conner and the Lenape*. Conner Prairie Museum, Smithsonian Affiliate Museum, Conner Prairie, Indiana. http://www.connerprairie.org/places-to-explore/lenape-indian-camp/learn-more-about-lenape-indian-village/captain-john-conner-and-the-lenape.

Hale, Duane Kendall. 1987. *Peacemakers on the Frontier: A History of the Delaware Nation of Western Oklahoma*. Anadarko: Delaware Tribe of Western Oklahoma Press.

Pommersheim, Frank. 2009. *Broken Landscape: Indians, Indian Tribes, and the Constitution*. Oxford, UK: Oxford University Press.

Chapter 22

Notes

1 State of Hawaii, "Annual Visitor Research Report, 2020."

2 The Hawai'i Tourism Authority (HTA) is the official agency for tourism in the state of Hawai'i. For more information, please go to https://www.hawaiitourismauthority.org/who–we–are/our–strategic–plan/.

3 In this text, I use the term "Kanaka Maoli" to reference Hawaiians. The use of this term is intentional because it includes kūpuna (ancestors) who were the first peoples of the Hawaiian archipelago. Equally this term is being used because I do not want to silence or diminish any of the voices within the Hawaiian community that utilize various terms such as "Kanaka 'Ōiwi," "'Ōiwi Maoli," or "Keiki Papa," etc. but want to recognize the diversity and celebrate the unique perspectives that Kanaka Maoli engages in our struggle for sovereignty, self-determination, and well-being. My decision to use this term has also resulted from the frequent and inappropriate use of the referent "Hawaiian," which is being used to refer to all residents in Hawai'i. This casual "borrowing" follows a practice whereby the state you reside in becomes your identity, as in Texans, Oregonians, and Californians. In the context of strong political awareness in Hawai'i, the use of the term "Hawaiian" should be carefully examined. It is an identity and culture of a specific people whose ancestors were the first peoples of the Hawaiian archipelago. Therefore, this referent does not apply and should not be used by those who cannot make this ancestral claim. This concern also includes those who are immigrants to Hawai'i. Immigrants who have settled in Hawai'i have contributed to a vibrant culture that is defined as "local culture." Oftentimes what is really "local culture" is mis-re-presented as "Hawaiian" culture. One example is the "shaka" that has received lots of national attention since the election of President Obama, who was born in Hawai'i. As a result of this occurrence, the image of the "shaka" is now synonymous with Hawai'i. While this is true, the "shaka" is clearly not a symbol of Hawaiian culture. Rather it is a symbol of "local" culture in Hawai'i.

4 The italicization of this phrase and its parts discerns the foreign ideology superimposed by such imaging.

5 Pemoni, "Hawaii's Favorite Spam Faces Competition from Denmark."

6 *Merriam–Webster, Collegiate Dictionary*: metaphor.

7 The use of this term in Hawai'i, refers to what Native Americans might call "Turtle Island."

8 A straw-like fiber used in craft projects. In Hawai'i, raffia has replaced the use of sennit (cordage traditionally made from the husk of coconut trees) and has multiple cultural uses that include hula.

9 Pukui and Elbert, *Hawaiian Dictionary*, 201: A lei worn on the head. Pukui is one of the most profound and highly respected scholars of the Kanaka Maoli community. This dictionary is but one example of her brilliance.

10 Ibid., 148: Hip.

11 Ibid., 185: Bracelet or anklet.

12 Aumack and Majka, *The Art of Hula Dancing*, 8.

13 Thoughout this text, I will also refer to this guide as a book.

14 Aumack and Majka, *The Art of Hula Dancing*, 8.

15 McAvoy, "Record Numbers of Tourists Come to Hawaii in 2012, Spend Record amounts of Money."

16 Aumack and Majka, *The Art of Hula Dancing*, 8.

17 Ibid., 17.

18 Pukui and Elbert, *Hawaiian Dictionary*, 179: Right, responsibility and authority.

19 Pukui and Elbert, *Hawaiian Dictionary*, 182: Hula teacher.

20 Ibid.

21 Kame'eleihiwa, *Native Land and Foreign Desires*; and Silva, *Aloha Betrayed*.

22 Pukui and Elbert, *Hawaiian Dictionary*, 186; Ancestor.

23 Keawe, "Ki'i Pāpālua: Imagery and Colonialism in Hawai'i."

24 Aumack and Majka, *The Art of Hula Dancing*, 13.

25 Ibid., 12.

26 Shelton, "Hula Found to Be a Promising Cardiovascular Therapy; and Seto, "Collaboration."

27 Gomes, “Hula Coffee Cards Earn Star Bucks.”

28 Ibid.

29 Disney Hawaii Aulani Resort, https://www.disneyaulani.com/#.

30 Sanders and DeBlois, *Lilo & Stitch*, Film, Walt Disney Pictures, 2002.

31 Brigante, Ricky, “Disney Opens Aulani Resort in Hawaii, Imagineers Describe Disney Connection to Magical Island Culture.”

32 Inside the Magic, Imagineers discuss Aulani, a Disney Resort & Spa in Hawaii.

33 Walt Disney Imagineers are the creative force behind the iconic Disney attractions and experiences. According to its website, it combines Disney’s rich storytelling legacy with the latest technology to breathe life into beloved Disney stories and characters in theme parks, resorts, cruise ships, and other Walt Disney Parks and Resorts experiences around the world. Imagineers continue to push the boundaries of creativity, innovation and possibility, creating new experiences and new forms of entertainment for guests of today, tomorrow and beyond (The Walt Disney Company, Walt Disney Imagineering website).

34 “Inside the Magic, Imagineers discuss Aulani, a Disney Resort & Spa in Hawaii.”

35 Pukui and Elbert, *Hawaiian Dictionary*, 254: Story.

36 Pukui and Elbert, *Hawaiian Dictionary*, 276: Family.

37 “Inside the Magic, Imagineers discuss Aulani, a Disney Resort & Spa in Hawai‘i.”

38 Solis, “‘he’ pane iki.”

39 Drexel, “‘a’ mini retort.”

Bibliography

Aumack, Suzanne, and Connie Majka C. 2005. *The Art of Hula Dancing*. London and New York: Running Press.

Brigante, Ricky. 2011. “Disney Opens Aulani Resort in Hawaii, Imagineers Describe Disney Connection to Magical Island Culture.” Inside the Magic. http://www.insidethemagic.

net/2011/08/disney–opens–aulani–resort–in–hawaii–imagineers–describe–disney–connection–to–magical–island–culture/.

Dewey, Matt, Erin Monnie, and Jesse Cordtz. 2005. "Semiotics: The Study of Signs," DigiMatt. http://www.youtube.com/watch?v=rEgxTKUP_WI.

Disney Hawaii. 2022. "Aulani." Disney Entertainment. https://www.disneyaulani.com/#, accessed March 29, 2022.

Drexel, April A. H. 2013. "'a' mini retort." In "'a' mini retort"—art exhibit at The ARTS at Marks Garage, Nuʻuanu Gallery, April 30, 2013—June 1, 2013.

Gomes, Andrew. 2005. "Hula Coffee Cards Earn Star Bucks," Honoluluadvertiser.com, Feb. 24. http://the.honoluluadvertiser.com/article/2005/Feb/24/bz/bz02p.html (site discontinued).

Hawaiʻi Tourism Authority (HTA). 2020. "Our Strategic Plan." Who We Are. https://www.hawaiitourismauthority.org/who–we–are/our–strategic–plan/.

Inside the Magic. 2011. "Imagineers Discuss Aulani, a Disney Resort & Spa in Hawaii." http://www.youtube.com/watch?feature=player_embedded&v=A8fo3AaMX38.

Kameʻeleihiwa, Lilikalā. 1992. Native Land and Foreign Desires: How Shall We Live in Harmony? Ko Hawaiʻi ʻĀina a me Nā Koi Puʻumake a ka Poʻe Haole: pehea lā e pono ai? Honolulu, HI: Bishop Museum Press.

Keawe, Lia OʻNeill M. A. 2008. "Kiʻi Pāpālua: Imagery and Colonialism in Hawaiʻi." PhD diss. Mānoa: University of Hawaiʻi.

McAvoy, Audrey. 2013. "Record Numbers of Tourists Come to Hawaii in 2012, Spend Record Amounts of Money." Associated Press, January 25, 2013.

Merriam–Webster. 2003. *Collegiate Dictionary*, 11th ed. Springfield, MA: Merriam–Webster, continually updated at https://www.merriam–webster.com/.

Pemoni, Lucy. 2004. "Hawaii's Favorite Spam Faces Competition from Denmark." Associated Press, March 7, 2004. http://archives.starbulletin.com/2004/03/07/business/story3.html.

Pukui, Mary Kawena, and Samuel H. Elbert. 1986. *Hawaiian Dictionary: Hawaiian–English, English–Hawaiian*. Honolulu: University of Hawaiʻi Press.

Sanders, Chris, and Dean DeBlois. 2002. Lilo & Stich. Film, Walt Disney Pictures.

Seto, Todd. 2012. "Collaboration." *The RCTR Newsletter*, November 1, 2012.

Shelton, Tina. 2012. "Hula Found to Be a Promising Cardiovascular TherapyThe Newsroom, August 30, 2012. http://www.hawaii.edu/news/article.php?aId=5265.

Silva, Noenoe K. 2004. *Aloha Betrayed: Native Hawaiian Resistance to American Colonialism*. American Encounters/Global Interactions. Durham, NC: Duke University Press.

Solis, Kekeha. "'he' pane iki." *Honolulu Star Advertiser*, May 11, 2013.

State of Hawaii. 2022. Annual Visitor Research Report, 2020." Visitor Statistics, Department of Business, Economic Development & Tourism. https://dbedt.hawaii.gov/visitor/visitor–research/.

The Walt Disney Company. 2023. Experience By Design. *Walt Disney Imagineering*. https://sites.disney.com/waltdisneyimagineering/our–process/.

Walt Disney Imagineers. n.d. Disney Careers. http://wdi.disneycareers.com/en/default/.

Chapter 23

Notes

1 US Census Bureau, "2010 Population and Housing Characteristics for Kodiak Island Borough."

2 Luerhmann, *Alutiiq Villages under Russian and US Rule*; Clark and Black, unedited draft document on the history of Kodiak's villages; and Crowell et al., *Looking Both Ways*.

3 Demidoff, "Ar'ursulek," interview.

4 Cajete, *Look to the Mountain*.

5 Crowell et al., *Looking Both Ways*; and Clark, *Afognak before Russians*.

6 Kawagley, *A Yupiaq Worldview*.

7 Mishler, "Kodiak Alutiiq Weather Lore"; and Crowell et al., *Looking Both Ways*.

8 Crowell et al., *Looking Both Ways.*

9 Leer Conversation with Pestrikoff, August 11, 1999, Tape 4, Side B.

10 Russell, *Alutiiq Plantlore*; Kelso, *Plant Lore of an Alaska Island*; Schofield, *Discovering Wild Plants*; NEAR, *Kodiak Alutiiq Spring Plants*; Garibaldi, *Medicinal Flora of the Alaska Natives*; and Kelso and the Ouzinkie Botanical Society, *Plant Lore of an Alaska Island.*

11 Crowell et al., *Looking Both Ways;* and Fortuine, *Chills and Fever.*

12 Afonsky, *A History of the Orthodox Church in Alaska (1794–1917).*

13 Martin, "No Refuge from Colonists;" Knecht et al., "Awa'uq: Discovery and Excavation of an 18th Century Alutiiq Refuge Rock in the Kodiak Archipelago"; and Pamintuan, "A Living Heritage: The Alutiiq Story."

14 Afonsky, *A History of the Orthodox Church in Alaska* (1794–1917).

15 Alutiiq Museum and Blanchett, *Generations*, CD Track 25.

16 Miller, *Kodiak Kreol.*

17 Shelikhov, *Officials' Instructions for Kodiak Island*, 1–2.

18 Ibid., 1.

19 Golder, 1900–2. (Personal Journals).

20 Golder, *Father Herman;* and Orthodox Church of America, *Saint Herman of Alaska.*

21 Afonsky, *A History of the Orthodox Church in Alaska (1794–1917).*

22 Crowell et al., *Looking Both Ways.*

23 Golder, *Father Herman: Alaska's Saint.*

24 Black, "The Konyag," 81.

25 Dauenhauer, *Conflicting Visions in Alaskan Education*, 28.

26 Davydov, *Two Voyages to Russian America, 1802–1807*, 181.

27 Black, "The Konyag," 81.

28 Dauenhauer, *Conflicting Visions in Alaskan Education*, 28.

29 Black, *Looking Both Ways*; and Dauenhauer, *Conflicting Visions in Alaskan education.*

30 Tyzhonov, *Alutiiq Primer*; Tyzhonov, *Holy Gospel According to St. Matthew*; and Tyzhonov, *Sacred History and Christian Catechism.*

31 Larionov, *Primer and Prayerbook in Kodiak–Alutiiq, c. 1855–1867.*

32 Dauenhauer, *Conflicting Visions in Alaskan Education*, 8.

33 Ibid., 12.

34 Ibid., 9.

35 Ibid., 28.

36 Fortuine, *Chills and Fever*.

37 Luehrmann, *Alutiiq Villages under Russian and US Rule*; and Mason, *Alutiiq Ethnographic Bibliography*.

38 Napoleon, *Yuuyaraq*.

39 Ibid., 17.

40 Ibid., 17.

41 Ibid., 12–14.

42 Russell, "Cultures in Collision"; Bolkhovitinov, "The Sale of Alaska"; and Golder, "The Purchase of Alaska."

43 Black, *Looking both Ways*.

44 La Belle, *Voices of Our Elders*; Hirshberg and Sharp, *Thirty Years Later*; Black, *Looking Both Ways*; and Dauenhauer, *Conflicting Visions in Alaskan Education*.

45 Counceller, "A Decade of Language Revitalization."

46 La Belle, *Voices of Our Elders*; and Hirshberg and Sharp, *Thirty Years Later*.

47 Lantis, personal notes.

48 Counceller, *Niugneliyukut (We Are Making New Words)*; and Crowell et al., *Looking Both Ways*.

49 Hirshberg and Sharp, *Thirty Years Later*, iii.

50 Pullar, "Ethnic Identity, Cultural Pride, and Generations of Baggage"

51 Gamble, "Crushing of Cultures."

52 Ibid., 22.

53 Mulcahy, *Birth and Rebirth on an Alaskan Island*, xxix.

54 Gamble, "Crushing of Cultures," 22.

55 Carrera–Bastos, et al., "The Western Diet and Lifestyle and Diseases of Civilization," 24.

56 Kawagley, *A Yupiaq Worldview*, 51.

57 Glavinic, "Neglected Responsibilities."

58 Drabek, *Liitukut Sugpiat'stun*, 111.

59 Hirshberg and Sharp, *Thirty Years Later*, 1.

60 Kleinfeld, *A Long Way from Home*.

61 Hirshberg and Sharp, *Thirty Years Later*.

62 La Belle, *Voices of Our Elders*; Kleinfeld, *A Long Way from Home.*

63 BIA, The Education Program of the Bureau of Indian Affairs in Alaska, 1971–72.

64 Hirshberg and Sharp, *Thirty Years Later*.

65 Ibid., iii.

66 Ibid., iii.

67 Clark and Black, Unedited draft document on the history of Kodiak's villages.

68 BIA, The Education Program of the Bureau of Indian Affairs in Alaska, 1971–72.

69 Barnhardt, "A History of Schooling for Alaska Native People," 22.

70 Ongtooguk, "Their Silence about Us."

71 Kodiak College, Kodiak College Informational Handout.

72 Counceller, "A Decade of Language Revitalization."

73 St. Herman Orthodox Theological Seminary, n.d.

74 Counceller, *Niugneliyukut (We Are Making New Words)*; Counceller, "A Decade of Language Revitalization"; and Knecht, Alutiiq language (Sugtestun) lessons.

75 Knecht, Alutiiq language (Sugtestun) lessons.

76 Counceller, "A Decade of Language Revitalization."

77 Kushman and Barnhardt, *Study of Alaska Rural Systemic Reform*.

78 Assembly of Alaska Native Educators, 1998–2003.

79 NEAR, Kodiak Alutiiq Cultural alues.

80 Drabek, "Blending Indigenous Story and Science"; and Drabek and Adams, *Red Cedar of Afognak*.

81 Barnhardt, "Creating a Place for Indigenous Knowledge in Education."

82 King, *The Truth About Stories*.

Bibliography

Afonsky, B. G. 1977. *A History of the Orthodox Church in Alaska (1794–1917)*. Kodiak, AK: St. Herman's Theological Society.

Alutiiq Museum, and S. Blanchett 2007. Generations. Kodiak, AK: Alutiiq Museum and Archaeological Repository. (Alutiiq songs and stories CD, 27 tracks).

Assembly of Alaska Native Educators. 1998. *Alaska Standards for Culturally-Responsive Schools*. Fairbanks, AK: Alaska Native Knowledge Network.

———. 2000. *Guidelines for Respecting Cultural Knowledge*. Fairbanks, AK: Alaska Native Knowledge Network.

———. 2001a. *Guidelines for Nurturing Culturally–Healthy Youth*. Fairbanks: Alaska Native Knowledge Network.

———. 2001b. *Guidelines for Strengthening Indigenous Languages*. Fairbanks, AK: Alaska Native Knowledge Network.

———. 2003. *Guidelines for Cross–Cultural Orientation Programs*. Fairbanks, AK: Alaska Native Knowledge Network.

Barnhardt, Carol. 2001 "A History of Schooling for Alaska Native People." *Journal of American Indian Education*, 40(1): 1–30. http://www.jstor.org/stable/24398586.

Barnhardt, Ray. 2005. "Creating a Place for Indigenous Knowledge in Education: The Alaska Native Knowledge Network." In *Place–Based Education in the Global Age: Local Diversity*, ed. G. Smith and D. Gruenewald. Hillsdale, NJ: Lawrence Eribaum Associates, 112–134.

Black, Lydia 1977. "The Konyag (The Inhabitants of the Island of Kodiak) by Iosaf [Bolotov] (1794–1799) and by Gideon (1804–1807)." *Arctic Anthropology*, 14(2): 79–108. http://www.jstor.org/stable/40315910.

———. 2001. "Looking Both Ways: Heritage and Identity of the Alutiiq People." In *Forgotten Literacy*, ed. A. L. Crowell, A. F. Steffian, and G. L. Pullar. Fairbanks: University of Alaska Press, 60–61.

Bolkhovitinov, N. N. 2003. "The Sale of Alaska: A Russian Perspective." *Polar Geography*, 27(3): 254–267.

Bureau of Indian Affairs (BIA). 1972. The education program of the Bureau of Indian Affairs in Alaska, 1971–72. (Unpublished document shared by Paul Ongtooguk via the Alaskool website). http://www.alaskool.org/native_ed/law/bia_edu.html.

Cajete, G. 1994. *Look to the Mountain: An Ecology of Indigenous Education.* Durango, CO: Kivakí Press.

Carrera–Bastos, Pedro, Maelan Fontes–Villalba, James O'Keefe H., Staffan Lindeberg, and Loren Cordain. 2011. "The Western Diet and Lifestyle and Diseases of Civilization." *Research Reports in Clinical Cardiology*, 2: 15–35. doi: 10.2147/RRCC.S16919.

Clark, D. W. 1998. "Kodiak Island: The Later Cultures." *Arctic Anthropology*, 35(1): 172–186.

———. 1990. *Afognak before Russians: Precontact History of Afognak Village and Vicinity*. Kodiak, AK: Native Village of Afognak.

Clark, D. W., and Lydia Black. 2002. Unedited draft document on the history of Kodiak's villages (unpublished manuscript.)

Counceller, A. G. L. 2012. "A Decade of Language Revitalization: Kodiak Alutiiq on the Brink of Revolution." (Unpublished essay.)

Counceller, A. G. L. 2010. "Niugneliyukut (We Are Making New Words): A Community Philosophy of Language Revitalization." Unpublished PhD diss. Fairbanks: University of Alaska.

Crowell, A., A. Steffian, and G. L. Pullar. 2001. *Looking Both Ways*. Anchorage: University of Alaska Press.

Davydov, G. I. 1977. *Two Voyages to Russian America, 1802–1807*. Trans. C. Bearne. Kingston, Ontario, Canada: The Limestone Press.

Dauenhauer, R. 1997. *Conflicting Visions in Alaskan Education*. Fairbanks, AK: Alaska Native Knowledge Network.

Demidoff, R. 1962. "Ar'ursulek—Whaler Story." (Typed transcripts and audio recording.) Interview by Irene Reed. Transcribed in Alutiiq by Jeff Leer. Fairbanks: University of Alaska.

Drabek, A. S. 2009. "Blending Indigenous Story and Science." *Journal of Australian Indigenous Issues*, 12: 1–4. (World's Indigenous Peoples Conference on Education [WIPCE] 2008 presentation.)

———. 2012. Liitukut Sugpiat'stun (We Are Learning How to Be Real People): Exploring Kodiak Alutiiq Literature through Core Values. Fairbanks: University of Alaska.

Drabek, A. S., and K. R. Adams. 2004. *Red Cedar of Afognak: A Driftwood Journey*. Kodiak, AK: Native Village of Afognak.

Fortuine, R. 1992. *Chills and Fever: Health and Disease in the Early History of Alaska*. Fairbanks: University of Alaska Press.

Gamble, D. J. 1986. "Crushing of Cultures: Western Applied Science in Northern Societies." *Arctic*, 39(1): 20–23.

Garibaldi, A. 1999. *Medicinal Flora of the Alaska Natives: A Compilation of Knowledge from Literary Sources of Aleut, Alutiiq, Athabaskan, Eyak, Haida, Inupiat, Tlingit, Tsimshian, and Yup'ik Traditional Healing Methods Using Plants*. Anchorage: University of Alaska.

Glavinic, T. 2010. "Neglected Responsibilities: America's Failure to Support Alaska Native Students." (Unpublished essay.)

Golder, F. A. 1900–2. (Personal Journals.)

———. 1920. "The Purchase of Alaska." *The American Historical Review*, 25(3), 411–425.

———. 2004. *Father Herman: Alaska's Saint*. Platina, CA: St. Herman of Alaska Brotherhood.

Hirshberg, D., and S. Sharp. 2005. *Thirty Years later: The Long-Term Effect of Boarding Schools on Alaska Natives and Their Communities*. Anchorage: Institute of Social and Economic Research, University of Alaska.

Kawagley, A. O. 2006. *A Yupiaq Worldview: A Pathway to Ecology and Spirit*. Long Grove, IL: Waveland Press.

Kelso, F. 2011. *Plant Lore of an Alaska Island: Foraging in the Kodiak Archipelago*. Bloomington, IN: AuthorHouse Publishing.

Kelso, F., and the Ouzinkie Botanical Society. 1985. *Plant Lore of an Alaska Island*. Anchorage, AK: Alaska Northwest Publishing Company.

King, T. 2004. *The Truth about Stories: A Native Narrative*. Minneapolis: University of Minnesota Press.

Kleinfeld, J. 1973. *A Long Way from Home: Effects of Public High Schools on Village Children Away from Home*. Fairbanks, AK: Center for Northern Educational Research and Institute of Social, Economic and Government Research, University of Alaska.

Knecht, R. A., S. Haakanson, Jr., and S. Dickson. 2002. "Awa'uq: Discovery and Excavation of an 18th Century Alutiiq Refuge Rock in the Kodiak Archipelago." In *To the Aleutians and Beyond: The Anthropology of William S. Laughlin*, ed. B. Frohlich, A. S. Harper, and R. Gilberg. (Publications of the National Museum Ethnographical Series, Vol. 20 ed.). Copenhagen, Denmark: Department of Ethnography, National Museum of Denmark, 177–191.

Knecht, P. H. 1995. *Alutiiq language (Sugtestun) lessons*. Kodiak, AK: Kodiak College.

Kodiak College. 2016. Kodiak College Informational Handout. Kodiak, AK: Kodiak College, University of Alaska–Anchorage.

Kushman, J., and Ray Barnhardt. 1999. *Study of Alaska Rural Systemic Reform: Final Report*. Portland, OR: Northwest Regional Educational Laboratory.

La Belle, J. Aqpayuq. 2008. "Voices of Our Elders: Boarding School and Historical Trauma." Presentation for National Resource Center, Anchorage, AK.

Larionov, C. 2010. *Primer and Prayerbook in Kodiak–Alutiiq, c. 1855–1867*. Kodiak, AK: Digital Typography. (Original work published 1865.)

Leer, J. 1978. *A Conversational Dictionary of Kodiak Alutiiq*. Fairbanks: Alaska Native Language Center.

———. 1990. *Classroom Grammar of Kodiak Alutiiq, Kodiak Island Dialect*. Fairbanks: Alaska Native Language Center and Kodiak Area Native Association.

———. 1999. Conversation with Florence Pestrikoff, August 11, Tape 4, Side B.

Ongtooguk, P. 1992. "Their Silence about Us: The Absence of Alaska Natives in Curriculum." (Unpublished manuscript.) Anchorage: University of Alaska: Institute for Social and Economic Research.

Orthodox Church of America. 1970. "Saint Herman of Alaska." http://oca.org/FS.NA–Saint.asp?SID=4&Saint=Herman.

Pamintuan, T. 2001. "A Living Heritage: The Alutiiq Story." *Humanities* (May/June) 22(3): 14–19.

Pullar, G. 1992. "Ethnic Identity, Cultural Pride, and Generations of Baggage: A Personal Experience." *Arctic Anthropology*, 29(2): 182–191.

Russell, C. 2009. "Cultures in Collision: Cosmology, Jurisprudence, and Religion in Tlingit Territory." *American Indian Quarterly*, 33(2): 230–252.

Russell, P. N. 2011. Alutiiq Plantlore: An Ethnobotany of the Peoples of Nanwalek and Port Graham, Kenai Peninsula, Alaska. Fairbanks: Alaska Native Knowledge Network.

Schofield, J. 2003. Discovering Wild Plants: Alaska, Western Canada, The Northwest. Anchorage: Alaska Northwest Books.

Shelikhov, G. 2006. *Officials'" Instructions for Kodiak Island.* R. A. Pierce, ed. Trans. A. S. Donnelly and D. Krenov. National Humanities Center (NHC). (Original work published 1786.) http://nationalhumanitiescenter.org/pds/amerbegin/settlement/text4/RussianKodiak.pdf.

St. Herman Orthodox Theological Seminary. n.d. https://www.sthermanseminary.org/.

Tyzhnov, I. 2005a. *Alutiiq Primer: In the Alutiiq language—Dialect of Kodiak Island.* St. Petersburg, Russia: Synodal Typography. (Original work published 1848.)

———. 2005b. Holy Gospel According to St. Matthew *(in the Alutiiq language—Dialect of Kodiak Island).* St. Petersburg, Russia: Synodal Typography. (Original work published 1848.)

———. 2005c. *Sacred History and Christian Catechism (In the Alutiiq language—dialect of Kodiak Island).* St. Petersburg, Russia: Synodal Typography. (Original work published 1847.)

U.S. Census Bureau. 2010. "2010 Population and Housing Characteristics for Kodiak Island Borough." www.commerce.state.ak.us.

Chapter 24

Notes

1 Pukui et al., *Nānā i ke kumu*, 188.

2 Ibid., 189.

3 Manu, interview July 30, 1970.

4 wa Thiong'o, *Decolonising the Mind.*

5 Ibid., 13–16.

6 Ibid., 10.

7 Unless otherwise noted, all Hawaiian terms are located in Pukui and Elbert, *Hawaiian Dictionary*. Throughout this piece, this term will be interchanged with Hawaiian language.

8 For more information about this topic please see: Kimura, *Native Hawaiian Culture*, 173–197.

9 Pukui, *ʻŌlelo noʻeau.*

10 Ibid.

11 Ibid.

12 The name of the person who posted the comment will not be revealed to protect the innocent (or as in this case, the not-so-innocent).

13 ʻauhuhu—n. A slender, shrubby legume ... used for poisoning fish (Pukui, 1986). This plant was used in fishing to "paralyze" the fish.

Bibliography

Kahinu, J. 1871. "E na hoa, e nihi ka hele i ka uka o Puna," *Ka Nupepa Kuokoa*, May 27, 1871, 3.

Kimura, L. 1983. "Native Hawaiian Culture." In *Report on the Culture, Needs and Concerns of Native Hawaiians, Pursuant to Public Law 96–565*, Title III. Final Report, vol. 1, 173–197.

Luehrmann, S. 2008. *Alutiiq Villages Under Russian and US Rule*. Fairbanks: University of Alaska Press.

Manu, R. 1970. Interview by C. Kanahele (on mp3). Clinton Kanahele Collection. Joseph F. Smith Library, Brigham Young–Hawaiʻi University (July 30).

Martin, B. 2007. "No Refuge from Colonists." *Kodiak Daily Mirror*, August 14, 2007.

Mason, R. H. 1995. *Alutiiq Ethnographic Bibliography*. Kodiak, AK: Kodiak Area Native Association.

Miller, G. A. 2010. Kodiak Kreol: Communities of Empire in Early Russian America. Ithaca, NY: Cornell University Press.

Mishler, C. 2001. "Kodiak Alutiiq Weather Lore." In *Looking Both Ways: Heritage and Identity of the Alutiiq People*, ed. A. L. Crowell, A. F. Steffian, and G. L. Pullar Fairbanks: University of Alaska Press, 150–151.

Mulcahy, J. B. 2001. *Birth and Rebirth on an Alaskan Island: The Life of an Alutiiq Healer*. Athens: University of Georgia Press.

Nākoa, S. K. 1979. *Lei momi o ʻEwa*. Honolulu: Tongg Publishing.

Napoleon, H. 1996. *Yuuyaraq: The Way of the Human Being*. Fairbanks: University of Alaska–Fairbanks, College of Rural Alaska, Center for Cross-Cultural Studies.

Native Educators of the Alutiiq Region (NEAR). 2002. Kodiak Alutiiq Cultural Values (Poster). Fairbanks, AK: Alaska Native Knowledge Network. Available from http://www.ankn.uaf.edu/publications/.

———. 2005. *Kodiak Alutiiq Spring Plants*. A. S. Drabek, ed. Kodiak, AK: Native Educators of the Alutiiq Region. Ngũgĩ wa, T. 1986. *Decolonising the Mind: The Politics of Language in African Literature*. London: James Currey Ltd.

Pukui, M. K. 1983. ʻŌlelo noʻeau: Hawaiian Proverbs and Poetical Sayings. Honolulu: Bishop Museum Press.

———. 1986. *Hawaiian Dictionary: Hawaiian–English, English–Hawaiian*, rev. and enl. ed. Honolulu: University of Hawaii Press.

Pukui, M. K., E. W. Haertig, and C. A. Lee. 1972. *Nānā i ke kumu (Look to the Source)*. Honolulu: Hui Hānai.

wa Thiong'o, N. 1981. *Decolonising the Mind: The Politics of Language in African Literature*. Harare, Zimbabwe: Zimbabwe Publishing House.

Wong, K. L. 2006. "Kuhi aku, kuhi mai, kuhi hewa ē: He mau loina kuhikuhi ʻākena no ka ʻōlelo Hawaiʻi." PhD diss. Manoa: University of Hawaiʻi.

Index

D

E

F

G

K

L

M

N

O

P

R

U

V

W

Y

About the Contributors

Vernon Finley (Kootenai)

While currently the director of the Kootenai Culture Committee, Vernon Finley has served his community in many ways. He has been a leader in language restoration efforts and served as the Tribal Chairman for the Confederated Salish and Kootenai Tribes. Vernon completed his doctorate program at the University of Georgia.

Donald Grinde, Jr. (Yamasee)

Donald is chair and professor of American studies at the State University of New York at Buffalo. He is a longstanding member of the American Indian Movement. Professor Grinde has published more than ten books and fifty articles since the early 1970s, and he earned his doctorate from the University of Delaware in 1974. Donald has received publication commissions from the US Congress and served on an advisory board of eight historians to plan the 200th anniversary of the Library of Congress. Professor Grinde specializes in Iroquois history and the history of Native American Thought.

Angayuqaq Oscar Kawagley (1934–2011) (Yup'ik)

Yup'ik scholar Oscar Kawagley was an anthropologist, teacher, and actor. During his doctoral work at the University of British Colombia, he published a paper, "Yup'ik Ways of Knowing," that expanded into his book, *Yupiak Worldview: A Pathway to Ecology and Spirit.* The book chronicles culture and traditional knowledge and the potential for impacting western education.

Norma A. Shorty (Tlingit)

Norma has been an instructor in Teacher Education Programs at the University of Regina and Yukon University. She has served as a researcher and cultural specialist for the Yukon Nation and a variety of schools and organizations. Norma's PhD in Indigenous studies is from the University of Alaska–Fairbanks.

Annette Ku'uipolani Kanahele Wong (Kanaka Maoli)

Annette was born and raised on the island of Ni'ihau and is the Graduate Chair and an Associate Professor of Kawaihuelani Center for Hawaiian Language. She holds her doctorate degree of philosophy of education in curriculum studies from the University of Hawai'i at Mānoa. Annette was the founder of Kaulakahi Aloha, Lā Mānaleo, and Ka Waihuna o ka Na'auao. Kaulakahi Aloha is a professional development opportunity for Kawaihuelani faculty and graduated students to participate in a Hawaiian language engagement with the Ni'ihau native speakers on Kaua'i.

Robert J. Miller (Eastern Shawnee)

Since 2013, Bob has been a professor at the Sandra Day O'Connor College of Law at Arizona State University. He is also the director of the Rosette LLP American Indian Economic Development Program and the Willard H. Pedrick Distinguished Research Scholar at ASU. Bob graduated in 1991 from Lewis & Clark Law School and then clerked for the US Ninth Circuit Court of Appeals. He is the Chief Justice for the Pascua Yaqui Tribe Court of Appeals and an appellate judge for other tribes. Bob is the author and coauthor of five books, including *Discovering Indigenous Lands: The Doctrine of Discovery in the English Colonies* (Oxford University Press, 2010). His latest book is *A Promise Kept: The Muscogee (Creek) Nation and McGirt v. Oklahoma* (University of Oklahoma Press, 2023).

George Price (descendant of the Assonet and Pokanoket bands of the Wampanoag tribal nation of Massachusetts)

George has been living with his family on their five-acre organic, polyculture farm on the Flathead Indian Reservation in Montana since the summer of 1985. He completed his PhD in interdisciplinary studies at the University of Montana. He retired from a thirty-three-year teaching career in 2018, which included teaching Native American Studies, American History, and African American Studies at the University of Montana for twenty years.

Annette Reed (Tolowa)

Annette currently serves as the Chair of Ethnic Studies at California State University, Sacramento, where she is Professor of Ethnic Studies and Native American Studies. She earned her PhD in ethnic studies from the University of California–Berkeley. Annette's areas of research and interest are Native American History, California Native People and Nations, Native American Women, and in general Native American Studies. She believes in preparing the next generations to become leaders within our communities through respecting traditional ways of knowledge.

Oren Lyons (Seneca/Onondaga)

Oren serves on the Grand Council of Chiefs of the Six Nations of the Iroquois Confederacy and as Faithkeeper of the Turtle Clan of the Onondaga Nation. Oren has a Doctor of Laws Degree from Syracuse University and holds the title of professor emeritus at SUNY Buffalo. A leading voice at the United Nations Forum on Human Rights for Indigenous People, Oren is the recipient of numerous awards—the United Nations NGO World Peace Prize, the Ellis Island Congressional Medal of Honor, and Sweden's prestigious Friends of the Children Award with his colleague, the late Nelson Mandela.

Jeane Breinig (Haida)

Jeane was recognized for her leadership in expanding diversity at the University of Alaska–Anchorage. She was one of the first Alaska Native tenure-track professors hired at the University of Alaska–Anchorage, arriving in 1995. Jeane earned her PhD at the University of Washington. Her research and teaching expertise included Indigenous language revitalization, oral histories, and decolonizing methodologies. Jeane served as a faculty member and administrator at UAA for twenty-four years, retiring in 2019.

Jonathan Kay Kamakawiwoʻole Osorio (Kanaka Maoli)

Jon is dean of Hawaiʻinuiākea School of Hawaiian Knowledge. He received his PhD in history from the University of Hawaiʻi. Jon has developed and taught classes in history, literature, law as culture, music as historical texts, and research methodologies for and from Indigenous peoples. His recent publications include *The Value of Hawaiʻi: Knowing the Past and Shaping the Future*, which he co-edited and authored, and *Dismembering Lāhui: A History of the Hawaiian Nation to 1887*.

Renya Ramirez (Ho-Chunk and Ojibwe)

Renya is a professor of anthropology at the University of California–Santa Cruz. Her research interests include Native feminisms, documentary film, settler colonialism, diaspora, transnationalism, urban Native Americans, gendered citizenships, critical mission studies, and Ho-Chunk and Ojibwe family/tribal history. Renya received her PhD from Stanford University. She is the author of two books, *Standing Up to Colonial Power: The Lives of Henry Roe and Elizabeth Bender Cloud*, and *Native Hubs: Culture, Community, and Belonging in Silicon Valley and Beyond*.

Steven J. Crum (1950–2022) (Western Shoshone)

Steve served as faculty and chair of the Native American Studies Department at the University of California–Davis. He previously taught at California State University–Chico. He earned his PhD in history from the University of Utah and published numerous scholarly articles and the book *The Road on Which We Came: A History of the Western Shoshone*.

Billy Frank, Jr. (1931–2014) (Nisqually)

A treaty rights activist and environmental leader, Billy devoted his life to fishing rights for his tribe, the Nisqually, and tribes in the Pacific Northwest. His leadership was significant in the Boldt Decision in *United States v. Washington*. He served on the Northwest Indian Fisheries Commission and in his lifetime was the recipient of numerous awards, including the Presidential Medal of Freedom.

Clayton Dumont (Klamath)

In 2022, Clay was elected as Chairman of the Klamath Tribal Council. Prior to his leadership service for his tribal nation, Clay was a professor at San Francisco State University. He earned his PhD in sociology from the University of Oregon. Clay is considered an expert on the historical and cultural conceptions of knowing and knowledge, and his work focused on the debates between scientists and Native Americans over the meaning of the Native American Graves Protection and Repatriation Act of 1990.

Joseph Whittle (Caddo)

Joe Whittle is an enrolled tribal member of the Caddo Nation of Oklahoma, and a descendant of the Delaware Nation. He is a photographer and writer who has gained notoriety as a freelance journalist bringing Indigenous representation to outlets such as *The Guardian, USA Today, Outside* magazine, *High Country News,* the *New York Times, HuffPost,* and many other publications.

Lia O'Neill Moanike'ala Ah-Lan Keawe (Kanaka Maoli)

Lia is an associate professor at Kamakakūokalani Center for Hawaiian Studies in Hawaiʻinuiākea School of Hawaiian and an affiliate faculty at the Center for Teaching Excellence at the University of Hawaiʻi–Mānoa. Her teaching focus and research interests are located in the intersections of comparative politics, historical and political "myths," body politics of Kanaka Maoli identity and culture, Indigenous studies, and cultural semiotics. Dr. Keawe holds a doctor of philosophy and master of arts degree in political science and a bachelor of arts degree in Hawaiian Studies.

Alisha Drabek (Alutiiq)

Author, artist, and Indigenous advocate, Alisha holds an MFA from the University of Arizona and a PhD from the University of Alaska–Fairbanks. She grew up on Kodiak Island, and most of her professional career was in her home state of Alaska. She has authored several children's books that incorporate Alutiiq language and culture.

Ron Kekeha Solis (Kanaka Maoli)

Kekeha is an associate professor at Kawaihuelani Center for Hawaiian Language in Hawaiʻinuiākea School of Hawaiian Knowledge at the University of Hawaiʻi–Manoa. He wrote his doctoral dissertation entirely in Hawaiian. Since 2020, Kekeha has co-edited "Kaukūkalahale," a Hawaiian-language column published in the *Honolulu-Star Advertiser*. He is considered an authority on the proverbial sayings in his language and is noted for his scholarship, creativity, and methodology in teaching culture and language.

About the Editor

Julie Cajune (Salish)

Julie holds a master's degree in education from Montana State University–Billings. After several years of classroom teaching on her home reservation, Julie began developing tribal history materials and curriculum and served as her Tribe's Education Director. Julie has collaborated with Indigenous scholars, knowledge keepers, artists, and musicians, as well as elders and poets to produce materials in a variety of media including DVDs—*Stories from a Nation Within, Art and Identity, Remembering the Songs,* and *Inside Anna's Classroom*—and children's books—*Gift of the Bitterroot* and *Huckleberries, Buttercups and Celebrations*, and a variety of other publications

Julie is a recipient of the national Milken Educator Award, the Montana Governor's Humanities Award, and two Lifetime Achievement Awards. She continues her work to add Native voices to the master narrative of American history.